D0842531

Anthropology and Roman Culture

Ancient Society and History

Translated by John Van Sickle

Anthropology and Roman Culture

MAURIZIO BETTINI

Kinship, Time, Images of the Soul

The Johns Hopkins University Press
Baltimore and London

Originally published as *Antropologia e cultura romana: Parentela, tempo, immagini dell'anima,* © Copyright by La Nuova Italia Scientifica, Roma, 1988.

This book has been brought to publication with the generous assistance of the David M. Robinson Publication Fund.

The Johns Hopkins University Press
701 West 40th Street
Baltimore, Maryland 21211-2190
The Johns Hopkins Press Ltd., London
∞

The paper used in this book meets the minimum requirements of American National Standard for Information Sciences—Permanence of Paper for Printed Library Materials, ANSI Z39.48–1984.

Bettini, Maurizio.
[Antropologia e cultura romana.   English]
Anthropology and Roman culture : kinship, time, images of the soul / Maurizio Bettini ; translated by John Van Sickle.
   p. cm.—(Ancient society and history)
Translation of: Antropologia e cultura romana.
Includes bibliographical references and index.
ISBN 0-8018-4104-6 (alk. paper)
1. Family—Rome.   2. Kinship—Rome.   3. Time—Social aspects—Rome.   4. Space and time.   5. Soul.   6. Rome—Religion.   I. Title.
II. Series.
HQ511.B47   1991   306.83—dc20   90-25887

Contents

Translator's Note

The publisher has requested that this translation be made accessible beyond the specialized field of classical studies. Thus, general readers will find translated into English in the body of the book the main argument and the illustrative materials, along with brief indications of their sources. Where details of the language are at issue, the original text also appears.

Specialized readers, then, will find in the notes subsidiary discussion and further illustrations, which are quoted in the original tongues. Whenever the bibliographic information given by the author seemed likely to be intelligible to the intended audience, I have not sought to impose strange conventions on a rather different editorial culture.

Preface

As I was writing this Preface, an old idea of Friedrich Schlegel's came to mind: "A good preface is both the root and the framework of the book."[1] Frightened, I decided not to write it after all and just briefly to announce the subjects treated.

The first part, then, studies family and kinship in archaic Rome, with focus on relations with the father and the four uncles and aunts: father's brother (*patruus*), mother's brother (*avunculus*), mother's sister (*matertera*), and father's sister (*amita*). These relationships were strongly differentiated, unlike those in our culture. They followed an interwoven complex of models—legendary, religious, and linguistic, among others—which is richly exemplified in our texts though often overlooked.

The second part addresses the problem of how Roman culture localized time: in other words, "where" it placed its future and the past (the future "before" and the past "behind," yet often just the contrary, and not by chance); also, how and why "first" was placed "before" or "above," whereas "then" stood "behind" or "below," and so on. This is a cultural perspective that leads to unexpected reflections not only on the plot of the *Satyricon* and other travel romances, and on the "Review of Heroes" in book six of the *Aeneid*, but also on the genealogical tree in Rome and on the procession of likenesses which accompanied the aristocratic funeral.

Part three treats some symbols of the soul after death—the bee, the moth, and the bat—and goes on to investigate ancient beliefs about the natural world, especially about the bee: What kills it? What brings it back to life—the "ox-generation" *(bugonia)?* Who are the bee's "friends" and "enemies"? Why does the bee so hate adulterers and scents? We then look at some literary episodes and mythic tales that are closely related to the world of the bee, the moth, or the bat. Tales, after all, often shape our understanding of the ancient world.

In preparing and writing these pages, the most time and trouble went into the search for examples. Because the subject lay slightly outside the beaten paths of classical philology, it was rarely possible to take advantage of published materials. Thus, the reader may add a number of examples or counterexamples. Indeed, so be it! Despite the difficulties, however, I willingly undertook this work. If it also gets read willingly, something will have been gained. Could this, even, be the "root and framework of the book"?

As I worked, many gave support, and I wish to thank them. Above all, I owe invaluable suggestions and concrete help to Lucia Beltrami, Gianni Guastella, Francesca Mencacci, Renato Oniga, and Licinia Ricottilli. And now, "with good luck," as the Greeks say.

Part One

"Uncle me no uncle!": Relatives in the Archaic Roman Family

My aim here may seem unusual: to reconstruct for the archaic Roman family the system of prevailing attitudes, by which I mean the patterns of conduct, feelings, rituals, and institutions, which linked individuals with their fathers, paternal uncles and aunts, maternal uncles and aunts, and also, in certain respects, with grandfathers. I focus, therefore, on so-called vertical and transverse relations, with a preference for contiguous generations, rather than on horizontal relations (such as "brother/sister," "husband/wife").

What do I mean by attitudes here? Very succinctly, I am referring to particular patterns of behavior which are expected to govern the personal relations that define one's role in a family. For example, the attitudes between father and son constitute one particular pattern of behavior that social norms attribute to a father with respect to a son (that which defines the paternal role in the kinship system), and vice versa. Thus, in the family system, a father will be assigned both a specific appellation (*pater*) and a precise legal or institutional function, as well as a set pattern of attitudes in reciprocity with a son. If, then, these "father/son" attitudes are integrated, as I have sought to do, into the group of the transverse relations (with aunts and uncles), so as to bring out analogies, differences, and correlations, we will get a first impression of the system of relations and attitudes.

To modern ears, it sounds strange that an individual should be expected to maintain different sets of attitudes toward each different aunt and uncle. In our culture, we could hardly claim that one must show a different attitude toward, say, a father's brother than a mother's brother. Our personal experience tells us the opposite or, rather, tells that, if such differences exist, they depend on contingent factors.[1] But we know that this is not so with many peoples whom anthropologists have studied.[2] Thus we also might expect such differences in archaic Roman culture: just reflect on the different terms used in Latin to designate uncles and aunts.

These four relatives are lumped together in Italian under the generic label *zio* (feminine *zia*), which means that one single term, with two gender marks, can indicate all four. Two terms also suffice in other Romance languages and in English. By contrast, Latin has a different term for each of them: *patruus* (father's brother), *amita* (father's sister), *avunculus* (mother's brother), and *matertera* (mother's sister). However, Latin did not include among the aunts and uncles (as we generally do) the respective husbands and wives of the siblings of parents.

The shift in terminology from Latin to the Romance languages (but the Germanic languages, too, now show the same pattern) can be described, from the standpoint of structure, as a shift to the bilateral principle in family relations, putting on one and the same plane relations from the father's side (agnatic) and the mother's side (cognate, in the narrow sense). The father's siblings become equal in every respect to the mother's (a mingling that we perpetrate also in the case of cousins, whom Latin still kept terminologically distinct).[3] In short, an original bifurcation in terms has given way to a linear model;[4] the two streams that had been separate have flowed into one; hence we ask, "Uncle on which side?" when we want to know a bit more (though to tell the truth, this happens rarely enough, which itself says something about our culture).

2

From the historical standpoint, this process of bilateralization, which created the undifferentiated and linear model, appears to have been completed toward the end of the Roman Empire; and, with all probability, the process presupposes broad social, economic, and political changes.[5] But, I repeat, this bilateralizing had not yet taken place in the period we discuss. We can therefore expect, and verify by analysis, that a culture which uses different names for various aunts and uncles will also differentiate the relations to be observed with each and assign to each a specific sphere of activity. This, then, will be our concern in the ensuing pages, beginning with the "father/son" relationship (not on the legal plane, which falls outside our interests here, but at the level of conduct and custom), because I believe that it is fundamental for understanding all the others.

Given the limited nature of the documentation available for such a study of the ancient world, it will be necessary to draw on literary testimony, as well as the data of the language, religion, and glossography. We are pushed into the realm of legend and artistic creation. If this sometimes makes our task a bit more tricky from the standpoint of history and anthropology, it repays us with the opportunity to reread many Roman texts and tales in a new, often unexpected, light. This, at least for me, adds to the rewards.

One

Father: *Pater*

So long as Aeneas's house holds the Capitoline rock
Unshaken and the Roman father keeps command.
Aen. 9.448–49

An Imperious Line

I t is widely known, because the texts tell us, that relationships
between father and son in the archaic Roman world tended to
be austere and severe. How greatly the constitution of Romulus
differed in this respect from that of the Greeks, and outdid
them, was pointedly remarked by Dionysius of Halicarnassus
(*Ant. Rom.* 2.26.1). In Rome, the power of a father over his son
lasted for life, not for a limited time. And often fathers of men who
were already famous and important hauled them away from the
tribunals in the forum's heart to undergo some punishment.
Ineed, the Greek historian rightly noted that the power of a Roman
father over his son exceeded that of a master over a slave (2.27.1);
because, whereas a slave could buy his liberty and get free, a son
sold by his father into slavery had to return twice under his father's
power, even if he had bought his freedom (and only after the third
sale and the third redemption could the son call himself free).

For the moment, however, I have been speaking of institutional
severity; I have said nothing concerning attitudes: and yet, given
certain characteristics of the institutions, it is easy to infer the attitudes. Not that evidence is lacking. Dionysius himself reminds us

5

how frequently fathers punished with death even sons who had covered themselves with glory, but who were guilty of disobedience to their fathers (2.26.6). Typical of its kind is the episode of T. Manlius Torquatus, with the examples of paternal severity cited by Valerius Maximus (5.8.1ff.).[1] We come even closer, however, to the attitudes and behavioral content of the father and son relationship in another piece of evidence from Dionysius:[2] here he comments on the behavior of the father of the Horatii after their death and underlines the frequency with which, in Rome, fathers "had donned garlands, offered sacrifices, celebrated triumphs immediately after the death of their own sons, whenever the community had received some benefit from them" (3.21.10). Evidently the behavioral code did not consider the loss of a son good reason why a father should hold back from the solemnity or the gaiety of certain community events. Add the case of Horatius Pulvillus, who was dedicating a temple when he heard of a son's death: in no way shaken, he merely ordered that the corpse be removed without interrupting the ceremony.[3]

Let me return for a moment, though, to Dionysius. In the just-mentioned report of the trial of Spurius Cassius for aspiring to tyranny, Dionysius also gives a version in which it was the father of Spurius who turned him in and personally carried out the sentence decreed by the Senate (8.79.1). Dionysius does not feel authorized to reject this version, given "the harsh and inexorable nature of fathers' anger toward guilty sons, especially among Romans of that time." This explicitly confirms, if there was need, that the pattern of paternal severity was above all archaic.[4]

The content of this behavioral pattern is most clearly revealed by the legend or, better, the chain of legends, of the Manli, which have the virtue of showing us not only some instances of unbending severity in fathers but also the reactions and the convictions on this subject of sons, all shown, naturally, in an exaggerated and exemplary form that represents the abstract ideals of the cultural code: the form, in a certain sense, of myth.

L. Manlius Imperiosus, dictator in 363 B.C., had exiled to the country his own son, T. Manlius, because of a "dull and brutish youth," as Seneca puts it (*Ben.* 3.37.4).[5] There the boy lived a rough and rural existence. Indeed, Livy adds, there "a dictator's son born to the highest station could learn through daily wretchedness that he was born of a truly imperious father" (7.4.5). But even in exile, the boy hears that his father has been summoned to court by M. Pomponius, tribune of the plebs, who accuses him of excessive hardness and cruelty, also with respect to his son. At this the boy, taking with him a knife, makes his way by night to the house of Pomponius and, threatening him with death, forces him to swear that he will withdraw his accusations against the boy's father. The act is considered a fine instance of *pietas,* says Livy (7.5.2 and 7.10.4), because, despite a certain roughness and brutishness, it places the boy in an honorable light. It does so above all, Livy adds, because "so much paternal harshness had in no way turned the boy from *pietas*" (7.5.7).[6] The boy, then, carries out a fearless, violent act to defend the very imperiousness that his father uses against him. The son is the best defender of his father's severity.

But let us go on with the tale. The young T. Manlius, as is well known, carries out a famous act of heroism, killing a giant Gaul in a duel and seizing his gold torque; this deed earns him the cognomen of *Torquatus.* Indeed, in Livy's version, the dictator finds a way of underlining, in the youth who asks permission to go out against the Gaul, the quality of "*pietas* toward father and fatherland" (7.10.4). Subordinate to his father, Torquatus is ready, for the same reason, to sacrifice himself for the *patria.*

Years go by, and now T. Manlius Torquatus is consul in the war against the Latins (340 B.C.): a father in his own right, whose young son fights in the army. Challenged by the chief of the Tusculan cavalry, Geminus Mecius, the youth disobeys the orders of his father and the other consul, who had forbidden anyone to fight the enemy outside the ranks. The boy kills the foe; but when he brings back the spoils, as once his father did with the spoils of the giant Gaul, he receives from his father not a reward or an honorific cognomen: Torquatus condemns his son to death for the infraction of military discipline.[7] He knows that by acting so he makes of himself a "gloomy example," but he considers it equally "sound for youth in the future" (Livy 8.7.17).[8] When the army returned to

Rome, only the elders (the fathers, who had understood his action) came out to greet the consul, because "the youth both then and throughout his entire life shunned him and cursed him" (Livy 8.12.1).

Now we can understand the reason for the *pietas* of T. Manlius Torquatus toward the father who kept him exiled in the country (that "rather grim" father, as Valerius Maximus called him, 5.4.3). By defending the uncompromising sternness of his imperious father, he defended the possibility of becoming imperious in his turn toward his son: he defended, in short, the existence and the prestige of the *pater*. In fact (still in Livy's account, 8.7.19), Torquatus addresses his son in these very terms: "Nor would I advise you above all, if any of our blood is in you, to refuse to pay the penalty for the breach in military discipline brought about by your fault." To have the blood of the Manli in one's veins means both to be stern and unbending as a father and to be ready, as a son, to undergo this same sternness. Indeed the son, Frontinus tells us (*Strat.* 4.1.41), before the army that threatened mutiny to save him, himself begs that his father be allowed to punish him. He thus repeats the gesture of his father when, still a son, he compelled Pomponius to drop the charges and to allow his father to go on being imperious toward him.

In this cycle of legends, the roles and the functions repeat with too much regularity for the message to be unclear. An imperious father has a son so submissive as to threaten with death someone who would aid him against his father's excessive sternness. The dutiful son, a brave fighter, winner in one-on-one combat, has in turn a son who carries out the same deed, going against, however, his father's commands;[9] and again punishment and imperiousness ensue, and again the son himself asks his defenders to allow his father to be cruel. In the course of three generations, the insistent repetition of the deeds lays the groundwork for the exaggerated, mythic model of the relationship between father and son. In this pattern, T. Manlius Torquatus stands as a crucial link, both son and father, summing up in himself the two faces of the same coin. Cicero says that this man, "harshly stern" toward his son, had shown himself exceptionally indulgent toward his father (*Off.* 3.112). No contradiction, of course: just the contrary. The one presupposes the other, the unbelievable *pietas* was prelude to the equally unbelievable sternness. The sons must be the most unbending defenders of the severity of the fathers.

This story has a sequel. Many years later, another T. Manlius Torquatus (consul in 165 B.C.) is called to judge his own son,[10] D. Silanus, who had been accused of corruption in Macedon. The same traditional Manlian severity recurs. Having ascertained that the charges were true, this Torquatus banished his son from his sight. Moreover, the son killed himself, for shame; but the father did not even attend the funeral: while it was going on, he stayed behind and held open house for anyone who might have need of him. It makes a fine literary moment, when Valerius Maximus shows him seated "in that atrium . . . where stood the image of the imperious Torquatus famed for sternness" (5.8.3) and as a grim guardian of the unbending Manlian tradition.

"They do not bathe together"

Severity, men "all of a piece," or is it, rather, indifference? Perhaps we have yet to come up with the right terms. It is always difficult to find words to describe the actual attitudes, complex and subtle, that are involved in a relationship;[11] and it is even harder when one is working with evidence handed down by historians or men of letters, or (worse still) by the indirect testimony of heterogeneous texts: not, in any case, the living voices of subjects to be interviewed. It would certainly seem reasonable to expect between son and father, alongside the severity and fear, and as their inevitable consequence, almost a basic lack of intimacy, communication, trust. Luckily, on this score we do have clear testimony, and it points to one of the favorite concepts of anthropology, avoidance.[12]

The meaning of avoidance is well known: the necessity that binds certain persons not to meet each other, the obligation to maintain hauteur or detachment, the bar to mutual intimacy and

9

trust, and so on. One of the most typical avoidances of this sort is that which recurs in many cultures between mother-in-law and son-in-law,[13] and which Freud studied.[14] But let us look at the evidence that concerns us here. Plutarch tells us that "it is neither proper nor fine for a son to undress in the presence of his father, or a son-in-law in the presence of his father-in-law. For this reason, in the old days, they did not take baths together" (*Quaest. Rom.* 40). Other sources, too, record the taboo.[15] I hardly need add that the elder Cato, as a stubborn cultivator of every custom from the good old days, scrupulously observed this rule, even as he also avoided using indecent language before his son.[16] The rule, as can also be seen from its association with indecent language, has a sexual base: structurally it looks like the taboo in many African societies that barred mention of sexual matters in the presence of the father or father-in-law.[17] The rule is a genuine mechanism of shame and distancing, which blocked the establishment of excessively close relations between sons and fathers.

An equally useful comparison may be drawn with Chinese society as described by Granet.[18] In China, too, severity and detachment marked the relations between fathers and sons: "Their relations do not belong to the realm of affect but to that of honor and etiquette," as Granet neatly puts it.[19] And another singular ban also fits in here: "Father and son may not hang their garments on the same hook, just as two persons of opposite sex may not, because of sexual prohibitions."[20] Once again we see avoidance like that of the bath, again with sexual content, and likewise associated with harshness and detachment between son and father. Moreover, avoidance of the bath itself also occurred in China, and again between individuals whose relations were governed by a like rule of mutually agreed severity: husband and wife. They also, like father and son, may not hang their garments on the same hook; furthermore, "it is the worst of scandals if husband and wife take a bath together."[21] Here, indeed, we should note that the detachment of father and son and of husband and wife shows the kind of structural parallelism that Lévi-Strauss has discussed.[22] The parallel not only casts light on the meaning of the two Chinese cases but also brings us to the relationship of mutually agreed severity that existed in Rome, too, between *vir* (husband) and *uxor* (wife). Here, however, we must keep to the case of father and son.

On the case of father and son, Caesar gives us some interesting information from the Celtic world. He reports that the Gauls bar fathers from appearing in public together with sons who have not reached puberty: "Unless their sons have reached puberty, so as to be capable of military service, they do not permit them to approach openly and they consider it disgraceful for a son while still a boy to be present in public in the father's sight" (*Bell. Gall.* 6.18.3).[23] The case is one of avoidance between father and son of the type seen in Rome, although the content differs; for in Gaul the ban appears to end once the sons reach military age: thus it affects only boys who are still small.

These reports of Caesar's may cast some light on another bit of evidence from Plutarch, again from that priceless anthropology handbook the *Roman Questions* (33): formerly in Rome, it says, fathers never dined away from home without their sons while they were still children.[24] Thus the situation in Rome seems just the reverse of that in Gaul, although it is difficult to be more precise about the matter: in Gaul, "father/son" avoidance was the rule during childhood and ended when the boy reached military age, whereas in Rome childhood seems to have been a time of close association, with avoidance taking effect later, at the son's adulthood. Evidence that the rule against bathing together applied essentially to sons beyond the age of puberty comes from a phrase in Valerius Maximus, "pater cum filio pubere" (2.1.7), as well as from the fact that an analogous ban existed with regard to the father-in-law. The latter would make no sense before puberty. Moreover, the sources underline cases of fatherly harshness (or indifference) toward adult sons.[25]

The same principle of balance in the relations between father and son seems to have inspired the elder Cato, if we believe Plutarch's *Cato Maior* (20). We hear that Cato rigorously followed the rule of not bathing together, as well as that of avoiding indecent speech in his son's presence. The regimen designed for the boy's upbringing must have been harsh, since its "excessive stiffness" had to be softened because of the child's weak constitution. Yet he grew up to be a brave soldier and a proud defender of traditional values (to mention only the loss and recovery of his sword during the Battle of Pydna). However, we are told that his father "set aside every sort of important affair, with the exception of public duties, in order to be with his mother when she washed the baby and wrapped him," that Cato himself taught the boy to read and wrote out history for him "in large letters," and so on. In short, Cato seems to have been a father who was especially close to his son's childhood, and yet he respects the traditional rules of avoidance at puberty and he forms the child's education along lines of discipline and rigor.

The avoidance of bathing together tells us quite explicitly that relations between fathers and sons in Rome were expected to show detachment and little intimacy, along with the enormous institutional powers of the father over the son and the habitual and notorious severity. With regard to severity, it may be interesting, as a close, to look at a case handed down to us in comedy. In Plautus's *Asinaria,* Demenetus is an indulgent father. Indeed, he has virtually switched roles with the mother: "His mother hems him in closely, as fathers used to do; I let all these things go" (78).[26] So the mother is strict; she acts the part of the father. He, instead, prefers to be loved rather than feared (67, 78). Now here we are expressly told that this goes against a norm, a customary severity ("as fathers used to do"): this is important for us, in our search for the traditions of behavior.[27] In the course of the play, however, this indulgent, understanding father, a kind of boon companion to his son, ends up, during a banquet, trying to steal the son's courtesan, whom the two together had obtained: the wife (and mother) has to intervene to shame the father and drag him away. What happened? Evidently giving up paternal severity and nonintimacy (the son tells his father all, keeps him up to date on his love affairs, etc.: 74ff., 80ff.) leads to an opposite extreme that the behavior code certainly does not permit: rivaling a son in love, entering on an equal basis a competition that is decidedly forbidden between men who share this degree of kinship. Thus we can infer, from the living example, the preventive value, so to speak, of certain types of avoidance, such as that of not seeing each other naked or using indecent language in the presence of sons: allowing intimacy and freedom in areas of a sexual nature can run the risk of creating embarrassing situations, which might even unhinge the system. Elsewhere Plautus says, in a similar case of amorous competition between father and son (*Merc.* 985ff.):

> For if that's your law, oldsters whoring in old age,
> to what pass has our public business come? . . .
> Youths rather used to do that business.

If old men start making love, taking women from their sons, even the republic trembles.[28] In short, certain scenes in Plautus, in which a father yields too much, but then demands too much, serve to reveal the traditional patterns of behavior: they let us see what can happen if fathers act like mothers, if they choose intimacy and indulgence rather than harshness.

This passage casts a particularly clear light on the models of behavior that have just been described, including severity, and lack of intimacy. They form a kind of cultural humus from which certain comic situations grow, or, at least, because Plautus was translating, they help to explain his choices and his successes with his public. His comedies are rooted in Roman culture and its traditional forms.[29]

Two

Father's Brother: *Patruus*

T his chapter might well open with a tribute to the *Adagia* of Erasmus. We read at Chilias 2, Century 3, Proverb 39,[1] *"Ne sis Patruus mihi. Sapere patruos"* (Don't be a father's brother to me. Smack of paternal uncles), which Erasmus explains: "The characteristic and genuine severity of fathers' brothers to their nephews gave rise to this proverb." As proof, he appends some of the passages discussed in this chapter. His venial mistake—the Latin *nepos* cannot mean "brother's son"[2]—should not keep us from acknowledging that he gets the gist of the matter. If the Romans use the proverb "Don't be a father's brother" to say, "Don't be severe," the reason must be that the paternal uncle was characterized by a particular and genuine severity toward his brother's sons. But in what did this severity consist? And why did the paternal uncle have to play this role? Thus we get started on a path that is narrow, as so often in philology, but unusual and interesting: to seek the roots of the proverb.

"Don't be a paternal uncle to me"

Early in his first satire, Persius makes a rhetorical gesture of uncertainty whether or not to speak (8–11):

And if it's lawful to speak. But it is, when I've seen old age, our gloomy life and what we do once leaving childhood games behind, when we smack of fathers' brothers . . .

Ac si fas dicere! Sed fas
tunc cum ad canitiem et nostrum istud vivere triste
aspexi ac nucibus facimus quaecumque relictis,
cum sapimus patruos. Tunc tunc—ignoscite . . .

Thus, to have the air of a father's brother, of a *patruus,* makes a good metaphor for old age and a gloomy life, in contrast with the joys and games of childhood.[3]

The scholiast notes: "Nicely put, when we smack of fathers' brothers, which means, 'when we have an air of true severity'. For *patrui* are severe to their brothers' sons." The *patruus,* then, is marked by his "true severity." Moreover, the poet applies the metaphor to himself on opening his book. But if "to be a paternal uncle" meant having a spirit like that of Persius, it was grim.

We then hear from Manilius what it portends to be born when Cepheus is leaving Aquarius (*Astr.* 5.450): a conjunction that does not inspire love of games and tricks ("non dabit in lusum mores"), but confers rather a stern mien and an expression mirroring the seriousness of the mind. Those born under this sign will grow up on worries, will ever carry the saws of the ancients on their lips, will laud the sayings of Cato, the haughty brow of the guardian, or the stiffness of the paternal uncle ("tutorisve supercilium patruive rigorem").[4] As we see, the *patruus* keeps good company. He frequents the *tutor superciliosus* and the *laudator temporis acti,* the lover of Cato's harsh apothegms. Above all, as in Persius, he seems to stand against the gaiety of play: *lusus* is a stranger to him.

Keeping to proverbial sayings, but seeking yet more explicit testimony to the characteristic severity of the *patruus,* we come to Cicero's defense of Caelius. Cicero perceives that the judges have shown great interest in the charges just launched against Caelius by L. Herennius Balbus; some charges they are! (*Pro Cael.* 11.25):

For much he said about luxury, much about lust, much about the vices of youth, much about character; and, in this case, he was a kind of gloomy paternal uncle, censor, schoolmaster, although in the rest of his

life he is mild in character and wont to revel playfully in that sweetness
of humanity which almost everyone now enjoys . . .

Dixit enim multa de luxurie, multa de libidine, multa de vitiis iuventu-
tis, multa de moribus et, qui in reliquia vita mitis esset et in hac suavi-
tate humanitatis qua prope iam delectantur omnes versari periucunde
soleret, fuit in hac causa pertristis quidam patruus, censor, magister . . .

The mild L. Herennius thus delivered himself of a harangue
against the luxury and debauchery to which youths such as Caelius Rufus gave themselves without restraint (to hear him tell it).
In this Herennius resembled, although in all else humane and
mild, a schoolmaster, a censor, a paternal uncle, and a particularly
gloomy one to boot ("pertristis"). Here, then, a bit more explicitly,
thanks to Caelius's loose life, we get a picture of the role of the
paternal uncle: his voice could easily be felt in the words of one
who screwed up his face like a pedagogue or censor and berated
the vices and effeminacies of the young.[5] This surely is a valid line
of interpretation. To confirm it, we have the testimony of Caelius's
contemporary Catullus, who certainly knew the reprobate life. His
epigrams portray one Gellius, who at least in this literary picture
summed up the worst imaginable sexual offenses:[6] lover of his
mother, sister, cousins (88–89), he seems not to shrink even from
fellatio (with Victor, 80). Yet he also thought up one worse, of
special interest for us: to become the lover of the wife of his *patruus*. So doing, he achieved two ends (74.1–4):

> Gellius heard his paternal uncle would find fault
>   if anyone enjoyed himself in deed or word.
> To keep that from himself, his uncle's wife herself
>   he softened up and shut his uncle up.

> Gellius audierat patruum obiurgare solere
>   si quis delicias diceret aut faceret.
> Hoc ne ipsi accideret, patrui perdepsuit ipsam
>   uxorem et patruum reddidit Harpocratem.

Not even a *patruus* wants to tell the world about a love affair between his brother's son and his own wife, so he becomes as "silent

as Harpocrates," the Egyptian god of silence (Plutarch, *Is.* 68), leaving Gellius free to pursue his illicit delights.

This text is important above all for the attack: it shows that a paternal uncle customarily ("solet," hence we have a custom, a rule) reproaches a nephew who says or, still worse, does anything loose. Here we may recall for a moment the pattern of father-son avoidance discussed earlier, by which the son may not appear naked before the father or use indecent language in his presence. With Gellius, the situation is similar: the presence of the *patruus* blocks each and every eruption, even verbal, of the erotic and sexual sphere. Moreover, the *patruus* turns directly to public denunciation *(obiurgatio),* to reprimand, when a young man dares so much as to speak of love. We shall come back to this prohibition when we discuss the "false *patrui*" of the comedies in Greek dress *(palliatae).* For the moment, it is enough to have clarified two matters: one, that the *patruus* has as a special role the repression of luxury and sexual pleasure; two (perhaps more important), that one expects this behavior from him, that a cultural model exists. Hence the epigrammatic ploy of Gellius, who silences the reprimanding uncle not by retreating from his passion for pleasures but by pushing it shamelessly to an extreme.

Before leaving Catullus, we may devote a word or two to another *patruus,* this time Gallus,[7] a rather indulgent uncle (78.1–6):

> Gallus has brothers, of whom one's wife
>   is very charming, charming the other's son.
> Gallus is dandy: for he connects sweet loves
>   as the dandy girl beds with the dandy boy.
> Gallus is foolish: forgetting he's a husband, the sort of
>   father's brother who promotes father's brother's shame.

> Gallus habet fratres, quorum est lepidissima coniunx
>   alterius, lepidus filius alterius.
> Gallus homo est bellus: nam dulces iungit amores
>   cum puero ut bello bella puella cubet.
> Gallus homo est stultus nec se videt esse maritum
>   qui patruus patrui monstret adulterium.

So Gallus, the paragon of savoir-faire, helps the son of one of his brothers in an amorous intrigue with his other brother's wife. Foolishly, for he fails to realize that, being both a husband and a *patruus* himself, he works against his own best interests when he undermines the integrity of his own family roles. A *patruus* has nothing to gain from teaching his brother's son how to commit adultery against a *patruus*. We sense again, behind the epigram, what a *patruus* ought to be if he respects the model; that is, what people expect of him: to be a severe reprover of a dissolute nephew, not a "dandy fellow" who seconds the young man's looseness. Besides, there are immediate implications. Gallus risks his own fall by giving up his role as paternal uncle. A "dandy" paternal uncle may find a dangerous rival in his spoiled nephew, somewhat like Plautus's indulgent father, who ended by disgracefully competing in love with his son. All this underlying dialectic (reversal of traditional roles, obtuseness of Gallus, and the rest) comes out like a lightning bolt in the epigrammatic form.

I wish to underline how the epigram, with its characteristic twist or point, thus interacts with the terminology of kinship. The technique of epigram depends on concise intersections of language, which are most successful when most economical. This aesthetic requirement finds an extremely apt tool in the system of kinship. Take the closing phrase, "forgetting he's a husband, the sort of father's brother who promotes a father's brother's shame." The utterance makes its point through the quickness with which the terms of kinship expose the trap that Gallus has laid for himself. A more explicit presentation would have to go something like this: Gallus, who encourages the love between his brother's son and the wife of his other brother, does not realize that he, too, inasmuch as he is a brother of the boy's father in the same way as the brother who has been betrayed, and like him possessed of a wife, risks the same shame. All this, thanks to the swift signals provided by the terms of kinship, is expressed in three words: "husband . . . father's brother . . . father's brother's. . . ."

Pursuing our survey of severe uncles, we turn to two passages in Horace's *Satires*. In an attack on the vice and luxury of the table,

Ophelius plays a large role, describing the ancient traditions, the sparing and simple nurture of another age (*Serm.* 2.2.94--98):

> You value reputation, as filling the human ear more pleasingly than verse: great plates and fish bring great disgrace with economic harm; add to that your angry paternal uncle, neighbors, you at odds with yourself and vainly wanting death . . .

> Das aliquid famae, quae carmine gratior aurem
> occupet humanam: grandes rhombi patinaeque
> grande ferunt una cum damno dedecus. Adde
> iratum patruum, vicinos, te tibi iniquum
> et frustra mortis cupidum . . .

If you give any importance to good report, he says, remember that expensive fish and rich dishes lead to disgrace and economic ruin. Also add your *patruus* outraged, your neighbors, your own self-hate. Thus the paternal uncle's sphere of action is more or less what we know (reprimanding vices and offenses), and yet slightly enlarged and focussed. What accompany the reproaches of the *patruus* in this case are the shame and loss that this dissolute nephew will suffer. Thus the uncle seems to watch over the family goods and repute. If his brother's son throws his money at frivolities, the uncle evidently feels obliged to intervene. And then there is the disgrace, the shame for a scion who neglects the discredit cast upon his name.[8]

In short, the matter appears to be one of judging how a brother's son should behave. This role of the paternal uncle would explain a passage in which Suetonius describes a stormy encounter between Claudius and his nephew Caligula (*Claud.* 9.3). When the plot of Gaetulicus and Lepidus against Caligula was unmasked, Claudius was included among the legates sent to Germany to felicitate the emperor on escaping the danger. But Caligula did not welcome the tribute: "Gaius was outraged and fumed, above all, that his father's brother had been sent as if to govern a boy, so much so that some threw Claudius headlong into the river, clothed as he had arrived." With the farce (and farce is frequent, when Claudius is concerned) mingles an important piece of evidence

19

about behavior. Caligula interprets as an intentional and institutional act (a father's brother could come for no other reason than to govern a nephew) what is merely a coincidence. Poor Claudius pays the price of a cultural model so deeply rooted that it becomes a distorting lens deforming reality.

It is remarkable that when Dio Cassius reports the same event (59.23.3), he makes it smoother, but also flatter: he says that the uncle's arrival "displeased Gaius, so much so that he renewed his prohibition on praises and honors for his relatives; and indeed he felt that he had not been honored as was his due" (cf. 59.22.9). For Dio, Gaius's anger depends merely on fear or on jealousy toward his relatives: he cannot bear to see Claudius among the ambassadors of Rome. Dio leaves it unclear why Gaius did not feel adequately honored. But precisely this feeling can be explained in the terms provided by Suetonius, who shows that the emperor felt reduced to the level of a boy corrected by his *patruus*. Dio appears to have reported the feeling without seeking its cause. Or perhaps, from the distant vantage point of his Greek culture, he did not consider causal something that seemed incomprehensible and irrelevant.

Further confirmation of the role of *patruus* appears in another passage of Horace, in which one Staberius has made a testamentary disposition that the sum total of his estate be inscribed on his tomb. If the heirs fail to do so, they will have to provide the public with one hundred gladiatorial shows, an extraordinarily luxurious entertainment, and, besides, all the grain that Africa grows. Staberius closes (*Serm.* 2.3.88):

> . . . whether wrongly
> or rightly I have wished this, don't be a *patruus* to me . . .

He asks not to be judged too severely, and thus that one not be a paternal uncle to him. Clearly a *patruus* would not have approved his conduct in making the will. Here again, then, a "father's brother" is cast in the role of worrying about the destination of family possessions and about the criticism that a brother's son may attract by improper use of them, by not conforming to the code of behavior accepted by tradition.

Having looked at the relations of the *patruus* with his brother's son, let us turn to the complementary relations with a brother's daughter. The uncle's attitude does not change substantially: if anything, it is more extreme. We might expect this, because here the uncle stands guard not merely over the good behavior of a male, disentangling him from enjoyments or spendthrift ways, but over the chastity of a girl. And so much family honor and respectability ride on that. Thus, in a Horatian *Ode,* Neobule complains of her situation as a girl without love and entertainment (3.12. 1–3):

> Pitiful girls either do not give play to love[9] and with sweet
> wine launder their ills or they are lifeless with fear
> at tongue-lashing from a paternal uncle . . .

> Miserarum est neque amori dare ludum neque dulci
> mala vino lavere aut exanimari metuentis
> patruae verbera linguae.

Neobule stands at a crossroads: either give up love and wine, which would dissolve her troubles, or live in fear of the blows that the tongue of her father's brother might inflict at any time. Clearly a *patruus* could not let a niece give herself up to love, or even wine.[10] Indeed, it seems strange that the commentaries here do not recall a Roman custom that must have haunted the anxious girl in this case: the specter of the *ius osculi,* "right to kiss," according to which a Roman woman was kissed on the mouth by her male relatives up to and including the sixth degree. This custom, as our sources explain it, arose from the need to see to it that the women of the family did not drink wine.[11] We ought then to imagine Neobule, desirous of wine and love, trembling at the thought of the kiss her *patruus* would exchange with her, unveiling to the stern guardian what should have remained concealed. That the *patruus* did exchange the ritual kiss with his brother's daughter is confirmed for us by a well-known passage in Suetonius, which describes the way in which Agrippina insinuated herself into Claudius's heart: "By the allurements of Agrippina, daughter of his brother Germanicus, through the right of the kiss and occasions for blandishments, he was attracted into love" (*Claud.* 26). The same story is told by Tacitus, without the detail of the kissing: "Promoted by Agrippina's allurements, these things gained the upper hand: she attracted her *patruus* by coming to him frequently in a show of family affinity" (*Ann.* 12.3). Thus the ritual kiss, owed by the girl to the uncle, testimony to her family affection and, at the same time, proof of her good conduct, gets subverted by Agrippina into its exact opposite: amorous allurement, disguised and seductive art.

The time has come to look back toward the confused mass of myths and legends which conceals the history of archaic Rome. By now we lack only this further step to reach the root of the Erasmian proverb. Having come a long way, we want to find in mythology a *patruus* in action, actor in a tale concerning his behavior. But first we would like to praise an insight by a great interpreter of Virgil, Juan Luis de La Cerda.[12] In book six of the *Aeneid,* Aeneas and the Sybil stand before Charon. To the curses of the old boatman, the prophetess replies that he has nothing to fear: the hero who asks to be ferried over the infernal waters is not Hercules, Theseus, or Pirithous (6.400–402):

> . . . let the huge gatekeeper in his grotto,
> barking for all eternity, terrify the bloodless shades,
> let Proserpine chastely keep to her father's brother's threshold.

So Proserpine will suffer no offense; the house of her uncle Pluto will remain unviolated. But La Cerda asked himself:

> Why in naming Pluto did he use the word *patruus?* I believe that the pride and severity of Pluto are marked. As if he said: let her keep to the threshold of the most severe god; never will he, though he be most harsh, find anything in us deserving of reproach. Thus it can be an allusion to the proverb "You are a *patruus* to me."

La Cerda's question was certainly right. And his answer, too, must contain some good. Let us restate the question, in the light of what we have seen thus far. How does it happen that, in a context concerning chastity, the poet refers to the god of the underworld by recalling his position as the *patruus* of the woman? For us, who have just reviewed the anxiousness of Neobule, a hint of the repressive function of a *patruus* in keeping a niece chaste and pure might not seem alien to the density of the Virgilian text, even though here (leave it to the gods) the *patruus* is not only uncle but also husband to the girl.[13]

Turning back to legend, we find markedly differing stories about the birth of Remus and Romulus. Even if we consider only the versions that relate the twins to Aeneas, the variants still are many: some make the twins directly sons of Aeneas, others make them sons of a daughter of his (the version that appears in Naevius and Ennius), still others (in the most widely adopted version) place between Aeneas and the twins the series of kings of Alba Longa, with Romulus and Remus as sons of a daughter of Numitor, the good but unlucky Alban king.[14] Naturally, the best-known version interests us; for it makes Numitor's brother, Amulius, the paternal uncle of the twins' mother. Not that we are so interested in how Amulius treats the twins: the rules of narrative require him to do all he can to get rid of them, because these children exposed but miraculously saved are destined to drive him from the throne and install a new civic order.[15] Equally outside our interest is Amulius's behavior toward the son of Numitor.[16] That Amulius has him killed, as we are told by Ovid, among others (*Fast.* 4.53ff.), corresponds again to the logic of narrative, which presents a usurper eager to remove any future dynastic threat to his reign.

To be sure, when Ovid writes that the youth fell by the sword of his *patruus,* we cannot rule out that the word plays to some degree on the traditional model of harshness and severity in the paternal uncle, almost as if that sword had been truly *patruus,* so to speak. But even if this interpretation were right, we would still be dealing with an artful play of style, not a real model of behavior rooted in the structures of myth. For no one will argue that the traditional harshness of the *patruus* consists of murdering his nephews.[17] The model *patruus* watches severely over his brother's sons in order to protect the good name and honor of the family, quite unlike a murderous tyrant who intends to get rid of every possible rival.

What interests us, instead, is the behavior of Amulius toward a person in a certain sense less important, the simple link of transmission between Numitor and the twins—she who merely receives the divine seed from which the grandeur of Rome is destined to sprout: Ilia, or Rhea Silvia.

We are told that Amulius turned this "brother's daughter" into a Vestal Virgin, fearing that she might renew his brother's line. But thanks to Mars's intervention (they say), Rhea Silvia conceived the twins. Concerning the reactions of her uncle to the discovery of her guilt, our sources give all too few details. Generally, they say no more than that he had her put to death (or in prison, or into the Tiber) and ordered the babies to be exposed. Only from Dionysius of Halicarnassus do we get a little more information (*Ant. Rom.* 1.77). His version is particularly long and rich. It tells that, when the girl's mother realized her condition, she tried to save her daughter by keeping her from going to the temple. The girl feigned illness and stayed home. But after a bit, Amulius became suspicious. He had the girl examined. When the truth came out, he put her in his wife's custody. Then he "summoned his brother to the Senate and, taking upon himself the responsibility for unmasking the guilt that had been hidden from all, accused her parents of being the girl's accomplices in the misdeed: let them cease, then, from hiding what has happened, and let them say clearly how things are!" At this Numitor, taken by surprise, asks for a delay and orders a quick investigation. He learns that his daughter is pregnant by a god and (as the god himself revealed to her) that she is to give birth to twins. Await, then, he says, the moment of birth. If twins really are born, this will prove that the girl has told the truth. The twins are born, but Numitor begs in vain that his brother not brutalize the innocent girl. The wrath of Amulius is inexorable ("aparaitetos") and he decides that "she who has spotted her body" be beaten to death with rods. Such is the king's will.

Amulius really is pitiless, no doubt about it. In the whole affair, other relatives play much milder roles, beginning with the girl's mother, who tries to save her by a trick. But her father, too, seeks to ascertain the facts before rushing to punish; then, having understood her innocence, he tries to save her, this although a Roman father would hardly forgive his daughter's rape, even if suffered through violence and against her will: only recall the conduct of the father of Virginia. Also supportive of Rhea Silvia was the daughter of Amulius, Rhea's first cousin on her father's side (*soror patruelis*), who in many versions, as Dionysius himself relates (*Ant. Rom.* 1.79),[18] asks and obtains from her father the life of her cousin with whom she had grown up and shared deep affection. In this story, the convergence of family sympathies on the raped girl suffices to show in especially cruel light the pitiless harshness of Amulius: faced with a niece who has "spotted her body with guilt," thus violating irreparably her status as a priestess, he insists unbendingly on the sentence of death.

It is well known that, in the organization of a story, an important role belongs to the motivations, as Propp called them.[19] These are the express reasons given by the storyteller to explain and to motivate the presence of a certain part in the narrative which the structural framework of the tale requires. Thus where the blank structure has it that a city's mythic founders have an irregular and tragic birth, motivations get found to explain why the infants had to be exposed and why, in our case, their mother met with the king's wrath and had to die tragically. In the version in which the part of the cruel king is filled by Tarchesius (Plutarch, *Quaest. Rom.* 2.4), we are told that this king of Alba had ordered his daughter to couple with a phallus that miraculously appeared on the hearth; she refused, and a slave woman mated with it instead. And so we have another means of assuring that the founders get born in irregular fashion: no longer a Vestal Virgin violated by a god, but a slave mated with a miraculous phallus on the hearth. But how does this version represent the motif of anger toward the children's mother?

When Tarchesius learned that his daughter had disobeyed, putting the slave in her place, he became so angry that he wanted to execute both women, Plutarch says. Here we see that the penalty inflicted on the princess is motivated by a different code: this time she has disobeyed her father. In the version of Dionysius analyzed above, the traditional figure of the *patruus*, inflexible guardian of the niece's chastity, may have worked as a motivation to explain the heroine's demise. Thus the guilty Vestal Virgin, although absolved by her father and other relatives, finds an unbending judge in her paternal uncle. In a certain sense, the readers of the tale would expect, would find it natural or plausible, that a *patruus* behave in a particularly severe manner with a girl who had been raped. Likewise, they would have found it natural for Virginius to kill his daughter once she had lost her honor, or that Brutus, without one glance in the direction of his traitorous sons, allowed them to be executed. Similarly, Amulius's being a *patruus* may have contributed to Ovid's portrait of him (*Fast.* 4.53).

Why not add a further datum, more as an invitation to reflect than a proof? Scholars have often tossed about the theory that Naevius had created a version of Amulius differing from Ovid's portrait of him as scorning one right (*Fast.* 3.49). In order to get around the many perhaps insoluble problems posed by the Naevian version, they posit an Amulius who "did not expose the twins out of wickedness but through his conviction of Ilia's worldly guilt."[20] In that case, one would have to suppose that in Naevius's *Bellum Poenicum* the character of *patruus* which Amulius dons, severe censor of his niece's morals, was meant to play a still more solid, call it structuring, role in the construction of the tale.

For another case of the "reprimanding uncle," we move down three centuries from Rome's origins to the age of the decemvirs: Appius Claudius, the leading spirit and the ruin of decemviral policy, gives us a chance to see in action, with plenty of details, a *patruus obiurgator*. Once again, however, our source must be Dionysius of Halicarnassus (2.2), for Livy has erased almost all trace of that intricate family behavior (so valuable for our purposes) that must have played a significant role in archaic Roman history, and thus also in the creation of stories about it.

In time, the rule of the decemvirs weighed heavily and discontent, ever more obvious, wound its way through Rome. They not only used illegal means to renew their rule but also let bands of youths take possession of their adversaries' goods, wives, and daughters. Amidst proscriptions and expropriations, many respectable citizens preferred to leave town, in hope of better times. And thus the traditional enemies of Rome returned to cash in: the Sabines set up camp at Eretus; the Aequi at Algidus. The Senate gets called into emergency session, but has to wait for the next day to give the absent members time to return from their voluntary exile in the country. At last the session begins. L. Valerius Potitus and M. Horatius Barbatus violently attack Appius Claudius. Someone tries to silence them. Appius in the end declares that each senator shall have the right to speak, but in canonical order and only concerning subjects that are on the agenda. He then yields the floor, first to his paternal uncle, Gaius Claudius Sabinus Inregillensis,[21] honoring him "because of kinship, as it was fitting that he do" (11.7). The uncle rises and begins a long speech. He seeks to explain the reasons for the war. Rome's enemies have raised their heads because the city is upset, ruled by arrogance and bullying. Let not the decemvirs become angry at him, if he speaks this way: he has the public weal at heart. And then, "Since I am the *patruus* [*onti theio pros patros*] of the leader of the decemvirs, it is clear that I shall be dearest of all when the state is well run, and more hateful than anyone else when things go ill" (9.2).

This *patruus* feels in some sense responsible for the behavior of his nephew: the citizens' hates and loves will be directed toward him, according to the political developments. But Gaius Claudius goes on in his harangue. The patricians are outraged at being shut out from their traditional prerogatives; the intermediate classes accuse the decemvirs of theft and of insults to their wives: "Your drunken outrages against their married daughters" (10.3). Appius must withdraw from this senseless policy. He need not fear the vengeance of the citizens, because the Romans will surely remember his services on their behalf, as well as his mistakes. But, alas, Gaius Claudius suspects that Appius's fear may be nothing more than a pretext (*prophasis*): Appius does not intend to withdraw from his office because he is in the grips of a vain love for power and of a passion for the ruinous pleasures that go with the tyrant's life (13.1). Let him draw an example from his ancestors! No one of them ever "desired tyranny or became enslaved to the blameful pleasures of the flesh" (13.3). In sum, the eyes of the *patruus* see Appius as a victim of luxury and pleasure. Hence the decline of his policy.

There follows is a consideration still more interesting for us (14.1):

> Often I would have wanted to give you this advice in private conversation, one to one: not only to instruct an ignorant person [*hos agnoounta didaxai*] but to counsel [*hos hamartanonta nouthetein*] one who erred. In effect I came to your house more than once, but your slaves kept me at a distance, saying that you had no time for private matters because you had more necessary things to do, as if there were anything more necessary than a religious respect for your family! . . . The situation has forced me thus to tell you these things before everyone, in the Senate, because I was not able to speak to you one on one. . . . After having carried out in your regard those duties that come to me from our line, I call to witness the gods, whose altars we descendants of the line of Appius honor with shared sacrifices. . . . And, wanting to correct your folly, I ask you now not to seek to remedy evil with further evil.

Here we can interrupt. The elements that characterize the figure of the *patruus* are all there. Reproaches to the nephew for the dissolute life he has chosen to lead, ignoring the customs of the ancestors; certainty that society holds the uncle responsible for the nephew's political conduct, good or ill; duty to rebuke him privately, to counsel him (like a teacher, or a father: Appius's father is dead, we learn incidentally, in 14.3); indignant amazement that the nephew finds things more necessary than the respect owed to his paternal uncle; feeling that the duty to counsel the nephew comes directly from the line—which is to say, from the sum of the obligatory behavior, the moral patterns handed down in a family system, with its cults and its legends. Without doubt, Gaius Claudius took up, with plenty of reasons and touches of feeling, the role of a reprimanding father's brother.

Moreover, we know from the rest of the story that this was the impression also of those present. After Gaius Claudius ended his speech, Appius remained silent, deigning to answer nothing to these things (*pros tauta ouden exiosen eipein*, 15.1). But Marcus

Cornelius, another member of the oligarchic faction, answered for him:

> We, Claudius, decide by ourselves concerning our own interests. . . . In fact by now we have reached the age most marked for prudence . . . and we do not lack friends to advise us when necessary. Therefore, stop doing something that does not fit our age [*pragma . . . aoron*], acting like an oldster who gives warnings to those who don't need them [It is as if he were turning against Gaius the proverb from which our inquiry began: "Don't be a *patruus* to me!"]. If you then want to counsel Appius, or better, if you want to insult him [*loidoreisthai*], for this is the right word, go insult him outside the Senate. And now declare your opinion about the war with the Aequi and the Sabines because you were given the floor to speak on this.

Then Gaius Claudius rises again and says (15.3):

> Appius does not consider me worthy even of a reply, senators, I, who am his uncle. I, too, then, am forced to leave the city because I can no longer stand the sight of one who has made himself unworthy of his ancestors. . . . I shall go to the Sabine country, to Regillus, the city from which my family came.

And to Regillus he goes (22.4), as promised, not to return before the fall of the decemvirs.

The reply of Marcus Cornelius also interests us. Refusing to accept the advice of Gaius Claudius, or rather denying his right to give advice, he claims for himself the status of an adult, who has no need for an uncle who counsels in an unseasonable fashion [*pragma . . . aoron*]. But it is clear that the words of Gaius were taken not so much as counsel as rebuke, as insult: in the manner of a true *patruus,* he reprimanded his degenerate nephew. We should note, however, that Marcus does not dispute the right of Gaius to revile his nephew. Marcus insists only that these are private affairs, to be conducted outside the Senate.

This long passage from Dionysius speaks for itself. At last we see a reprimanding uncle, and we can even follow his actions, weigh the reactions that his behavior provokes in his nephew and in the judgment of those present. A few words will suffice, now, to evaluate Livy's version of the same event (3.40.2). As we foresaw, almost every trait that interests our particular angle of vision has been wiped out. Livy gives us a fleshless summary in indirect discourse, a few lines in which Gaius Claudius, fearing for his nephew the grave dangers from the wrath of the citizens, warns him to stick more closely to family tradition rather than to his perverse alliance with his collaborators. And yet, for one familiar with the behavior of a *patruus* under certain conditions, it is rather interesting how Livy introduces this brief account: "The speech of Gaius Claudius, who was the paternal uncle of Appius the Decemvir, was more like a plea than a reprimand," which is just how it did not strike Marcus Cornelius and actually was not in the version of Dionysius. However, this opening comment of Livy's may suggest that a reader, or the writer, would have expected reprimands from a *patruus* (the kinship role expressly remarked) and that he had come across instead something so bland as to seem more like a plea.[22]

False Patrui *in Roman Comedies with Greek Characters*

Before we look at a paternal uncle in Plautus and one in Terence, it is useful to focus briefly on the ideal figure of the uncle as delineated by Plutarch in the *Peri Philadelphias* (*Concerning brotherly love* = *Moralia 491 D*), so as to get at least a preliminary understanding of how the Greek and Roman models differ. Just before the passage that concerns us, Plutarch writes that the wife of one's own brother should be praised and prized as much as possible. He goes on to prescribe the behavior appropriate toward the brother's children: "One must show affection toward the children of one's brother as if they were one's own, but with even more kindness and sweetness, so that whenever they commit any of the typical mistakes of youth, they don't run away and end up in dangerous company, for fear of their own parents, but have an aid, a refuge, where they are mildly reproved and one intercedes on their behalf."

Plutarch continues with some examples.[23] Aleva Thessalus, "being proud and scornful of the law," was punished by his father "with unbending harshness, while his uncle [his father's brother] took him in with great kindness" and even helped him to become king against his father's will. In short, "it pays to exalt and praise the successes of one's brother's children. . . . To praise the children of one's brother is a noble and unselfish thing, truly godlike [*theion*]: in fact, it seems to me that the name of uncle [*theios*] pushes us exactly toward kindness and love for nephews."

After the severe paternal uncles we have seen at Rome, this page of Plutarch's comes as a surprise. Here the paternal uncle does not rebuke harshly; he even acts as a feeling and kindly protector for nephews who have been rebuked too harshly by their parents. The duty of Plutarch's *theios* is diametrically opposed to that of the Roman *patruus*: his fields of action are affection and tenderness, and his main weapon is indulgence. What Plutarch sketches here is a portrait that would fit the maternal uncle at Rome, but certainly not the *patruus*, who has nothing in him of the divine, of *theios*, if to be divine means to forgive and to shield one's nephews like a kind divinity.[24]

What we have, in short, is a reverse type: evidence of a culture with a system of behavior very different in this respect from Rome's. And yet Roman comedy, which thrived by translating and imitating Greek models, did not hesitate to present the type of the kindly and forbearing *patruus*. The closest affinity with Plutarch appears in the *Adelphoe* (*Brothers*) by Terence. In the familiar story, Demea has two sons, Ctesiphon and Aeschines. The latter has been adopted by Micio, Demea's brother: adopted, in a word, by his *patruus*. The comedy then plays on the comparison between two different types of child-rearing: one stiff and traditional, the other more elastic and modern, relying more on the inner resources of youth than on the harshness of imposed discipline, preferring indulgence to reproach, friendship to constraint. But the interesting thing, from our viewpoint, is that the indulgent role falls to Micio, a *patruus*.

It is really unusual to hear a *patruus* say: "It's no scandal, believe me, for a young man to whore and drink, no, it's not, nor to break down doors" (101ff.). What has become of the *patruus* who had charge of reprimanding his nephew at every sign of enjoyment in deed or word? This *patruus* even takes upon himself the blame whenever his brother comes to remonstrate for the loose upbringing of his adopted son: "I suspect now, as usual, he will reprimand" (79ff.). Thus we have a text that takes for granted a cultural context different from the Roman one. This paternal uncle is truly *theios* in the Plutarchan way: more kindly and forbearing than the father, able to allow his nephew the chance to grow and develop without giving up the "mistakes that are typical of youth," as Plutarch calls them. In short, we have a further, specific innovation in a play that already looked so culturally progressive. Not only does the play present a new type of upbringing which is more flexible and tolerant, more suited to the needs of a society with changing tastes and values, but it does so in the person of a *patruus*. To be sure, this novelty is unintentional, as it were, because it is determined by the plot and characters. And yet the goodly, tolerant *patruus* must have surprised and intrigued the Roman public, which found itself facing a distribution of family attitudes which was quite unconventional.

Even before Terence, Plautus also had staged a rather strange *patruus*, with no didactic purpose, of course. And yet the public can hardly have been less bemused on seeing the liberties that Agorastocles, the youth in *Poenulus,* took with Hanno, his *patruus*. The story takes place in Greece, at Calydon; the characters are Carthaginian; and the plot presupposes a rather tight web of kinship. We learn that Iaon and Hanno were *fratres patrueles,* "first cousins" (1068). Iaon had a son, Agorastocles, who had been kidnapped at Carthage while still a baby. Having lost his son, Iaon falls ill and six years later dies, leaving everything to his cousin Hanno. Meanwhile, Agorastocles had been taken to Calydon and sold to a rich old man, a misogynist with no children. As for Hanno, his two adolescent daughters, Adelphasia and Anterastiles, had been kidnapped and sold to a pimp, Lyco, who took them to Calydon, where Agorastocles, of course, falls in love with one, not knowing that she is his cousin. Passing over all the tricks and stratagems devised to get the girl away from the pimp,[25] we come to the moment when Hanno, who has set out to seek his daughters, arrives in Calydon. He and Agorastocles discover each other at once, and henceforth the boy always calls him *patruus*.[26] Next they have to take the girls to a court to have them recognized as free and subtract them from the pimp. The recognition gets delayed deliberately, to allow the characters to show off in an amusing skirmish that does not require analysis here.

How does the youth behave with regard to his *patruus?* We see him in ecstasy at the beauty of the girl, punctuating his admiration with appeals to his uncle, "o patrue" and even "mi patruissime," which frankly do not seem advisable for someone thinking of erotic delights (1195–99):

AGORASTOCLES: O uncle, o uncle mine.
HANNO: What? Child of my brother. Child. What do you wish? Tell.
AGORASTOCLES: But I want you do this.
HANNO: But I'm going do it.
AGORASTOCLES: Unclest uncle mine!
HANNO: What now? AGORASTOCLES: She is charming and elegant.

A little further along he calls the girl "mea voluptas!" (1214), to say nothing of the wordplay to come: his uncle, about to take the girls to court to obtain their freedom, says, "I call you before the law" (1225), and Agorastocles picks up the cue: "Do you want me to get hold of this one?" (1226), and, "I'll stand witness for you, then I'll kiss her and hug her" (1230). But then he falls into genuine lovers' wordplay: "Give me a kiss for the morsel, put out your tongue from your mouth" (1235), and "Give me a pledge for a kiss, don't forswear, let's each give to the other" (1242). To see a *patruus* permit such conduct, in his presence, by his brother's son, and with his own daughter to boot, must have seemed quite singular and amusing to the Roman public. What has become of the *patruus* that reprimands a nephew who so much as dares to speak of enjoyments in his presence? In all probability, this subversion of the figure of the paternal uncle must have made a not unimportant contribution to the efficacious and amusing finale of the comedy.[27]

What a pity that practically nothing survives from the comedy in toga (*comedia togata*) and the Atellan farce: we might perhaps have been able to meet, in these theatrical works on purely Roman themes, a real *patruus,* as severe and reproachful as tradition could wish; for when we look at the *commedia togata,* we do find a maternal aunt, *matertera,* acting out her affectionate and protective role, which fits the general tendency of this type of theater to deal with roles and plots drawn from kinship relations (see chapter 4). To tell the truth, an Atellan farce called *Patruus* is mentioned among the works of Pomponius. And in view of the fact that this kind of work liked to base itself on rather marked characters (e.g., Gamblers, Suing Heir, and Miser), we may suspect that the *patruus* invoked by this title was the Roman type of the severe old grouch. What survives of this farce (a lone fragment) lets us go no further than a hunch. Yet, strangely enough, it contains a reproach: "Mirum facies, fatue, si stud nimium mirabis diu" (108 Ribbeck[3]).[28] Must we imagine a *patruus* who reprimands a nephew, calling him "silly"?

Cicero as Paternal Uncle

What then, really, is a role of kinship attitude? Surely the proverb or the epigrammatic turn can give us only the outer shell, the stereotype. Underneath, however, there are real people, who live a whole complex of family relationships and have to meet life's chances with whatever is on hand, not only from tradition but also from their own special position, their character, or simply destiny, and so on. That is why it is so difficult to describe an attitudinal relationship, and it would be silly to pretend that everything works, every time, as in a well-organized little handbook of phonology. In one sense, any attitudinal relationship would allow endless study. It would only take endless documentation. In a system of kinship relations, life comes with full hands, adds, removes, mixes in according to each concrete situation, according to what is there and is not, to what happens and has not.

This is not to say that a tendency, a regular furrow, does not continue to exist. The pattern alters but, in general, tends to hold. As Ascoli used to say about the phonetic rules worked out by the new grammarians: not free of exceptions, no, but tenacious. Hence, then, the reason why we have left the next example for last: not so much because of the unusual nature of the person in question, but because of the story's complexity. We can imagine what would have happened, in the many examples studied thus far, if we had not found relatively few fixed traits, apart from the fuller case of Gaius Claudius, but had had wide access to the countless "uncle stories" that make up the endless stuff of Roman history.

Cicero's letters put before us a relationship between paternal uncle and brother's son which we can follow, step by step, from its origin to its crisis, rich in quite specific events, tendencies of character, and all the rest. It is an individual story, true, as they used to say. From it, however, emerges the role of *patruus* pretty much as we have come to know it, as if, despite all, the paternal uncle knew that, beyond stereotypes or happenstance, his behavior had to follow a pattern, that he had duties.

The young Quintus Cicero was the son of Cicero's brother and Pomponia, sister of Cicero's most intimate friend, Titus Pomponius Atticus. The boy, born in 66 B.C., thus had Cicero and Atticus as uncles, paternal and maternal, respectively.

Here it would be impossible to report point by point the whole tortuous biography of this young Roman, from childhood to his troubled political choices.[29] We shall make do, then, with a few hints related to our angle of observation.

To be sure, the swift glimpses of his childhood show us a brother's son enjoying a *patruus* who is extraordinarily affectionate, almost tender. To his brother, Cicero writes: "For I don't admit that you love him more than I do myself" (*ad Quint. frat.* 3.1.7). And he not only loves but also can even feel the duty to love: "I love him as you ask and as he deserves and as I ought" (*ad Quint. frat.* 3.9.9).[30] But time goes by, the child grows, and something quite unexpected happens: the boy turns out badly. He has a difficult character—moody, untrustworthy, suspect. He proves quite different from his first cousin Cicero's son, of whom his father can write confidently: "No one is more tractable than he" (*Att.* 10.11.3).

Forced by these circumstances, Cicero, as both *pater* and *pa-*

truus at the same time, has to ask himself the reason for the failure. And his answers are quite different from those that Micio gave the disappointed Demea in a similar case. Writing to Atticus, the boy's maternal uncle, Cicero says that too much permissiveness, not too much severity, has spoiled Quintus. The boy has all the faults of today's youth ("hac iuventute"), who had been brought up permissively (*Att.* 10.11.3). To blame, first of all, is the boy's father, Cicero's brother Quintus, who has always shown himself weak and indulgent with the boy (*Att.* 10.4.5, 6.2, 11.3, etc.). But Cicero also blames himself: "Spoiled by our indulgence, evidently he has gone where I scarcely dare admit" Yet Cicero hastens to make a distinction, as if to distance himself from the "our" that identified him too closely with the others responsible for the failure: "My every kindness to him was joined with much severity, and I squelched not one and slight but many and great offenses of his" (*Att.* 10.4.5). Thus we learn that Cicero also acted as a severe *patruus,* carried out the role of stopping ("comprimere") his nephew's misdeeds, punishing not only the slight ones once in a while, but often, habitually, and when they were serious. The affectionate *patruus,* who felt the duty to love his brother's son, and who loved him more than did his own father, thus took up the burden of punishment, of pinning back, when faced with the boy's errant ways. It would be wrong to see in this a contradiction or an abrupt turnabout. Merely because his role entails severity and judgment, a *patruus* need not detest or not love his brother's son.

In this light, now, we can understand what Cicero wrote to Atticus about his son and his nephew, when they were with his friend in Laodicea: "But the one has need of reins, the other of spurs" (*Att.* 6.1.12). And, shortly thereafter, Cicero writes: "Indeed, the boy's gifts are great, and yet many-sided: in governing him I have plenty to do" (*Att.* 6.2.2). The *patruus,* then, governs ("regit") the boy (remember Caligula, who sees in Claudius not the Senate's ambassador but his own *patruus* sent "to govern the boy"). Cicero had already become worried about the boy's character and inclinations and seeks to straighten him out. In truth, Cicero would be willing to keep up this severe role, if it were not that his brother, with his excessive indulgence and weakness, gets in the way: "For the boy's father, too indulgent, loosens whatever I have tightened: if I could do so without him, I would govern the boy" (*Att.* 10.6.2). And, above all, the times are certainly not the most favorable for the task of rearing him: the boy's vices "have their roots, which nevertheless I certainly could pluck out, were it allowed. But the times are such that I have to put up with everything" (*Att.* 10.11.3).

Because the father is weak, too permissive, Cicero confesses his own impulse to play the *patruus* to a youngster with errant ways and, furthermore, to tell us that he really did play *patruus,* joining severity with kindness, not forgetting systematically to stop the misdeeds, trying to govern and to tighten. Only that it did no good. On this, Cicero and his brother appear to confirm an opinion Porphyry expressed in his commentary on Horace, who explained uncles' severity toward their nephews: "For in reproving young men, fathers' brothers appear more stern than fathers, from whom nature itself usually extracts indulgence" (*Carm.* 3.12.2–3). In the case of Cicero's brother Quintus, we cannot say whether it was the "nature" invoked by Porphyry, or merely character, discord with his wife,[31] or whatever else that made him weak and too permissive as a father: very far, in short, from that tradition of paternal severity which stamped the archaic period. Instead his brother, the *patruus,* ended up quite close to the traditional role that we know.

Moreover, it is interesting to see how Cicero, in his role of severe corrector, was left pretty much on his own by Atticus, the boy's maternal uncle. From a letter, it is clear that Cicero would very much have liked to ask the *avunculus* to rein in the young man, but then he has second thoughts: "I might wish you had undertaken to govern the youth, . . . but I forgive you; it is, I admit, a great task" (*Att.* 10.6.2). Atticus indeed asks Cicero to be measured rather than harsh. In the same letter, Cicero remarks on Atticus's advice about the boy: "What you, then, advise me, and with friendly foresight you advise me; but all will be easy, if I just get assurance from him [*si ab uno illo cavero*]." When, finally, the relations between Cicero and his nephew have gone thoroughly bad,

Cicero asks Atticus how to behave: "Shall I spurn and reject the fellow openly or with hypocrisy [*skoliais apatais*]?" (*Att.* 13.38.2). Atticus clearly recommended the latter course: "But I shall follow your advice, for I see that hypocrisy pleases you" (*Att.* 13.39.2). In sum, Atticus prefers indirect means. We shall recall this attitude in the next chapter when we discuss the role of greater moderation and indulgence which seems to fall to the *avunculus*.[32]

Three

Mother's Brother: *Avunculus*

Preliminaries

Avunculus presents a dense and knotty problem, perhaps the knottiest we have to face—but also the most suggestive. We must try to understand why the maternal uncle came to be called by a diminutive, "wee grandfather" or "grandfather-kin" and why, in a singular metaphor, the noun *nepos* passed from "nephew" to "wastrel": a metaphor that appears explicable precisely in terms of the relationship between "maternal uncle" and "nephew." But we have to try to understand much else as well, so let us take each thing in turn.

The linguistic opposition between *patruus* and *avunculus* is fairly plain. The term *patruus* comes from *pater* and reflects the fact that the "father's brother" is the like relative; that is, the one with the same sex as the parent, in this case the father, who provides the kinship link. On the mother's side, however, *avunculus* differs totally from *mater*, the linking parent here; this reflects the fact that the mother's brother is the unlike relative; that is, the one whose sex differs from that of the parent providing the kinship link. Something similar occurs with the aunts: on the mother's side, the like relative, "mother's sister," is *matertera*, like *mater*, while, on the father's side, the unlike relative, "father's sister," is *amita,* unlike *pater.* All this may look, to the eyes of believers in evolutionary explanations, like a development from an archaic stage in which all the like relatives were called "fathers" and "mothers"; in other words, "father" and "mother" were the classifying terms, which happens in many cultures. It matters little from our viewpoint. The remarkable fact is that the Roman system of classification so clearly differentiated between like and unlike relatives.

So we may grant, then, that the system itself, for the sake of recognition, required that maternal uncles be called something different from paternal uncles and from the mother; but why call them *avunculus,* "grandfatherkin"? The old explanations hold scant interest;[1] but we must look at what Benveniste had to say.[2] The great French linguist traced the origin of *avunculus* to a supposed custom of marriage between cousins, although he used the terminology somewhat loosely: in particular, he posited a matrimonial preference for the daughter of the father's sister (see chart).

According to this diagram, Dupont II and Durand II each marry a daughter of a father's sister.[3] As a result, the offspring, Durand III (*ego*), has his father's father, Durand I, as his grandfather (*avus*) through his father, but as his great-uncle through his mother. Now Benveniste postulates an ancient rule of filial descent through the mother's line,[4] so filial relations would follow not from father to son, but from maternal uncle to nephew. Proceeding thus, in the diagram, one passes from Durand III (*ego*) to Dupont II, who is Durand III's mother's brother (*avunculus*), to Durand I, who is in turn the mother's brother (*avunculus*) of Dupont II; Durand I, thus, is at once for *ego* both maternal great uncle and paternal grandfather.

For this reason Dupont II can be called "little grandfather": because for *ego* one person is both grandfather and great uncle, his uncle can be considered a kind of "lesser grandfather." Of course, Benveniste had to postulate that in Latin *avus* meant only "grandfather on the father's side,"[5] otherwise his case would have been greatly weakened; indeed, he felt it necessary to propose that *avus* had meant "maternal great-uncle" before it came to mean "paternal grandfather."[6]

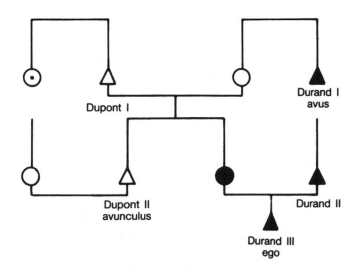

As attractive as Benveniste's proposals seem, they are wholly un-founded.[7] Beekes, for one, has already remarked how the hypothesis of matrilineal descent is baseless and dogmatic in this case.[8] I do not know whether Benveniste felt it was justified by the work of certain historians of Rome, among them a compatriot.[9] But the matrilineal model leaves no trace in the Roman world, which, to the contrary, is strictly patrilineal and paternal from the Twelve Tables down (5.4.5 and 7a).[10] We should recall, against every attempt to infiltrate matrilineal filiation into archaic Roman culture, the stricture of Canuleius: "Naturally, children follow the father" (Livy 4.4.11). Equally weak is the view that *avus* in Latin means only "paternal grandfather," which is just not true;[11] we have to resign ourselves to admitting that Latin, at this level, lacks a bifurcated terminology. But an even more serious objection remains to be raised. If Roman culture had ever known a matrimonial preference for the daughter of the father's sister, so well established as to give rise to a whole set of terms, we ought to find cases in which *amita,* "father's sister," means *socrus,* "mother-in-law," or vice versa: instead, this never happens.

Beekes offered anther criticism of Benveniste; it will allow us to go into the matter still more deeply. Touching the heart of Benveniste's argument, Beekes refuses to allow that traces of marriage between first cousins survive in the Indo-European world: more exactly, traces of that which Benveniste postulated, which was a marriage preference for the daughter of the father's sister. There is nothing unusual about this. Indeed, we can add that a reading of Lévi-Strauss's *Elementary Structures*, which Beekes does not cite, shows that this type of matrimony is rather rare in any culture: Lévi-Strauss also says that this rarity is because of the instability and narrowness of its structure.[12] Clearly, then, Benveniste chose a type of marriage which is too rare, refined, and problematic to allow it to be inferred simply through guesses: symmetrically, then, it is too unstable and passing to have been able to found a whole system of terms, as Benveniste would have it do.

Beekes, however, by his own admission, supposes that marriage with the daughter of the mother's brother would be "much more frequent" than marriage with the daughter of the father's sister.[13] In this fashion, he risks crediting the position he opposes. To be sure, Benveniste was a bit too brief and imprecise in his assumptions; he formulated the question in a distorted perspective, so the resulting debates also have been deformed.

Turning again to Lévi-Strauss's *Elementary Structures*, we see that there are three basic types of marriage between first cousins: marriage with the daughter of the father's sister (Benveniste's preferred type), marriage with the daughter of the mother's brother, and marriage with the father's sister's daughter who is also the daughter of the mother's brother. These three types of marriage coincide with three different patterns of matrimonial exchange. The second type corresponds to so-called generalized exchange, which is a long, interlinked cycle in which several social groups share women according to a definite progression. The third type, in contrast, corresponds to so-called restricted exchange, in which two social groups share women to the exclusion of other groups; whereas the first type (Benveniste's) carries out a kind of mediation between the others, seeking to introduce restricted exchange into the process of generalized exchange, thus creating a more complicated and unstable system. Here we have neither the space nor the need to chart these diverse situations. We can limit our-

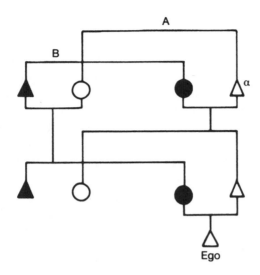

selves to showing what happens in a restricted exchange; that is, in marriage with the father's sister's daughter who is also the daughter of the mother's brother. We posit, then, two groups, B (black) and A (white), that exchange sisters:

Evidently also in a system of this type, in which brothers exchange sisters, "alpha" is to "ego" both paternal grandfather and maternal great-uncle at once. This is just what Benveniste wanted, but no longer are we forced to postulate a marriage type that is unstable and rather rare. At this point, however, having replaced Benveniste's chart with an equivalent, but substantially improved, version, we must look again at Beekes's objections, some of which no longer hit the mark.

Beekes, for instance, objected that in the Indo-European world we find no traces of marriage with the father's sister's daughter, but, if anything, traces of marriage with the mother's brother's daughter. Now, however, our modified chart indicates marriage precisely with the mother's brother's daughter who is also the father's sister's daughter: in other words, Beekes's objections risk turning into an argument for the modified chart of Benveniste. All these are the paradoxical consequences of the failure to attend to structure that was discussed earlier. Be that as it may, Benveniste's proposal, even having been made internally more consistent and closer to the marriage rules discovered by anthropologists, still does not wash.

The objections to matrilineal descent persist, although it would have to be supposed in some fashion to maintain Benveniste's thesis; and *avus* does not mean just "paternal grandfather," as Benveniste would have it: still less could we go along with guesses such as the one that *avus,* even before meaning "paternal grandfather," must have meant "great-uncle on the mother's side." Naturally, too, by this line of speculation, we ought to expect to find *amita,* "father's sister," meaning *socrus,* "mother-in-law," this time with the addition of *avunculus* meaning *socer,* "father-in-law," which is still less likely. All in all, then, we must be resigned to seeking another explanation, which is what we shall do.

But before closing with Benveniste, it may be useful to try also to understand better why he ever came to get caught in such an erroneous construction, capable, too, of confusing his critics. It all depends on an unfortunate interpretation of Granet,[14] to whom Benveniste expressly refers in his notes. From Granet comes the rule of identity between paternal grandfather and maternal great-uncle, which he postulates as necessary to explain the kinship organization in old Chinese society. Granet also believes in the idea of an ancient matrilineal structure behind the patrilineal,[15] on which Benveniste's argument hinges. But Granet postulated a structure quite analogous to the one just presented,[16] even though he did so with charts that are rather sketchy and difficult to read.[17] It may be, then, that Benveniste took Granet's ideas only in part and then constructed, on his own, a system that is apparently identical with the Chinese, to which he expressly refers, although differing radically from it and of a sort to cause a host of difficulties when applied.[18]

Leaving Benveniste, and I hope having also understood the reasons for his reconstruction, we can turn to other explanations. Szemerényi has easily destroyed the frail foundations of a proposal by Lounsbury,[19] picked up later by Friedrich,[20] then by Gates,[21] which employs a classification of the Omaha Indian type for the entire Indo-European world.[22] However, Szemerényi's own proposal does not seem clear. Taking up Lévi-Strauss on the so-called atom of kinship,[23] Szemerényi seeks to integrate into this basic structure also the maternal uncle as guardian of the woman who is given in exchange and is the mother of *ego,* the third generation in our chart. In Szemerényi's view, the maternal uncle would thus come to be identified with *ego*'s grandfather (maternal in this case) because in the "not infrequent situation in which he (the maternal uncle) lost his father (who was the grandfather of *ego*), he (said maternal uncle) inherited the position of his father." This line of reasoning would imply as well that the father of *ego* could be called "little grandfather": is it not, after all, the case that when *ego*'s paternal grandfather dies, *ego*'s father inherits his position? This evidently would be absurd. In reality, kinship classifications contain a sound rule, that of the slippage of roles: each father becomes a grandfather, each son becomes a father, and so on. But precisely because the entire structure hinges on the slippage, we can in no way move up its application: that would vitiate the system. It would be like wanting to place one's queen on the chessboard before one's pawn reached the opposite edge: "That's not how it's played!" one's opponent would shoot back.

How, then, shall we explain *avunculus,* this "little grandfather"? We have to agree with Beekes[24] when he makes it a matter of affective relations—in other words, what we have called attitudes—which is where we started. He proposes to solve the terminological riddle by postulating that the maternal uncle and the nephew were joined by a tender attitude like that between the grandfather and the grandson. In this sense, the maternal uncle would be called "little grandfather" because with him *ego* enjoys bonds of affection quite like those with the grandfather. It is interesting to note, in support of this, what Radcliffe-Brown reports from the Thonga:[25] the mother's brother is called grandfather (*kokwana*) because with these two individuals one shares an identical attitude of affection. The linguistic situation closely resembles that of Latin. But if postulated in these terms, such a hypothesis about the Roman world, though fairly plausible, might remain a dead letter, arbitrary and unproved. Thus, we must ask: Did an attitude of intimacy, freedom, and familiarity between maternal uncle and nephew exist in

Rome? And did the same attitude recur between grandfather and grandson?

In Great "Familiarity" with the Avunculus

Starting with the first problem, what we have seen in the Roman world of relations between fathers and sons marked by severity and lack of intimacy is enough to invite us to believe in advance that the reverse must obtain between maternal uncle and nephew; that is, relations of intimacy and affection. That the two relationships complement each other has been known since Radcliffe-Brown: when fathers are severe, uncles are usually affectionate and permissive, and vice versa.[26] But more evidence is needed. We can hardly hope to solve a problem of kinship terms without trying to correlate the linguistic givens with evidence from the society's history and legends. This is what makes so frail all the attempts to reconstruct Indo-European kinship on the basis of comparisons among the various languages. Thus, let us reformulate our aim: if the linguistic terms, as well as the general anthropological typology, lead us to expect relations of intimacy between maternal uncles and nephews in Rome, what do the ancient authors tell us in this regard?

Taking the evidence backward, as it were, from nearest to farthest, we may begin with Seneca speaking to Helvia about her maternal uncle, "that very indulgent *avunculus* . . . you have lost" (*Dial.* 12.2.4). Helvia's maternal uncle, then, was "very indulgent," a significant trait for our purposes. One might object, of course, that just because Helvia's was like that does not prove that others also were. So let us look back a bit further in time, to the age of Cicero. In one of his polemics against Marc Antony (*Phil.* 8.1), Cicero says that L. Caesar spoke less harshly than he ought to against Antony because of kinship, even though L. Caesar himself urged the Senate not to follow his lead on the path of moderation because he would have given quite a different opinion, had it not been for his kinship. Now Lucius Julius Caesar was the brother of Marc Antony's mother, Julia, and thus Antony's *avunculus*. And Cicero presses the point: "He then is a mother's brother: but surely

you're not all mother's brothers, you that agreed with him?"
(8.1.27). To understand Cicero's wit, we must remember how he
used *patruus* too, figuratively, calling L. Herennius a "gloomy paternal uncle, censor and schoolmaster," in the familiar metaphorical use of *patruus* to mean any person who is severe and harsh (*Pro
Cael.* 25). So any particularly unbending and aroused accuser can
be called a *patruus;* by contrast, excessively indulgent judges risk
being styled *avunculi,* for the same reasons that apply to the actual
maternal uncle seated among them on the benches. The behavior
of L. Caesar also drew Cicero's attention elsewhere: "L. Caesar
judges well, but, because he is a maternal uncle, he does not state
very harsh opinions" (*Fam.* 10.28.3). In short, another indulgent
avunculus, like Helvia's.

Another example from Cicero may be even more interesting.
Lepidus married Junia, the sister of Junius Brutus; but by 43 B.C.,
alignments in kinship and politics no longer match as they should.
Lepidus is a little too close to Antony and is now considered an
enemy by Cicero. Hence Cicero, writing to Brutus, says he cannot
aid Lepidus's sons as Brutus's sister (their mother) and mother
(their grandmother) want him to (*Ad Brut.* 1.12). Brutus replies:
"You should forget that my sister's children are sons of Lepidus,
and you should consider that I have entered into the place of a
father for them" (1.13). And he goes on: "Some live one way, others another, with their own: there is nothing I can do for my sister's
children that could fully satisfy my duty or my will" ("quo possit
expleri voluntas mea aut officium"). Certainly, "against the father
Lepidus, Brutus the maternal uncle" ought to be worth something.
Brutus adds that a case of this kind needs no words, that Cicero
ought to grasp at once his feelings and concerns: "Write much to
you, I neither can because of worry and anger, nor should I." He
should not write more because if his interlocutor does not get his
sense thus, without too much talk, there is little hope that he really
wants to help.

The text commands interest and merits comment. The bond
between Brutus and his sister's sons is very close. He feels the duty
to assume the father's role in an especially trying time. Brutus even
says that by his lights nothing can exhaust his will or his duty

toward his sister's sons. But in circumstances of this kind, the live-liest and most interesting witness is silence: if an *avunculus,* forced to seek help for his nephews, feels unable to say more because of worry and anger ("prae sollicitudine et stomacho"), and if, above all, he considers that he ought not to speak ("neque debeo") to explain the reasons for his request, his motive can be but one: a duty so clear, so deeply rooted in the culture, that there is no need to describe the feelings that accompany it. To do so would be em-barrassing.

We are beginning to find some explicit contents, the kinds of attitudes which existed in Rome between maternal uncles and nephews: Helvia's *avunculus* is *indulgentissimus;* L. Caesar is behav-ing like an *avunculus* when he speaks mildly against Antony in the Senate; Brutus, the stern and unbending Brutus, can imagine nothing that would exhaust his duty toward his sister's sons, al-though they are the children of a rebel: full of concern, Brutus considers it inappropriate to speak too much in seeking aid from his friend. Relevant, too, may be what Valerius Maximus says of the close attachment of Hortensius to his sister's son (5.9.2), amidst a difficult relationship with his own son, which risked complicating his will.

All these instances, however, leave us rather far down in history from the archaic culture we set out to study. It is further back, then, much further, that we have to look for evidence that can fill out fully our anthropologic-linguistic model of the *avunculus.* Luckily, we have the evidence of a legend that takes us back to the dawn of the republic. Here, too, interestingly enough, we find a conflict between the demands of kinship and the loyalties of polit-ical faction, just as in the two cases from Cicero. This similarity is not pure coincidence. A narrative of attitudes between family members, of the emotional contents of kinship bonds, can emerge only at the moment when the family comes into conflict with an outside emergency: this is how our historical sources get made. No ancient historian would set out to describe the feelings of a maternal uncle toward his nephew in an everyday situation; that is, for example, when they were together at a family celebration such as the *cara cognatio* or met in the street. Such events do not usually make history, I am sorry to say. In order to get talked about, everyday feelings, the affective code, have to clash with some outside circumstance that does make history: civil war, confiscation, plots. Otherwise, to find these descriptions of behavior which are so valuable for us, we have to look at the history of the "others" in ethnographic writings, such as Tacitus in the *Germania* describing the institution of the maternal uncle among the Germanic folk. Thus, it is interesting to look at an earlier Brutus, who played the role, not of an *avunculus* strongly concerned with his nephews, but of a *pater,* and thus came into conflict with an *avunculus.*

When the Tarquins were driven out, Rome's government passed to the first two consuls, Collatinus and Brutus. But Tarquin did not mean to give up and soon reentered the road to power. According to Plutarch's narrative (*Publicola* 3ff.), the Tarquins won over to their cause two Roman houses, the Aquilli and the Vitelli, as well as no less than Titus and Tiberius, two of Brutus's sons. All these Roman worthies were relatives, which is the important thing for us: the Aquilli and Vitelli were nephews of Collatinus on the mother's side (so Collatinus was their *avunculus*); and the Vitelli, in turn, were related to Brutus, because he married a sister of theirs (which made the Vitelli the *avunculi* of Brutus's sons Tiberius and Titus). To put it graphically:

Plutarch says expressly that Titus and Tiberius were not only

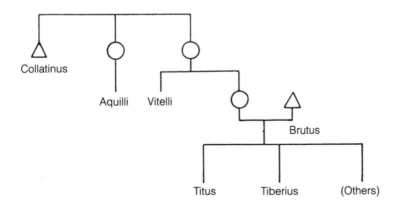

relatives but also were intimate (*synetheis*, 3.5) with their uncles the Vitelli. Thus these uncles persuaded the two young men "to free themselves from the obtuseness and harshness of their father" (3.5) and side with the Tarquins. A first sign of conflict thus emerges between a harsh *pater* and an *avunculus,* with whom intimacy can be shared. This should suffice to guide us: the *avunculus* here functions as the reverse of the *pater.* But to go on. The plot failed and the traitors were accused. The Aquilli and Vitelli, as well as the two sons of Brutus, were brought before Brutus and Collatinus.

What interests us is how the behavior of the two consuls, Brutus and Collatinus, differs when they are called to judge respectively their own sons and their sister's sons. Collatinus shows weakness and uncertainty, even letting himself weep (6.2), whereas Brutus displays harshness and severity, which befits what we have seen of the behavior code for fathers in the archaic period: Brutus implacably has his sons condemned to death, and for the whole time "he never turned aside his gaze, nor did any pity alter the wrathful severity stamped on his countenance" (6.4). After this, Brutus goes off, leaving Collatinus to judge his nephews. Once again the consul shows weakness and hesitates, arousing the disdain of Publicola, who cries out that Collatinus is behaving unworthily, because "after forcing his colleague to execute his own sons, he, instead, to do something pleasing to certain women [his sisters], wants to spare the enemies and betrayers of the fatherland" (7.4).[27] Brutus is called back and makes a stern and noble speech ("for his sons he was judge enough: as for the other citizens, who are free, let them express their will," 7.5), after which the other traitors are also condemned. Following this unfortunate test, Collatinus of his own accord goes into exile.

The first serious risk to the fledgling Roman republic reveals a counterpoint of conflict between two cultural roles: on the one hand, the maternal uncle sharing intimacy with the nephews and knowing how, at the right moment, to be permissive, even weak, even to the point of risking his own position in society for the nephews' sake; on the other hand, the harsh father, who shows himself the sole and implacable judge of his guilty sons. Tiberius

and Titus were ruined by their intimacy with their *avunculi,* the
Vitelli; the weakness of Collatinus toward his sisters' sons caused
him to lose power. The bond between maternal uncle and nephew
thus stands out for us in the legend and gets made visible and
plain from both viewpoints: that of sister's son toward maternal
uncle (intimacy), and that of maternal uncle toward sister's son
(weakness), all against the backdrop of severity in the *pater.* Indeed, Plutarch may give us a useful key to the roots of the maternal
uncle's feeling for his nephews, when Publicola accuses Collatinus
of wanting to spare the traitors "in order to please certain women
[that is, the sisters of Collatinus]." Sister-brother relationships have
as a kind of consequence those between maternal uncle and
nephew,[28] which regularly correlate with them: if relations between brother and sister are tender and intimate, then so are those
between her brother and her son.

This tissue of relationships looks rather similar in the version
by Dionysius of Halicarnassus (*Ant. Rom.* 5.9.1ff.). After Titus and
Tiberius are executed, it is the turn of the Aquilli, who are asked
by Brutus to speak in their own defense; but "they fall at their
uncle's knees, as if it were his responsibility to save them" (5.9.1).
Brutus, seeing that they have no intention of defending themselves, wants to have them led straightaway to die, but Collatinus
delays the lictors and takes his colleague aside: "If only Brutus will
grant him the life of his kinsmen, he asks only this favor, he will
not ask for any others" (5.9.2). But Brutus cannot be moved; he
refuses to grant even a lightening of the penalty, not even a delay.
Then Collatinus, exasperated, tells him: "Because you are intrac-
table and cruel, I shall spare these boys, for my power is just as
great as yours" (5.9.3). Whereupon Brutus summons the people,
tells every in and out of the plot (including his suspicions and the
unworthy requests of Collatinus), emphasizing that he, Brutus,
has already forced his own sons to die, and says that among the
condemned men are the brothers of his wife (remember that Brutus was married to a Vitellia), but that he has been and still is
determined to stop the guilty. And now, he says, Collatinus "wants
to snatch the Aquilli from me; he is unwilling to let them suffer the
fate of my sons, although they conspired in the same plot"

(5.10.3ff.). And Brutus announces his intention to deprive his colleague of power. Collatinus answers, shouting that "he rejects the accusations against him and again asks for pardon for his nephews" (5.11.1), but the people are full of rage toward him. Then his father-in-law, Spurius Lucretius, intervenes, advising him to leave the city of his own free will. After this, Collatinus, vanquished, "lamenting his fate, that he had been forced to give up his country because of his compassion for his own kinsmen, renounces his power" (5.12.1), and he goes to exile in Lavinium.

The tissue of relations remains substantially the same here in Dionysius as in Plutarch:[29] on one side, a father, determined and severe; on the other, a maternal uncle, weak and compassionate, who ends up losing his honors and his homeland through love of his nephews. Thus this legend, along with Cicero's strikingly similar evidence, guarantees us something that Radcliffe-Brown's work and other anthropological studies had already let us expect: in Rome, too, in correlation with a stern father appears a maternal uncle who is indulgent, even weak.

A rather different case looks equally interesting: the legend of a cruel *avunculus*. Tarquinius Superbus killed his sister's son, the brother of Brutus, who was Tarquin's nephew; and if Brutus pretended to be "brutish," it was because he had learned that Tarquin had dirtied himself with this crime (Livy, 1.56.7). We must not forget, however, that this murderous maternal uncle is the same one who had crossed the threshold of the realm by killing his good brother, his sister-in-law, and even his father-in-law, Servius Tullius. The myth darkens the colors of this figure and multiplies the wickedness. Thus finding among his outrages the killing of his sister's son only further confirms what we already knew: that the link between maternal uncle and nephew is very close in the world of archaic Rome, so that only a desperado such as Tarquin could have the audacity to violate it.

"Grandsire/Grandson" and the Intimate Diminutive

Let us come back to the linguistic riddle from which we started: what to make of the term *avunculus,* "grandfatherkin." We have

seen enough historical and legendary evidence for intimacy between a woman's brother and her son that we need not use one
rather dubious datum about the indulgence of the maternal uncle,
although it is the sole witness called, as far as I know, by previous
students of the matter. I refer to the metaphor that *nepos* equals
"wastrel," mentioned at the beginning of this chapter. The linguistic usage is fairly well attested,[30] but it deserves a preliminary defense, because the suggestion has been made that *nepos* (wastrel)
is a homophone, radically different from *nepos* (nephew):[31] it
would be derived from *potis* (able) in the manner of *impos* (unable)
and *compos* (enabled); the alternation between *impos* and **nepos*
would be of the type found in *inscius/nescius* (not knowing/un-
knowing). Semantically, at least, the hypothesis would appear
credible,[32] but it bumps up against a prosodic objection difficult
to meet: if *nepos* derived from *potis*, we would expect forms in
short *o*, **nepŏs, nepŏtis*, of the type well known as *compŏs, compŏtis,
impŏs, impŏtis*, rather than the forms in long *o*, *nepōs, nepōtis*,
which we actually get.[33] If, then, one wants to invoke the criterion
of analogy (which would be a bit strange in the case of a minimum
pair of quantities) and argue that **nepŏs* became *nepōs*, on the
model of *nepōs*, "nephew," then one would have to admit that semantic reasons motivated this attraction: in other words, that *nepōs*, "nephew," had already some traits that associated it with dis-
sipation. Thus, after a rather long detour, we return to where we
began.[34]

So the metaphor *nepos* equals "wastrel" stands, but why? For
Benveniste,[35] the metaphor was a consequence of the free and indulgent relationship between maternal uncle and nephew: the
nephew became a kind of spoiled child. This would be quite be-
lievable; again, we should refer to famous pages by Radcliffe-
Brown.[36] Yet there is a problem, already underlined by Beekes.[37]
For Benveniste's postulate to work, *nepos* from the start has to have
meant "sister's son," which instead it only begins to mean in late
Latin.[38] Earlier, it means only "grandson of grandfather" and not
even "nephew of uncle." Thus we are obliged, once again, to give
up a hypothesis of Benveniste's in favor of a conclusion that appears more banal: if *nepos*, "grandson of grandfather," took on the

meaning of "wastrel," relations of indulgence and familiarity must necessarily have existed between grandchildren and grandfathers (paternal and maternal, for all we know).[39] In other words, the metaphor implies that the grandchild must have handled with a certain carelessness and a lack of inhibition the grandfather's goods, so much so as to give the impression that his grandfather was spoiling him. Porphyry writes, explaining Horace, *Epode* 1.34: "The ancients spoke of the grandchild as spendthrift and dissolute, because in reality those who are reared by a grandfather usually live looser and softer lives." Grandfathers spoil grandchildren, give what a father never would, and thus transform their own *nepotes* into loose and spendthrift persons, hence our metaphor.

This somewhat simple conclusion has a rather important implication for us. It puts into our hands the rest of the argument we were building: now we know that relations marked by indulgence and familiarity must have existed also between grandfather and grandchild. In other words, where before, on the basis of Seneca, Cicero, and some legends, we could say that relations of familiarity and intimacy existed between maternal uncles and nephews, after our analysis of the metaphor we know that analogous relations must also have existed between grandfathers and grandchildren. Now this justifies in full the designation of the maternal uncle as a *avunculus* (little grandfather).

The point becomes clearer if placed within the whole framework of kinship relations and attitudes. A given *ego* found, among his male relatives in the first generation above him, two examples of severity and reserve: *pater* and *patruus*. It must have seemed natural, then, to shift the maternal uncle, who was the third male relative at the same level, but with whom the relations were familiar and intimate, to the still higher level, that of the grandfather, with whom relations were equally indulgent. Thus it was that the maternal uncle, under the pressure of the system of attitudes, underwent a linguistic shift toward the grandparents, just as in the societies studied by Radcliffe-Brown,[40] in which one and the same term designates both grandfather and maternal uncle because of the system of attitudes.

That relations with the second older generation should be affectionate and indulgent hardly is surprising. Our societies, too, do something similar; but, above all, the pattern is common in those societies that go by alternate generations; that is, by setting close bonds between the first and third, rather than first and second, generations. On this score, too, Granet offers interesting examples from ancient China,[41] where the pattern of alternate generations created, on one side, a marked familiarity between grandfather and grandson and, on the other, a chilly severity between fathers and sons. So, too, in Rome, the succession of the ancestors was marked by a similar pattern, with strong bonds between the first and third generations, grandfather to grandson, and weak bonds between the first and second generations, father to son; we owe this observation to Benveniste's study of "grandfatherhood" in Roman kinship.[42]

Let us turn again to the Roman patrimony of legend. The story of Numitor and his daughter's sons, Romulus and Remus, illustrates the relations between grandfather and grandson. But the legend does not say much on our specific theme. More promising, then, may be another hint, which has at least the merit of making us reflect on the cultural reasons behind an extraordinarily rich text, Virgil's *Aeneid*. Every Virgilian reader remembers the figure of Evander, aged and unlucky father, highly noble. There is no need to be reminded of the scene in which he bids farewell to his youthful son Pallas (8.554ff.), which is a picture full of tenderness and emotion, as likewise his heartbreak before his son's corpse (11.148ff.). How different is Evander from the Roman fathers described by Dionysius, unfeeling at the death of their own sons! Virgilian tenderness, sign of a poetic nature and of a new culture? Surely, surely it is so.

Yet something strikes us in the Virgilian legend which might make us wonder whether the poet, rather than merely inventing, perhaps redirected to the channel of this paternal role certain feelings that, originally, had run in a different stream. Evander is old (8.560; 11.165); he differs greatly, for example, from Mezentius, who also is the father of an unlucky youth; he differs greatly from

Aeneas, who has a son not that much younger. Mezentius and Aeneas, to be sure, are warriors in full force, fearsome and strong, whereas Evander for a long time now has been far from the moil of battle, from men in armor. Mothers, rather then fathers, complement his feelings of love for his son, who is all that he has. Virgil's strokes are quick, like some mute chorus of extras: "The mothers redouble with fear his prayers" (8.556), and, as his son leaves, "the mothers stand fearful on the walls and follow with their eyes" (8.592). And when the corpse of Pallas comes home, this chorus breaks out in grief, making a mournful prelude to the aged father's lament: "After the mothers have seen it approaching the house, they fire the city with their cries" (11.146). Evander, then, is a very old father, with a very young son: a tender father echoed and accompanied by fearful Arcadian mothers. Can it be, then, pure chance that Dionysius calls Evander "metropator" (*Ant. Rom.* 1.32.1);[43] that is, the "maternal grandfather" of Pallas, not the father? Certainly the intense concern of a grandfather would somehow be more fitting for the aged Evander of Virgil. Or better, not more fitting, because the fatherly guise is also fitting, which Virgil, guided by a different sensibility, gave to feelings that perhaps in the legendary model belonged to an aged grandfather.

We have reached the end of our inquiry. By now the network of attitudes, with their linguistic consequences, should be clear. As in other societies, so in Rome an indulgent maternal uncle is set over against a stern father, and this avuncular concern appears to leave substantial traces later, outside of legend. As for the name *avunculus* (little grandfather), the designation appears based on the fact that with the grandfather, as with the mother's brother, one had familiar and permissive relations: from *nepos* as "grandson of grandsire," too, comes the sense of *nepos* as "wastrel." Because such intimate relations were impossible with the father and his brother, who were the other members of the contiguous generation, the maternal uncle, as the sole contiguous male relative with whom one did enjoy familiarity, came to be shifted linguistically to the generation of the grandfather.

How did this linguistic shift take place? With what morphological means? We realize that we have gotten to the bottom of the

term *avunculus* only in regard to the root, which is to say its relation with *avus;* but the suffix also requires a brief concluding note.
Clearly diminutive in form, it was already so identified by Paulus-
Festus (13 L); and it transforms *avus* to *avunculus* ("grandfather"
to "grandfatherkin"). Such formations are well known for their generically affective character, to use Hoffmann's old category, which
is difficult to do without:[44] affectivity can show up in contexts of
intimacy, as Hoffmann still termed them:[45] pleasing, playful, also
subtly ironic, as when Cicero describes Clodius, "the pretty little
boy gets up" ("surgit pulchellus puer," *Att.* 1.16.10), and so on.
Therefore, the simple fact that a maternal uncle is named by a
diminutive, the only one among kinship names, allows us to sense
an intimate, affective glow that must have surrounded this personage. The linguistic register in which maternal uncle moves is that
of certain playful or affectionate passages in Plautine comedy or
Catullan lyrics, all too familiar. Just think of the *patruus:* in no way
could one refer to him in the diminutive.

We can push our analysis a bit further. The normal diminutive
of *avus,* which we might expect, would be **avolus.*[46] The ending
-unculus would presuppose **avon-,* a stem that is never attested.[47]
Thus we shall have to suppose that *avunculus* also belongs to the
number of the irregular diminutives in which the ending *-unculus*
does not result from a stem in *-on* + *-culus,* but functions as a
suffix in its own right and hence can be attached to differing stems,
though generally those ending in *-o* or *-a.*

We have *furunculus* (little thief), derived from *fur,* thanks to Cicero (*Pis.* 66).[48] Here, of course, an analogy may have been at work
with the regular *latrunculus* (little thief). Then there is the intricate
problem presented by *lembunculus* (little boat), often found in the
form *lenunculus.*[49] As for *lucunculus,* a kind of sweet, it appears to
be found in diverse combinations with *lucuntulus* (cf. *lucuns -untis,*
TLL 7.1750). Other cases, however, are quite clear, such as *ranun-
culus* (froglet), from *rana* in Cicero (*Div.* 1.15), used also metaphorically of *clientes* in Cicero (*Fam.* 7.18); like *domuncula* (houselet), from *domus* (Vitruvius 6.7.4; Valerius Maximus 4.4.8 and
16).[50] And, finally, *aprunculus* (little boar), from *aper,* used in an
inscription to designate a military standard.[51] The regular form of

this diminutive, *apriculus,* appears in Ennius (*Var.* 38 Vahl[2]: *apriculus piscis;* cf. Apuleius, *Apol.* 34). Two diminutives of this kind also come from Petronius: *statuncula* (statuettes) (50.6), a form also found in inscriptions,[52] and *sangunculus* (66.2),[53] from *sanguis* (blood); the form *sanguiculus* appears in Pliny (*Hist. nat.* 28.209).

We can sense an affectionate and playful touch in "houselet" and "froglet," and even more so in "little thief." We learn more, however, from the other forms because of their distribution. *Aprunculus* (boarlet) seems to belong to soldiers' jargon: the only examples come from inscriptions, whereas literary sources give the regular form *apriculus.* Both of the other examples come from Trimalchio's Dinner in Petronius: *sangunculus* is a nonce word, doubling the regular form, *sanguiculus* (blood pudding); and *statunculum* has parallels only in inscriptions or glossographies. In short, it would seem that the irregular diminutive in -*unculus* enjoyed a certain fortune at linguistic levels of the lower sort, to the extent of being prized by Petronian ex-slaves or by soldiers. Something of this kind might apply also to *avunculus,* to be thought of, then, as a diminutive of markedly colloquial and trivial character.

Be that as it may, we have an explicit witness for the stylistic level of *avunculus,* given us by Daniel's Servius in a gloss on Virgil: "'Both *pater* Aeneas and *avunculus* Hector arouse': some consider *avunculus* rather lowly for an epic poem (*humiliter in heroico carmine dictum*)" (*Aen.* 3.343). Evidently some purists considered *avunculus* a bit too humble, too abject,[54] to appear in epic language, and they criticized Virgil for this. Thus *avunculus* was not a kinship term with a neutral function, as could have been the case with *patruus* or *consobrinus.* The diminutive character, perhaps particular lowly, was still strongly felt: alongside the denotation of "maternal uncle" survived the playful connotation of "grandfatherkin."

To add the obvious corollary at this point seems hardly necessary: a kinship term has to be considered from the viewpoint of its users. Thus a sister's son who used a formation of this kind to designate his mother's brother must have enjoyed relations of great familiarity with him. The narratives of legend and the behavior of every day agree in this with the data of historical linguistics.

The Maternal Uncle, "Defender" of the Nephew

Having dealt thus far with the relations between maternal uncles and nephews, let us take a moment, before adding the last link to our chain, to look at the relations between maternal uncles and nieces. Two Roman legends, among the best known, merit attention also from this standpoint.

The first legend is that of Virginia, the girl threatened by the decemvir Appius Claudius. We recall how Appius fell in love with the lovely maiden, either noble or plebeian, according to the source we choose; how he bribed one of his people to claim her as a slave; and how her father, Virginius, giving himself up for lost, preferred to kill her rather that yield her to rape. In Livy (3.44) and Dionysius (*Ant. Rom.* 11.28), unlike the other sources, which are much more laconic,[55] alongside the father of Virginia appear her fiancé, Icilius, and Numitorius, her maternal uncle.[56] Numitorius appears in Dionysius's account—which, as usual, is fuller—engaged in a lengthy defense of the girl: indeed, in his role as uncle (30.1), he claims the right to keep her in his custody while awaiting the sentence, because Virginius is still with the army. We are told that Virginia, "under those circumstances, took refuge with him, being long since orphaned of her mother and lacking, too, her father" (30.3). Then, once Virginius has done his tragic deed, Numitorius and Icilius, gathered around the corpse with other friends and relatives, "call the people to freedom" (38.2). In Livy the scene is more pathetic still: "Icilius and Numitorius show the bloodless body to the people: they bewail the crime of Appius, the girl's unlucky beauty, the father's obligation" (3.48.7).

What we have, then, is a maternal uncle who seeks to defend his niece from rape and who, after her tragic death, makes it his business that the people take revenge on the tyrant. His presence, however, could be of little meaning, pure happenstance, even though in the personages of a myth or legend it is difficult for cultural traits to be due to chance. But in matters of violence to a niece and revenge, maternal uncles have a tendency to intervene, and the pattern is repeated and thus acquires meaning.

The second legend, Lucretia's, shares more than one trait with that of Virginia. The resemblance leaps to the gaze,[57] and ancient sources underlined it.[58] Again a tyrant uses violence on a free woman, causing her tragic death; her relatives take revenge, raise popular support, and provoke the tyrant's fall. The framework is the same in all respects, except each function changes greatly in practice. This time the violator is Sextus, son of the king, not himself the tyrant; the heroine is not a maiden, but a married woman and, furthermore, the wife of a cousin of the violator.[59] The device for getting at her is not a juridical fiction (that which makes the Virginia legend paradoxically like some comedy in Greek dress, albeit with another outcome):[60] no, Sextus cleverly takes advantage of kinship; he manages to get into Lucretia's presence just because he is "joined by blood" (Ovid, *Fast.* 2.788; Dionysius, *Ant. Rom.* 4.64.4). Then he turns against the married woman even her sense of shame and good repute: if Lucretia does not accept, Sextus will kill her and place beside her the lifeless body of a slave. Then he will say that he surprised them together in adultery. Here, then, the rape is consummated; in the legend of Virginia, only threatened. In short, we have two stories substantially the same, and yet substantially unlike.

If we look at the avengers who stir up popular ire, they are three, as in the Virginia story:[61] to the father, Virginius, corresponds Lucretius Tricipitinus; to the fiancé, Icilius, the husband, Collatinus; but to the maternal uncle, Numitorius, nothing corresponds directly, for the third avenger, Brutus, appears to share no direct bond of kinship with Lucretia, even though, as cousin of Sextus on the mother's side, he is also related in some way to Collatinus.[62] And yet in Livy (1.59.9), it is Brutus, not the father or the husband, who merely stands by and cries out, and Brutus who pulls the dagger from Lucretia's corpse and swears by this blood to drive out the tyrants, a scene that Ovid retells (*Fast.* 2.837ff.). And again it is Brutus, like Numitorius with Icilius, who displays the body of the wretched victim to the Romans: "He displayed the woman to the multitude of the people" (Zonara 7.11). One version of the legend, however, casts a different light on the network of relations around Lucretia. In Servius's commentary on Virgil, among the relatives summoned by Lucretia are her "husband, Collatinus; father, Tricipitinus; and *avunculus, Brutus*" (*Aen.* 8.846).[63] Hence the analogies with the story draw closer: here the third avenger is likewise the maternal uncle.

This Servian note forms part of a series of departures and differences from Livy and Dionysius; together, they amount to more than happenstance or mistake.[64] In Servius, Sextus, rather than Arruns, is the rapist, and, furthermore, Sextus gets to Lucretia not by means of kinship, but with a faked letter from Collatinus. Again, this rapist brings with him to the chamber the slave that will serve his turn to blacken the wife's posthumous honor, and this time, indeed, the slave is specifically called Ethiopian. Thus we certainly have another version of the legend, in which, among the other departures, must be numbered Brutus's role of *avunculus*.

Naturally, we could ask at this point: Do we have here an early section of the tale, preserved by Servius and erased by our other sources? Or do we have a late section, tacked on in this version, perhaps even taking after the model of Virginia? The question is quite legitimate, but the answer need not be overvalued, as if it were the only one of importance. When we analyze legendary narratives, we ought not to consider the criterion of their earliness and lateness as principal, and rarely is it the best to employ.

In studying the variants of a legend, it can be disastrous to adopt the model of textual criticism with its reconstructed pedigree or stemma,[65] which supposes an original version or archetype that gradually degenerates through successive copies, becoming more and more corrupt, so the most genuine state of the text can automatically be equated with the oldest. In legend, every variant has its structure, which means its worth, and must be studied with a view to the system in which it organizes its specific traits. Hence the question we asked above has to be reformulated in the following terms: Even granting that one or another particular was written later or tacked on, why did the one who did so feel that he could? He evidently found that a maternal uncle, as defender and avenger of his niece, fitted in: indeed, he found it right to assign

61

just to the maternal uncle, rather than the husband or the father, the main role in the revolt and vendetta. The narrative, in short, when grasped in terms of its system of anthropological and cultural premises,[66] counts on a Brutus *avunculus,* which has to be of interest. It has been suggested that the story of Virginia had, in the avenging *avunculus,* a trait to underscore:[67] namely, that being an *avunculus* constituted a worthy motive for a person to take the lead in a revolt. This in itself would suffice, for us, to judge the Servian variant as important.

I tend to consider Brutus's avuncularity more a trait removed by the other sources than added from the model of Virginia. First, the two narratives are as like in framework as they are unlike in actual detail, so that influence is difficult. Second, the very logic of the narrative leads the reader to expect, in a way, that Brutus have a special link with Lucretia: indeed, the reader's expectation of a motive is somewhat disappointed when no justification emerges for Brutus's central part in the revenge and in the sequel, except for a vague friendship or closeness. But even more than these generic needs for motivation, there is a passage in Livy that has been difficult to interpret and would become clearer if one supposed that Brutus was an uncle. And here we would stand on much firmer ground.

When Brutus snatches the bloody dagger from Lucretia's corpse, he shouts, "By this blood most chaste before [it suffered] regal wrong, I swear that I . . . " (1.59.1). This oath by Lucretia's blood troubled Oglivie,[68] who unerringly noted that it is "unparalleled in Latin" and sounds quite unusual. He takes the oath to be a false archaism that, with other elements also linguistically suspect, betrays the "imaginative reconstruction" that characterizes this stretch of the story. At the same time, however, Oglivie, with his fine knowledge of the language, reminds us of the practice of making oaths "on the highest honour" that one knows, as well as on the gods below and above. He gives the example of "father's bones" in Horace (*Carm.* 2.8.10; Propertius, 2.20.5, etc.), the eyes could be added from Plautus (*Men.* 1060), the eyes and head from Ovid (*Am.* 2.16.43), and the right hand from Virgil (*Aen.* 9.298), to mention only these. In short, it would hardly strike me as strange that an uncle swore by the blood of his niece who had been raped and killed: what unites them is the blood, and it is this blood that, uniting, drives and in a way obliges the uncle to revenge. As will have been remarked, bones, eyes, head, and hand are all strongly symbolic parts of the human body, which thus specifies and directs oath-taking in a particular cultural sphere: and the same can be said, with good reason, also of blood, especially when the oath is sworn by one whose blood is the same.

Indeed, Brutus's oath "on blood" appears well motivated in Livy and by no means out of place in view, also, of the way it gets expressed: not merely by Lucretia's blood, but "by this blood that was most chaste before (it suffered) royal wrong." Her blood, then, was unsullied up to the moment when Tarquin forced her to unite with him. The married woman, even when she undergoes violence against her will and even though she nobly killed herself, loses the purity of her blood. In this regard, Ovid's account is more straightforward and nobly celebrative: Brutus simply says, "I swear for you by this strong and chaste gore" (*Fast.* 2.841). The oath is sworn on the gore (*cruor*), the "spilled blood"; that is, the blood Lucretia poured out by her noble deed.[69] This blood is chaste and strong, a concrete and visible symbol of her virtue. Livy speaks of blood rather than gore, and he furthermore emphasizes that it, after the "royal wrong," has lost its precious chastity.

We can hardly consider happenstance that, in the crime of female adultery, it is precisely the blood that gets befouled. Thus, Atreus in Seneca, when he discovers that his brother Thyestes has seduced his wife, remarks bitterly: "The blood's uncertain" (*Thy.* 341). The blood's purity wavers when a women unites with two men; she makes uncertain that which should be clear and simple by nature. Pliny says the Psilli, the legendary snake charmers, tested the virtue of a bride by exposing her offspring to contact with reptiles, "because the snakes did not flee those born of adulterous blood" (*Hist. nat.* 7.14). It is blood that becomes adulterated, as we still say, by adultery.

Moreover, we know that, after the death of her husband, a Roman widow could not remarry until ten months in order to avoid disorder of the blood, *turbatio sanguinis,* as Ulpian calls it (*Dig.*

1.2.11). The maximum time for gestation was ten months. After that time, a woman no longer risked mingling the two unions in herself, the risk described by the expression "disorder of the blood."[70] In short, Lucretia disordered her blood, even though her union with Sextus was forced. For this reason, to put it bluntly, she was practically forced to kill herself. Once her blood was polluted, there could be no further room for her in the household of Collatinus. It is this pollution of the blood that Brutus underscores so harshly in Livy. This brusque frankness would be much better justified in the spirit of a maternal uncle: a blood relative who sees his own blood polluted and humiliated by the offense to his niece.

Although we cannot get beyond hypothesis, however well rooted in the culture and the text, we can at least cling to the Servian note. Here Brutus is Lucretia's maternal uncle; in the legend there are two instances of an *avunculus* who stands up as defender and avenger of a niece threatened by rape or raped. With this figure, then, the triad of avengers is complete. And they correspond, in their grades of kinship, precisely to those three groups in terms of which the identity and status of a woman are defined: her father (her relatives on the paternal side), her maternal uncle (her relatives on the mother's side), her fiancé (relative by marriage, *adfines*). The three groups that join through her, associating their own blood in her, gather at once around her to defend and avenge her. But let us stay with the uncle.

In the light of these two stories, and the role of defender and avenger played in them by the maternal uncle, we have to reread a gloss in Paulus-Festus which purports to explain why the *avunculus* is so called (13 L):

> *Avunculus*, brother of my mother, drew this form of address from the fact that he is third from me, just as my grandfather [*avus*], but is not of the same right [*eiusdem iuris*]: and for that reason the diminution of the word was made. Or he is addressed as *avunculus* because he takes the place [*optineat locum*] of the grandfather and, by his closeness, watches over his sister's daughter.

The gloss, which closely resembles a following one on the father's sister *(amita)*, first interprets in a way that we call positional, explaining the diminution of grandfather to "grandfatherkin," *avus* to *avunculus,* on the basis of the identity of kinship grades that separates each of them from *ego*. Second, the diminution is interpreted on the basis of an analogy of functions between *avus* and *avunculus:* the *avunculus* can do certain things the *avus* also does, and because of this he is named in relation to *avus* (a type of explanation sometimes used by modern scholars).[71] But why, among all the things an *avunculus* can do in place of an *avus,* does he choose to "protect the sister's daughter"? There is no (pseudo-)etymological reason that could suggest this role for the *avunculus*. However, it all fits very well with what the legend tells us. So we have to infer that Roman custom knew of a tutelary function, protective or defensive, that the maternal uncle exercised toward his niece, which is exemplified by Brutus and Numitorius and explicitly declared by Paulus-Festus. The maternal uncle protects his sister's daughter.

We must remember that the role of mother's brother as guardian and protector of his niece corresponds to a well-known anthropological pattern shared by many cultures. Thus the Roman case only constitutes a chapter in the huge typological novel that links nieces with maternal uncles. Think only of the Gyljiaki legend in which a maternal uncle frees his niece from a bear that had carried her off and raped her, told in the framework of a system of matrimonial exchange that assigns to the maternal uncle a leading role in the wedding of the niece.[72] Among the Lushai, the term *pu* means not only "grandfather, maternal uncle, and every other relative on the side of the mother and the wife,"[73] but also "person expressly chosen as protector or guardian."[74] We also have the evidence of *The Tale of Genji,* the eleventh-century Japanese novel, to the effect that "even a girl of royal blood would lack a future if she had no maternal uncles to defend her, to whom she could turn."[75]

In America, among the Sherente, "the bride's maternal uncle performs the following functions: He organizes and carries out the abduction of the bridegroom as a preliminary to the marriage; he takes in his niece in the event of a divorce and protects her against her husband; if the niece's husband dies, he forces her brother-in-law to marry her; together with her husband, *he avenges his niece if she is raped.* In other words, he is his niece's protector with, and if necessary against, her husband." [76]

Having gathered these comparative scraps, we must draw the line, leaving to others, if they so desire, the task of interpreting this bond from a standpoint of general anthropology which we cannot take up here. [77] When we think of the examples of archaic Roman history studied so far, one fact stands out: the *avunculus,* tender and watchful guardian of his sister's son, also has the function of defending his sister's daughter in matters that are perforce more risky and treacherous for a female: matrimony and sexuality. We shall see in chapters 4 and 13, when we analyze in general the theme of matrilineal temptation in Rome, how this role of the maternal uncle fits into the wider dialectic between takers and givers, between paternal and maternal, and constitutes one of its most suggestive manifestations.

In closing, let us reemphasize how extremely interesting, in view of the maternal uncle's role, is that cycle of legends which entwines the expulsion of the kings and the creation of the first consuls in Rome. Collatinus, only too tender a protector of his sister's sons, had earlier found in Brutus an *avunculus* who made common cause with him, showing readiness to avenge his sister's daughter. Brutus, for his part, who is a sister's son persecuted by his maternal uncle Tarquin, finds himself forced to kill, as a Roman *pater,* his own sons, who had been led astray by the strong bond of familiarity which bound them to the Vitelli, their maternal uncles.

Four

Mother's Sister: *Matertera*

"Almost another mother"

For the maternal aunt to be a figure of great affection for the nephew seems rather likely in itself: what could be more natural than for a child to sense in its mother's sister someone with affections like the mother's? On this, the ethnographic parallels are interesting. Among the Arapesh of New Guinea, children's training is strongly geared to affection and to trust in the world.[1] To this end, the Arapesh seek to make children, from their infancy, familiar with everyone who surrounds them and, in the first place, with their relatives. Thus, the mother introduces her own sister: "This is your other mamma . . . other mamma, other mamma. See your other mamma. She is good, she brings you something to eat. Smile, she's good."[2] We sense that, for speakers of Latin, "other mamma" was conveyed by the word *matertera*, "almost another mother" (*quasi mater altera*), as Paulus-Festus (121 L) notes.[3] It is also quite understandable that from time to time the maternal aunt may help her own sister to carry out the chores of mothering. Indeed, precisely this attitude of maternal aunts is cited by the Baggara of the Sudan in order to justify the practice of marrying inside the clan: "The women say that a son gets better care when his mother lives in her own household with her sisters, and that they can help her if she falls ill."[4]

We are fortunate to have good evidence about the attitudes of maternal aunts to nephews in Rome. This role of women seems to have been particularly marked in Roman society: it filled an affective dimension that lasted a particularly long time in the social structure. Its importance, moreover, can be inferred from its prominence in myth. The role of *matertera* gets encoded culturally in the very events that define the mythic foundation of the community: Queen Amata is the first *matertera* in Rome.

Wife of King Latinus, Amata is the sister of Venilia, mother of Turnus, and thus is Turnus's maternal aunt (Virgil, *Aen.* 10.29; Servius on *Aen.* 6.90, 7.366, and 2.29).[5] And so this particular institutional and affective bond between Amata and the young Rutulian king must account for the exceptional love she bears him, which is well known to readers of the *Aeneid.* The unusualness of her behavior shows through the very words of the poet, when he describes the force with which Amata sought to push the wedding between Turnus and her own daughter, Lavinia: "To have him joined as son-in-law, she hastened with amazing love" (7.57). Her feeling for Turnus is not just the generic affection toward a future son-in-law, or the bond that links, in our view, an aunt with her nephew: her feeling takes on the look of a real and true mother's love. With the same words a mother would address to her son, Amata urges Turnus not to go into battle, where she would risk losing in him the sole stay of her life (12.54ff.). And Turnus, himself caught up in the emotional level of her words, can do no less than answer, addressing her as "o Mater!" Not dissimilar is Ovid's story of Ino, when she finds herself with her sister's son up against the raging Bacchants and shrieks to the gods, "Aid a wretched mother!" (*Fast.* 6.473ff.). The *matertera* is in some sense like the nephew's mother, and the nephew can so address her.

Like a mother faced with a son's death, Amata wants to pay with her own life for the wrong she believes she has done Turnus by, through her obstinacy, causing war between the Trojans and the Latins, resulting in his death. Between the two exists a relationship almost better described as that between mother and son rather than that between nephew and maternal aunt. This deeply felt connection ought perhaps to be given more weight in reading the *Aeneid* because it both underlies and moves the whole unfolding of the story in the so-called Iliadic part of the poem.[6] In any case, the close overlapping of *mater* and *matertera* which emerges from the Amata myth is further confirmed by the following evidence.

The *matertera* figures in another Roman myth, but more impersonally, only because the names of the two sisters are unknown. In the clash between the Horati and the Curiati, as Dionysius tells it, the mothers of both sets of brothers were sisters (*Rom.* 3.15.2). Tullus describes their relationship: "For the mother of our Horati is the sister of the mother of the Alban Curiati, and the children were nursed on the bosoms of both women and love each other no less that their own brothers." Further along, the Horati and Curiati are called "cousins reared together." Thus, in the background of the tragic affair, in which brothers' blood will spill, there emerge the figures of the two sister-mothers, who nursed each other's sons without discriminating among them. This function of nourishing, in a broader sense, by the *matertera* of the nephew will require our attention later. Certainly, in the picture of the two women, each holding the other's sons at her breast, we find the same symbolic expression of the bond between maternal aunt and nephew which is performed ritually in the action of the *materterae* at the *Matralia*.

Let us leave myth for its logical continuation in literature. Even the careless reader can hardly fail to realize how much the plot that underlies from time to time one or another ancient comedy owes its energy to the workings of relationship and kinship. Children lost and recovered, unknown nephews, severe fathers, and so on make up now and again a kind of working generator for the individual text. Naturally, in this respect the plots of the comedy in Greek dress (*palliata*), with their various Greek models, differ from those of the comedy in toga (*togata*), which are based on Roman domestic situations (and, of course, have Roman dress). And to the latter, naturally, our study must turn, trusting that the paucity of surviving fragments will be compensated by the Roman authenticity of the themes.

Among these themes, the very problems that spring from kinship relations must have figured, and to a preponderant degree.
We can confirm this simply by reasoning from the surviving titles
of Greek and Roman comedies: among some 159 titles of the
Greek, only 5 (about 3 percent) specifically refer to kinship or a
related theme, whereas among the 71 surviving titles of the Roman, 11 (about 17 percent) refer to relations of this sort. If the
authors favored such themes even in the titles, we may suppose
that the public, hence Roman, culture liked seeing on the stage
that network of human relations which springs from cousins (thus
the *Consobrini* of Afranius), from in-laws (thus *Fratriae,* again of
Afranius), and so on. We should also place, within this frame of
attention to the knots deriving from kinship and affinity, the two
toga comedies called *Materterae,* one by Afranius and the other by
Atta.[7] Only a fragment of the former has survived (207ff. R[3]):

> When she sees that she
> is at this pass, she entrusts her tiny daughter
> to her sisters

In Ribbeck's brief reconstruction, this scene appears to provide
background, whether in a prologue or a later flashback: the main
character must have been the baby when grown. Her mother appears in the passage at the point of death, entrusting her tiny
daughter to her *materterae*. In view of the mother's decision, and
knowing something of the workings of comedy, we can easily infer
that the baby's father is absent, at least for the time of the background scene: will he be the usual missing person who later turns
up and recognizes the child abandoned all those years before? This
circumstance will also help clarify the context for some of the in-
scriptional material we shall analyze later. We may assume that the
materterae played a decisive role in the rest of the play, justifying
its title. The function of the *materterae* consists precisely in acting
as mothers in a situation in which the real mother is missing; that
is, taking care of such a little child.

Such a particularly affectionate relationship between the *matertera* and the baby—almost that of the nursemaid and the nursling,

or grandmother and grandson (a similarly institutionalized closeness)[8]—also appears in a passage of Persius which deals with in-
considerate prayers (2.31–39):

> Look, a grandmother or god-fearing maternal aunt
> takes the boy from the cradle and purifies his brow
> and lips, wet before with naughty finger and drool to clean,
> because she is skilled in stopping eyes that burn.
> Then she claps her hands and sends with prayerful vow
> her skinny hope to Licinus' fields or Crassus' shrines:
> "Him as son-in-law may king and queen desire, may girls
> steal him, roses spring up where he walks!"
> But I to my nursemaid don't trust vows . . .

Interesting also for the folkloristic evidence of jingles that
grandmothers and maternal aunts addressed to children in their
charge, the text brings to the foreground the figure of the *matertera.* Her role here runs over into that of the nursemaid, as the poet
shows, both because of the motherly concern toward a child not
her own and because she is the very personage who desires the
rosiest pleasures for the little one, coddling him.[9] The *matertera,*
who nursed her little nephews in the myth of the Horati and Curiati, here also shares certain affectionate qualities of the nursemaid, verging on an almost complete overlap of functions.

With this overlap in mind, we can now reread an episode from
the *Golden Ass* of Apuleius, the tale of Cupid and Psyche, just at
the moment when the wicked sisters learn that Psyche is about to
become a mother: "How much good you think you're bringing us
in that sack! With how much joy you'll cheer up our whole household! O happy us, whom the golden child's nurture will make
happy! If he matches his parents' beauty, as he should, he shall be
an absolute Cupid" (5.14).

The two *materterae* clearly do not resist taking on the role of
nursemaids for the little one: they will have the responsibility for
nurture and the related joys. Moreover, in the words of his maternal aunts, the child becomes a "golden child," a "Cupid," although
Psyche has said nothing to them about its parentage, so they do
not know that the baby "really" is the son of love. Also, recalling

the jingle of the *matertera*-nursemaid in Persius, we find precise parallels. "Golden child" is quite comparable to the boy who makes "roses spring where he walks!"; and "Cupid" is identical to the child whom, one day, the girls will go for. In short, in the very language of the future *materterae,* their feeling of being nursemaids to the little one blossoms. Even before they say expressly that the responsibilities of nurture will fall to them, they are already mouthing the formulas that nursemaids use to coddle children in the crib. Therefore, that we know these wicked sisters are just pretending only goes to prove that their words fit the appropriate model. One who pretends has to be as true as possible: an evil *matertera* must try to hide her wicked feelings under the mask that best conforms to what is expected of a maternal aunt *comme il faut.*

From the Silent World of Inscriptions

What the relationship between maternal aunts and nephews was supposed to be emerges clearly enough, I think, from the examples gathered thus far. Other examples may be sought by widening our horizons in place and time. Reaching into the entire body of Latin inscriptions, we shall interpret the relationships between maternal aunts and nephews in some of the most significant texts. Naturally, there is no dearth of generic inscriptions, in which only the act of dedication itself testifies to the mutual affection of a maternal aunt and her nephew. Clearly, in an undertaking of this sort, the specific meaning of each individual case depends on the presence or absence of the defining members of the family unit, as well as on the words, both kinship terms and proper names, employed in the system created.

Take an inscription from Velletri: "Titedia Apicula, hateful to no one, mother of Colpus and *matertera* of Themis" (*Not. Scav.* 1926, VI, vol. II, 426). Or take a similar case: "To Turania Vera, *mater,* Turania Quarta, *matertera,* and Cornelia Optatina, most revered cousin" (*CIL* VI 27831).[10] Generally, in these epitaphs a nephew, with other members of his own family, wished to memorialize his own *matertera* either with others or alone. The case differs when the *matertera* makes a dedication in honor of her dead nephew.[11] Here the sociological plot thickens, because generally in such cases one or both of the parents is lacking: it is as if the *matertera* has to take up the slack left by one or both of the main players.

The missing parent is the mother in the following two cases, the first of which is from Vienna: "Perseus, *pater,* and Primigeneia, *matertera,* to Perseus, most sweet son" (*CIL.* XII 5866). Note that Primigeneia, the *matertera* of young Perseus, stands at the side of father Perseus, in the place usually taken by the mother, and that young Perseus is classified simply as "son" to them both. It is unclear if this is due to the linguistic confusion of trying to say something like "to Perseus the most sweet son of him and of her sister," or if it reflects some unspecifiable history of family feelings: maybe both. The second case comes from Luceria: "For L. Vitorius Fortunatus, [who] lived thirteen years, nine months, Vitoria Briseis, his *matertera,* and P. Tamullius Eros, his *tata,* and for themselves set up" (*CIL.* IX 899). Here again, alongside the father—if this is what *tata* means[12]—is not the *mater,* but the *matertera.* The placement of the *matertera* next to the child's father amounts to a functional analogy that is especially striking when found in locations that are thousands of kilometers apart. I would not rule out the possibility that parallels of this sort presuppose a cultural institution such as sisterhood.

We also have the converse situation, in which the father is missing: "Cornelia Ferocilla and Coelia Oclatia to Coelia Marcella, who died at age 35, *mater* and *matertera* for (their) daughter most unhappily and faithfully offered" (*CIL.* III 2738, Colonia Claudia Aequum, Dalmatia). Here the dead woman is classified as daughter of both her *mater* and her *matertera,* just as the dead man discussed above was referred to as son of his *pater* and *matertera,* which further underlines the closeness of *matertera* and *mater.* Still more singular is the fact that the dead woman, if we trust the order and placement of the words, has the same family name as her *matertera,* rather than that of her *mater.* The family tree would appear to stand as follows:

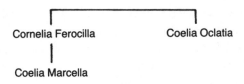

Cornelia Ferocilla   Coelia Oclatia

Coelia Marcella

The fact that two sisters have different family names can be interpreted by supposing that one was born before the marriage that produced the other.[13] Not wholly clear, however, is the closely shared bond that the identity of family names seems to imply, in the father's absence, between the daughter and the *matertera*. Similar to the previous example is another inscription from the same place: "Cornelia Ferocilla. For Cornelia Ferocilla, most faithful daughter, her *mater* and *matertera* offered" (*CIL*. III 2737). This situation, too, appears to lack a male figure, and it places the mother and *matertera* together, with the dead woman once again called daughter of both sisters. Indeed, if this Cornelia Ferocilla is the same as in the previous example, or belongs to the same family, there would be a sort of materteral lineage, in which twice consecutively a mother and her sister join together in shared affection for a daughter, who is at once both daughter and sister's daughter, in one family group, almost as if by a tradition.

In still more complex cases, lacking both father and mother, the *matertera* appears to fulfill the whole system of family relations: "For Clodia Rufina, Quintus's daughter, her grandmother Furia Helice and Rufina, her *matertera*, most dutifully" (*CIL*. II 4352, Tarraco). Again, the relationships may be charted, assuming that Furia Helice is the maternal grandmother:

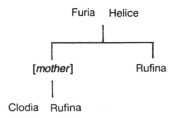

Furia Helice

[*mother*]   Rufina

Clodia Rufina

It is striking that the niece shares the cognomen Rufina with her *matertera*. A quite analogous case appears in another inscription: "For Saturninus, (who) lived 4 years, 11 months, 10 days, Pomponia Saturnina, his *matertera*, did this for herself and for her own and their posterity" (*CIL.* VI 25913). Again, the cognomen links the child with its *matertera*. Indeed, these last two cases also invite reflection on a case mentioned earlier (*CIL.* III 2738), in which the dead woman and her *matertera* shared the family name Coelia. And, finally, we have the following: "For Quintus Aemilius Maximus, Aemilia Restituta, *matertera*, did this; (he) lived 49 years, 41 days, 5 hours. Aemilia Cupita. Lived 14 years, 40 days, Aemilia Restituta did this *mater*" (*CIL.* VI 11086). Here, it is the same person at the same time who performs the roles of *mater* and *matertera:*

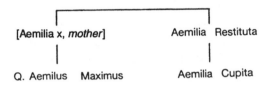

[Aemilia x, *mother*]   Aemilia Restituta

Q. Aemilus Maximus   Aemilia Cupita

Restituta carried out both of her duties, even if her nephew died at nearly age fifty. The family names of the daughter and the nephew are those of the mothers. It also may be worth recalling in this context the situation of Afranius's comedy, in which the father is clearly missing and the dying mother entrusts her little daughter to her sisters, hence the title *Materterae*.

The evidence presented thus far shows something more than a generic bond of affection between nephew and maternal aunt. The *matertera* can appear at the father's or mother's side, filling one or the other's absence and sharing in the dedication to a dear dead one simply classified as daughter or son; and, in the absence of both parents, the *matertera* can appear alone. If we are on the right track, we can begin to infer from these skeletal remains of language a constant functional value of the *matertera*, similar to that which we had seen already in other texts: she is the trusted stand-in. Like the unnamed *materterae* of Afranius, Pomponia Saturnina, Coelia Oclatia, Aemilia Restituta, and other maternal aunts perhaps had the task of rearing and supporting children who had lost one or both of their parents. That old institution of fondness, shaped at the dawn of the Roman family, found, in the vicissitudes that the family nucleus unavoidably encounters, the historic food for its survival in practice.

We have before us, then, an anthropological model well marked out and unusually solid, by which I mean founded on objective premises, which emerge without intermediaries from the social and emotional needs of the family group. How else can we explain why such a relationship persists without a break from the myth of Amata to the family of a Gallo-Roman living during the empire's decline? In his *Parentalia*, Ausonius gives us invaluable evidence: rarely does a poet feel the need to make explicit, through a set of epigrammatic vignettes, the whole system of fond relations which linked him to his own family. The complex web of affections and familial institutions cannot be analyzed in its entirety here, although it certainly deserves better than the officious and rather parochial perspective applied to it by certain scholars.[14]

Focusing, then, on the poet's relationship with his *materterae*, we read these words to the first, Aemilia Hilaria (6.1):

> And you, maternal aunt in degree of family, yet merit marking
>   by a son's pious fondness with a mother's place
>
> . . .
>
> Because as a mother with loving counsel you cherished me,
>   I give in turn these honors with last rites as a son.

So Aemilia Hilaria nurtured Ausonius with love and advice, like a mother. This is also true of the other *matertera*, Aemilia Dryadia (25.1ff.):

> You, too, Dryadia, maternal aunt, . . .
> I of your sister born nearly son
>   with pious mouth adore
>
> . . .
>
> In me you learned, *matertera*,
>   a *mater* to become.

Once again, the word "son" returns; but above all, now, there is the singular interpretation of the usual tasks: Dryadia seems to have performed the familiar roles of second mother and nursemaid for the little Ausonius, which he interprets as her apprenticeship for the role of mother: "Discebas in me, matertera, / mater uti fieres." From the viewpoint of family life, this suggests a further general reason for the traditional role of maternal aunts.

A Ritual of Maternal Aunts:
The Feast of Mater Matuta

The relationship between maternal aunt and sister's son now leads us to new ground, perhaps unexpected: the history of religion. The figure of the *matertera,* with its social and emotional vectors, underlies one of the most fascinating rites in Roman tradition, the *Matralia,* which was the festival devoted by Roman woman to Mater Matuta on 11 June. During the festival, women prayed not for their own sons, but for those of their sisters. So they addressed the goddess not as mothers, but as maternal aunts. Here we shall discuss the terms of the problem, although we cannot go into all the questions posed by the rite.[15]

So who was Mater Matuta?[16]

1. She was a goddess honored from early times in Rome; her temple was said to have been built by Servius Tullius (Ovid, *Fast.* 6.480; Livy, 5.19); another devotee of hers was M. Furius Camillus (Livy 5.19.6 and 23; Plutarch, *Camillus* 5).[17]

2. She received particular honor at Satricum, south of Rome. Excavation at the site of her celebrated temple has made it possible to reconstruct roughly two different phases:[18] one that goes back to c. 6-c. 5 B.C., the other to c. 4-c. 3 B.C. Particularly interesting for us are the contents of one of the three deposits found, dating to c. 4 B.C. It contains reproductions of heads and other parts of the human body, like the objects also found in a still older votive deposit near the temple; it also contains seated female figures, with an infant nursing at the breast or sitting on the lap. In other words, together with the typical representations of mothering are

votive objects, the heads and other body parts, typically associated with gods related to human health.[19]

3. Lucretius identifies Mater Matuta with a goddess of the dawn (5.656): "Also at the established time Matuta spreads rosy dawn / throughout the shores and unfolds light." And we recall, of course, the adjective *matutinus* (of the morning).

4. *Matuta* also is an epithet of two goddesses: Juno, who was honored as Juno Matuta in a temple that the consul G. Cornelius Cethegus built in Rome in 194 B.C. (Livy 34.53.3);[20] and Pales, in a dedication of 167 B.C. by M. Atilius Regulus (Schol. Virgil, *Geo.* 3.1).[21] Also, Augustine tells us that the goddess Matuta presided over the ripening grain (*Civ. dei* 4.8).

5. Poets and writers often identify Mater Matuta with Ino-Leucothea, the sister of Semele and the nursemaid and stepmother of Dionysus (e.g., Cicero, *Tusc.* 1.28 and *Nat. deor.* 3.48; Ovid, *Fast.* 6.476; Hyginus, *Fab.* 2 and 223).[22] Perhaps the Eileithya-Leucothea honored at Pyrgi is also to be identified with Mater Matuta.[23]

6. In Rome, she was worshipped on 11 June during the *Matralia*. This festival gets us to the heart of the problem. The ritual had singular features, which have long tormented philologists and historians of religion. The two most remarkable are the following:

a) The women who took part in the ritual offered prayers and showed fondness, by hugging, not their own children, but those of their sisters (Plutarch, *Camillus* 5.2, *Quaest. Rom.* 17, *Frat. Amor.* 21).[24]

b) A slave woman was introduced to the temple, struck, and driven out (Plutarch, *Camillus* 5.2 and *Quaest. Rom.* 16; Ovid, *Fast.* 6.479ff).[25]

Radke offers the most recent and organic interpretation of *Mater Matuta*.[26] He believes that *Mater Matuta* means something like the following: the *mater* (mother), who has done good. He sees in play a root element, **Ma-*, meaning "goodness," here in the form of **ma-tus*, which he supposes to mean "good" and to be an adjective in form like *ma-nus*, by analogy with the alternation between *plenus* and *ple-tus*. He supposes, from this new **matus*, the derivation

of a verb, *matuo,* "to do good," having a participle, *matutus,* on
analogy with *statutus,* and so forth. Only in this case the past participle would not have the usual passive value, but would be active, so the feminine Matuta must mean "She who has done good."
In this fashion, the Mater Matuta would be connected with the
goddess of the first level in the excavations at Satricum, although
this assertion is somewhat unusual, given that the offerings belonging to a divinity that brings health also appear in the second
level of excavations. Also, in Radke's view, Iuno Matuta and Pales
Matuta would be so called only because they have, in a sense,
"done a favor" to the persons who prayed to them, allowing them
to win in war. As for the mother goddess of the second level at
Satricum, she would be only a specialized form, as well as ob-
scured by Hellenizing reinterpretations.

Radke's proposals would require some discussion, especially on
a linguistic grounds; for example, the assumption of an active past
participle.[27] For us, however, it suffices to emphasize that *manus/
manis* means "tame," "domestic," "civilized," not simply "good."[28]
Thus, Radke's argument, based wholly on *manus* meaning "good,"
no longer stands up: could Mater Matuta be the "Mother that
tames"?

One wonders, in Radke's reconstruction, about the role in the
Matralia of the prayer for the sisters' children. It has none. In other
words, Radke has studied the divinity and said nothing of the ritual in which her worship unfolds; no doubt he took over an unlucky guess by Rose.[29] Rose found the verb *soriare,* "to grow
breasts," in Festus's descriptions of pubescent girls. Thus, Rose
imagined a prayer of this type: "Mater Matuta, I pray and beseech
that you be willing and propitious to boys and sisters," with reference to "boys who are developing, growing," rather than "sisters'
children." Rose thought, in short, that our sources had mistaken
the adjective *sororius,* which he must have believed to have been in
the formula; from this mistake must have come the report of a
prayer and hugs for the sisters' children. This veritable gallimaufry
is implausible on its face: based only on a made-up prayer. Alas, it
has found credit in some of the best works on Roman religion. It
reappears not only in Radke but also in Latte's *Römische Religion-*

geschichte.[30] Because of these circumstances, then, we must give it more time than it deserves. Our compensation will be the chance to go a bit deeper into an anthropological problem that lies to one side of our main purpose, although it contains many interesting points in itself.

"To Sister/To Brother" (An Intermezzo)

On the verb *soriare*, Festus gives us the following (380 L): "The breasts of girls are said 'to sister' when first they swell, just as 'to little brother' of boys. Plautus in *Frivolaria* d . . . ⟨Then⟩ nipples fir⟨st little brothered: that⟩ I wanted to say, si⟨stered. What⟩ need of word[s]?'" The gloss takes this form in its abbreviation by Paulus: "The breasts of girls are said 'to sister' when first they swell, just as 'to little brother' of boys. Plautus (fr. 85 L) 'Then nipples first sistered; that I wanted to say, little brothered'" (381 L).[31] In the *Frivolaria*, then, someone was talking of *papillae* that were just starting to *fraterculare* or *soriare*: "nipples" beginning to swell, in other words. But why use these kinds of expression for that?

The most natural explanation would seem to be that "to little brother" and "to sister" serve to designate the analogy between two things—here, body parts—that grow up resembling each other like sisters or brothers.[32] But Rose wanted to use *soriare* to mean simply "develop" and to rule out its relational sense, and thus he had to detach it from *soror* (sister). Taking counsel with the linguist Whatmough,[33] he fell back on a root, *suer-*, identical with that of the German *schwellen* and the English *swell*. This is the hypothesis that Radke takes up and works out to the full under the heading *sororia*:[34] he would have us see *sororia* as a reduplication of the root **suel-* (*schwellen*), according to a putative process of derivations of the following sort, viz. **sue(l)-sul-ia⟩ *so-sol-ia⟩ *so-rol-ia⟩ sororia*: which is, if I understand it, with *-l-* dropping out before *-s-*, with *-s-* between vowels becoming *-r-*, and with assimilation at a distance of *-r- . . . -l-* into *-r- . . . -r-*. This is ingenious reconstruction but a quite unnatural one, especially considering that **suel-* occurs nowhere else in Latin. But, leaving that aside, it goes against all we know about the phonetic tendencies of the Latin tongue.

Grant, for instance, that Radke's presumed redoubling of *suel-* did take the form he wants, *suel-sul-:* here -*l*- in the middle before -*s*- should not have fallen out but, if anything, might be expected to become like the following -*s*-. Look, for example, at the case of *vel-se* becoming *velle,* or *col-sum* > *collum:* in Latin the unvoiced sibilant generally assimilates to a preceding liquid, -*r*- or -*l*-, probably also becoming voiced in the process.[35] Which is to say, the result, if anything, would have been *sollolius,* not *sosolius.* Thus vanishes the possibility that -*s*- between two vowels became -*r*-, because, for one, we no longer have an intervocalic -*s*-; nor can there be any "assimilation at a distance" of a putative following -*l*-. The phonetic environment for it could never have existed, pace Radke, but, if it had, the assimilation could not have occurred as Radke thought. A sequence of the type "V *r* V *l* V-" is quite stable in Latin: only think of words such as *feRaLis, corpoRaLis, cuRuLis.* Moreover, so little are such sequences prone to assimilation that they can be themselves the result of dissimulation, as in the type *Parilia* from *Palilia* or *caeruleus* from *caeloleos.*[36] The supposititious *sorolius,* even if it could have come into being, which it could not, would in all likelihood have remained as it was, *sorolius,* especially given the need imposed by the dynamics of the linguistic system to mark itself off against *sororius* coming from *soror.*

Phonetics apart, it makes no sense to detach Plautus's *soriare* from *soror.* It should be enough to think of the verb *fraterculare,* with which it plays, to realize that both verbs come from the pair sister and brother; that is, the image comes precisely from the idea of relatedness implicit in both: growing together as sisters and brothers do. Someone might, however, think that, given the comic context, Plautus coined *fraterculare* by analogy with *soriare* to amuse the crowd, so the real verb is *soriare.*

That Plautus is capable of coinage, we know, for example, from: "Hey, what a body! Like a buzzard. . . . Whoops! Like an eagle, that's what I wanted to say" (*Rudens* 421ff.). In structure, both syntax and language are identical with the passage we are studying:

Fraterculabant. . . . Whoops, *sororiabant,* that's what I wanted to say." In the *Rudens,* the real adjective—*subaquilum,* "brunette"— comes second, and *subvolturium* is a dig, perhaps to imply the grasping power of certain feminine attractions. The process is exemplary, creating the adjective *subvolturius* from *voltur,* "buzzard," with play on the similarity between *aquilus* (dark-colored) and *aquila* (eagle).

That such is not the game, however, in the case of *fraterculare* and *soriare* is shown by the fact that *fraterculare,* unlike *subvolturius,* is not a unique form. *Fraterculare* connects with a verb *fratrare,* meaning the same thing, in another gloss of Paulus-Festus: *"fratrare* the breasts of boys are said to do, when first they swell, because just as equal brothers they rise, which also in grain the ear is said to do" (80 L). Here we can be certain that the gloss does not invent or merely double the other gloss on the passage from Plautus just discussed (381 L). Here we not only have *fratrare* rather than *fraterculare,* but also a field of application wider than could have been inferred from the other passage: the reference to growing grain is completely new. To reconstruct, then, the entire pattern, we must also cite two other passages that constitute a unitary scheme, passages that students of this matter have ignored heretofore. Both come from Pliny's *Natural History:* "Mammas *sororientes,* praecordia maciemque corporis piscinae maris corrigunt" (31.66), and "Undulata vestis prima e lautissimis fuit; inde sororiculata defluxit" (8.195).

In the first instance, *soriare* or, rather, a variant, *sorire,* if the text is sound, is applied once again to the breasts; in the second, there is talk of a female garment called *sororiculata* because, plausibly enough, it had two enlargements at the level of the bosom: it was not straight,[37] and thus it was seen as a logical development from an undulating dress. Taking a hint from Pliny, we can also reconstruct the verb *sororiculare,* analogous to *fraterculare,* inasmuch as it, too, comes from the diminutive: thus the two pairs, *fratrare ⟩ fraterculare* and *sororiare ⟩ sororiculare.* Formally speaking, the paradigm is quite compact, which makes it still more absurd to seek to take it apart.

What we have, then, is an interesting cultural scheme that bases itself on the idea of *pares oriri* (paired growth), typical not only of brothers but also of breasts and of ears of grain. The idea is hardly unnatural; in Latin, objects that resemble each other are called brothers, especially in regard to height: for example, consider Plautus: "I seem to have seen here someone very similar to you in form, with the same stature: indeed, could be your brother" (*Persa* 698). Or, again, the seven hills of Mauritania, "which are called Seven Brothers because of their similar height" (Pliny, *Hist. nat.* 5.11).[38] Then there is the recherché expression with which Apuleius, quite in keeping with his style, describes the progressive growth of libido between two lovers: "With emulous lust to parity of love siblingizing [*congermanescenti*] with me" (*Met.* 10.12). In order to reach parity of pleasure, a kind of erotic fraternizing takes place: once again, equality is metaphorically expressed as brotherly.

In the light of the evidence gathered to this point, the opposition between *fratrare (fraterculare)* and *sororiare (sororiculare)* seems rather specifically linked to the female bosom, as we infer from Pliny. Evidently, the swelling breasts could only be perceived as two sisters, because they are the feminine attribute *par excellence.*

What comes to mind is Mephistopheles's remark in Goethe's *Faust* concerning Gretchen's breasts: "Ich habe Euch [to Faust] oft beneidet / ums Zwillingspaar, das unter Rosen weidet!" (3336ff.). Her breasts, then, are like twinlets that graze among roses. The metaphor may well derive from the Song of Songs: "Your two breasts, like twin fawns of roe deer that graze among lilies" (4:5).[39] The breasts are siblings, evidently a symbol so obvious that it forces itself and is found in the most diverse literary cultures.

The symbol is not only literary; it appears in dreams, with a brief, but specific, elucidation by Freud:[40]

Here is a example of a symbol which I have not yet mentioned: *He met his sister in the company of two women friends who were themselves sisters. He shook hands with both of them but not with his sister.* No connection with any real occurrence. But his thoughts took him back, rather, to a period in which his observations led him to reflect on how late girl's breasts developed. So the two sisters were breasts; he would have liked to take hold of them with his hand—if only she were not his sister.

Here, also, the two breasts become two sisters, showing once again, if there was need, how silly it was to try to use a linguistic hypothesis, ill made at that, to destroy a symbolic system that is so widespread and deeply rooted in culture. From this standpoint, the poetic practice of Plautus, which is so rich in verbal inventiveness, and Latin usage in general become the invaluable witnesses for anyone who wishes to trace the threads of this symbolic web.

Coming back, then, to the specifically anthropological function in Roman culture of this trait of parity (be it ears of grain or breasts), perhaps we can grasp it better if we glean some other evidence to flesh out the lean testimony of the glosses. Augustine mentions the goddess Hostilina, who had the task of "leveling" (which is what *hostire* means) the ears of grain among themselves (*Civ. dei* 4.8).[41] The sight of one set of ears higher than the others is a well-known cause of panic among certain primitive peoples.[42] So the Romans actually had a goddess who presided over the *fratrare* of the ears, their growing in parity among themselves: clearly, an irregular growth violated the order of nature; namely, the order that the culture sought to impose on nature. Likewise about the breasts, considered in their development at the problematic moment of puberty: "first they swell"—an analogous anxiety must have been felt. In this liminal moment between childhood and the new sexual status of the individual,[43] the development of breasts must have been followed with particular concern. Such attention may perhaps be related to the popular superstition that disparity of breast size marks the hermaphrodite[44]—denoting, still more explicitly, sexual confusion. Nor does it seem accidental that Latin even had a specific term to name a breast that was smaller than the other: the adjective *minus, -a, -um.* Paulus-Festus reports: "Aelius says that *mina* is what one of the breasts is called when it lacks milk, as if it had been made less (*minorem*)" (109 = 10 L). In all this evidence, we perceive the traces of an anthropological classification of the breasts that is more developed than in our own culture.

Plautus was not making up words in the *Frivolaria:* he simply forgot to use the feminine term at the right moment,[45] and employed the masculine term instead. The comic effect must have been inevitable, as it always is when we skirt the breakdown of difference between the sexes. Procedures of this sort, a slip and a correction, are frequent in Plautus; for example, *Pseudolus:* "I've brought him::What have you brought?::Led him, I wanted to say" (711), in which the wit depends on the fact that "brought" could be said of things, but not people. Or, again, there is *Miles:* "Or ivory in India, at which I broke his arm with my fist::What arm?::Oh, thigh. You know what I mean" (25ff.).[46]

The Role of the Matertera *and*
the Structure of the Rite

Although this study of sibling verbs has stretched the thread of argument rather far, now at least we can be sure that Rose's guesswork had no grounds. More credit, then, will have to go to the ancient sources, which assign a central role in the *Matralia* to the fond relationship between maternal aunt and nephew, in keeping with what emerges from study of the other elements as well. Moreover, if we start from the structure of this particular kinship bond, it is possible, or at least plausible, to explain the role of Mater Matuta as goddess of the dawn. That this role does not depend on mere poetic imagination in Lucretius is shown by the existence of the adjective *matutinus,* indicating things related to morning and actually deriving from *matuta:* the word *matutinus* is found regularly in association with substantives such as *dies* (day), *tempus* (time), and *lumen* (light), clearly to indicate those moments in the day that, insofar as they occur in the morning, belong to the sphere of Matuta as goddess of the dawn. Dumézil has suggested that this very function of Mater Matuta be interpreted precisely in terms of the relationship between nephew (namely, "day") and maternal aunt (namely, "dawn, sister of night, who in turn is mother of day").[47] Dumézil observes that the Vedic dawn, Usas, often is called the sister of the night, Ratri, and that they often are indicated as mothers of the same son, the sun or heavenly fire. The

succession is the following: Night gives birth to Day, of whom
Dawn, the sister of Night, takes care.

If things stand thus, the ritual models may also be transposable
into terms for the atmosphere and thus, in general, frame the
functions of Mater Matuta. Even without this thesis, however, we
do have more specifically documentary materials that suggest a
special role for the maternal aunt in relation to Mater Matuta. Here
I wish to point to an inscription that, although known, has not
been given enough weight in previous studies. The text I refer to
was found in Pesaro and can be dated to about the beginning of
the second century, close to when the colony was sent out in 184
B.C.[48] Hence, here we have evidence much older than that from
our other oldest source, Ovid, even though Plutarch, too, must
have drawn on older material: "Matre Matuta / dono dedro / ma-
trona(s) / M(ania) Curia / Pola Livia deda(s)"; or, recast into classical Latin, "Matri Matutae dono dederunt matronae M(ania) Curia
Pola Livia dedae" (*CIL.* I²2.379 = I, 24 *ILLRP* Degrassi); the inscription may be read in this way: "To Mother Matuta as a gift gave
the married women Mania Curia Pola Livia aunts"; that is to say,
"in their role as aunts."[49] The word *deda(s)*, although occasionally
misunderstood,[50] has for some time now been identified by linguists as the plural of *deda* (aunt).[51] The word occurs in this sense
to this day in some north Italian dialects.[52] Therefore, it seems best
to combine the linguistic data with what we already know about
the role of maternal aunts in the cult of Mater Matuta and to translate as we do. We have to imagine, then, that the two married
women, as sisters of women with children, gave to Mater Matuta a
dedication that underlined this status: in conformity with the ritual, they indicated not only that they were *matronae* but also, in
the end, with special emphasis, that they were maternal aunts.

We must better describe the structure and workings of this ritual complex. Its irreplaceable moment is the display of fond concern for the children of one's own sisters. This takes for granted,
obviously, that the participants have sisters, who have children.
Hence, those who do the praying belong to the category that the
Romans termed *materterae*, aunts on the side of the mother. Be-

cause the rule of the rite requires that one pray only for one's nephews, not for one's own children, this clearly is the feast of *materterae,* not *matres.* However, it does remain a festival of *matronae;* that is, of women who are married and themselves capable of having children. Our sources make the point that the prayers are not for one's own children, but for those of others: it is taken for granted that the women themselves are mothers, as well as maternal aunts. In this way, the rite shapes up as a perfectly balanced organism, in which each sister prays for the other's children through a mechanism of exchange. On this basis, the children, who are at stake, after all, seem perfectly well protected, though not through the usual relationship of child and mother, but through the link of nephew with maternal aunt.

We must therefore recognize that, underlying this structure, is the very model of the *matertera* as it has been unfolding here: the quasi-mother, linked to her nephews by a motherly fondness, on occasion acting as nursemaid or trusted stand-in:[53] in short, a relationship of cultural contiguity between *mater* and *matertera,* which is defined at the level of religion by the ritual of the *Matralia.* Thus, when we read about the extraordinary attachment of Amata to her sister's son Turnus, or the mothers for whom it made no difference whether they were nursing their own or their sister's babies (the little Horati and Curiati), or the unknown *materterae* in Afranius to whom a dying mother entrusts her little girl, we must imagine all this in a society that practiced—verified, as it were—these bonds in ritual, too, every year.

"If care for mother-right torments"

A special case is constituted by the relationship between maternal aunt and niece when marriage is concerned. What applied in the case of uncles, both paternal and maternal, also pertains for the *matertera:* relationships take on a special character when it comes to matrimony and the sexual nature of the child. This was only to be expected. Analyzing, then, the evidence about the role of the maternal aunt in these cases, we shall also take up the threads of an argument already underway concerning the maternal uncle and carry them to their conclusion. Our way leads back to Queen Amata.

If we look, then, at a *matertera* and a niece who is *iam matura viro, iam plenis nubilis annis,* as Virgil says, "ripe now for a husband, now marriageable in fullness of years," we see that the nursemaid of before seems to perform in this phase a role almost of god-mother with regard to the girl's matrimonial options. It fell to the maternal aunt to take the nuptial omens for her niece, according to a custom that two sources call "ancient." The information arrives rather incidentally, in the course of a narrative about unintended omens. Caecilia, wife of Metellus,[54] wishing to place her sister's daughter in marriage, went with the girl a night by the shrine to take the nuptial omens, in keeping with the ancient custom. But the signs failed to arrive, and so the girl began to feel tired. Then she asked her aunt, who was sitting down, to give the seat to her. "Willingly," said her aunt, "I give you my place!" After a few months, Caecilia died and the girl became the bride of Metellus, the widower of her aunt. The *matertera* really had "given her place" to her sister's daughter.

Concerning this "ancient custom," the sources speak as follows: "[They say that] Caecilia of Metellus, when she wished to place her sister's daughter in marriage, went out to a certain shrine for the sake of taking the omen, which used to be done in the custom of the ancients" (Cicero, *Div.* 1.104; cf. 2.83); and "But Caecilia of Metellus, when she was seeking the nuptial omen for her sister's virgin daughter of adult age, according to pristine custom in the dead of night" (Valerius Maximus 1.5.4). It therefore seems that the *matertera* had the task, according to ancient usage, to take omens for the wedding of a girl suitably aged to take a husband.[55] If so, we must keep in mind that this particular privilege implies certain rather interesting things.

Clearly, the aunt goes to take omens for the opportunity or the prospect of marriage, rather than for a wedding that is about to occur; the latter task fell instead, so it seems, to certain nuptial seers or attendants.[56] As Valerius Maximus says, we are dealing with a girl who has reached marriageable age, to whose matrimony thought has to be given. The very openness of the situation, how-ever, is shown by the story itself, in which the omen brings the most unforeseeable of outcomes. Hence, we must conclude that the sister of the mother possesses rather specific prerogatives re-garding the choice of her niece's future marriage. And if the *mater-tera* is really the one who gets the fateful word, the omen[57]—or if, at least, it must be taken in her company—that means that she can have a certain influence on the choice of a match. The omen, naturally, is an empty and shapable form. Thus, there must gen-erally have been a need for settling, getting the real possibilities for marriage—such as social position, family tradition, alliances, and interests—to coincide with the divine signal, which is the interest-ing thing. Through the "ancient custom," the maternal aunt, to-gether with her niece, has the chance to work within and around the choices dreamed of or proposed. The maternal aunt holds a very high card.

This privilege, translated into the terms of matrimonial ex-change, means that the girl's maternal line has a rather strong weight in the choice of matrimonial connections. Unsure how far the custom was really practiced, by what classes—though our ex-ample comes from the aristocracy—we do know one thing: any-one who applies such a custom gives the maternal side consider-able weight in the choice. Naturally, we do not forget that the right to give a daughter in marriage belonged to the father; the rule is only too obvious.[58] But neither should we overlook, because the custom is called old and is little known, that the mother's side could counterbalance the father's choices to a degree by means of the omens taken by the mother's sister.

This is not just folklore or irrelevant and half-forgotten *Aber-glauben*. Instead, the omens of the *matertera* may actually consti-tute one of the many chapters in the long dialectic in Roman soci-ety between givers and takers of women: in this case, too, we find givers who are not wholly disposed to give up the woman they have handed over, or her offspring. These givers want to have their say about the future of the niece. Indeed, we should note one final detail. More explicitly than Cicero, Valerius Maximus lets us know that Caecilia was Metellus's wife ("Not so long after Caecilia died, he led the maiden of whom I am speaking into matrimony"). Hence, we have to infer that Caecilia had contracted marriage with one of her relatives on the father's side, because both are Caecili.[59] As for Caecilia's sister's daughter, her father is unknown,[60] and so is her family name; but one thing is sure: by marrying Metellus, widower of her *matertera,* she makes a match that is doubly tilted toward her mother's line: he not only was the husband of her maternal aunt but also bears the same family name as her mother, who clearly was also a Caecilia. Thus, the matrimonial situation must be:

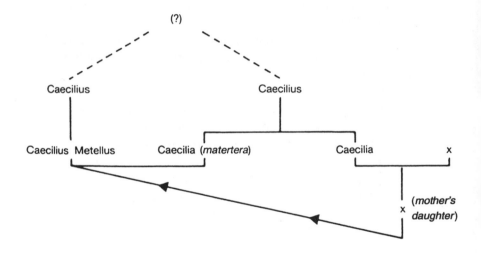

The omen pronounced by the *matertera* tells against her, unwittingly on her part, of course, but certainly not against the maternal line of the girl. Such an omen, indeed, could have been a good card for the Caecili to play, to push the wedding between Metellus the widower and the young daughter of one of their women. The situation, to be sure, is paradoxical and looks like a deliberate testing of the outer limits of the "ancient custom." But we can reasonably speculate that on other occasions the *matertera,* without having to give up her own husband, must have given priority to omens that steered toward choices welcome to the maternal group.

We have been suggesting that the privilege of the *matertera* in matrimonial matters forms part of a more general dialectic between paternal and maternal interests over the girl's matrimonial destiny, corresponding rather well to the relationship between the maternal uncle and his sister's daughter, that *avunculus* who protected and defended his niece precisely in the matrimonial context, in which the father might have been expected to appear. This was the case, above all, of Brutus and his strong link with the blood of Lucretia. The maternal uncle feels called upon to defend his blood in the daughter of his sister, on a par with the father or, in Brutus's case, with almost greater zeal. The solidarity between members of the maternal group is so strong, in this case at least, that it nearly overshadows the paternal group. Other times, as in the case of Virginia and her *avunculus,* Numitorius, the maternal group assures its own presence at the side of the threatened girl, leaving to the father the difficult role of the executioner. Plausibly, then, we have an ongoing dialectic that, by its very nature, cannot admit a final settlement of accounts.

Festus knew that the maternal uncle "protects the sister's daughter." The omens of the *matertera* and the protection of the *avunculus* point to a cultural matrix that could be most accurately characterized as solidarity through the female group: a kind of bridge, a privileged link that products of the same womb *(cognati)* project to further their own line on the female side. It is as if the kinship that passes through a woman, which is what *cognatio* means—as opposed to *agnatio,* that which passes through the male[61]—stimulated solidarity, watchfulness, or interest for the marriage of the daughters of this woman, to assure respect for some undercurrent perhaps of "mother-privilege" in the matrimonial arrangements of girls. If "mother-privilege" provokes any suspicion of "Bachofenomania," it will be answered. What we want to emphasize in speaking of "mother-privilege" is simply that such a solidarity through the female line must have taken hold in the first instance between daughter and mother. And hence, within that deep dialectic of maternal and paternal groups, there are numerous cases in which a mother intervenes directly in her daughter's matrimonial choice, by no means always in agreement with the father. Kroll mentions some instances of this kind, from Cicero's time, which evidently was an age of relatively advanced freedom for women.[62] Other instances have been brought out more recently.[63] In such cases, the figure of a mother who decides directly, or wants to, about her daughter's marriage must be added to those of the *avunculus* who protects or avenges his niece in matters of marriage and to the *matertera* who channels the signals from the gods.

From this viewpoint, too, *mater* and *matertera* seem to share a remarkable affinity in function, which it may be well to reemphasize, in a return to the theme of this chapter. Livy recounts the marriage between Scipio's daughter and Tiberius Gracchus (38.57).[64] Scipio had promised her to Gracchus in the Senate, under the unexpected pressure of the senators. Hence, Scipio had not spoken to his wife in advance. Coming home, he told her of the news. With wifely indignation, because she had not been consulted about their daughter, Aemilia says she should not have been left out of the deliberations, not even if Scipio were giving the girl to Tiberius Gracchus. Scipio, delighted with such unwitting agreement, answers that Gracchus is actually the one to whom he has promised the girl. Livy does not say if Scipio thus took his wife's words for an omen, but her outburst certainly has the structure of one. Unwittingly, believing that she is saying something else, Aemilia utters the right name: thus her unconscious simplicity confirms the choice made by her husband.[65] In the same way, the *matertera* Caecilia had pronounced the fatal word, thinking that she was simply talking about a place to sit. Omens have a notoriously strong meaning in Roman culture. Thus, it can be important to see an omen as the basis of decision about a girl's wedding, both for a *matertera*, acting in accordance with an "ancient custom," and a *mater,* who considers it her right to be consulted about her daughter's marriage.

Having added the *mater,* now, to the *matertera* in our inquiry, we will return to Amata[66] and look at her behavior not only as *matertera* but also as *mater,* because surely both these roles, with their respective attitudes, are presupposed in her figure. And this new look at her will allow us to clarify yet further the cultural significance of "mother privilege" and "solidarity through female groups" in the Roman way of thinking.

As Virgil tells it, Amata's relationship with her sister's son is very troubled. The relationship, however, takes the form, above all, of her energetic will to get her daughter, Lavinia, married to him: "That he be connected as a son-in-law, she urged with amazing passion" (*Aen.* 7.57), which Servius glosses with "renewed intemperance." Hence, Amata is not only a *matertera* who wants, with exceeding love, her nephew as her son-in-law, but also a *mater* who stops at nothing to carry out her plans for her daughter's marriage, which fate itself, however, blocks. Dim and fearsome prodigies compel Amata's husband, Latinus, to consult the oracle of Faunus, and the response is unambiguous: the girl must not take a mate from her own folk. Latinus must wait for a son-in-law "come from afar" (7.96ff.; 268ff.): Aeneas, of course, whose qualifications as an outsider had been expressly highlighted, in symbolic language, by the prodigy of the bees, as we shall see further in chapter 15. However, Latinus gives in to his wife's pressure; hence the war. Indeed, the old king sums up for Turnus what has happened, when matters are finally rushing to their close (12.27):

> That I join my daughter with any of the former suitors
> was not fated, and this both gods and men all prophesied.
> Yet won over by love for you, won over by family blood,
> and by my mournful wife's tears, I broke all the restraints:
> The girl, though pledged, I took back from a son-in-law; despite the
> gods I took up arms.
> From that, what luck befalls me, Turnus, what wars
> ensue, you see . . .

Latinus let himself be won over by his wife's love for her nephew, by her related blood. In so doing, the king preferred an especially near son-in-law, a blood relative, to one "from afar," the outsider that the oracle had foretold. On this contrast turns the deepest articulation of the story, in which a new civilization to be founded requires the most clearly new marriage possible from abroad:[67] marriage between Turnus and Lavinia, first cousins on the mother's side, is the exact opposite of what is needed to found the greatness of a new city.[68] But Latinus, on his own testimony, let himself be won over also by Amata's tears. The queen has played the leading role in defending the wedding with Turnus: she herself feels that she is the "chief cause of the ills" (12.600), just when, believing Turnus dead, and aware at last what misfortunes her insistence has caused, she decides on suicide.

In the story, her action unfolds as follows. Shaken by the serpent that the Fury Allecto placed in her bosom, Amata will intensify her passion, but at the start she speaks to Latinus rather softly and in the usual fashion of mothers (7.357). She complains that he wants to give Lavinia to an outsider, who, like a thief, will carry her away with him, at the first favoring wind (7.359). Then she tries to show her husband that Turnus, if his origins are studied well, is not of Latium, but an outsider. And hence the will of the oracle shall be in any case carried out (367ff.: here Servius, more clever than Amata, improves on her case by adding that Aeneas, as a descendent of Dardanus, also stems from Latium!). But she gets nowhere. And so the queen, spurred further by the foul Fury in her heart, decides to give herself up utterly to mad rage, dragging along with her, in a Bacchic orgy, the Laurentian mothers (373ff.). The scene of this madness led by Amata is the woods, where the god's wands echo. The queen, brandishing a flaming pine branch—symbolizing the torch of Turnus and Lavinia's wedding, which she wants to celebrate perforce—shrieks to the women gathering around her (373–76):

> Io! Mothers, hear, where any Latin women are,
> if in any god-fearing souls unlucky Amata's influence
> remains, if care for mother-right torments,
> loosen bands from your hair, take up the holy wands with me!

Hence the queen claims the existence of some mother-right (*si iuris materni cura remordet*):[69] this right gives the mother the privilege of determining the matrimonial fate of her own daughter. The denial of this right, the frustration of maternal privilege with regard to Lavinia, has provoked Amata's crisis and her madness in the woods.

The setting, too, for this invocation of *ius maternum* deserves notice: the Bacchic orgy, the "outside" *par excellence,* breaking with every sort of cultural order. Especially interesting, in this regard, is the word Virgil used to indicate this return of mother-right to consciousness: *cura remordet* (literally, "care bites again"), suggesting that the consciousness of maternal privilege comes, then, as a kind of remorse the female group harbors in its soul.[70]

Thus a social and existential problem of the female condition underlies Amata's crisis. An illuminating comparison can be drawn with the phenomenon of seizure or possession attributed to the bite of the tarantula, which was recorded in Apulia by De Martino. Surprisingly, in *La terra del remorso,* his extraordinary book,[71] De Martino does not include Amata among the precedents for this so-called tarantism, even though, more than Euripides' Phaedra, or the despair of Aeschylus's Io, it is Amata's crisis that prefigures what he describes. Here we can hardly hope to synthesize, in a few lines, the riches of content and symbol in tarantism, which De Martino reconstructs. But perhaps we can make a synthesis more simply for Amata.

Amata's crisis, as we said, has existential and social roots in the female condition, motives that appear with equal strength in the explanation of tarantism,[72] which also shares an identical mythic origin with her crisis. A woman from Galatina under the spell attributes her "trouble" to the bite of a spider that stung her once and that, by its presence or that of its descendants, puts into effect the successive "ri-morsi" (bites again) that cause new crises to arise. Thus the tarantula figures as the mythic and symbolic origin of the "trouble." In the same fashion, Amata has in herself the burning fire that was instilled by the serpent of the Fury Allecto. Thus the existential and sociological sufferings of Amata are assigned a symbolic origin that coincides in all respects with that employed by the model of tarantism: the action of a mythic animal. The analogy becomes all the more astonishing if we consider that, in many cases in the stories of possession, the tarantula is replaced by a serpent;[73] in one instance, a blue serpent,[74] even as "sky blue" is the color of the serpent growing like hair on the head of Allecto, who rips it from her head to fling it at Amata (7.346).[75]

The way the crisis unfolds and ends also presents many analogies with the model from folklore. De Martino himself emphasized the accessories used in tarantism, such as boughs and water, that bring to mind Dionysiac practice;[76] they are signs of a tension that finds relief most easily in natural or naturalized places, which is, of course, what happens with Amata and the mothers. Amata's whirling movement, in the famous simile that compares the maddened queen to a top (7.778), brings to mind with unbelievable immediacy the movement of an exhausting dance.[77] I cannot imagine that Virgil, with this symbol of the top spun by the whips of entranced children, meant to describe anything other than a woman possessed who whirls, slows, accelerates, stops, starts up, amidst an anxious crowd, just like the setting for a crisis of tarantism.

Among the characteristic movements in the crisis, as De Martino emphasizes, is swinging, the to-and-fro of the swing. It brings to mind, as he points out,[78] the theme of suicide by hanging, which underlies the ritual of *aiwresis,* for which the story of Erigone is the myth of origin, to say nothing of other Greek cases of female crisis that find their denouement in this particular form of suicide. Amata also, of course, at the end of her madness, finds nothing better to do than tie a "knot of ugly death" to a high beam.[79]

The madness of Amata hence runs point for point through a model of crisis like that found in the tarantism of Apulia and other Mediterranean regions:[80] the mythic cause (venom of an imaginary beast), the deep and real cause (frustrations inflicted on her condition as a woman), the setting (the woods), the maenad's whirl (the top), perhaps, too, the final noose. In thus describing Amata's behavior, Virgil seems to have given new actuality to a set of cultural contents and attitudes whose framework must have formed part of the religious horizon of his age: a framework that continues to function, more or less altered, long after and to gather the same kind of anxieties and troubles.

The parallel hardly makes Amata a women bitten by the *taranta*. Rather, we can see, in the humble *tarantata* of Galatina, a poor, obscure descendent of Virgil's grand queen, one who shares, in her fashion, in the symbolic model that the *Aeneid* used to describe the events of a rebellion, a madness, by women.

Amata's words return: *si iuris materni cura remordet.* This is the mothers' privilege: a form of remorse, a hidden spur, a burning regret for what is denied a mother, which can explode into destructive crises. The remorse of Amata quite embodies, in our view, the matrilineal temptations, which, in a rigidly patrilineal society such as the Roman one, can only be repressed, except when, unforeseen, they "bite back." The privilege ceded to the *matertera* to take the nuptial omens, the protection by the *avunculus,* Aemilia—not consulted about her daughter's wedding and thus indignant, but then reconciled by the omen: all these tendencies to solidarity "in the women's group" find in Amata their most dramatic and violent representative. She is truly the reverse, the remorse of Roman patrilinealism, which is one of the most deeply structural reasons for the tragic and grim fascination of her figure in the poem. Her struggle for the success of "mother privilege" is, of necessity, destined to fail: the patrilineal world of Rome has no room for a mother who insists on the *ius maternum.* In this respect, Amata is a typically Virgilian hero: defeated, condemned.[81] But her defeat is not merely historical, not merely a matter of making room for a new world that ineluctably is coming. No, outside of time in a way, Amata's defeat is cultural. Her model of "mother privilege" is authentic, justified, with staying power, but its life can only remain hidden. It is and has to be simply a remorse. Any effort to make it win out turns it into a rout.

Never forget that in Amata the will for the mother's line reaches its extreme. The queen means not only to decide, she herself, about her daughter's marriage; she also wants to keep the girl in her maternal group, making her marry a member of the group itself. In terms of matrimonial exchange, Amata plays the dual role of loving *matertera* and exclusive *mater:* the result is a female personage obsessed by "mother-lineage," a woman who seeks to counter her daughter's father's paternal group by both deciding herself (as mother) about the marriage and imposing (as maternal aunt) her sister's son as the groom.

This matrilineal obsession, which already characterized Amata in the legend, is indeed reemphasized by another undertaking of the queen, one that Virgil did not choose to utilize in the poem, but which Servius, luckily for us, took the trouble to transmit in his commentary (on *Aen.* 7.51):[82] he tells us that Latinus also had two male children, who were killed or blinded by Amata:[83] "For Amata with a conspiracy (*factione*) killed her two sons, who at their father's behest were betrothing their sister [Lavinia] to Aeneas, [others tell that they were blinded by their mother, after Lavinia was joined to Aeneas when Turnus was dead]." The episode interests us because it shows the irreducible, I would say systematic, character of the matrilinealism of Amata. Her female solidarity pushes her so far as killing or blinding her own sons, as much hers as Lavinia is, when they make common cause with their father in selecting a marriage for their sister. The principle of "mother-right," once accepted in all its implications, seems hence to lead to this tragic and paradoxical consequence: that the sons are no longer like the daughters, that the family solidarity follows other lines than those traced by normal bonds between parents and children. The sexual determinant prevails over the blood determinant: even one's own sons, because male, come to be perceived as belonging to the father's group, against which women's solidarity must struggle and fight.

Matrilineal remorse does not occur only in Amata or only in Roman culture. It also is in our culture. And hence, to continue the metaphor to the end, I think that this remorse may have affected many scholars. They have wanted to see in practices such as those of the maternal uncle,[84] the bond with the maternal aunt,[85] and the ambitions of the mother so many vestiges or survivals of an ancient matrilineal order that was sunk by triumphant patrilinealism.[86] As if one had somehow to grant to women that there has always been a world in which their rights and lineage triumph over those of men, a mythical golden age that the scholar discovered in the "before" only because he saw no way for it to come into being in the "now": or because he feared this might come about (come again), or even utopistically dreamed of its return as a possible yeast of liberty.[87] But to speak of matrilineal remorse in our culture—a remorse that is ambiguous, perfidious, an often masked and contradictory return—would carry us afar. We are speaking, after all, of Roman culture, and of Amata. And it would be absurd to want to see in the legendary queen of Laurentum the proof of a previous matrilineal world, in which mother-right celebrated its holy days. No, Virgil's formulation must be our guide: matrilinealism in Rome is a remorse, a temptation, a risk. Its life is not that of a resplendent maternal dwelling, collapsed and buried in memory, but rather of an unseen current that continually blocks and redirects the course of the maternal group, ready to stop it, or to let itself be overrun, able to bend, according to circumstances and times, in a relationship always dynamic with the force or weakness that from time to time typifies givers in the face of takers.

Like any society in which one model of filial descent predominates over the other, Roman society daily experienced the impossibility of ignoring the existence of the overshadowed line; in this case, the impossibility of ignoring the existence of the maternal side.[88] Despite that or, better, because of it, Roman society was always a society in which the paternal-line prevailed.[89] Thus Amata's story, far from hinting at a lost dominance of mothers, warns exactly the opposite: the mad queen, who stirs up the mothers in the woods to assert her own privilege, who wants to marry her daughter to her sister's son and reject the marriage with a foreign king which fate intends, who kills her male children because they are too close to their father. Amata gives an express warning, with the inward force of facts, of narrative, to keep the aspirations of women's solidarity within the bounds that the traditional code assigns. Amata's myth sanctions the express impossibility of lineage through the mother. To yield to this remorse, this temptation, would have meant giving up the very foundation of Rome.

Five

Father's Sister: *Amita*

Our luck runs out when we turn from the mother's sister to the father's. Evidence is scanty and rarely yields characterizations that are specific and well defined. The *amita* remains an elusive figure. If we look, for example, to the inscriptions, which were so rich in clues and witnesses about the maternal aunt, we find a rather discouraging poverty of information.[1] But also, at the other end of the spectrum, in the legends of the archaic period, things are little better. Anyone who expects to find, in the guise of *amita,* a personage such as Amata, or even anyone comparable to the *materterae* of the Horati and Curiati, will be disappointed. In the legends of Rome's origins and regal period, there appear to be no paternal aunts. Or, if there are, no particular bond gets emphasized between them and their brothers' children. Such is the case of Tarquinia, daughter of Tarquinius Priscus and wife of Servius Tullius, penultimate king of Rome.

Old Tarquin's death left in the palace two little Tarquins, still infants (*nepioi*), the grandchildren of Tarquin by one of his sons, according to Dionysius of Halicarnassus (4.6.1), who echoes Calpurnius Piso Frux.[2] These children risk being left prey to the Marci. Tarquin's widow, Tanaquil, their grandmother, makes a long speech urging that the boys be protected and educated. Her appeal, however, goes not to Tarquinia, her daughter and the sister of the father of the boys, thus their *amita,* but to Tarquinia's husband, Servius Tullius. Tanaquil urges him to act as father to the boys and bring them up till such time as the older of the two can resume the kingship (4.4.4). She makes no mention of any role their *amita* might play in their regard, no appeal to Tarquinia as a natural nurse for her brother's children. And yet the little Tarquins, as presented *(erema . . . kai orphana),* appear to lack a mother as well: they are presented to their grandmother by nursemaids (4.4.3), and a mother is nowhere mentioned. But for all this, even though Tarquinia, as well as her husband, hugs the children with emotion (4.5.1), she remains a mute and secondary figure.

Nor does the *amita* stand out later when the two Tarquins marry the two daughters of Tarquinia and Servius. It is Servius Tullius who arranges the marriage (Livy 1.42; Dionysius 4.28.1), evidently intending thus to restore the throne to the family of the previous king. But we hear neither of any move by the *amita* to foster the union between her daughters and her brother's sons, nor of any special bonds between the nephews and the aunt. Only after her death does Brutus, in his speech against the younger Tarquin, allude to the relations that ought to have obtained between the latter and his aunt (Dionysius 4.79.4): Tarquin should have honored her like a mother because she was his father's sister and busied herself on his behalf *(spoudaian . . . genomenen).*

Naturally, no interpretation can be built on silence. But we do continue to meet the same paucity of evidence and of specific emotional characterizations as we move down into history, beyond the legends. We have seen that the writers of comedy and farce took an interest in the maternal aunt and the paternal uncle. By contrast, no titles survive regarding paternal aunts. Nor can it be said that other Latin writers tell us a great deal on the matter. However, we may at least look at what does remain.

The young Aebutius finds himself in a bad way (Livy 39.11). His mother and his stepfather, with whom he lives, because his father is dead, intend to initiate him into the Bacchic mysteries.

But the boy resists, warned by Hispala Fecennia. So his mother and stepfather drive him away from home (39.11.3):

> Hence the youth betook himself to Aebutia, his paternal aunt, and told her the reason why his mother had driven him out. Hence, on Aebutia's authority, the next day he denounced the affair to the consul Postumius without the presence of others.

The result, of course, will be the scandal of the Bacchic rites and the Senate's prohibiting decree (c. 2 B.C.), which do not concern us here. What we have is a youth in conflict with his mother and without a father's support. Into this situation comes the *amita*: her role, however, is characterized not by affection, but by authority (*auctoritas*). On the basis of her authority, the boy betakes himself to the consul to make his dreadful revelation. The *amita* steers the behavior of her brother's son. Thus, Livy shows us a figure marked by concern for reputation more than affection or motherly conduct.

In another case, Seneca speaks of certain instances in which suicide might not be opportune (*Ad Lucil.* 70.8–10): Why take upon oneself, in advance, another's cruelty? By way of example, he cites the behavior of Scribonia, the *amita* of Drusus Libo: she is described as a weighty character, in contrast to her dull, lightweight nephew, who had naïvely tried to conspire against the emperor Tiberius (Tacitus, *Ann.* 2.27; Suetonius, *Tib.* 25). Feeling abandoned by all, Libo considers himself as good as dead. He asks, then, if it would not be better to kill himself, to get it over with: "To whom Scribonia said: Why does it amuse you to carry out another's business?" Her wit may show firmness, even elegance, anything but the feeling of affection or compassion.

Faced with her nephew's desperate situation, the aunt prefers the efficacy of paradox, almost cynicism, to any other expression of feeling. Her words might be expected of a Roman father exhorting his son to die well, rather than of an aunt showing tender concern for a nephew: an aunt, at least, as we would like to imagine her: woman, and thus inevitably dedicated to the anxious and compassionate role of mothering. But the point may lie just here, in the paternal characterization of this aunt. The authority of Aebutia and the mordant wit of Scribonia may make us think that between the *amita* and the nephew intervenes, like a filter, the figure of the *pater* and the gravity of the paternal line, which impose on her relations with her nephew a coloring that makes them necessarily differ from relations with a sister of the *mater*.

This paternal presence interposed between *amita* and nephew appears also in other clues. Both *amita* and *matertera* have definitions in the glossary of Paulus-Festus. For *matertera*, we read: "maternal aunt, mother's sister, almost another mother" (L 121) and, further along, "*Mater Matuta, manis, mane, matrimonium, mater familiae, matertera* seem so named, as Verrius says, because they are goods" (L 151). Although clearly improbable from a linguistic point of view,[3] these pseudo-etymologies have a remarkable cultural interest: they reveal an underlying model, a complex of hidden attitudes and behaviors which guides the etymological choice. Hence *matertera* is so called because she is like a second mother, or because, like the *mater familiae*, she belongs to the family goods.

What a contrast with the definition of *amita:* "*amita*, sister of my father, can seem to be said for this reason, that she used to be called *avita* by the ancients, because, like my grandmother [*avia*], she is third from me. Or *amita* is said, because she is loved by my father [*a patre meo amata*]. For brothers usually love their sisters more than their brothers" (13 L). The interpretation has something singular about it. The first part, which derives *amita* from *avita*, involves the nephew as *ego*, the one who says *amita*. He establishes an equivalence on the basis of the degree of kinship between grandson and grandmother, on the one hand, and brother's sister and brother's son, on the other.[4] And it is obvious that a kinship term must be interpreted with reference to the viewpoint of the person who employs it.

In the second part of the interpretation, however, a sharp shift in viewpoint occurs. Noting the similarity between *amita* and the verb *amare* does not lead to an explanation of the sort, "*amita* because loved [*amata*] by me," which is what we might expect if the previous viewpoint continued. Instead we are told, "*amita* because *amata* by my father," so the father's presence upsets at very least the point of view. It is strange that an aunt should be defined as such because loved not as an aunt, but as a sister "by my father." The paternal figure gets interjected into the relations between aunt and nephew and seems to call away to itself the affective dimension, as if one could be loved as sister, not as aunt.

Things seem to go somewhat similarly even when an *amita* is maternal and concerned. The wife of the younger Pliny, Calpurnia, lost her parents and was brought up by Calpurnia Hispulla, her paternal aunt. At a particularly critical time for the young bride, when a pregnancy failed, Pliny speaks of the state of mind in which the aunt must find herself: "When I think your affection for your brother's daughter is even softer than a motherly indulgence" (8.11.1). The *amita*, then, feels for the orphan she has reared a tenderness that is more than maternal.[5] But to fill out the picture, here is Pliny's account elsewhere of the role of Calpurnia Hispulla in rearing her niece (4.19): "Since you are an example of piety and have cherished with reciprocal love your brother most excellent and fond of you and cherish his daughter as your own, and you represent for her not so much the affection of an *amita* as of her lost father."

Here the affection of the *amita* takes the form not only of a woman's motherly feeling toward an orphan but also of a substitute for the affection of a father: Calpurnia Hispulla, inasmuch as she is *amita,* can represent, can make live again for the girl, the father's figure. What we see, then, has a structural quality and is implied directly by the system of relations: beyond the specific shape that a relationship may take in individual cases, the *amita* remains inescapably a "sister of father." However much a woman, like the *mater* or the *matertera,* the *amita* cannot be linked with her niece if not by means of the paternal figure. The *amita* finds herself in the situation of woman of the father's branch, a figure that must join in herself the characteristics of the female with those of the male line. Although a woman, she remains always a link in the patrilineal chain; the patrimony of characteristics and traditions which marks the genus speaks also in her: hence, in all likelihood, the role of some authority that Aebutia takes on, or the severe saying of Scribonia. This paternal and patrilineal mediation must have much less effect on a specific bond in a situation such as that described by Pliny, which presupposes the absence of both parents, and certainly does not assume a detached and stern father in the archaic style: Calpurnia Hispulla can show true maternal concern and, indeed, play a double affective role. But if we extrapolate this structural model back to the time of the Bruti and Torquati, we will find in all probability the reason why the *amita* plays no affective role in the legends of the archaic period.

From this viewpoint, it would certainly be very valuable to have the funeral laudation delivered by Julius Caesar after the death of Julia, his paternal aunt. It would show us what were the characteristics of an *amita* which an official occasion allowed to be underscored. But even the few words of this speech that Suetonius reports in his life of Caesar allow us to see clearly the nature of the *amita* as a woman in the paternal line, with a marked relationship to the *pater* (*Div. Jul.* 6):

> And, indeed, in the praise of his *amita,* he speaks thus of his father's and her origin: of my paternal aunt Julia, her line on the mother's side descended from the kings; on the father's side it was joined to the eternal gods. For from King Ancus Marcius descend the Marci Reges, which was her mother's name. From Venus descend the Julii, to which clan our family belongs. Thus in her line there is both the sanctity of kings, who have the greatest power among men, and the prestige of the gods, in whose power are kings themselves.

Here is the point: praising the origins of the paternal aunt, one praises automatically, inescapably, also the origins of one's father. The *amita* can be chosen as representing the line to which one, as well as one's male relatives, belongs. This male lineage puts her in structural opposition to the *matertera.* In a patrilineal society such as the Roman one, in which the paternal figure had such a particular importance, the *amita* and the *matertera* could not help but find themselves on two different shores, just as in the case of the *avunculus* and the *patruus,* even if, because they were women, and hence the weaker links in the chain, their contrast does not appear so marked as in the case of the two male uncles.

Six

Conclusions

The system of attitudes which little by little we have delineated seems sufficiently clear. The father's side and the mother's side are differentiated from each other according to a consistent pattern: it contrasts the detached severity of the former (*pater, patruus,* perhaps *amita*) with the intimacy and affection of the latter (*avunculus, matertera*). The pattern appears to reproduce the stamp of the father and mother, who are the linking parents through whom the indirect relationships are established: it is as if these two links assured not only the inheritance of differentiated kinds of kinship (*agnatio* through the father and *cognatio* through the mother) but also a different flow of feelings. That the Roman mother was indulgent is fairly obvious and well known, and it has not seemed worthwhile to dwell upon that here. The point was made by Terence: "Mothers all are wont to be aids to their sons in peccadillos, of help when fathers hurt" (*Heaut.* 991–93). And we remember what happens when mother and father switch these roles (see chapter 1). Seneca says it yet more explicitly (*Prov.* 2.5):

> Do you not see how greatly in one way fathers, in another way mothers, indulge? Fathers order that their children be awakened to undertake

their studies on time, and do not permit them to be at leisure even on holidays. Fathers shake from them sweat and sometimes tears. But mothers want to fondle them in their bosom and keep them in the shade [namely, idle], never to be saddened, never to weep, never to work.

Yet a system of attitudes, like every kinship set, is a complex structure, with circuits that can be entered and followed in multiple ways. In consequence, it often gives the impression that it could be written and rewritten ad infinitum, as ever-new combinations allow us to infer ever-differing meanings and motives. And this impression depends on the nature of the system (besides the inevitable uncertainties of analysis): in the system, any one individual may find himself from time to time in relations that may be oblique, horizontal, vertical, and thus changing roles, names, statutes. In short, we must not forget that the same person undergoes our analysis as *pater, patruus, avunculus,* and *frater* according to the point of view we adopt. Consequently these roles must be given a hierarchical arrangement and correlated among themselves in an ordered system: a subject does need to know how to behave, to have an identity defined and definable. Thus probably the contrastive model, father/mother, worked as a kind of generative scheme for the relations that, through his father and mother, the nephew established with his own aunts and uncles. But the model can be rewritten still further, because "father's" and "mother's" in Roman culture form an opposed pair not only in the family nucleus, father/mother, but also in the more general, and more overtly and immediately social, context of the paternal group *(agnati)* and maternal group *(cognati)*. The *patruus* is not only the "brother of my father" but also the nearest, after one's brother, of one's relatives on one's father's side *(agnati)*. In the same way, the *avunculus* is not only the "brother of my mother"; he is also very likely the most prestigious representative of one's relatives on one's mother's side.

The opposition between *agnatio* and *cognatio* plays a fundamental role in Roman culture, also from a juridical viewpoint: think only of an inheritance in which a will is lacking, how different is the treatment of relatives on the father's side from that of the relatives on the mother's side: the *agnati* are entrusted with one's name, with the family goods, with the ancestral cults, with one's traditions. Nothing of the sort instead can be said of the *cognati*, at least officially and institutionally, although we have seen that in fact the dialectic between receivers and givers is never resolved. This fundamental disparity of social statutes cannot fail to have directly influenced, too, the attitudinal relations we have analyzed thus far: the *agnati,* those who own and define one's identity, through the chain of wealth, name, cults, residence, and so forth, are severe; the *cognati,* outside this institutional stream that has been sanctioned since time immemorial, are indulgent. It is as if the lack of an official part for the maternal lineage were compensated in some sense by a greater familiarity and intimacy in relations. And such behavior is especially striking in the case of relations with the male representative of this group; that is, the maternal uncle. In other words, it is as if the continuity of one's line on the maternal side—a continuity that does not aim to preserve a name, residence, particular cults—has the need in order to maintain itself, or can allow itself the luxury, of a cohesion based on intimacy and affection.

By way of closing, I wish to cite a system of attitudes studied not in a society ancient and long since rounded off in a limited body of evidence, but in the field, asking the members of a living community directly about the nature and motives of their family relations. The time for this comparison may be ripe, because the philologist, or the scholar of antiquity in general, sometimes seems a little like someone forced by absurd rules imposed by a wicked host, like the magic prohibition in a fairy tale, to play billiards always off the cushions, with never a direct shot. How many times we have to make the best of some myth or gloss or suffix in cases where all an anthropologist or sociologist would have to do is ask!

Let us conclude with the opinions of their uncles and their aunts that the Nuer of the upper Nile confided to Evans-Pritchard. The comparison will serve, in each case, to suggest some further slight rewritings of the system of attitudes in Rome.

1. The Paternal Uncle[1]   The *gwanlen,* particularly the father's paternal half-brother, is portrayed by the Nuer as the wicked uncle and is contrasted with the good uncle, the *nar,* particularly the mother's uterine brother. Both youths and maidens have often told me that they are more at one with their mother's brothers than with their father's brothers and with their mother's sisters than with their father's sisters. "Wa! Your *nar* is far better (than your *gwanlen*)," said a Nuer to me once, expressing with force this common partiality. When I asked him why the maternal uncle was better he gave no further answer than the usual reply to this question: "Because he is the brother of your mother". . . . If your paternal uncle is angry with you he may split your head open with his club, but however angry with you your maternal uncle may be, he would never strike you, for you are his sister's son.

2. The Paternal Aunt[2]   The *wac,* father's sister, is not so prominent in the picture of family portraits, . . . but the Nuer say that she is like the father's brother: "Your *wac* is your *gwanlen* also." She may treat you badly when you are little, and even if she is kind she does not love you: "The ones she loves are her grandchildren and the children of her sisters. . . . Your father's sister blesses you with her mouth, meaning nothing, but she cares nothing for you in her heart." The Nuer contrast her, especially the father's paternal half-sister, with the mother's sister, as they contrast the father's brother with the mother's brothers. When you visit her she lets you remain hungry till evening instead of preparing a meal for you at once as a mother's sister would do. They also say that it is very likely she was resentful of your mother and takes it out on you.

3. The Maternal Uncle[3]   Nuer say of the maternal uncle that he is both father and mother, but most frequently that "he is your mother." He is a man's great supporter when he is in trouble. If a youth has committed adultery, . . . he goes to his maternal uncle for help. He will help his sister's son for his mother's sake. . . . The relationship between sister's son and mother's brother is one of tenderness. The Nuer have often told me how indulgent a mother's brother is with the little children of his sisters. They say, for example, that if a boy living at his maternal uncle's home feels out of sorts and does not want to spread out the cattle-dung to dry or to perform some other domestic task of boyhood, and the sons of the home think he is shirking work and abuse him, their father will admonish them to leave his sister's child in peace. If this happened at the home of a paternal uncle he would support his own sons and upbraid his nephew for laziness and even beat him.

4. *The Maternal Aunt*[4]   The *manlen,* the mother's sister. Nuer say of her that she is like the mother's brother, that "she is your mother" and that she will love you as a son. "Your mother's sister is your friend. Is she not the sister of your mother?" If you live at her home she will not, like the father's sister, favour her own children at your expense. You are her son and will eat with her own child and share and share alike with him like brothers. When you visit her from a distance, she sees that you are hungry from your journey and at once leaves off what she was doing to prepare a meal for you, and she pours her best butter over the porridge she has prepared for you. It is the mother's sister relationship that the Nuer mostly invoke when hurling their spears in hunting and fishing: "*Tet cueda malene,*" "My right hand, my mother's sisters."

Clearly, the distribution of attitudes closely resembles what we have sketched in archaic Roman culture. Here, too, a good, indulgent, protective maternal uncle contrasts with a quite unlikable and suspect, even nasty, paternal uncle. Likewise, with the maternal aunt, the nephew enjoys relations of intimacy and affection, to say nothing of the remarkable ritual bond, invoking her when throwing the spear. In short, her functions, refreshing the tired nephew and so forth, really overlap the role of the mother. In contrast, relations are not very good between the paternal aunt and the nephew: but in Rome, too, the function of the *amita* does not compare with that of the *matertera.*[5]

Yet it would be a mistake to linger over a comparison that, however much it really does surprise for the likenesses, might also just for this reason deceive. Frankly, what interests us most in Evans-Pritchard's accounts are the motives the Nuer give in explaining the reasons for their different attitudes. We are told that the paternal aunt does not love the children of her brother because she loves those of her sister; so, too, the maternal uncle, out of regard for his sister, aids a nephew in trouble. In other words, the presence of a very caring and concerned maternal aunt, a sister who loves her sister's children, rules out in some way the presence of a paternal aunt equally concerned and affectionate, who would represent the nonexistent category of sister who loves the children of her own brother. In the same way, a maternal uncle loves the children of his sister for the simple reason that he loves his sister. In short, to interpret the feelings and attitudes that obtain between aunt or uncle and nephew or niece, one also has to reintegrate into the system the relations that obtain between brother and sister, sister and sister, and brother and brother: this is what the words of the participants seem to suggest.[6]

Hence, it may be possible that the Roman system could be further rewritten in the light of horizontal relations that in some sense precede the indirect ones. In other words, the very presence of a maternal aunt who is affectionate and concerned toward her sister's children would in itself rule out the existence of a paternal aunt of the same sort; namely, the sister that loves the children of her sister, rather than those of her brother. The vast quantity of surviving material on the role of the maternal aunt already predicts, in a certain sense, the scantiness of evidence about the role of the paternal aunt. Nor should we forget that the Matralia was an important festival, even as Mater Matuta was an old and important goddess: if the Roman matron celebrated these rites in her role as a *matertera,* this meant that in some way she preferred to present herself as "sister who loves the children of her own sister," rather than "sister who loves the children of her own brother."

As for the maternal uncle, Plutarch's Publcola said that his fellow consul, Collatinus, sought to spare dangerous traitors, the Aquilli and Vitelli, "in order to please certain women [namely, their mothers, who were the sisters of Collatinus]." One loves as an *avunculus* because first, as a brother, one loved one's own sister. Behind the legendary *avunculi* Numitorius and Brutus himself (of Virginia), it is very likely that we should discern in the first place brothers who love sisters. Surely, this rule underlies the passage in Paulus-Festus which was quoted in chapter 5: "For brothers usually love their sisters more than their brothers" (13 L). Such is the case in the legend of Horatia, killed by her brother Horatius upon his return from battle with the Curiati, which tells of a sister killed by a brother because she refused to kiss him after he had killed her fiancé and cousin, Curiatius.

111

This, however, is not the place to explore the system of attitudes horizontally, which I may do in another work. At this point, instead, we should seek to reintegrate in a single explanation the diverse motives we have been finding one after another in the affective system as we discover differing but complementary rules. We should seek to imagine a paternal uncle who is severe and unlovable by virtue of resembling the father's model, by virtue of belonging to the agnatic, the male, line, by virtue of being a brother who prefers the children of his sister to those of his brother and who thus elsewhere can be an affectionate and indulgent person in his relations on the maternal side. The network is dense and unbroken, capable of revealing from changing viewpoints ever-deeper ties and combinations. The same effort, of course, ought to be repeated for each of the other kinship roles we have studied thus far, until we are sure that a system of attitudes, deriving as it does from the system *par excellence*—that is, from kinship—constitutes one of the most inexhaustible and complex of social objects.

Part Two

"The future at your back":
Spatial Representations of
Time in Latin

Time exists, undoubtedly. Yet it cannot be seen. Without body, incorporeal, is how Seneca once defined it on the wave of his Stoic philosophy (*De brev. vitae* 8.1),[1] but that is too little. We have to resign ourselves to confessing that, for us, Time is only a confused mass of hints: that little, or much, which has always made lonely hunters run the tracks of its trails. And Seneca among them. But are they, then, really trails? Is there really a fleeing Unseen that leaves its mark on everything it touches? Its most advertised and unmistakable signs, the sun, moon, and seasons, do nothing but come back regularly the same, and hence are outside of Time. As for the throng of Time's smaller and grimmer signs, such as change or death, they may even be false messages, signals without a source. Maybe nobody is there at the end or out back tapping the keys. Maybe the signs themselves are Time, but with a small *t,* and that is all there is to it.

When it comes down to it, if we want to speak of Time (and Lord knows how much we need to every living day!), if from this ensemble of passion and culture we call Time we want to make an object of discourse, we have to represent it for ourselves. Thus, in our cultural and linguistic imagination, we make out Time as space.[2] We arrange its implications and effects "near" or "far" and "before" or "behind" and "above" or "below." Time's disasters or gifts are imagined sliding along a line or still awaiting our passage, like milestones along the highway of life. Time presupposes a topography; but it is conferred by language, which was the first to give place to Time. And perhaps this is no mere play on words.

Seven

Localizing Anterior and Posterior

Augustine says, "I speak of position when we see each thing's right, left, above, below, before, after, far, near" (*dexteram laevam, superiora inferiora, ante post, longe iuxta, Cat.* 10). Among these categories that define the position of something, only the last three pairs serve to represent time. Right and left in time do not exist. A "right time" (*dextrum tempus*) is a favorable moment (Horace, *Serm.* 2.1.18), but it has no particular position in a chronological order. Instead, one can say that an event is before or after (*ante/post*), farther up or farther down (*superius tempus/inferius tempus*), or far or near (*proxima nocte*, etc.). Not distinguishing right and left in time fits with the observed fact that temporal processes extend along a line without reference to the lateral extension of the plane.[1] Hence, time is space without right and left; this trait, perhaps most directly, marks its representations.

By way of compensation, the complementary pair of "before/after" enjoys wide employment in the temporal field. As Varro noted in discussing why temporal expressions such as "in the morning" (*mane*) and "at evening" (*vesperi*) do not form comparatives and superlatives: "But in time of day there can be no 'greater' [*magis*] and 'lesser' [*minus*]. There can be 'before' [*ante*] and 'after' [*post*]" (*Ling. Lat.* 9.73). Quantitative relations are not admitted in hierarchies of time. One time of day is not greater than another. In compensation, the times do relate to one another as "after" and "before."

Varro's remarks take us directly to what may be the most direct and famous application to the temporal field of the pair "before/after": its use to express the relationship of "anterior/posterior." This relationship, which is definable in terms of sequencing,[2] expresses the position of an event relative to another. Given two events, A and B, if A is "before" B, then B is "after" A. The chronological determination is in a sense objective because it does not depend on the position of the speaking subject. To express this relationship, Latin uses principally, but not solely, the pair *ante/post*.

In the spatial field, *ante* and *post* contrast as "before" and "behind": "The spirit of each man assigned him the order of fighting before or behind" (Livy 22.5.8). From *ante* and *post* come many derivatives that continue the same contrast; thus *antela* (horse's chest), contrasts with *postela* (horse's croup). Similarly, in augural language we frequently find the derived adjectives *anticus* and *posticus*: "Of that heavenly division [*templi*], four parts are named: left to the east, right to the west, before to the south, behind to the north" (Varro, *Ling. Lat.* 7.7).[3] So there is the part before and the part behind.

In the temporal model, the pair continues to contrast. Here *ante* indicates what came first, whereas *post* indicates what came later, "after." Clearly, the notion of anterior, coming first, is expressed through the idea of "before"; posterior, coming later, is expressed through "aft, behind." In the case of two events, A and B, if A comes earlier than B, it is defined as coming "before" B. In correlation, B, which comes later than A, will be defined as "behind, more aft than" A. To treat all this as obvious would be the worst thing we could do if we wish to undertake the study of such relations. Instead, it behooves us to gather and analyze the main expressions in the Latin language that witness to the association of "first" and "before."[4]

Consider the adjective *antiquus* (ancient). It clearly derives from *ante* (before). Hence, whatever is old or ancient must stand before. Other forms in *-quus* cover the field of spatial determinations: *obliquus* (that is across), *aequus* (that is even); and also, with a nasal infix, *longinquus* (that is far) and *propinquus* (that is near). In this series, *antiquus* (that is before), meaning "ancient," fits very well. As for its relations with *anticus,* which is the form with a simple velar, many examples occur in which *antiquus* (ancient) is written simply *anticus.* Similarly, we often have *aecus* for *aequus,* and *oblicus* for *obliquus.*[5]

We therefore can infer that the form *anticus,* "anterior," exploited for functional ends the shifting between *-quus* and *-cus,* the evidence for which we have seen. At the time when *antiquus* took on an enriched and ramified set of temporal values, the simple velar form got restricted to the purely spatial meaning, with the resultant creation of a minimal pair in which a nonfunctional variant was preserved.[6] As for *post* and its derivatives, the spatial-temporal differentiation was carried out in another manner: *posticus,* which is the correlative of *anticus,* covers the spatial axis, whereas the temporal dimension is covered by *posterus,* in which the ending expresses "position in space," as it also does in *superus* and *inferus.*

We are accustomed to feel, in the adjective *antiquus,* simply the sense of "ancient" and "past," no longer with any reference to space and arrangement, to one thing standing ahead of another. But this sense still is felt in a use of *antiquus* remarked by Fronto: "that which is preferable is commonly called senior [*antiquius*]" (162.9 Nab.). The examples of this usage are many,[7] including those, some archaic, gathered for the heading *antiquior, melior,* "senior, better," by Nonius (688 L), among them Varro, "Nor do good citizens hold anything senior to the common safety" (*Rerum humanarum* 20).

Likewise, Cicero writes: "It behooves to hold nothing senior to the laws" (*De inv.* 1.142). Here "senior" (*antiquius*) means "preferable," as Fronto has explained. But to translate more closely to etymological dictates would require: "Nothing must come ahead of the laws." In short, *antiquus* here does not have its habitual sense of "ancient"; it has nothing to do with the past as in its most common use. What is activated here is its direct link with *ante* and its ability to establish an order, a hierarchy. For this reason Pease,[8] for example, is quite misleading when he draws a parallel with analogous uses in Greek of *presbyteron* (senior), as in Euripides: "I consider nothing senior to moderation" (fr. 959 N). This use of *presbyteron* implies instead the notion of "venerable," and "commanding respect," which belongs to the meanings of *presby*.[9]

Instead, *antiquius* or *antiquior* implies a more abstract notion of order, of positional hierarchy in space and time. Cicero, for example, speaks of a "place further before [*antiquiorem*] for declaring an opinion in the Senate" (*Verr.* 5.36), where it is a matter of "coming first" or "being before" in the order of speakers. Similarly, Velleius Paterculus writes that "he held nothing earlier or further before than . . ." (2.52.4).

Likewise, Aulus Gellius can say, "Massurius Sabinus assigned his guest a place further before than his dependent" (5.13.5), which means placing the guest before the *cliens* in the code of obligations. Gellius then says: "Among our ancestors, when obligations were at issue, the observance was thus: first guardianship, then hospitality, then dependents, then relatives, afterward neighbors" (fr. 6 Huschke). The code of obligations thus had its own hierarchy of precedence, in which Masurius Sabinus believed that the guest came before (*antiquior*) the dependent. Naturally, this "stand before" implies being preferable, *potius*, as Fronto says. Everything that stands "before" is considered better than what is "behind," thanks to the cultural predominance of "before" over "behind."[10]

The comparative use of *antiquus* shows, then, that in this adjective the link with *ante* and its positional value remains quite alive. For us, that which is *antiquus* is simply "ancient, belonging to the past." So we have to be reminded that, yes, it is "old," but with less metaphorical detachment from the original "before in position" than our habits of language might make us think. Thus, in the famous line of Ennius, "moribus antiquis res stat romana virisque" (*Ann.* 500 Vahl.²), we need to see a reference to the Roman state as sustained by customs and heroes that stand before others, which in turn stand behind and come later. Not that we can reduce *antiq*-

uus to its simple original sense, "that stands before"; however, the existence of such a sense must be underlined.

Now that we have seen how the model of "before/behind" works for *ante/post* and the adjectives derived from them, we can continue our analysis of anterior and posterior with a look at the similar system formed by derivatives with *pri-*, such as *pri-die* (day before); *pri-dem* (long since); and *pri-scus* (primitive).

The pair *pridie/postridie*, "the day before/the day after," occurs in reports of things, in the discourse of third-person narrative.[11] It differs from the discourse of dialogue between first and second persons, "I/you," in which the adverbs of time are so-called shifters.[12] For example, *heri* and *cras*, "yesterday" with respect to "tomorrow," are bound to the position of the speaker (I/you) and are able to change content continuously. By contrast, with *pridie*, a third person indicates "the day before" and with *postridie*, "the day after." In the case of *pridie*, we have no reason to doubt what we are told by Paulus-Festus: "Instead of *prae* [before] the ancients said *pri*" (252.25 L). For example, if *pri-mus* is "the first," that one in the series who is "tout à fait en avant,"[13] clearly *pri-* does not differ in function from *prae-* as it appears in compounds such as *praefectus* (made before); *praetor* (going before); *praeses* (sitting before); and so forth: in short, all those cases in which *prae* is used to indicate an extreme position, as we shall see in chapter 12. We should recall, too, those uses of *pri-mus* and *pri-mor* that designate the fore or extreme part of an object:[14] *primus digitus*, "fingertip"; and *primora labia*, "lips' edge." Here it is easy to recognize the sense of extremity found in *prae*. Hence *pri* and *prae*, as Paulus-Festus says, are clearly equivalent. That means that *pridie*, which is the "yesterday" of narrative discourse, is properly the "day that stands before," toward the part before, whereas *postridie* is the "day behind." The same holds for *pri-dem, pri-scus, pri-stinus*: the "first" is always a "before": the speaker imagines that the *prisci Latini* or the *pristini mores* are located before, toward the part that is before those who came behind and who thus stand behind. Similarly, *prius* means "further before" and thus "prior to": the adverb plays the same syntactic role as *ante* or *antea*.

Hence, we can be sure that Latin expresses anteriority and posteriority in terms of before and behind. Indeed, we can italicize for further notice later, that the terms to designate "before" and "first" are more frequent and emphatically marked than those for "behind" and "later": thus the workings of the adverb and preposition *ante* with its derivative *antiquus,* also the prefix *pri-* and its multiple ramifications in *pridie, priscus, prius;* and so, too, *prae-,* as in *prae-sentire* (cf. presentiment), *prae-cavere* (cf. precaution), *prae-dicere* (cf. predict), and so forth, where what is perceived, feared, or said first is something felt or said before, *prae-*.[15]

Against this abundance of terms for "first" and "before," the "last" and "behind" can boast in Latin of only *post* and its derivatives. Thus, the expression of anteriority, of beforeness, seems to have stimulated or required a greater linguistic articulation. This is the problem we shall come back to in chapter 12, with the question why, when we think of it, does "first" get associated with "before" and "later" get associated with "behind." But for now, the evidence.

Eight

Localizing Future and Past

Having dealt with the placement of two events in respect to each other, we turn now to the placement of "first" and "then" as they are reckoned in respect to an indicating subject: a subject, that is, conceiving of these two dimensions as its own past and own future. Such a situation could also be expressed in terms of tense,[1] which is the semantic category that expresses the relationship between the time of the description and the time of the event it describes.[2] Putting it thus, however, would risk impoverishing the model, by cutting it down solely to a matter within language. Instead, I am convinced that the ways in which language represents time have to be set in their specific cultural context in order to be understood. Hence, I prefer to put the case at once less specifically and more fully, as follows: not only a linguistic subject, dealing in language with relations between the time of description and the time described, but also a cultural subject, dealing with its own future and past, hence bringing into play a broader range of anthropological models from religion, philosophy, literature, and the rest. Naturally, even when we put it this way, temporal relations maintain their character as shifters,[3] changing contents and placement in relation to the speaking subject.

We saw with the pair "anteriority/posteriority" that "first" got linked with "before" and that "then" got linked with "behind." This placement, however, gets inverted when we come to "past/future": what is "passed" gets linked with "behind," and what is to be (the future) gets linked with "before." That is to say, the relationship "first/then" gets expressed in different, in reversed, spatial terms: whereas the pair "anteriority/posteriority," equated "first" with "before" and "then" with "behind," here the pair "past/future" equates "first" with "behind" and "then" with "ahead":

anteriority/posteriority: first = before, then = behind
past/future: first = behind, then = before

These two symmetrical schemes will return again and again in the following pages, so I hope that the reader has visualized their contrast.

The following passages exemplify the localization of "past/future": "For when you regard the whole past space [*omne praeteritum spatium*] of immeasurable time" (Lucretius 3.854); "How much further can my mind regard the space of past time [*praeteriti temporis*]?" (Cicero, *Pro Arch.* 1). In both passages, the verb "look back" [*respicere*] leaves no doubt that, to look at one's own past, one must "turn around."[4] Seneca, a writer extremely concerned with time and its passing,[5] gives us the most abundant examples of this localization: "Nor do those who are busy have leisure to look back at what has gone before [*praeterita respicere*]" (*De brev. vit.* 10.2); "No one gladly . . . twists himself back toward the past" (10.3); "The spirits of the busy, as if they were under the yoke, cannot bend themselves and look back" (10.5). Here the traditional "look back" is varied by the ideas of twisting back and bending back.[6]

Horace, too, provides an interesting case (*Carm.* 3.29.43–47):

> . . . Let Jupiter tomorrow with black
>   clouds preempt the sky
> or bright sun: yet he will not cross out
> whatever is behind or redivise
>   and make undone what once
>   the fleeting hour has brought.

Jove will not be able to make vain that which has already taken place, the "passed," which is "behind": the same idea gets expressed then, too, in the image of that which the fleeting hour has brought already. Similarly, Juvenal can say: "For behind his back, he has left sixty years" (13.16). The sixty-year-old has left his years at his back. Hence, there seem to be no doubts. The past locates itself behind the subject. In human time, behind each person is a certain quantity, greater or lesser, of time, thus the need, if one wants to think again of one's past, to turn around, look back, twist back, and so forth.

The theme of "looking back" invites a brief parenthesis. To be sure, *respicere* one's own past implies that the past stands behind. But what specifically does it mean to turn around to look at it? In Seneca's reckoning, looking back becomes the express sign of being able to reflect on the passage of time and hence on the value of life: in short, the invitation to look back is an invitation to be wise, and the busy person's inability to do so becomes the greatest existential failing. Thus, we have one of those cases in which the location of time in space intertwines inextricably with philosophical reflection or literary creation.[7] To get to the bottom of these Senecan philosophical images, it may be necessary to recall that traditionally, including in folklore, to "look around," *respicere,* has the symbolic significance of establishing contact with the interlocutor. For example, a divinity that "looks back" is favorable, disposed to care for one.[8] Among the many manifestations of Fortune at Rome, one actually had the name Fortuna Respiciens, "Luck Who Looks Back," so called for bringing aid.[9] If Fortune turns back and looks, then she also brings help.

In general, *respicere* actually means "to think of" and "to care for," as in Terence, *Andria* 975 and *Adelphoe* 932. Indeed, the phrase "to look back at oneself" means caring for oneself, considering one's own condition, in Plautus, *Pseud.* 612, and Terence, *Heauton.* 70. The premise, in short, is that one who turns around to look, who accepts in some way the exchange of glances, is available for contact. This trait in all likelihood distinguishes the action of *respicere*.

Turning around or looking back might be said to constitute, at the level of cultural expressions, of nonlinguistic behavior, the equivalent of what Malinowski and Jakobson defined in speech as the phatic function, which serves to keep open the channels necessary to communication. From this phatic role of turning around derives, in all probability, the theme—also familiar from fable— of the prohibition against turning around: the condition imposed, for instance, on Orpheus leaving the underworld in Virgil's *Georgics* (4.485).[10]

To turn around means to establish contact, which is precisely what ought to be avoided with the world of the dead. That is why one must not turn, for instance, when fleeing from the appearance of a ghost. Thus, we hear Tranio shouting to Theopropides in the *Mostellaria* of Plautus when they hear the "voices from within the haunted house": "Don't look back! Flee! Cover your head!" (523). By contrast, in celebrating a triumph, one was told: "Look behind you! Remember that you are human!" (Tertullian, *Apol.* 33.4), just in order to keep one who was at the center of attention and at the peak of glory from "feeling like a god."[11] The triumphator, in short, was not to advance looking only ahead. He must turn, must maintain contact with his mortal human nature. Clearly, in this case also, to turn around to look amounts to a metaphoric contact, the phatic function performed by the symbolic gesture. By turning, the triumphator avoids cutting the ties that bind him, like everyone else, to his natural condition. Hence, when Seneca urges looking back at what has passed, he is really urging that contact be maintained with one's past: not to think only of the present, or of one's own tenuous future (a thought that is, moreover, one of the main threads in his tract on the shortness of life).[12]

Putting behind us our parenthesis on the wider implications of looking back, it is certain that the past gets localized metaphorically behind the subject, which takes for granted, of course, that the future is ahead, as one experiences it, too, in contemporary language and culture. We may recall the use of *pro-*, meaning "forward" rather than "first," as a prefix with verbs such as *videre* (see) and *-spicere* (look). If "look forward" can evolve into meaning "foresee," then the future surely is located ahead. Take the examples of Pacuvius, "For if anything is to come out, let them foresee" (407 Rib.[3]); Cicero, "which I . . . before I began to speak . . . perceived and foresaw" (*Vat.* 2.4); and, very clearly, Lucretius, "Nor does anyone begin to do anything before the mind has foreseen what it wants. That which it foresees, of that thing the image exists" (4.883–85). The mind, then, sees before, first, that which it intends to do, and this is called *providere*, "to look ahead."

The most interesting example comes, again, from Seneca, because, as usual with him, the localization of time and reflection of culture go hand in hand: "For in this we are deceived, that we look ahead to death: . . . whatever is behind in age, it holds death" (*Ad Lucil.* 1.1–3). Clearly, in the usual scheme of things, death is located ahead of the subject (*prospicimus*): in reality, death is the future event *par excellence*. It follows that the past is located behind the subject. Seneca, however, inverts the common localization, breaks the scheme, and liberates an existential reflection: death is in the past; it stands behind, not ahead as everyone supposes.

Placement of the future ahead can also be inferred from the temporal use of the adverb *porro* (ahead, further), also discussed in chapter 11. Take, for example, Terence, "What do you offer me here, why do I hope, further not to be?" (*Heaut.* 298); Cato, "I was disturbed and shall be further" (*Or.* 39 Malc.); a famous Catullan passage, "Unless I love you with no holds barred and am ready to love further without stopping through all the years" (45.3–4); and Livy, "Nor could they . . . divine what the Celtiberi had in mind, or what they were going to have further" (40.36.2).

The difference between "further" (*porro*) and "afterward" (*post, postea*) in contexts of this type deserves a brief clarification here. From the viewpoint of purely correct language, in the Catullan passage just quoted, the speaker, Septimius, could also say, metrical considerations aside, "and to love ever after [*post*]": he would thus still assert his intention of loving Acme "then," as well, "in the sequel," for his whole life. The matter interests because it would give us both "further ahead" (*porro*) and "after, behind" (*post*) employed with the same function. In fact, by replacing *porro* with *post*, one shifts automatically from the module "future/past," which we are analyzing here, to the module "anterior/posterior," which we discussed in chapter 7. But in passing from one to the other, the temporal localizations get reversed: that which is behind in one (*post*) passes ahead in the other (the future before). This implies that "to love after [*post*]" and "to love further [*porro*]" are equivalent only in a very superficial way. "To love after [*post*]" would mean to love "then" with respect to a "first" (*ante*: a relative position between two events); "to love further (*porro*)" would mean instead to love "ahead," implying forward movement that is a progression, a continuation toward the future love of Septimius (position of the future, "ahead" with respect to an indicating subject).

What we have are two models that mirror each other in structure, which is why, unexpectedly, the "after" and the "before" can play a similar role in each. Later, we shall see in detail how a word such as *porro* works in a temporal model that localizes movement. For now, we need only establish that the use of this adverb, too, presupposes the placement "ahead" of the future: "ahead" of the subject with respect to which it is reckoned.

The scheme for localization in space of past and future seems to be:

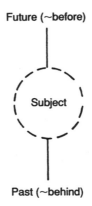

Future (~before)

Subject

Past (~behind)

At this point, we can ask how the movement of time gets represented: does the change of time, transforming into "after" what stood "before," appear as the subject moving toward the future (a passage) or, conversely, as time running to meet the subject? Both kinds of representation are well documented. For time running, we can see, for example, Virgil, "Time will come, when . . ." (*Geo.*

1.493) and "The age will come, when . . ." (*Aen.* 1.283); Horace, "The years coming bring many advantages with them; going, take many away" (*Ars* 175); "Time glides away . . ." Ovid (*Fast.* 6.771); or, again, there is Seneca, "The present time is very brief, . . . for it is always on the run; it flows and falls away" (*De brev. vit.* 10.6). Here, too, we can quote again the Horatian ode, "Yet Jupiter will not cross out whatever is behind [*retro*] or redivise and make undone what once the fleeting hour has brought" (*Carm.* 3.29.45–47). The past is represented as "behind," and the hour as fleeting, in images that are closely juxtaposed. In such cases, we clearly have a temporal flux in which the future, about to happen, is in a certain sense in arrival before the subject, whereas the past gets placed behind him:

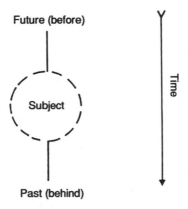

This model allows us a remark concerning history and religion. It is well known that Janus is considered the god of the beginning year: Ovid, "Origin of the silently gliding year" (*Fast.* 1.65), underlining that in the god is the source of the year's quiet flow. More precisely, in Janus coincide the end of the old year and beginning of the new. Again, for Ovid the *bruma*,[13] understood broadly as year's beginning and end, is at one and the same time "first of the new and newest of the old sun" (*Fast.* 1.163). On this day, the "head" and the "tail" of the annual cycle hook onto each other; beginning and end coincide.

However, Janus is also a god with spatial relevance. He presides specifically over all "passings." Thus, Cicero expressly writes, "From 'going' [*eundo*] the name Ianus is drawn, from which open passageways are called *iani,* and doorways over the thresholds of profane dwellings are named *ianuae*" (*De nat. deor.* 2.67). What interests us here is not the etymological relationship between Janus and "going" but that passageways are called *iani,* with the same name as the god of transitions, and that so, too, are the doors. Precisely the exits and returns were in Janus's power, according to Servius (on Virgil, *Aen.* 1.294), and this was the meaning of Janus's image with two faces, which presented itself as a guide to those going out and to those coming back. Indeed, this god receives frequent dedications of the type "for the sake of going out and coming back," which are accompanied by the images of footprints pointing in opposite directions.[14] These footprints actually represent the anthropological category embodied by the god. Indeed, this kind of representation is quite the equivalent of the double-faced image of the god, only shifting to a different part of the anatomy the doubled and contrastive character of the divinity.

In turn, we can make a useful comparison between the spatial and the temporal ranges of Janus, precisely in terms of our study of the ways that temporal relations get localized in space. If time is conceived as a flow, as movement that has an "ahead" and "back" in space, we can well understand how crucial points in time come to have a spatial god, one presiding expressly over passages and over going and coming, a god with one face before and another behind. We must recognize, in other words, that the spatial model of time, with distribution and hierarchy along spatial lines, also works in the religious sphere.

The model finds its place in religion in the person of the god that joins space and time in his powers. It is as if there were a solid movement, holographic so to speak: drawing time in language in spatial terms, the same drawing gets repeated in the tableau of religious representation. God of spaces, Janus gets set also at the articulations of time. Thus, we recall that one way of referring to the year's beginning is "the year coming in," *ineunte anno* (Suetonius, *Tib.* 54; cf. 61), just as one spoke of "summer coming in" (Cicero, *Att.* 4.2.6) and "spring coming in" (Cicero, *Imp. Pomp.* 35). In the same way, the year's end gets referred to as "the year going out" *exeunte anno* (Cicero, *Div.* 1.53; Ovid, *Fast.* 3.43; Paulinus, *Dig.* 15.3.19), and there is a frequent formula, "the year's exit" (Cicero, *Fam.* 8.10.3; Livy 6.4.1), even as the end of a given day is called "day's going out" (Livy 4.30, 30.25, and etc.).

So a year, a season, or a day "comes in" and "goes out": and Janus, straddling the end and the beginning of the year, guarantees the passing. Because the temporal representation is nothing but a localizing, a transposition into spatial terms, one and the same god presides both over passing beneath the entries of the city and over the exit and entrance of the year. We, too, in today's culture, employ localization in space to represent relations in time. What we do not have, however, unlike the Romans, is the possibility of employing specific religious figures in this capacity.

Let us look at the other model that gets applied to the passage of time: the subject "on the way" toward the future. The type emerges clearly from passages such as these in Seneca: "We see that you have come through to the last moment of a man's life, the hundredth or more year is pressed on you" (*De brev. vit.* 3.2); and, "Consider the shortness of this space, through which we run so very fast" (*Ad Lucil.* 99.7). Or there is Juvenal, cited earlier, "For behind his back, he has left sixty years" (13.16). Here, too, the temporal use of *porro,* "further," fits in with cases such as those cited above: if he pledges to love Acme "further . . . through all the years," Septimius apparently is imagined as "on the way" along his love, which goes on. It becomes a matter of "going ahead" with love for his whole life. To this type of representation, too, must be related the so-called future passive infinitive; for example: "Remember you promised that all the silver was going to be given back [*redditum iri*] to me" (Plautus, *Curc.* 490); and "When a rumor comes that gladiatorial shows are going to be given (*datum iri*)" (Terence, *Hec.* 39).[15] In such cases, the notion of future gets expressed directly by means of a "going" of the subject involved.

The latter construction, however, merits a brief analysis. It contains a supine; that is, the accusative of a verbal noun ending in -*tus,* which, as such, indicates the capacity, disposition, and possibility of bringing about the idea of the verb:[16] thus the possibility, potentiality, and so forth of "giving back" the silver and the potentiality of "giving" the gladiatorial show. These substantives in -*tus* appear as a goal toward which the action moves. Then comes the subject, the passive form of the infinitive of the verb "go." Altogether, such a structure can express the future quality attributed to the realization of the event. Literally, "the money become gone toward being given back to me."

Clearly, the infinitive mode in Latin has no lack of forms to express both variants of the pair:

passive   − / +
present   + / +

Thus, we find both of the following:

argentum reddere, "to give back silver" (= present⁺, passive⁻),
argentum reddi, "silver to be given back" (= present⁺,
   passive⁺)

Forms, instead, are lacking to construct both variants of the following pair:

passive   − / +
future   + / +

Here we find only the future active (future⁺, passive⁻):
   argentum redditurum esse, "to be going to give back silver."
There is no future passive (future⁺, passive⁺).

In the latter case, then, the lack of a form gets made up by lexical means, introducing a periphrasis centered on the verb "to go" and the "movement" expressed by the accusative of the verbal substantive.[17] This particular lexical choice, of course, is what interests us. It shows that where forms are lacking to express a notion of futurity, Latin has recourse to the notions of "going" and of "movement," which means that the future is seen as something toward which the subject goes. In this kind of representation, as in the Senecan phrases cited above or in the employment of *porro,* time's passing manifests itself as a movement by the subject toward the future.[18]

Hence, we can begin to outline the model that complements the one described above. While keeping unaltered the coordinate "before/behind," we change the subject and the direction of movement:

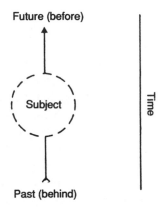

What remains, now, is the delicate task of seeing why, on any given occasion, we select one of these two models: the subject that moves toward his own future, or time that moves toward the subject. The matter involves a complex of cultural representations on a ground where metaphors in language, reflections in philosophy, and creations in literature all grow shoulder to shoulder. From a very general standpoint, any given choice of models may depend on whether one takes part in the events described. In other words, choice can fall on one or the other model according to whether we want to underline the active part of the subject in the temporal process or his detachment from it.

For instance, the "times" actually differ in two passages cited earlier. In Catullus 45, Septimius commits himself to "love further," thus seeing himself in progress toward the future. But in the *Ars Poetica*, Horace says, "As the years come, they bring with them many welcome things; many, as they go, they take away" (175–76): here time in its running enriches and impoverishes a subject who is essentially motionless. The same goes for constructions of the type "silver is going to be given back to me." In such cases, the subject is imagined as directly involved in the temporal process: it is the silver that goes toward being given back (*redditum iri*). The inverse model would call for solutions of the kind *tempus venturum in quo argentum mihi reddatur,* "time going to come for silver to be given back to me," or some such.

Seneca, with his continual soundings of the nature of time, again furnishes especially useful examples. He writes, "You are busy, life hurries on: death meanwhile will approach, to whom, willing or not, one must give way" (*De brev. vit.* 8.5). The busy man, as usual, is not aware of time's passing; he is outside it: "he has no time for time," one might say. But life runs fast, and death overtakes us by surprise. However, Seneca also describes the behavior of the wise man who does not waste time and uses it to the fullest because he knows that "however small life is, it amply suffices," so, when the last day comes, "wisely, he will not delay to go to death with unflinching step." Unlike the busy man, who is outside time's flow and whom death will approach unexpectedly, the wise man himself will go toward death with a sure pace. The one is time's victim, and the other is time's master; the two ways of understanding the approach of death, the future event *par excellence,* define two ways of life.

Elsewhere the prospect can stand out in a few lines, even in the turn of a few words: "Look back on the swiftness of devouring time [*rapidissimi temporis*], think on the shortness of this space, through which so very quickly we are running" (*Ad Lucil.* 99.7). Seneca shifts abruptly from the image of a time that is swift, and that snatches human life away with him in his flight,[19] to the image of the rush of the human race, breathlessly using up the short allotted way. The two symmetrical models cohabit, each adding emphasis to the other. The choice, then, of one or the other may depend on a writer's culture, his need for philosophical reflection, or even his simple and momentary feeling, whether man runs and uses up his time, or whether time runs to meet us. Between these two representational models runs a kind of continental divide which separates two different ways of understanding schools in philosophy, genres in literature, life itself. The contrast between those who endure time and those who seize it creeps unnoticed into the hidden folds of expression, the sinuous richness that is called "style," even in daily life; but it builds, too, the plots of stories and novels, dictates poems.

Nine

"On the way":
Reflections in Literary Anthropology

n Goncharov's *Oblomov,* the lazy Russian landowner of that name lives buried in his bed, busy shunning a string of experiences, in the form of friends, messages, and troublemakers, which try to get at him from outside. How different from an ancient novel such as Petronius's *Satyricon!* Quite the opposite of sluggish Oblomov, Petronius's heroes Ascylton, Encolpius, and Giton go out themselves to encounter experiences, which they meet along a meandering line like a progress through a maze:[1] the Greek city, with its internal wanderings among the brothel, the tavern, the house of Trimalchio, and so on; then the scene on the seashore, with the gallery of art, the ship of Lyca and Tryphena, the shipwreck, Croton bristling with legacy hunters.

In Petronius, as in all ancient storytelling, there is the journey that serves as the framework of the tale. It coincides in practice with the plot. The very unfolding of the narrative consists of the shifts in scene, the encounters, and, above all, re-encounters, which are what makes the plot seem like a maze. All this clearly is just the opposite of the tale of Oblomov, in which, by a brilliant paradox, immobility forms the framework, even at the deepest levels. Not by chance, one of the best chapters in the book consists of the so-called dream of Oblomov, which describes the little Russian village where the protagonist lived as a child: it is a small place, remote, in which "regularly, without shocks, the year completes its course," and where travel and encounters with new things are so strange that a foreigner who happens to come there gets mistaken for nothing less than "a snake or a werewolf" and is ringed in by peasants armed with pitchforks.[2] It is not difficult to recognize here, in the difference between these two novels, the same kind of contrast which separates the two models of temporal representation that we have just seen: in *Oblomov*, time and events come upon the protagonist like a torrent that tries to overwhelm his calm; in the *Satyricon*, as in all the other ancient and modern novels that employ the framework of the journey, the protagonists themselves are directly involved in creating the narrative time.

Speaking of the *Satyricon* and the ancient novel, we can do no less than really turn back, right to the start, to the very prototype, as it were, of the novel: the *Odyssey*.[3] It is here that the journey celebrates its triumph, but, not by chance, so also does time. The type of the hero who after many years returns to his own home, but so changed that he has to be recognized through proofs and private signs,[4] finds in the supporting frame of the journey its most firm temporal premise. One has lived much and changed much who is "of many turns": he who has wandered much.[5]

The journey is Time. Indeed, in the *Odyssey*, Time is really a character. To turn itself into narrative, into time that has been told, it has to become a way. Let us say that, in terms of cultural models, the representation of time as movement by the subject, which we studied in chapter 8, does not differ from a plot of the Odyssean type in which the journey is the narrative frame. If time as represented in language makes itself into space, in literature and storytelling it makes itself into travel.

Clearly, the analogies between language and literature remain very close. Seneca, with his rich vision, represents human life or human time in the metaphor of the way ("We see that you have come through to the last moment of a man's life," *De brev. vit.* 3.2):

and, so doing, he suggests, in hints and tidbits, possible plots of stories. Only stretch them out, put in all the encounters that give time its substance, and a story would already be born.

Let us, however, stay with the Homeric epos. Time receives markedly different treatment in the *Odyssey* and the *Iliad,* as several studies have shown.[6] Such differences strike me as all the more interesting because the two poems, with regard to real, objective, time, show a practically identical framework. The events told in the *Iliad* take place at the end of the tenth year of the Trojan War, and they last for about fifty days.[7] Similarly, the *Odyssey* picks up its hero in the tenth year of wandering, and the events told by the poet in the third person, not the long first-person reminiscence by the hero, encompass about forty-one days.[8] Thus, the two frameworks seem commensurate, from the same temporal mold. And yet how many differences emerge if one goes to look at the time as it gets told! To begin with, in the *Iliad,* indications of time like "the shadows set down upon the earth" are generic and, above all, serve to delimit the action more than the passing of time. Their character thus is metaphorical;[9] they signal shifts or breaks in the unfolding events without seeking to build a chronological picture in the background. Hellwig states that "the individual references to time serve not so much to mark the present moment as to symbolize the point at which the action stands."[10]

Such, however, is not the case in the *Odyssey,* in which "the events become perceptible in their real movement in time. . . . Duration is no longer strictly subordinated to the needs imposed by the scope of the action, but gets represented perceptibly for itself to the listener's ear."[11] And the *Odyssey* treats time with greater care in another respect as well: it uses the flashback, which suspends the forward motion of the plot and recovers after the fact events prior to the present action. True flashbacks differ, according to Hellwig, from the practice of the *Iliad,* in which we find only reference backward;[12] in other words, mention of previous events that do not, however, directly set the stage for the present action, which is not their sequel. By contrast, the *Odyssey* employs a compositional device that Hellwig calls an actual grasp backward:[13] a literary form that recovers previous events that are decisive for the understanding and unfolding of the present action, constituting its premises. This is what happens in the account of Odysseus to the Phaeacians, a rather long account that, practically speaking, sets at the end of the story a deeper knowledge of everything that came before. Not only, then, does the *Odyssey* represent time in a clearer and more autonomous fashion; the treatment also has a sort of multiplying effect, which reinforces time's weight in the action described.

With respect to space, too, the two poems differ in like fashion. In the *Iliad,* the scenes of action seem strictly divided in two halves: the human (city, ships, et al.) and the divine (Mount Olympus, Mount Ida, et al.). Naturally, sometimes the gods move over into the human half. In the *Odyssey,* however, the space is almost entirely human. When the gods appear, they generally make their entry onto the common scene of action:[14] in short, we cannot speak of a true divine scene. But what counts even more is that the scenes in the *Odyssey* receive, through the descriptions of the places, a precise spatial configuration,[15] unlike those in the *Iliad.* We customarily speak of Odyssean landscapes, certainly not of Iliadic landscapes, as Reinhardt long ago remarked,[16] and with good reason.

The *Odyssey* is far richer than the *Iliad* in spatial references inserted into the course of action, the so-called indirect descriptions.[17] In the *Iliad,* places are made visible only together with the developing action. Hellwig notes that "in the same moment in which the actions unfold and the characters act, one or another image of the place falls under our gaze. The result is a representation in which . . . some details can remain unclear or contradictory."[18]

In this regard, the *Iliad* seems to invite comparison with the spatial system in the plots of the Russian *bylina,*[19] which Nekljudov describes: "The static parameters of space . . . are linked not in a direct fashion, but through what is taking place." As a result, the "spaces in which the epic action takes place possess . . . a concreteness not so much of place as of plot (situational)."[20]

In the *Iliad,* the prime concern is action. Thus, just as the temporal signs serve more to symbolize the point reached by the narration than to indicate an actual moment in time, so the spatial indications delimit a piece of the action, in metonomy for it, more than a real and actual location. By contrast, the *Odyssey* takes care, even in the indirect descriptions, to provide much more precise indications of the scene, as, for example, in the meeting between Odysseus and Nausicaa.[21] In the *Odyssey,* the dimensions of space and time enjoy a role that we might call more autonomous; they take their own course, which is not so strictly meshed with the mechanisms of the action.

At this point, we can understand Hellwig's assertion that "in the *Odyssey,* not only space but also time gets discovered as a category."[22] Her intellectual toolkit, too close to German *Geistesgeschichte,*[23] leaves us rather unhappy today, but her observation of the facts, as it were, remains worthwhile. Suffice it to recall that we are not dealing with historically revealed categories of the spirit as much as, if anything, with different implications of structure. We should not forget that the *Odyssey* is built on the pattern of the journey and that the *Iliad* is not. And with the journey, time makes its entry at once. In other words, we may reasonably hold that the attention paid to spatial and temporal references in the *Odyssey* depends also on the basic fact that the heroes move, travel, constantly change scene and place. Odysseus is a man "of many turnings," he has wandered, he has seen countries and cities: thus he has gone out to meet his time, he has set himself on the way.

The *Iliad* contains no journey. The wrath of Achilles, the arrogance of Agamemnon, the pride of Hector, the pride of Priam, all constitute a bundle of exemplary cultural models around which the story of the poem gets organized: or, better, a series of repeated heroic moments, battles, conflicts, taking place in the narrow space between the walls of Troy and the ships, becomes the bearer, in the concrete language of epic representation, of a cultural code in which archaic Greece recognizes itself. The places are more or less always the same, the battles and duels repeat according to preset modules. But this has a reason: it is that the paradigmatic, exemplary stamp actually gets created by means of *repetition;*[24] by reiterating, however, one amplifies but does not create development. Repetition as such tends to *negate* time, certainly not to mark its progression.[25]

Relevant here is the example of what folklorists call "trebling,"[26] action repeated thrice, as often in fairy tales. It would be naïve to hold that the classic attempt twice botched by older brothers, then carried to a successful end by the younger bother, constitutes a temporal structure. To the contrary, the pattern merely serves to signal the exceptional importance attached, against all expectation, to the younger brother, who is shown capable of getting a particular good or handling a given task. Trebling, indeed, really consists of not a ternary but a binary structure, as Meletinskij has shown:[27] TWO (the botched tries) versus ONE (the successful try), an opposition that actually emphasizes the extraordinary importance attached to a Cinderella or Jack and the Beanstalk.

For the heroes of the *Iliad,* time will come, in a certain sense, only afterward; the "return home" is such that the action embodies the pattern of the journey. Only after Odysseus has wandered among the Lastrygonians, Circe, the Cyclopes, the Lotus-eaters, will he be able to change, to return home different from what he was, heavy with space and time.

This relationship between time and action gets inverted in Virgil's *Aeneid,* which sums up both the *Iliad* and the *Odyssey,* as we know. Aeneas is a hero who wanders first, fights afterward. Such an inversion perhaps indicates the truly unique fashion in which Virgil conceived his hero. Combined in this way, the two foundation epics of the ancient world yield an invincible fighter who has already, however, in his search for a new homeland, experienced the time of distance and loss. In one sense, it is as if Odysseus had had to face the Cyclopes, Circe, Calypso's love, and all the rest before the Trojan War. Would he have been the same hero? The question is awkwardly put. But it is equally certain that the dutiful Aeneas interprets his italic *Iliad* in such an unforgettable, Virgilian way also because, before he reaches the Latins, he has long tried the adventures and sufferings of the journey. While he is setting out for Lavinium, to fight and found the new civilization, Aeneas is a hero already heavy with time. No Achilles of the short and perfect youth, lacking any past that is not the inescapable sentence to an early death, Aeneas is an Odysseus who gets to Ithaca, bringing with him a long past, having traveled far. Indeed, by now, Aeneas has before him more an impersonal future, of descendants, than a further stretch of the road to pass. In this appearance late on the field of epic conflict, in this warlike ability of his, which is, at the same time, ripeness of time and journey journeyed through, Aeneas is truly "Father."

Perhaps we are getting a little away from the thread that guides our reflections: this metaphor of time as way, as journey, which we see at work in the literary plot, as before we saw it working metaphorically in the language. In the plot of literature, the journey seems ever more likely to be a metaphor of time. But let us look at one more example.

Further back than the *Odyssey* is hard to go; but at least we can try to get further beneath in a structural sense. It is an important fact that the journey pattern plays a quite canonical role in the most general narrative genre that we have, the fable. If we follow the order of the narrative functions defined in the morphology of Propp, we find that, on the threshold of the story proper, which means the end of what Propp calls the initial situation, there is the departure, dispatch of the hero (XI: ↑). Similarly, after getting the magical agent (F)—which closes a well-defined segment of the fable, in which the "proof" is contained (E)—the hero next gets to another place (XV: G). Finally, when the enemy has been defeated and the original harm has been repaired, the hero gets back to the point of origin (XX: ↓). In short, the framework of the fable consists of the displacements in which the hero gets involved.[28]

The unfolding of a given cycle in time, which brings about a situation at the end that differs from that of the start (harm versus repair of harm), coincides with a hero's involvement in certain basic displacements. These assure, in the simplest possible way, the presence of so-called narrative time. In sum, the need to organize in temporal succession a sequence of events that forms the intrigue—to give time, that is, to the plot—gets met by using the most tellable of the representations of time that the language offers to literary creation: the journey.

In the style of fable, two formulas are so frequent as to seem almost proverbial: "He goes and goes . . . " and "One day goes by, and then another, and another. . . . " These formulas belong to our personal memory of old stories; it would be superfluous to cite texts or quote examples. They are the typical formulas that any one of us would use if required to tell a story. We know that the formulas are used in moments that connect one episode to another, acting as both markers and frames for the narrative. But now, however, we can see that there is a reason, if one formula covers exactly the same space as the other. Evidently, these formulas are identical and perform the same function. If, then, the spatial formula, "He goes and goes, . . . " and the temporal formula, "One day goes by, and then another, and another, . . . " have homologous uses, it is because, in the structure of the tale, movement through space is movement through time. The second formula, directly temporal, is only the more abstract, explicit form of the first. As such, the temporal formula gets used in static contexts (e.g., waiting), whereas the spatial formula gets used in dynamic contexts.[29]

Naturally, these displacements by the hero can also stand out more clearly than they do in the elementary motif grammar of Propp, depending on simple narrative choices or the pressure of the material to be told. Among fuller versions, a famous case in ancient literature is the tale of Cupid and Psyche, told by Apuleius in his *Metamorphoses,* or *Golden Ass.* In order to remedy the harm that she herself caused, Psyche has to undergo a long series of wanderings that, of course, take her even to the world of the dead, until at last she regains her lost love. The structures are ample and bring to mind the plot of the *Odyssey,* as well as that of the *Metamorphoses* itself, in which one part of the central fable has a similar structure, and the plot of the *Satyricon* of Petronius, which is the point from which we began. But we hope, now, to have a greater awareness that the journey, in the plot, makes the hero encounter time in his narrated life.

Ten

"On the way": Generational Time and the "Review of Heroes" in Book Six of Virgil's *Aeneid*

ho journeys, and how? If one or some, we have a novel. If one and all, a whole community or human kind delimited no more closely, then we have history, or life itself. Once again we return to Seneca and his representations of time (*Ad Lucil.* 99.7):

> Look at this company of humankind tending in the same direction, set apart from one another by the slightest intervals. . . . One whom you think has vanished [*perisse*] has just been sent ahead [*praemissus*]. What, then, could be more mad, because this same way you, too, must measure out [*idem tibi iter emetiendum*], than to weep for one who has gone before?

Life, then, in its passing, is represented as a kind of procession, a company that goes forward set apart by brief intervals: evidently, the years that separate the generations, because shortly thereafter Seneca remarks: "By intervals we are set apart; by our exit we are made even." The procession moves toward one and the same end, death; and one who is already dead "has been sent ahead" (99.9).[1] Indeed, Seneca describes the law of death in his *Consolation to Marcia:* the oldest, not the youngest, are expected in the natural order to die first, "all of ours, . . . both those whom we want to survive us by the law of birth and those whose own most just vow is to go ahead" (10.3). In this movement toward death, the elders go ahead of the young, who by the law of birth *(lege nascendi)* must die after those who went before them.

Representations of this sort, describing time as human, with the orderly turns of generations one after another, place the elders ahead, closer to the goal. The young, in turn, stand behind, and whoever dies (the eldest according to the natural law) has been sent ahead *(praemissus)*. Thus, in this model, clearly we follow our ancestors, who are those who have gone before: as Publilius Syrus puts it, "Best it is to *follow* elders, rightly if they've *gone before*" [*App. sent.* 33 R³].

Hence the past, if conceived in terms of those who have gone ahead along the way, is placed *before:* correspondingly, the future, if seen as those who are younger than we, who hence follow us in the journey, is placed at our back. In other words, generational time, the journey of the whole community, seems to invert the usual localization: it makes our posterity into people back of us.

In reality, no inversion takes place. The image of generational time, as we have seen in Seneca and shall see in Virgil, simply shows the great complexity with which the game of representation unfolds in a field as culturally important as time. We go ahead toward a future that stands before us as the finish line of the way. But because we do not move alone, but in company, it is obvious that within the procession an order gets defined: some are further ahead, some further back. In other words, in the image of the company are mingled the two temporal models described in chapters 7 and 8: the relative model, which contrasts before and behind (anterior/posterior); and the absolute model, which contrasts past and future. In this way, the future is ahead of the whole procession, but, within the procession, those who came first must necessarily have a place further ahead than those who came after. The structure is complex; the relations between "before" and "behind" provide human depth—the generations—to the metaphysical and abstract movement toward the finish line that evens one and all.

Let us look at a fine example of this combined structure (combined both formally, with the play of the two relations, and humanly, substantially). In book six of the *Aeneid* (6.752–892), Virgil describes the procession of Aeneas's descendants. All Roman history, in the guise of Rome's future kings or commanders, unfolds here before the eyes of the hero and his father, Anchises. The setting is as follows. Aeneas and Anchises climb to the top of a rise (*tumulus*, 754), and the descendants, one after another in a long procession (*longo ordine*, 754), come to meet them (*venientum discere voltus*, 753). Naturally, each time the on-comers present themselves face to face to the watchers (*adversos legere*, 755). In sum, there is a real procession that marches before the eyes of the two heroes. And here, too, the most ancient are ahead, while the younger, who are still far from the goal, come behind. Thus, first in the series comes Silvius, the posthumous son of Aeneas. Next to Silvius stands Procas (*proximus*, 767),[2] then Capys, and so on. On and on winds Roman history, in the guise of its representative figures, as far as the age of Virgil. To close the series, last, the furthest back with respect to his ancestors, comes Marcellus, the young hero torn too soon from the life of glory which awaited him among the poet's contemporaries.

We see here that Virgil represents generational time in a manner quite like Seneca's, only that, in Virgil's hands, the brief verbal image actually becomes narrative. But then, as emphasized in chapter 9, the boundary is very fluid between the verbal image of the way and the story of this way. And here, in all likelihood, we touch the strongest structural reason for the extraordinary literary effect that the "Review of Heroes" has on its readers.[3] Very probably, by representing Roman history as a way, a company of heroes which advances slowly toward its future, Virgil has somehow conferred a kind of verisimilitude on a metaphor, giving unexpected voice to a quite strong virtuality that underlay the cultural representation.

Many models and parallels have been proposed for the "Review of Heroes." There is Homer's so-called *Teichoscopia* (Wall Watch),[4] the scene in which Helen, high on the walls of Troy, shows Priam the outstanding heroes of the besieging Greek army (*Il.* 3.161ff.). There is the catalogue of the heroines who come to meet Odysseus during his descent into the underworld (*Od.* 11.225ff.).[5] And there is the catalogue of the heroes who sailed on the Argo, running for some two hundred lines in Apollonius's poem (*Arg.* 1.20ff.).[6] Also, a generic inspiration in Roman statuary has been invoked.[7] Finally, and perhaps the most interesting,[8] a similarity has been suggested to the procession that took place during the aristocratic funeral: the parade of the ancestors' images, along with the bier of the dead man, when the entire noble line came momentarily back to life to accompany its latest death (a theme we shall return to in chapter 13). However, spontaneously, the "Review of Heroes" also invites comparison with other episodes in the *Aeneid* that share strong thematic similarities. Such, for example, are the prophecy of Roman destiny by Jupiter (1.257ff.) and, above all, the description of Aeneas's shield (8.626ff.). These are two episodes in which Roman history, in the guise of expectation, of prophecy, plays the role of narrated subject.[9]

No doubt each parallel has interesting features: it is very likely that Virgil was reenacting, in the poetic culture of the "Review of Heroes," suggestions from earlier masters; just as it is undeniable that the internal parallels with Jupiter's prophecy and Aeneas's shield constitute a kind of complement to this scene.[10] At the same time, however, one can claim with equal truth that each of the parallels ends by seeming inadequate to account for Virgil's elaborate structure: it seems able to contain them all, as it were, one by one, and yet always maintain something besides. Thus, although Homer's *Teichoscopia* shares the motif of standing on a high place explaining the names of heroes to one who does not know them, we can easily note that it lacks Virgil's movement, historical arrangement, prophecy, and so forth. Or again, for the heroines in the *Odyssey,* if Odysseus's preceding encounter with his mother resembles, in some respects, that of Aeneas with his father, every-

145

thing that differs from Virgil is only too easy to emphasize. Although in some fashion the parade of the Argonauts does contain the motif of movement,[11] its heroes are still present, all alive at the same time, with no story yet to come. Nor can one argue that an assemblage of statues is the same thing as a procession.

Finally, we need hardly add that even the internal parallels can be considered as such only if we first underline all the diversity, because a brief and inspired prophecy such as that of Jupiter, or the string of tableaux described for the shield, with their "here is . . . , there is . . . , nearby is . . . , not far from there one sees . . . ," which Lessing found so unbearable, certainly have precious little to do with the advance of the "Review of Heroes" in book six, apart from, obviously, the mere canvas of the historical subject.

The parallel with the Roman funeral remains surely the most suggestive. Yet differences here, too, are not wanting. The Roman aristocratic funeral paraded the images of only one clan, the family of the dead man, not the entire population,[12] as in Virgil's "Review of Heroes." If the model of the funeral is really active, clearly here it has expanded into a meditation on the whole of Roman history. Moreover, if the parade of images in the funeral served to reconfirm, to reflect on, the past of the clan, we must say that in Virgil this chronological bent, which does exist, at once gets complicated by its opposite, which is meditation on the future, a sense of expectation and prophecy. The citizens who took part in an aristocratic funeral, looking on the visages of so many noble figures, may well have conceived a sense of expectation, of hope, reassured by so much past excellence.[13] But we must not forget that in Virgil's narrative there is one personage for whom hope and expectation of the future are not a mere ideological deduction from the models of the past: for Aeneas, the parade of heroes really is the earnest of a glorious future. It is not an inference, more or less contradictory or tortuous; it is prophecy.

Turning, then, to our more immediate theme, we can certainly say that the separate parallels we have seen thus far all share a defect on one point. Each lacks that kind of ordered movement which translates into spatial terms a temporal succession:[14] from the nearer to the more distant future. This is the most distinctive trait, the defining mark of Virgil's "Review of Heroes," and for this reason the closest parallel remains that of the aristocratic Roman funeral.

On this note, we come back to the metaphor of the company, that procession on the march which represents generational time. In other words, we believe that the unmistakable charm of Virgil's creation is his success in grafting onto the scheme of the catalogue something that transformed it into a living thing, time.[15] The heroes to come are shown by Virgil on the march, as if the future promised to Aeneas had already begun its course and the company were preparing to let the first in the series get started toward the light. Concerning the hero who heads the column, Virgil writes: "By the next lot he holds the place of light, first to the breezes of the upper world will he rise, mingled with Italic blood" (761ff.).

Thus, customary words—old and colorless metaphors—reclaim new force in the narrative. At the end of the scene, Virgil says that Anchises, with his explanations, kindles the spirit of Aeneas "with love for the coming fame" (899). But whoever reads this comment, after seeing pass before him the parade of heroes, no longer finds only a metaphor representing time to come: the reader finds a concrete, real movement, the metaphor made narrative. The heroes have come to meet the founder. That which in the language of metaphor was only a "coming fame" becomes, in the literary invention, the picture of Aeneas mounting on the mound so that "he can take in and learn all the countenances of those who come toward him in the long column" (754).

Now that we have reached this point, we can achieve a better focus and take a further step. As we said, Virgil brings together a series of great literary moments (the epic catalogues) with material that is both history and celebration at once (Rome's accomplishments). These two threads polarize in a structure that follows the spatial model of time in its form as generational time. This scheme joins the relationship of anterior and posterior, expressed as before and behind, and the relationship of future and past, in the form of a "before" toward which the whole procession moves, a procession that is Roman history itself, a time made up of famous men who pass one after another, bringing with them the events of which they were protagonists.

What is the role of Aeneas here? Who, in structural terms, is this spectator, this pupil instructed by his father? In reality, Aeneas, as founder of the Roman race, ought to be ahead of the whole procession, the unwitting leader of a parade that winds behind him, like Virgil in Dante, who made light for the one who followed. This would require a blind or, shall we say, mechanical application of the metaphor of the company. In fact, the literary fiction, the angle chosen by Virgil, brings it to pass that the leader is outside his column: a spectator at one side who commands his future generations from the top of a mound. Aeneas, in short, is a leader who has had the rare occasion of stopping and, in a certain sense, turning around to know what will happen after himself. This is the plan that Virgil has given to Anchises' prophecy:

Temporal Directions* in the "Review of Heroes"

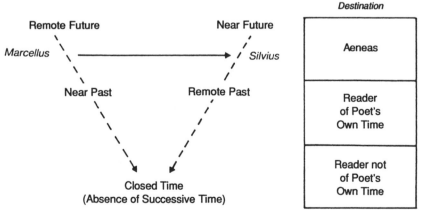

*The coincidence of two temporal directions in one and the same movement, which makes "Remote Future" and "Near Past" correspond with "Remote Past," produces the "Closed Time": a closure that becomes "Absence of Successive Time" for the reader who is not contemporary with the poet.

Let us employ coldblooded analysis to follow the structural lines of this plan to their end. We are aware that extreme complexity thus gets assigned to the play of time. Aeneas is a leader who has turned around, letting run toward him the very generational time that is fated to follow him and that otherwise he ought not to know. Instead, the poet and his contemporary reader ought to place themselves at the end of this same procession. In other words, the procession of the "Review of Heroes" amounts for Virgil to an account of those who have already gone before him: those who have been sent on ahead, as Seneca says. Hence, Virgil's scene must be read in two temporal and spatial directions: for Aeneas, what comes to meet him is the future, from the closest one (Silvius) to the farthest (Marcellus); for the contemporary reader, a past comes back to him from its beginnings to the present time.

These two diametrically opposed views, that of the recipient of the prophecy and that of Virgil's contemporary who has to relive the history, by their simultaneous presence confer on this scene a temporal tension that is truly exceptional. In reading the scene— and by this we mean not only the reading of a recipient who reads the poem but also the reading of Aeneas, who "reads" (*legit*) the countenances of those who come toward him[16]—a kind of double game is played: the reader knows that whatever is farther from him is nearer to Aeneas, and vice versa. The recipient reads in the past what lies in the future for Aeneas. From this perspective, the figure of Marcellus grows perhaps still richer in pathos: the handsome youth is so far from his mythical precursor, who therefore is all the more amazed at him, and is yet so near, in his death, to the contemporary reader. In Marcellus, the tape breaks. Narrative time overtakes prophetic time. Beyond this, not even Anchises, from his privileged observation post in the other world, can dare to look.

Just here, at the parade's end, a third time arises: ours, the time of readers who do not belong to the temporal horizons of Virgil and whom he could imagine only as posterity. But this time of ours is empty. It is the absence of a procession that we know kept on, and for a very long time. Like a kind of homesickness, it is the certainty that prophecies of it do not get made. Neither near nor far, the reader of "today" (but what does the word mean?) compacts into one sole farness the founder and his descendants and then looks on in wonder at the fascinating play of contraries set in motion by Virgil to give the impression that, with him and his poem, time stood still.

Eleven

Other Aspects of Time: "The future at your back"

To have "a future behind you" was a witticism that Freud attributed to Herr N. (perhaps J. Unger?) long before a celebrated Italian actor, with acute self-irony and without, I think, benefit of Freud, called his memoirs *A Great Future at Your Back.*[1] The wit, or self-irony, of course consists in playing with the model we have been studying: one's future is before one, not behind. At one's back lies the past, and hence. . . . But before it became wit, this way of representing the future had been a key to interpreting dreams, a folkloristic hint, a religious sign: many things.

First dreams. Borghini has called attention to a dream of Domitian's,[2] reported by Suetonius, in which the usual localization of the future as ahead and the past as behind, to which by now we have become accustomed, appears completely reversed: "For they say that Domitian himself dreamed that a golden hump had grown behind his neck and that he took it as certainly portending a more prosperous and happy condition of the state after him" (*Dom.* 23.1).

The golden hump appears behind the neck and gets read at once as a symbol of the future. To this dream, moreover, we can add another, rather famous one, of Hannibal's. Right after the capture of Saguntum, Hannibal gets called before the council of the gods, where Jupiter commands him to carry the war to Italy and provides him with a divine guide, as Cicero tells it (*Div.* 1.49ff.):[3]

> Then that guide bade Hannibal not look back. He, however, could not keep this up any longer and, carried away by desire, looked back. Then he saw a beast huge and monstrous all entwined with snakes, and wherever it went it overturned all the trees, bushes, buildings. And Hannibal, marveling, asked about it what such a monster showed. And the god answered that it was the devastation of Italy and bade him go forward, lest he be troubled by what was occurring behind and at his back.

The folkloric mechanism of this dream is clear. Above all, we have seen that the ban on turning back was a very popular theme in ancient folklore.[4] But what interests us here is that Hannibal has behind him the ruin he is destined to bring to Italy and of which he should be absolutely unaware according to the prohibition set by his guide. Indeed, once the prohibition has been broken, the guide urges him to go straight on without thought for what lies at his back. Like the hump of Domitian, what lies "behind" expresses what will happen "then" and is not known yet, or rather, in the folkloric rendering of Hannibal's dream, should not be known.

This model of placement in time, as it emerges from the two cited dreams, finds a precise and express parallel in the rules for interpreting dreams of Artemidorus: "Everything that stands behind symbolizes the future" (1.21); and, "To dream of having the head twisted to the rear, so as to see behind one, keeps one from leaving his homeland, . . . and prohibits undertaking anything else. In fact, it forces one to look not merely at what is pleasing in the present but at the future" (1.36);[5] and, perhaps not dissimilarly, "We hold that the back and all the posterior parts symbolize old age" (1.49). Hence, this particular kind of placement of temporal relations was in some ways canonical and current in the interpretation of dreams. The dream tales and the categories of dream interpretation match perfectly. In the dream, time is turned around. That which normally stands "before" gets placed behind.[6]

This reversal of the temporal model is very likely owed to the presence of a new element, which until now we had not seen in action: knowledge. In other words, if the future is seen as something that must be known, then its position has to be turned around at once; it can only be at the back. The future is the unseeable, the unknowable *par excellence*. And that which cannot be seen has an excellent chance of standing behind the one who is looking for it. An explanation of this kind emerges from the dream of Hannibal, when the general on his way to Italy "must not know" what his expedition will bring to the enemy land. Formally, we could say that knowledge stands in a hierarchy above the spatial location of future and past and that, whenever it enters into play, the usual localization gets inverted at once.

Another piece of evidence can be cited, again from a work by Borghini. Toward the end of the nineteenth century, there was a superstition in the region around Modena: "On Christmas Eve, when getting up from the table, many superstitious country folk look behind their back; and if they see their shadow projected on the wall merely in part, they take it as a sign of death within the year; if, instead, it is projected wholly, then they don't have to fear misfortune."[7]

We hardly need to remind ourselves that Christmas Eve is a typical moment of passage, a space in which one gathers signs of the future, given that in a certain sense a new future presents itself along with the new year. Thus, the behavior of the country folk from Modena acquires meaning: in the act of taking an omen about the coming year, they look at the shadow that lies behind their back, and from this they draw signs for the future. Here the divinatory direction, revealing of the future, comes into play. And hence the location behind the subject becomes relevant.

To clarify this point further, we can turn once again to Seneca's *On the Shortness of Life,* that really and truly fundamental text for us in this study: exhorting his reader not to throw away his most precious possession, time, Seneca argues: "If, as with our past years, so also the number of our future years could be set before us, how few that they are we would see and tremble, how we would not waste them!" (8.3). Here doubtless the matter is one of

"putting before" each person the number of his future years; however, the text says clearly that usually what we have before us are
the years already lived, the past, which evidently inverts the model
we saw earlier: the past no longer stands at our back, but before
our eyes. It is the future's lot to "stand behind"; and if only one
could have it before, like the past!

The reason for this is simple. We do not have a common question of meeting our own future: we demand to see it. And thus its
place can be no other than the unknowable, the behind. Instead,
the past is localized ahead because it is well known. In the same
manner, Seneca insists: "One must hasten, it presses from behind.
Wretches, you know not how to live in flight" (*Ad Marc.* 10.4). Life
is flight. That which must come, and of which there can be no
certainty ("nothing is promised for this night," he has just written,
"nothing for this hour"), presses on us from behind, like everything that is unknown. And he writes: "Death follows me, life
flees" (*Ad Lucil.* 49.9). But is not death the future event *par excellence?* The event, that is, that one goes to meet? But if death is
imagined as the unknown, the unforeseeable, the hidden foe, then
its place can be nowhere but behind us.

Let us move into the area of archaic Roman religion. Here we
find perhaps the most full and interesting evidence for the model
of temporal localization which we are reconstructing. We begin
with Macrobius (*Sat.* 1.7.20):[8]

> [Janus] is believed to have borne a twin countenance so that he might
> see what was before and what was behind his back: which undoubtedly
> must be explained as referring to the foresight and diligence of the king,
> who is to know what has passed and foresee what will be. Just so, the
> Romans worship Antevorta (Fore-turned) and Postvorta (Back-turned),
> certainly the most fitting companions of Janus.

In this passage, the two faces of Janus are associated with the
past and the future, but the word order leaves no doubt: to see
"ahead of oneself" (*ante se*) is equated with knowing the past,
whereas seeing "behind one's back" (*post tergum*) is equated with
foreseeing the future. In short, here, too, the past lies ahead, the

future behind; and again we have a question of being able to divine, of a possibility of knowing that belongs to the superior foresight of the god.

Naturally, we might imagine that Macrobius made a mistake, or played a trick. But the text also refers to two divinities that are known from other sources, too, and are conceived according to one and the same pattern of temporal localization. Thus, Ovid speaks of the two goddesses who are companions to the prophetic deity Carmentis[9] (*Fast.* 1.631–36):

> If you love old rites, stand near the one who prays:
> you will hear names not known to you before:
> Porrima is being placated and Postverta, both sisters
> and companions in your flight, o goddess of Maenalus.
> The former is said to have sung what was before (*porro*):
> the latter, whatever was to come after (*postmodo*).

Thus there was a goddess Porrima, who knew how to make utterances about the past, and a goddess Postverta, who could prophesy about the future. The differences with Macrobius are minimal: he writes *Postvorta* where Ovid has *Postverta*; and instead of Ovid's *Porrima*, Macrobius has *Antevorta*, which Ovid could not have used in his verse, because it contains a long-short-long sequence (cretic). In meaning, however, *porro* (forward),[10] corresponds perfectly to the *ante* in *Antevorta*. Likewise, here the goddess of what is "ahead" knows the past (*quod fuerat*), whereas the goddess of the "behind," of what is "backward," knows the future (*quidquid venturum*).

The same situation occurs in the commentary of Servius on the *Aeneid*: "Others say that Carmentis's companions are Porrima and Postverta, because prophets know both the past and the future" (8.336). Again, the word order leaves no doubt. There is one goddess of "turning backward" (Postverta), who knows how to prophesy about the future, and another goddess of "forward" (Porrima), who knows how to prophesy about the past. The situation corresponds perfectly to the temporal functions of the two faces of Janus as described by Macrobius. And here, as there, the matter concerns the cognitive aspect of past and future: Antevorta (or Porrima) and Postvorta (or Postverta) constitute a pair of deities concerned with knowing.

The singularity of this religious representation of time stands out. It is proven, we may note parenthetically, by the recurrent error of modern scholars, who assign to Antevorta (or Porrima) knowledge of the future, and to Postvorta (or Postverta) knowledge of the past, reversing the sense of the sources.[11] Evidently, scholars unwittingly apply the classic model of temporal localization, which is described at length above (in chapter 8); they do not realize that the models of spatial representation of time are numerous and complex.[12]

What we have, then, is archaic evidence: Ovid himself underlines the remote antiquity of the goddesses:[13] "old rites . . . names not known to you before." The old Roman religion thus presents a pair of deities constructed according to the same pattern of spatial localization of time that we saw at work not only in the dream and dream interpretation or in folklore but also in Seneca's philosophical reflections. And the same pattern, according to Macrobius, can give a sense, a positional meaning, to the two faces of Janus: the one "ahead" symbolizes knowledge of the past; the one "behind" symbolizes knowledge of the future. Also, in the religious sphere, the issue of knowledge seems to take precedence over placement in space. Both Janus and his two companions divide the future and past as they do because they are deities of prophecy: they have to do with the past and future from the viewpoint of foreseeing and knowing.

Hence, we find confirmation for the idea that the future gets imagined as "behind" when there is a question of wanting to know it, so one who can foresee it must have a face behind, or be able to turn backward. Behind the back stands what we cannot know. Horace says so quite expressly: "He will learn to look back at what is pending behind" (*Serm.* 2.3.299). And we may recall the fable of Phaedrus: "Jupiter loaded us up with two sacks: one he set on our backs, full of faults of our own; the other he hung in front, heavy with others' faults" (4.10).[14] The representation is the same. That which one does not know (does not want to or cannot know) is behind; that which is well known is before. And a similar argument occurs in the scholiasts to Homer, when they interpret the pair *prosso/opisso* (before/after): "One says *prosso* [before] for the past because one sees what stands before; one says *opisso* [after] for the future because it cannot be seen" (*Schol. Il.* 18.250; Eustathius, *Comm. Il.* 81.45 and 389.3). To be sure, the explanation is wrong.[15] The scholiast confuses the relationship between anterior and posterior (the relative chronology of two events), with the absolute relationship between future and past. We, however, by now know how things stand. But it is also interesting to observe how the confusion arises. Everything stems from applying the divinatory, cognitive model of time to a the usual relationship of anterior and posterior. If the scholiast erred, it was because he knew that the relationship between future and past also had a specific cognitive localization, in which the sign of what is visible and of what is invisible shaped according to its needs the various spatial locations of time.

Twelve

The Cultural Preeminence of "Before": Linguistic and Anthropological Analysis

Thus far we have been concerned with the play of time that employs the pairing of "before/behind" to represent diverse temporal hierarchies and single changes in function. Because we have used the pair with such frequency, perhaps the moment has now arrived to look a bit more closely at it for its own sake. Our analysis is both linguistic and anthropological. On the linguistic side, we look at the main prepositions used in Latin to express the idea of "before"; on the anthropological side, we underline some of the more important cultural values of the oppositional pair "before/behind" (which receives further, specific treatment in chapter 14). Readers who are not specialists and who find the ensuing analyses a bit too technical may skip directly to the end of the chapter or to the following chapters without losing the main thread of the argument.

The three main prepositions used by Latin to signify "before" are *ante, prae,* and *pro.* Of these, *ante* indicates that one particular thing is in front of another, which is understood as a point of reference. Thus, in the language of comedy, a character is said to be *ante aedes,* "in front of the house" (Plautus, *Cist.* 543), whether the speaker himself is within the house (*Merc.* 808), or outside the house and coming toward it (*Amph.* 406), or happens to be the very one who is "in front of the house" (*Tri.* 824, etc.). In all these cases, the point of reference is always the house, and the person is said to be in front of it. This quality of being in front of something gives rise both to a temporal sense and to a metaphorical sense of superiority. Thus Plautus can say, "Know that he before all is the most worthless of mortals" (*As.* 858); and Cicero can use expressions of the sort, "Whom I cherish before myself" (*Ad Att.* 8.15A.2). As a preverb, *ante* appears with this meaning in *antecello, antepono,* and so forth: again, Plautus can say, "This man is outstanding among all men, foremost [*antepotens*] in delights and enjoyments" (*Tri.* 1115).

The situation with *prae* differs greatly. As Benveniste has explained,[1] this particle indicates priority in the form of "forepart" or "head-part" of a particular object: the object in question is generally understood as a continuous whole, and the viewpoint seems to be considered "posterior" to that which is *prae.* Take, for example, the expression *prae manu* "on hand," used especially of money: it means that one has the money at the tip of one's fingers, ready to be paid. This character of "forepart" or "extremity" emerges clearly from forms of the type *praecingere, praecidere,* and *praeferratus,* in which *prae* acts as a preverb: the action affects the forepart of the object. Also in the case of *prae,* as with *ante,* the idea of priority leads, on the one hand, to a temporal function as in *praecox, praevideo,* and *praenosco,* but, on the other hand, to a meaning of "excellence, superiority," as in *praefero, praeficio,* or in *praealtus, praeclarus,* and *praefervidus.*

In the comparative function, then, it becomes particularly evident how the two particles basically differ. Only compare two expressions such as Cicero's "Whom I cherish before myself [*ante me*]," cited above, and Plautus's "I consider myself less than him [*me minoris facio prae illo*]" (*Ep.* 522). We see that in the comparisons, *prae* and *ante* have symmetrically opposed functions. Thus, *ante* governs the lesser term in the comparison ("myself" loved less than the other), whereas *prae* governs the greater term (by compar-

159

ison with his great worth, I am less), which is the usual use of *prae* in comparisons.[2] When coupled with *ut, quam,* and so forth, a proposition introduced by *prae* is always the greater term, as in Plautus: "little . . . by comparison with what it will be [*prae ut futurum*]" (*Amph.* 374), or "a matter of quite little pleasure by comparison with what trouble [*prae quam*]" (634).

These differing uses of *ante* and *prae* can be explained perfectly in terms of the model we have proposed. *Ante* designates simply being "in front of something," and thus "coming first" ("being more important") than something: whatever stands "behind" has less value, is left over. In contrast, *prae* designates the extreme point of something, or something seen in all its extent, its expanse. That which stands before it, therefore, appears in some way surpassed by it. As a result, an expression such as *omnium unguentum odor prae tuo nautea est* means "By comparison with the extremity of your perfume [with its extraordinariness], that of the others provokes nausea" (Plautus, *Curc.* 99).[3] Here it is worth remembering that this value of *prae* occurs in Latin from a truly venerable age. In fact, a fragment of the Saliar Hymn is *Quome tonas, Leucesie, prae tet tremonti* (When you, Jupiter, thunder, before you they tremble) (fr. 2 Morel). Evidently, this "before you" implies disproportion, superiority of the other: before the dreadful greatness of Jupiter thundering, they tremble. In a case such as this, *ante te* would not have expressed the same meaning. It would have had a purely local force, lacking the connotations of majesty, on the one hand, and inferiority, on the other, that make up the special religious significance of this formula.

We can, however, give another example. Only compare "Whom I cherish before myself [*ante me*]," cited earlier, with "He considers no one before himself [*neminem prae se ducit*]" (*Ad Herenn.* 4.28). In the former case, the subject places another ahead of himself, thus considering himself at once outclassed; he loves the other more than himself. In the latter case, the subject considers the others from the extreme point of himself, and thus he finds no one who can equal him. What we have are two different and complementary ways of seeing "before": "before" as being over and beyond, "before" as extremity.

Between the symmetrical opposites of *ante* and *prae, pro* shows a certain neutrality. At first sight, the function of *pro* as preverb seems less interesting: in *procedo, progredior,* and so forth, it indicates a coming "forward" or "outside" of something. As a preposition indicating state, it occurs in expressions such as "battle fought . . . before the camp [*pro castris*]" (Cato, *Orig.* fr. 91 Peter[2]), or "sitting before the temple of Castor [*pro aede*]" (Cicero, *Phil.* 3.27), which might make one think of an equivalence with *ante.*[4] But this proves not to be the case when we look at the metaphorical uses of the preposition, which can be charted as follows:

1. "In place of": *pro me responsas tibi* (Plautus, *Cist.* 507).
2. "In the role of": *hanc illam habebat pro ancilla sua* (Plautus, *Bacch.* 45).
3. "In exchange for": *huic pro te argentum dedi* (Plautus, *Per.* 838).
4. "In conformity with, as befits, in proportion to": *pro dignitate opsoni haec concuret cocus* (Plautus, *Bacch.* 131), or *pro virili parte,* and so forth.
5. "In defense of, in favor of": *factumst abs te sedulo pro fratre* (Terence, *Phor.* 1001).

From what kind of "before" can meanings of this sort develop? They certainly do not come from a generic "in front of" such as *ante,* or from the "extremity" of *prae.* Here, too, there is putting oneself "before" something, but we need to look at its function. At one time or another, we get "before" so as to take something's place, to constitute its value or price, to protect or favor it. All these uses postulate a fundamental equivalence between the two terms that are related by *pro:* "in place of, in the role of, in conformity with, in exchange for," all indicate that there is nothing extra or any extremity, but a responsion and a parity. *Ante* diminishes the value of its complement and *prae* increases it; but *pro* maintains it as it was, in parity, respects it. In this sense, we could also say that *pro* is a way of designating "before" without implying "behind": this opposition, from the cultural standpoint, is neutralized in a certain sense.

This specific quality of *pro* can be illustrated well by an example from Plautus, *Par pari datum hostimentum est, opera pro pecunia*

(Like for like weight was given, work for pay). The *hostimentum* is the "stone with which weight was equalized" (*Asin.* 172):[5] a counterweight, one could say. A transaction—work for money—has taken place between two parties. And the matter gets expressed in these terms: the work stands "before" (*pro*) the money, just as two perfectly equal weights balance each other. This is the "before" expressed by *pro*.

In keeping with this pattern, *pro* never develops a meaning of superiority, as happens with *ante* and *prae*. Clearly, then, this is a "before" without a "behind." Look at this example: "That Cato of ours who for me is one equal to a hundred thousand (*unus pro centum milibus*)" (Cicero, *Ad Att.* 2.5.1). Equivalence, not superiority, is expressed: Cato alone by himself is worth as much as a hundred thousand. Here we might say that, although *pro* itself is neutral, superiority or excellence does get expressed by the hyperbolic contrast between "one" and "a hundred thousand." The effort would not have been needed with *ante* or *prae*. It would have been enough to say, "Who is before all to me (*ante omnes*)" or, with the usual symmetry, "Before whom (*prae quo*) all are of no account."

It may be interesting to experiment with substitutions in this expression: the *differentia* emerge forthwith. *Qui mihi unus est ante centum mila* (Who by himself is worth more than a hundred thousand) at once implies superiority. *Qui mihi unus est prae centum milibus* (Who is one by comparison with a hundred thousand) instead implies devaluation: he is only one with respect to a hundred thousand.

For the same reasons, *pro* in Latin does not give rise to the notion of precedence in time. Certainly, such a sense is not implied by the use of *pro* in terms of kinship such as *proavus* or *pronepos*, although this is what Ernout and Meillet seem to be saying in the *Dictionnaire*.[6] The kinship line is something that runs through space, in the family tree (as we shall see in chapter 13). Thus the spatial *pro* operates here, in the meanings of "onward from" or "out from." The line goes onward, whether climbing, as in *proavus* or *prosapia*, or descending, as in *pronepos*, but also in *prognatus*, *proles*, and so forth. Priority in time has nothing to do with it. What counts is only the going onward, the following through. Nor should we be deceived by forms such as *providere* or *prudens* (**providens*). The *pro* that operates here is certainly not temporal, but spatial. The capability of looking ahead characterizes *providere*: "Indeed, I say that you have ascertained and foreseen it" (Plautus, *Capt.* 643). At issue is not having first seen what is said but, if anything, having done something like ascertaining, *explorare*: that is, having looked carefully ahead, gone into it deeply, without being short-sighted.

A sense of priority develops only with verbs (e.g., "see") that allow a movement forward, as Kranz has remarked:[7] thus we get *providere* ("see" ahead) and *prospicere* ("look" ahead), but not **pro-cavere* ("beware" ahead) and **prosentire* ("feel" ahead). What will be required here, obviously, are *prae-cavere* and *prae-sentire*. Given the fact (as we saw in chapter 8) that things to come are placed before the subject, it follows that "to look ahead" (*providere, prospicere*) can take on the meaning "to know the future in advance." Priority, as seeing something "before" an "after," has nothing to do with it: what does is the movement ahead.

As for *prudens*, what a pity that Ernout and Meillet in the great *Dictionnaire* explain it in terms of "qui prévoit" (even though they then have to admit that "dans l'usage courant, *prudens* s'était détaché . . . de *provideo* et avait pris le sens large de 'qui sait,' 'qui est au courant de.'" Here, too, the starting point is wrong. *Prudens* has the meaning of "expert, wise" (and then also that of "foresighted") simply because there is always a question of seeing "well; ahead; to the end" how things stand, not of seeing them "first." Naturally, the Greek *pro* of priority always lay there in ambush to push its Latin homophone toward the idea of priority. This is what happened with *proludo, prolusio* (prolusion) on the model of the Greek *proagon*; and think, too, of the importance of such Hellenisms as *proemium* and *prologus,* although the long *-o-* in *prologus* shows that Latin placed it close to *proloquor* (speak before all; clearly).

Hence, *ante, prae* and *pro* express in Latin three diverse modes of "before": a generic "stand out in front of" (from which eventually comes "outstanding"), extremity, and equivalence with respect to what stands behind. The system is rather articulated, as we see. Nor is that all. We can cite again the adverb *porro,*[8] which indicates movement forward: Cato, "From there I continue to go forward [*pergo porro ire*] to Turta" (fr. 40 Malc.); Livy, "Either the same road has to be taken back again or, if you continue to go forward [*ire porro pergas*]" (9.2.8). As such, *porro* practically equals *pro-* as preverb (*porro ire = procedere*).

More interesting still is the adverb and preposition *coram* (in the presence of). It probably can be analyzed as an amalgam of *co-* (with) and *os, oris* (mouth) (with the same ending that is found in *palam*).[9] Hence, *coram* indicates a "before" that is "face to face" (like the Greek *kata prosopon*). From here comes the sense of "before" as specifically "in the presence of" and thus also able to imply "openly," *palam* (in Ulpian, *Dig.* 50.16.33, *palam* is glossed by *coram pluribus*).

For *coram* with such implications, see the following: Terence, "I fear to praise you further openly to your face [*coram in os*]" (*Adelph.* 269); Cicero, "Shame kept him from trying repeatedly to take up these same things with you in my presence [*coram me tecum*]" (*Ad fam.* 5.12). It is important to underline that we have here a "before" that is solely human, personal. One cannot be *coram* with an object. What we have is the "before" of individual persons or collectives (e.g., *coram populo, coram militibus* [before the people, before the troops]). And as such *coram* implies, too, the activation of a series of social obligations, which are guaranteed by the one or by those before whom one stands *coram*: this is the "before" of the cultural code, the "before" in which a continual judgment takes place: one is before the eyes of the others and has to stick to the rules.

Now this richness of linguistic specifications for "before" finds its counterpart in a singular poverty concerning "behind." We have only *post* (*pone*: *post-ne) to indicate the state, and the particle *re-*, *red-* (from which comes *retro*) to indicate movement "backward": nothing else. Indeed, it is worth recalling the names of the deities of prophecy and birth which were discussed in chapter 11. If the goddess of "turning back" is regularly called *Post-verta* (or *Post-vorta*), the goddess of "turning forward" or "forward" is sometimes called *Ante-vorta* (from the "before" of *ante*), sometimes *Porr-ima* (from the "forward" of *porro*), and sometimes *Pro-(ve)rsa* (from the "before" of *pro-*). In this case, too, the range of versions of "before" is much richer than that of "behind," which is reduced to the sole *post*. And observations of this kind could be multiplied.

The unequal distribution of linguistic riches between "behind" and "before" leads us to a simple but useful remark, one that can hardly be avoided: from the standpoint of cultural patterning, "before" is much more important than "behind" and gets expressed through a very subtle network. One who counts stands "before": thus the *praetor* (chief), the *primus* (first), and thus, too, the verb *praesum* (preside). One who does not count stands "behind" is *post-positus, post-habitus,* and so forth. It is useless to heap up obvious examples; we shall confine ourselves to a few of the more interesting. In a house with two doors, the main one is simply called *ostium;* the secondary one, however, which in comedy opens on the alley and is smaller, more hidden, and so forth, is called *posticum (ostium)* (door behind). No need is felt for **anticum*[10] because it is taken for granted that the real and proper door must be "before."

Likewise in the code of warfare, not only are the wounds received "before" *(adversa vulnera)* the honorable ones, worthy of a soldier, but fighting (or dying) in the fore is what characterizes heroic conduct. At the end of his history of the Catilinarian conspiracy, Sallust describes the disposition no longer of the armies drawn up for battle, but of the corpses left on the field: "Then truly might you perceive how much boldness, how much force of spirit, there was in Catiline's army" (*De coniur. cat.* 61), because not only did each man in death keep the post assigned to him in life,[11] but Catiline "was even found far ahead of his own men, among the enemy corpses": in this he proved the greatness, dark though it was, of his warlike *virtus.* Catiline lies ahead of his own lines, hence he is courageous, a hero: "On the basis of the rhetoric of position, and by means of a distributional criterion, one builds the rhetoric of individual heroism."[12]

The preeminence of "before" over "behind" undoubtedly derives from cultural patterning carried out by projecting the plan of

165

the body. The attribution of "before" or "behind" to separate objects or groups of objects is carried out by projecting onto them the "before" or "behind" of the person, just as happens in attributing "sidedness," "left" or "right."[13] But along with the spatial coordinates, cultural coordinates also, as it were, get projected. And because, in a human being, the principal organs, as also by far the greatest number of actions, are located "in front, before," no wonder that "before" maintains its cultural dominance even in projections beyond the body. In this way, "before" and "behind" can work also as symbolic categories able to carry a whole series of cultural oppositions such as "important" and "secondary," "brave" and "base," "frank" and "sneaky," and so on. The situation is identical in every respect to that of the category "right" and "left": here, too, the pair of spatial terms becomes the carrier of cultural oppositions that, thanks to the well-known predominance of right over left,[14] can take the form of "favorable" and "unfavorable," "capable" and "incapable," "honest" and "dishonest," and so forth.

In conclusion: space is assimilated to culture, also in what regards "before" and "behind." To assert a placement, to localize something, does not mean merely itself. Very often it intends to involve the cultural hierarchy, which becomes the significance of the spatial signifier, the meaning of the sign of place. Nor do placements in time fail to obey this rule.

Thirteen

Vertical Time: From the Genealogical Tree to the Aristocratic Funeral

I s time, then, horizontal only? Does the order of time, in other words, receive spatial expression only in the paired terms "before/after" and their possible combinations? Of course not. Time can be represented spatially also by the paired terms "high/low" (although not by "left/right," as noted in chapter 7). This can be seen particularly clearly in language, but there are also other cultural models, of another order, that employ the same pattern of representation.

It is well known that ancestors are called in Latin *maiores* (greater), and descendants are called *minores* (lesser). In between, logically enough, are the *aequales* (equals, of the same age). A few examples will suffice: Horace, "To hearken to the greater [sc., older, *maiores*], to tell to the lesser [sc., younger, *minori*]" (*Epist.* 2.1.106); or, better yet, Ovid, "As I have cherished the greater [sc., my elders], so have the lesser [sc., those younger] cherished me" (*Tris.* 4.10.55). Here the chain from "great" to "slight," from "greater" to "lesser," emerges with special clarity.[1] As for *aequales*, we may recall, for example, Quintilian, "When he spoke, Trachalus seemed to stand out among his equals" (12.5.5) (see also

Cicero, *Orat.* 105, *De sen.* 10, etc.). In other words, the relationship of "before/after" can arrange itself either along a horizontal axis, as we saw, or along a vertical axis. The vertical axis appears divided into three segments: the highest belongs to "first, before"; the middle (which is even, neither high nor low) belongs to the present; and the lowest belongs to "after, then."

An interesting aspect of this way of representing time should be remarked at once. Unlike "before/after" (*ante/post*), this formula of "greater/lesser" makes it possible to represent an intermediate position within the same system, between its extreme terms; this middle position can be identified with the standpoint of the speaker, as contemporary, that is. If one can call that which comes first "high" and that which comes after "low," one can very well call that which comes at the same time "even with, on the same plane" (*aequalis*).

This localizing of before and after as "high" and "low" does not serve only to mark generational time (being born *ante* and descending from). In the form of "above/below," it can also be applied to any kind of "beforeness/behindness." Look, for example, at Cicero, "What you did the night before [*superiore;* literally, 'higher']" (*In Catil.* 1.1); and "In the life before [literally, 'higher']" (*De sen.* 26); and Suetonius, "Concerning what was done the year before [again, literally 'higher']" (*Div. Jul.* 23.1). For Caesar, "the higher days" are those past (*De bell. gall.* 7.58); whereas the "last five days," those at the end, after the current time, are called the "lower five days" (*inferiores*) by Varro (*Ling. lat.* 6.13). The same goes for "lower times" in Suetonius (*Div. Claud.* 41.2). Here, too, we see that what comes before stands above, is higher, and that which comes after stands below, is lower. On the same model, both *supra* (above) and *infra* (below) can function directly as "first" and "after" in temporal terms: see, for instance, Livy, "Let it be sought out above [sc., before] the seven hundredth year" (*Praef.* 4); Cicero, "Homer was not below [sc., younger than] the higher [sc., elder] Lycurgus" (*Brut.* 40), a particularly interesting case because, next to the temporal use of "below" (*infra*), it has the temporal use of "higher" (*superior*) for older.

A not dissimilar discourse regards the adjective *altus* (high, deep). For example, take Virgil, "from Teucer's high blood [*alto sanguine*]" (*Aen.* 6.500 = 4.230). Here "high" means "ancient"; indeed, Teucer, as founder of the Trojan race, gets called the "most great father" of the Trojans (*Aen.* 3.107). Likewise, Ovid says that Claudia Quinta could trace her line from "high Clausus" (*Fast.* 4.305), and Silius Italicus speaks of the memorable name from "high Saturn" (8.439) and of "high antiquity" (*alta vestustas*, 1.26). Because the Latin *altus* also means "deep," we might suspect that here "depth," more than "height," is at issue. We cannot rule out the presence of "depth" at the connotative level; yet the denotation must be perforce "height," if Horace can speak of "a race sent down from old [sc., 'high'] Aeneas" (*Serm.* 2.5.62). In the verb "sent down" (*demissum*), *de-* makes it certain that the antiquity of Aeneas gets represented as a position on high from which one comes down, descends.[2]

This image of the past as something that stands "on high" brings to mind what is perhaps our most interesting vertical model of time: the genealogical tree, or stemma. Without getting into complex antiquarian problems, which for obvious reasons we do not wish to deal with here, we know that Roman noble families kept in the hall a visual representation of their own genealogy. The custom presents certain similarities with the "right to images" (*ius imaginum*). This was the privilege of keeping, in cupboards made for the purpose, funerary portraits of forebears who had won particular honors:[3] portraits that could be brought out for certain ceremonial occasions.[4] In genealogical representations, the painted masks or the names of forebears were linked by a complicated network of lines, the stemmata, which defined their relationships in the genealogy. Pliny describes these stemmata (*Hist. nat.* 35.6):

> How different were the images to be seen in the halls of our ancestors! They were not made by foreign craftsmen, not of bronze or marble. The features were rendered in wax and placed in cupboards, so that the images could accompany family funerals and always each dead man had the company of all who had ever belonged to his family. But the stemmata ran down with lines to the painted images.

Pliny relates the usage of stemmata joining painted masks to the practice of keeping ancestral masks in the hall so that they could accompany the clan funeral; note also Seneca (*De ben.* 3.28.2): "Who displayed images in the hall and placed in the first part of the dwelling their family names in a long line and tied together with many windings of stemmata." Here it is the names of the forebears which appear in a long line interconnected by the windings of the stemmata.

Also in the stemma of the ancient nobility (as in the modern genealogical tree), the head of the line appeared at the top and his descendants were placed farther down.[5] See, for example, Statius, "Calm old man, you have no famous line of clan or stemma sent down (*demissum*) from great-grandfathers" (*Silvae* 3.3.43); and Seneca, below the passage just cited, "Boldly lift up your hearts, and whatever baseness lies among you, leap over it: great nobility awaits you on high" (*De ben.* 3.28.3); also Plutarch, "Stemmata led down to Numa from the beginning" (*Numa* 1). Also very interesting from this viewpoint is a passage in Prudentius, "Coming down through six times seven names of men and weaving a vein of high blood from ancestors by a long thread through stemmata" (*Apoth.* 984–86). Here language representing time in terms of "high/low" joins with the flow of the noble family stemma downward from the ancestors to the descendants. Indeed, the stemma is identified directly with the blood that symbolizes and identifies the family: as if the genealogy displayed on the wall were in reality woven by a thread of blood that runs through it all.

Hence, the "high" character attributed to earlier time and the "low" character attributed to later time find a precise correspondence and illustration in the structure of the genealogical stemma. When Virgil calls Deiphobus "race from Teucer's high blood" (*Aen.* 6.500 = 4.230), we must remember that, in a noble stemma, ancient Teucer would really be "up high" by comparison with Deiphobus. Only recall Ulpian, "Some use the word parent as far as the fourth generation; those higher [*superiores*] are called greater [*maiores*]" (*Dig.* 2.4.4.2). As for the other end of the stemma, we have Gaius, "Whether they get the first degree of children, such as daughter, son, or a lower degree, such as grandson, granddaughter, great-grandson, great-granddaughter" (*Inst.* 1.99).[6]

Having reached this point, it may be well to clarify, or forestall, a possible ambiguity. Our usual language would lead us to speak not of a genealogical stemma, but of a tree. In effect, the network of direct and collateral lines in a genealogical representation may bring to mind, iconically as it were, a trunk with branches. At the same time, we know that Latin does not use *arbor* in the sense of "tree of genealogy." We do find, however, scattered occurrences of *ramu* (branch), in contexts of this sort: thus Persius, "Does it become you to burst a lung with pride because you derive your branch from a Tuscan stemma, though thousandth down?" (3.27–28); and Isidore, "Stemmata are called branchlets (*ramusculi),* which lawyers derive in a clan, when they distinguish the degrees of relationships" (*Orig.* 9.6.28). Hence, the stemma is something that has branches or itself corresponds to a branchlet, when it is short and bounded, like that which a lawyer traces in reckoning the degrees of kinship.

This kind of language might lead us astray should we forget that the tree metaphor, if applied to genealogy whole hog, as they say, would impose a change in orientation: no longer the line from high to low, but an idea of development from low to high, with the "head of the line" placed at the foot, at the roots, and the descendants in the place of branches. To the contrary, our genealogical charts usually work from high to low, like the branch of the stemma mentioned by Persius, and like the well-known tree diagrams employed by linguists and others. Thus, to speak of a "genealogical tree" is to utilize a metaphor that is good only by half: a genealogical tree resembles an actual tree only in form, purely as an image, iconically; but it grows and develops with just the opposite orientation.[7]

With this point clarified, we can turn to the genuine tree metaphors that do occur in Latin representations of genealogy. Traces only remain, not a complete picture; but they deserve a glance. In first place is the word *stirps* (stock, stalk), as in Virgil, "He wished

171

that he had come from the ancient stock of the Teucers" (*Aen.* 1.626); or Nepos, "He enumerated the Junian family in order from the stock to this age" (*Att.* 18.3). Particularly interesting in this connection is a passage concerning the Scipios from Cicero's *Brutus*, "O noble stock, and like one tree grafted with many races, so that house has been grafted and enlightened with the canniness of many" (213). Clearly, the "stock" of the Scipios is compared to a tree, which has undergone a series of various grafts.[8] To the same order of representations must be assigned the use of the word *suboles* (outgrowth) to indicate offspring and descendants. *Suboles* in fact designates the shoot of a plant, the *rejeton*, as Ernout and Meillet say in the *Dictionnaire*. Look, for example, at Pliny, "Of many plants at the roots with thickly sprouting outgrowth" (*Hist. nat.* 17.65); and Columella, "Onion that did not bush out or have outgrowth sticking to it" (*Rer. rust.* 12.10). But *suboles* can also mean "continuation" in the form of descendancy, as in Cicero's *Offices*, "Which propagation and outgrowth gives rise to republics" (1.54); and Justin, "Would wipe out the whole stock of the royal outgrowth" (16.1.5).

These are only hints. But they might lead us to think that Roman culture, in representing the relationship between ancestors and descendants, used real tree metaphors, which would presuppose an orientation from low to high in lineage, as in the plant. Such does seem to be the case with *stirps,* or with *suboles,* the outgrowth that comes up from a root that is located lower down. Thus, we would have to reckon with another case of inversion in the spatialization of time. For that which stands high in the genealogical stemma seems to be placed low in the tree metaphor.

The development of generational time, with the ordered succession of ancestors and descendants, as represented by true tree metaphors, brings with it a host of added cultural signs that have nothing to do with the figure of the stemma. Above all, there is the organic, living nature of human development; then, too, there is the concreteness of the stock, its somehow unstoppable continuousness, like that of an unconscious vegetal growth, the possibility of making "grafts" in the body of the race (as in the passage from *Brutus* just cited), and so on. In short, the stemma and the organic-vegetal model are very different cultural tools: the former is a simple means of display, which respects the direction of writing itself in its orientation from high to low; the latter is an organic metaphor, able to convey a greater richness of anthropological contents in representing generational time.

Precisely the dominance of these cultural contents very likely explains the change in orientation we have seen in this particular representation of genealogical time: no longer "high to low," but "low to high." Here, too, as with "the future at your back" (chapter 11), time is inverted so as to express various cultural values that are somehow dominant, overpowering the mere localization of time. Wishing to transpose into visual terms not only the succession of generations but also its continuousness, its life, its internal growth, one chooses a metaphorical scheme that is the reverse of the other. Once again, we see how the localizing of temporal hierarchies has implications for anthropology, for a communication broader than itself.

The Romans themselves were well aware that, where trees are concerned, the usual orientation is inverted, as we see in an interesting passage from Varro: "A tree's feet and shanks one calls its branches; its head, its trunk (*caudex*) and stock (*stirps*)" (fr. 145 Fun.). In fact, a tree has its head, the upper part in human terms, set down low at the roots, while its limbs, the lower part in human terms, stand up high and are the branches.

The upper third—that is, the branches—is linked with the future and with descendants in figures of the universal tree in many cultures, according to Toporov.[9] So it is well known that, in the tree figure, time moves from below to above.

From what we have seen thus far, it is clear that both the modern metaphor of the genealogical "tree" and the use of "branch" to indicate the derivatives of a stemma are cultural expressions far more complex than they first appeared. On the one hand, these cultural expressions keep the orientation "high to low," which is typical of the stemma and which conforms to the model of writing and to the established usage in language that associates "above" with "before" and "below" with "after." On the other hand, the cultural expressions implant in their interwoven patterns all the organismic force of vegetal images, reinforced by the iconic analogy between the network of lines of descent and the tangle of branches on a tree. What results is a representation that is complex to the point of contradiction, because it assigns to the development of the tree an orientation of growth which is just the reverse of its natural one.

Leaving behind the tree model, let us return to the noble stemma. If we take it as a cultural symbol, as an image that a given family desires to convey of itself, and not merely as a convenient means of display, it invites us to reflect a little further, even though we do not presume here to deal with all the aspects of a problem as complex as that of genealogy.

One may suppose that the stemma constitutes a kind of label for a memorial, a guide or legend for the masks kept generation after generation in the cupboards. Although each mask was marked by its own inscription,[10] it still would have been difficult to find one's way through the crowd of visages and honors, especially to work out their relative chronology, ordering them in time with respect to one another. From this viewpoint, the genealogical stemma could serve as a chronological key, an organizing structure for the family image storehouse.[11] In a society like the Roman one that practices the "right to images," genealogical tables are necessary.

What is more, the stemma in its sinuous web represented the basic stages of a family's descent through the male line, its adoptions, its relations through mothers (*cognationes*) and daughters (*adfinitates*) contracted from generation to generation.[12] And by this very fact the stemma presented in tangible form the degree of prestige and social importance enjoyed by the family in the course of time. Most important were the honors of the males, and the strong deeds evoked by the names woven into the web; but there were also the female connections, women brought in from more or less prestigious families and bringing with themselves in marriage the *imagines* of their own forebears. In other words, the stemma could show, at every single stage of development, which other families had considered it fitting to their own honor to associate themselves with the family whose stemma it was. In this way, the stemma could be a kind of chart that displayed by means of matrimonial alliances the ongoing progress of family prestige, as it developed through time. Both the agnatic prestige, the official, if you will, which gets inherited along with the name and the dwelling place, and the cognate prestige, which we might call subterranean, deriving from the echoes of the maternal branch and the contracted marriages of daughters of it, got melded in the stemma into one image.[13] As a visual device for reconstituting time, as the organizing structure of the family image storehouse, the stemma directly rose to the role of symbol of the family. The stemma was a representation at once abstract and yet full of the prestige that fed the pride, really the identity, of the stock. Where, then, to put it, if not, as Seneca says, in the forepart of the dwelling, where it could identify, like a modern coat of arms, the household and the family?

Combining the principal male line with the various female grafts, and the adoptions, must have produced a picture both tangled and very complex. In the passage cited above, Seneca speaks of family names not only in a long line but also fastened into the many windings of the stemmata (*De ben.* 3.28.2). And Pliny, as we have seen, says that the lines of the stemmata ran in various directions (*discurrebant*) to the painted masks (*Hist. nat.* 35.8).[14] Naturally, we must not imagine a complete and exhaustive family enrollment. It is precisely genealogical structures that are most subject to what has been called to good effect "generative memory."[15] In other words, such structures are activated according to shifting, unequal criteria that are imposed by practical requirements—such as the possession of certain property, the connection with certain families instead of others, the membership in a certain class, and so forth—rather than being true to some precise standard. Indeed, "to counterfeit images [*mentiri imagines*]" (Pliny, *Hist. nat.* 35.8) is to some degree ingrained in the very genealogical custom. The language spoken by genealogies comes into being with strongly defined intentions, quite the contrary of the impassive impartiality we might be inclined to attribute to it. The stemmata and genealogies belong to the order of discourse: they constitute single language acts, bound as such to diverse communicative intentions, to the variable context, and so on. They serve not so much to communicate the bare and objective genealogical structure of a family as to express the abstract, often impalpable but always decisive, notion that is a family's prestige, which is a social value *par excellence,* and thus above all a relational value. As the privileged symbol of social prestige, the genealogical stemma has to change. The language of a genealogy cannot be uttered one time for all.

It is perhaps most striking that a moment came in which the genealogical stemma poured out onto the streets, as it were, and the abstract tissue of names and pictures became the solemn progress of a cortege: this was the moment of the aristocratic funeral. Polybius writes in his famous description (6.53):

> When a distinguished member of the family dies, they carry [the waxen masks] in the cortege, donned by the men who are most similar in stature and general appearance. These put on a purple-bordered toga if they are representing a consul or praetor, a purple toga for a censor, a gold-bordered toga for a triumphator or someone who accomplished deeds of that sort. They go forward on conveyances, preceded by the fasces, by the axes, or by whatever other insignia are usual for magistrates, according to the degree of honor that each man while alive enjoyed among his fellow citizens. When they reach the rostra, they sit in a row on ivory seats.

The spectacle impresses, as Polybius underlines more than once. It elicited from Pliny a remark almost epic in its simplicity: "Always each dead man had the company of all who had ever belonged to his family" (*Hist. nat.* 35.6). The ancestors are there, they have come, in the form of the masks that reproduce as closely as possible their ancient accomplishments. They wear the costumes of their ancient honors, carry the insignia. The inscriptions that faithfully registered their ancient offices came back to life and became purple borders, fasces, and the rest. Never will it be possible to emphasize enough the epic grandeur of the Roman funeral, in its cultural imagination. One who dies does not pass to his ancestors only metaphorically: his ancestors are really there to accompany him. One dies in the presence of his own past, of its proud grandeur.

With death a crisis opens, the equilibrium breaks. The anxiety of this crisis, the empty horizon that gapes before the living when they actually touch their own mortality and the feeling of irreparable loss gets filled not only by the praise of the dead before the rostra, or by the laments chanted by the hired female mourners. There is a mute population of the great, majestic, proud, to comfort the living: there are the ancestors who file by, a sign that there will be yet others, that the stock will not end, that its greatness will last. If the symbols of Christianity, carried in procession, are the pledge of individual rebirth and salvation, the comforting presence of the ancestors is a more secular sign of continuance, of emulation. Here the salvation is impersonal: it comes from the past, not from an individual expectation of the future.

The drama of the masks passing in procession brings us back to the problem of time and its localization in space; for the question arises, Is there an order in which the images pass? Movement in the genealogical stemma runs from high to low. But in the cortege? It is a pity that Polybius gives no clue. But, luckily, other sources come to the rescue, albeit indirectly. We know that the bier with the corpse regularly followed the procession of the ancestors: "May they lead your funeral and triumphal masks" (Horace, *Epod.* 8.11), where Porphyry comments, "In the funeral, the masks were usually carried first"; also we read, "Not with customary proud biers did the old mask going before adorn the rites" (Silius Italicus 10.566–67); and, "The masks of twenty famous families were carried before" (Tacitus, *Ann.* 3.76). Hence, we must imagine a dense crowd of images heading the cortege, with the bier behind.[16]

Was there also a relative order among the images? On this, too, Polybius gives no help, but again Tacitus does, describing the funeral of Drusus: "The funeral was very distinguished with the parade of masks, because Aeneas, the origin of the Julian race, and all the Alban kings and Rome's founder, Romulus, then the Sabine nobility, Attus Clausus, and the other effigies of the Claudii were seen in the long line" (*Ann.* 4.9). Two lines join in Drusus: the Julian, which goes back to Aeneas, and the Claudian, which goes back to Attus Clausus of Regillus.[17]

The order described by Tacitus is clearly chronological. First comes Aeneas, followed by the Alban kings and Romulus, in the order of the city's mythical history. Then *(post)* come Attus Clausus and the noble Sabines. The passage unfolds in a long line *(longo ordine)*, in an ordered series; we may recall the long line of the procession of Aeneas's descendants in the sixth book of the *Aeneid,* which likewise was arranged according to a criterion of chronological succession (cf. chapter 10, and the image of Romulus at the funeral of Augustus, mentioned in note 16). Thus, the founder opens the procession, as would be natural, followed by the descendants and, last of all, the bier of the dead man.

Here it seems worth remarking that the internal arrangement of the cortege bears a certain resemblance to the structure of the funeral oration that was pronounced in honor of the dead, as Polybius describes it (6.54.1):

> When the Orator has completed his speech about the dead man, he turns to speak of those whose images are there present, beginning from the founder, and he describes the successes and the undertakings of each. In this way the reputation for valor, which distinguishes the heroes, is renewed, and the renown of those who have completed noble deeds becomes immortal.

At the moment of the oration, with the dead man in the forum, at the rostra, it is clear that the speaker begins with him. However, when the speech turns to his lineage, to the chain of ancestors who are present, the order of the elogium follows the same sequence as the cortege: first, at the head, comes the founder *(ho progenestatos,* Polybius calls him), then all the others follow. One could say that the internal arrangement of the cortege is transformed into a rhetorical figure. Both the symbolic language spoken by the images in procession, so eloquent that it inspires courage and virtue in the young men who are there, as Polybius also says, and the solemn words devoted by the official orator to the glory of the clan, hero after hero, follow the same outline.

Let us return to the internal order of the cortege, with the bier behind the images and the arrangement with respect to them; that is, the founder ahead, and the individual descendants progressively farther behind. This order has a certain interest for us because we can relate it to the local arrangements of "before/behind" in space, with which by now we have grown familiar. We know that what comes first is defined as *ante* (before) and what comes after is defined as *post* (behind; see chapter 7). This system is perfectly applied in the funeral cortege. "Before" is where the founder comes—for example, Aeneas, who is the most distant ancestor, representing the very first in the line. Behind the first, then, follow the more recent ancestors, who came after him; and last of all, farther behind than everyone, comes the latest member of the line to die.

We should not forget that, with the close of the funeral rite, the mask of the newly dead man takes its place in the cupboards in the hall (Polybius 6.53.4): it is ready to be carried in procession whenever there is a new funeral in the family. When the procession occurs, this mask will come right after the file of the other masks and right before the bier. But as successive deaths occur, it will stand ever farther from the bier. By this principle, we can suppose that the name of the dead man was added to the bottom of the noble stemma, and that, following further deaths, it would progressively become a little higher in the stemma. Indeed, let us underline one fact that we can use later: whatever is placed "high" in the noble stemma is placed "ahead" in the funeral cortege and represents the "first," whereas whatever is "low" in the stemma is placed "behind" in the cortege and represents "after." In other words, "high" and "ahead" correspond, as do "low" and "behind." This will give rise to some concluding remarks in chapter 14.

Let us return to the way in which new names get added to the stemma, or new masks to the cortege. What we encounter is a substantial difference from the functioning of the Divine Parents and the terms of kinship. In the cult of the Divine Parents, there are only three ascending degrees: father, grandfather, great-grandfather (*pater, avus, proavus*), with their respective wives.[18] Hence, we must suppose that each new death pushed the top of the list beyond the range of the cult in a continual renewal: when a father entered the ranks of *dei parentes,* a great-grandfather had to leave. In the same way, the terms for ancestors reached only to the seventh degree in ascendance; that is, *pater, avus, proavus, aba-*

vus, atavus, tritavus (father, grandfather, great-grandfather, great-great-grandfather, great-great-great-grandfather, great-great-great-great-grandfather), after which one entered the generic category of *maiores*.[19] Thus, in the terminology as well, as the line grows longer, the farthest member loses his identity and passes over into the category of the indistinct.

By contrast, the aristocratic stemma and the procession of masks seem to share the characteristic of preserving or, rather, wanting to preserve, all the members of the clan, arranging them in a spatial order from high to low, and fore to back, that could indicate, at least summarily, their order of succession in time. Naturally, this is a preservation and a registration of the generative sort, which means that it can expand or shrink, take in or exclude names and masks according to contingent needs. For example, Julius Caesar ordered that the funeral cortege of his father's sister, Julia, include the mask of Marius (Plutarch, *Caes.* 5); the funeral of Cassius's wife was remarkable for the absence of the masks of Cassius and Brutus, masks that "glittered too much because of the very fact that they were nowhere to be seen," as Tacitus says so aptly (*Ann.* 3.76). Each of these instances illustrates precisely the generative character of this kind of genealogical memory, in which one is remembered or not according to what is opportune for a context; not for what one was, but for what one means. Nor does it matter whether certain images get left out of a cortege, or someone creeps into a stemma where, properly speaking, he does not belong (Pliny, *Hist. nat.* 35.8), or someone is removed from the winding web who might better never have been inserted at all.[20]

In effect, the scheme of the Divine Parents, like the ascending series of six kinship terms, is an empty vessel, a neutral mechanism. Hence, these schemes are limited but stable. Instead, the genealogical stemma or the order of the images constitutes a subtle symbolic whole, which can convey, as we have often seen, a multitude of social values: the genealogical symbolism is both totalizing and shifting, ambitious and shifty. As in historical recording or the totalizing glance of the epic poet, so in genealogy we find at work a mechanism familiar to literary critics: viewpoint, with its deforming partiality.

It would not, however, be right to close this chapter without referring to one last but basic trait shared by the funeral cortege and the aristocratic stemma. Both of these symbolic wholes work as sources of identity for anyone who establishes a relationship with them. Thus, one is identified as "following" in the cortege or "lower" in the stemma by one's placement in the spatial and temporal scheme. One finds "high" in the stemma and "ahead" in the cortege the very reason for one's *cognomen* (name),[21] the origin and meaning of his family cults, the basic characteristics, traits, and politics of the clan. And one also finds a complex of particular body traits which constitutes the storehouse of family resemblances: a suggestive and often so deceptive method of identification that sanctions or confirms membership in a certain group, often to a decisive degree.[22] Whoever is high or ahead also bears one's features: already, then, there is someone, recalled by that countenance and those body traits, who predicts one's features or determines them. Thus, one is a Manlius or a Cornelius just because high up in the stemma and far ahead in the cortege stand figures with clearly paradigmatic functions. Their presence, their having existed, does not mean only that in itself, but is capable of conferring meaning also on those who come after. This is because the ancestors, the "greater ones," who are higher and farther ahead, enjoy the double status of being both code and message at once.[23] Communicating themselves—for example, communicating the imperiousness of the old Torquatus—they communicate also an ensemble of rules which can influence or predict the behavior and the social characteristics of descendants: in short, their identity as a group. It is by looking up that models are found.[24]

The masks carried in the cortege constitute the express embodiment of the rules of behavior which are required, or would be required, of descendants. Consider, for example, Cicero, who tells how once, when Crassus was publicly berating Brutus, there passed near them, by an incredible coincidence, a cortege bearing an old woman of Brutus's family to her last resting place; Crassus, with consummate dexterity, took advantage (*De orat.* 2.225):

> Brutus, why do you sit there? What do you want that old woman to tell your father? What do you want her to tell all of those whose masks you

see being carried there? What do you want her to tell your ancestors? What tell to Lucius Brutus, who freed this people from royal domination? That you are doing what? That you are pursuing what business, what glory, what manliness?

I would like to end this chapter by citing a text that illustrates in exemplary fashion, to my way of thinking, the relationship that joins the identity of the individual with that of the family in aristocratic culture. I refer to the two couplets written for Cn. Cornelius Scipio Hispanus, who was praetor peregrinus in 139 B.C.(*CIL* I², 15):

> The merits of my genus, with good character I enhanced,
> progeny I generated, took aim at my father's deeds.
> I have kept up my elders' glory, so my growth from them
> delights them: my honor has marked the stock.

The last praise of Scipio Hispanus, the one that entrusts him to posterity, is thus the true one,[25] and it is truly generic, because the praise is of the genus, not of him. He seems to have done practically nothing different or new. This Scipio is happy to have increased with his character the store of virtues which his family already possessed, to have preserved the praise of his ancestors, to have ennobled the stock with honor. Nothing else. His life seems to have been devoted to the tenacious effort to stay at the level of his predecessors, as if he had lived with his glance forever fixed on high, toward those who stood above him in the stemma. Indeed, one phrase is even more striking than the others: "took aim at my father's deeds" (*facta patris petiei*). His aspiration embodied itself in the glorious paternal accomplishments. In short, Scipio Hispanus had his father before him; his own identity, now that he is dead, can be summed up as his constant commitment to reproduce him.[26] Because he has always maintained the level of his ancestors, they can be glad (*laetari*) to have given him life. The rules that ancestors dictate to their descendants, by the mere fact of having existed first, have been scrupulously observed throughout an entire life. Scipio Hispanus is, in the chain, a link that held up well: he guaranteed the biological continuation of the stock (*progeniem genui*), even as he guaranteed its social and cultural continuance by his character, actions, praise, and honor.

No one will be surprised to see that something as solid and massive as the nobles's notion of genus became a butt for comic parody. In the *Persa*, Plautus depicts the parasite Saturio, a great eater and drinker like all parasites, ready even to feign the sale of his daughter (clever and likable as her father) for the sake of money. Saturio introduces himself with mock solemnity as follows (53–61):

> The age-old, timeworn business of my sires
> I save, keep up, and cultivate with care.
> For never have there been forebears of mine
> who did not fill their bellies as parasites.
> Father, grandsire, great-grand, great-great,
> great-great-great, great-great-great-great,
> like mice were always eating other people's grub.
> Nor could anyone outdo them in sheer greed.
> And so they won the *nom de guerre* of Bighardhead.
> Hence I keep up this business and ancestral place.[27]

Parasites and gluttons for seven generations, the forefathers of Saturio have never known another occupation, nor did anyone ever outdo them in the virtue of gluttony. Indeed, the parasites can claim their own characteristic *cognomen*, "Bighardheads" or "Hard-pates" (as one might render *Duricapitones*): emblem of the blows to the head which parasites took during banquets, the better to amuse the guests, who were disdainful and not a little sadistic. Saturio, too, is a man at the level of his genus, nor does he mean to betray the virtues of his fathers. Just as Scipio Hispanus kept up (*optinuit*) the honors of his ancestors, so Saturio maintains (*optineo*) the traditional and inveterate trade of his; indeed, he preserves (*servo*) and cultivates it with great care (*magna cum cura colo*). His proud identity as an eater at others' expense is likewise a family identity. The reasons for this life of his are also higher up, reaching as far as his fourth-great-grandfather.[28]

Fourteen

Spatial Localizations of Time: Closing Remarks and Anthropological Reasons

By now we have reached the close of this part of our work. And in closing I would like to try to formulate a rather probing question: Why, in the relationship *ante*/*post* (anterior/posterior, "in front/in back") does the front, "before," get linked with "first" (cf. antique), whereas back, "behind," gets linked with "then" (cf. posterity)? And, why, instead, in the representation of "past/future," does past get linked with back, "behind" (cf. retrospective), whereas future gets linked with front, "before" (cf. prospective)? We could also formulate these questions still more simply: Why, in the passage from "anterior/posterior" to "past/future," does the placement of time in space get turned around?

The problem suggested itself to Traugott, though not perhaps quite so expressly.[1] And she answered in a way that might be called "naturalistic" or "objective." Above all, this kind of placement in space constitutes a typology and is practically universal, a fact that emerges clearly from the copious evidence in Traugott's excellent work. Now she supposes that there must be a general rule, which can be defined as a "canonical encounter," according to which, as

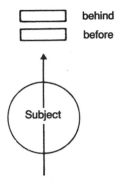

one moves along a way, whatever one encounters first is "in front, before," and what is encountered after it is defined as "after, behind" (see chart above).

If time's passing, then, is represented as a movement by the subject along a way, or as the coming of events to meet the subject (which amounts to the same thing, though not treated by Traugott), it follows that the events encountered first will be considered as "in front of, before" those encountered "after," which must be behind. In other words, the placement of "anterior/posterior" would be derived directly from the placement of "past/future" by a metaphor of the naturalistic sort (see chart below).

The explanation is respectable and highly economical. However, it is not particularly useful. To the contrary, its very simplicity runs the risk of masking grounds that are deeper and especially inter-

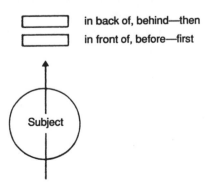

esting, which are concealed behind these placements of time. Moreover, the explanation presents two problems.

First of all, the representation of "anterior/posterior" really occurs independently of the temporal development in which the subject is involved. In other words, such a relation can stand by itself and can involve events anterior to the direct temporal experience of the subject: If I say something like, "Troy was founded before Rome," clearly I set up a relationship of "anterior/posterior" between events that are both before any "canonical encounter" of mine with them. The situation is quite different if we have the pronouncement made by someone older than the foundation of Troy, who thus speaks of it in the future; for example, an oracle: "Troy will be founded before Rome." If the speaker comes before both these events, it is clear that on his imaginary way he really does meet Troy before he meets Rome. Hence, one has to allow, in order to follow Traugott's explanation, that the device of the "canonical encounter" in time could also slip backward: that is to say, toward events that are prior to the subject. Once the device is set up, it must carry out a real movement of transference;[2] it must place itself also behind the back of the subject.

The explanation of Traugott puts great store in what we might call the "body set":[3] in other words, she derives "anterior/posterior" from "past/future" by giving particular value to the bodily aspects of temporal determinations: I meet, with my body, along my way, certain events before others; hence these, in the model of "anterior/posterior," are before, and what follows is behind. If this is how things are, one must also take into account, given this same "body set," that the transference spoken of a moment ago presents some problems. The placements in space of "anterior/posterior" will necessarily differ from the subject's; they will be inverted, depending on whether the relation at issue is one of "anterior/posterior" in the past or "anterior/posterior" in the future. Let us use again the example of "anterior/posterior" between the foundation of Troy and that of Rome seen by a subject placed respectively earlier and later than both.

In the first instance, the subject defines "before" as that which is near to himself, and "behind" as that which is far from himself:

1. Future

Rome (behind): *post*
Troy (before): *ante*

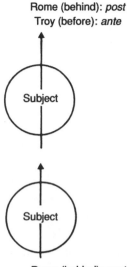

2. Past

Rome (behind): *post*
Troy (before): *ante*

In the second instance, the subject defines "before" as that which is farther from himself, and "after" as that which is nearer to himself. These are the consequences of the transference that we described as necessary in order to derive the model of "anterior/posterior" from that of "past/future."

Frankly, this reckoning would invite us to reduce the importance of the "body set" in interpreting the matter, or, rather, to give up the rule of the "canonical encounter" as an interpretive device. It actually seems better to seek an explanation that does not try to derive the placement of "anterior/posterior" from "past/future," as Traugott does in using the "body set" of the "canonical encounter."

Here lies the second big difficulty with her interpretation. It presupposes a derivation: in other words, she believes that the spatial representations of time can be derived from each other, can be combined one with another in a model that contains them all. In reality, however, our analyses make us certain of just the opposite. How, indeed, to combine among themselves a temporal representation in terms of "high/low" with one in terms of "before/behind"? To be sure, both exist and can work at the same time in language: one can perfectly well say *ante Catonem maiorem* ("before the greater—that is, elder—Cato"). But the one cannot be derived from the other; they are not interchangeable modules. What they are is a pair of diverse and independent ways of localizing time. But even within the set of "before/behind," the modules are not interchangeable. On one and the same page, a few lines apart, the passage of time can be represented as a "running" toward the subject, or as a movement of the subject toward time (see the end of chapter 8). In the same way, the placement of "past/future" can be inverted so the "future" ends up "behind the back" when the element of "knowing" comes into the picture (as we saw in chapter 11). How can we "derive" these diverse localizations one from the other through naturalistic metaphors or by applying the "body set"? It is impossible. To the contrary, these changes in the orientation of temporal placement all can be traced to anthropological motives. In other words, the orientation of temporal placement gets inverted in order to communicate certain cultural meanings. The future will come to meet the subject in a so-called passive representation of time, time endured, undergone (see the end of chapter 8); the future will get located behind the back of the subject to express its character as unknown (see chapter 11).[4]

In short, what we have to look for behind the variants in temporal localization are anthropological motives. The localizations do vary in ways that communicate the different cultural ramifications that the different images of time bring with them. Hence, we can expect that motives of an anthropological nature will also explain how the most basic localizations arose: *ante/post,* "in front/in back," in the category "anterior/posterior," or "before/behind" in the category "past/future." This brings us back to our original question: Why is "first" linked with "before," and "then" with "behind"? And why, instead, does "past" link up with "behind," and "future" with "before"? Because Traugott's naturalistic explanation is unsatisfying,[5] let us start over. However, we must add a further question about the basic categories of localization: Why does "first" get associated with "high," and "then" with "low"? This question, too, is legitimate.

The question is also practically the answer. For, if we compare the vertical model of time with the horizontal one, we see at once that, in both, "anterior" is expressed by the stronger member of a pair: "high" and "before." And we know that "before" shows a clear anthropological dominance over "behind." We have seen clear examples (in chapter 12). As for "high," obviously, though not therefore inconsequentially, it is quite predominant with respect to "low." Here, too, as in the case of "before" and "behind," there must be a projection of "body set" onto the surrounding space. Like "before/behind" and "left/right," "high/low" must get attributed to the surrounding space by projecting the "high/low" set of the person.

Together with the spatial coordinates, what also get projected are cultural coordinates, so to speak. Just as, in a person, the principal organs, the noblest, reside in the higher parts, the head with the mind, ears, eyes, so the higher part maintains its dominance in the cultural projections of the "body set." Just as the head (which not by accident the Stoics called the "sovereign part") is superior to the feet in the interior hierarchy of the individual, so all the higher parts of an object tend to be placed in a position of dominance, dominance that continues to operate also in the applications of this contrastive category that we may call metaphorical. In this way, the opposition between "high" and "low" can also convey cultural oppositions such as "noble/ignoble," "refined/vulgar," "divine/human," and "human/bestial." The same kind of operation also characterizes "right/left" and "before/behind."

A few examples will suffice. In the sociological code, the opposition *summi infimique* ("highest and lowest"; e.g., Livy 3.34) works to distinguish the dominant from the dependent class. Nor do we need to recall expressions such as *humilis* (literally, "of the earth"), "lowly," both in position and in cultural terms, or expressions such as *fastigium*, which is both the "upper part" of something and the "loftiness" of power (as in "the *fastigium* of the dictatorship was always rather high," Livy 6.38.13). As a sign of the degree of honor, "high" works in a way that is wholly equivalent to "before." For example, in the city the *summates*, "those who occupy the higher positions" (Plautus, *Pseud.* 227 and *Stich.* 492), are the same as the *primores,* "those who stand to the fore" (*pri-*; see chapter 7).

As cultural categories, "high" and "before" naturally correspond in many respects. Take an example from the field of religion, in which it is very clear that the higher part and the forward part enjoy quite special importance, so much so that they can be elevated to the special sphere of influence of deities: "Firsts are in the power of Janus, highests in the power of Jove" (Varro, *Ant. rer. div.* 16, fr. 15 Agahd., from Augustine, *De civ. dei* 3.9). Naturally, thought will seek, then, to set up among these cultural categories a further hierarchy that corresponds, no less, to the same hierarchy that functions among the religious practitioners themselves. The text from Varro continues: "Firsts are surpassed by highests, because, although firsts precede in time, highests exceed in honor."

Examples abound of "higher" as a dominant category in culture, and they could be multiplied endlessly.[6] Let us choose one last one, which interests because it shows how this cultural category can serve to solve questions of etiquette and precedence. The relative importance in the priestly hierarchy of the different *flamines* in Rome was reflected in the higher or lower placement of their thrones (Festus 198 L):

> The order of the priests is calculated according to the importance of each god.[7] The greatest is the *flamen* Rex; then the *flamen* of Jove; after him comes the *flamen* of Mars; in fourth place is the *flamen* of Quirinus; in fifth place is the Pontifex Maximus. And so, on the thrones, the Rex is permitted to recline above all, the priest of Jove above those of Mars and Quirinus, the priest of Mars above his neighbor, and likewise all above the Pontifex.

The internal hierarchy of the priestly college is visibly codified in terms of relative height. Parenthetically, something of this sort may account for the way in which the importance of banquet guests got codified through an elegant and sophisticated interplay of the categories "highest/middle/lowest."[8]

If, then, as seems clear from the anthropological perspective, "before" resembles "high" in expressing the stronger member of a cultural opposition, we have to conclude where time is concerned that in the relation "anterior/posterior," the "first" is considered culturally dominant over "then." That which follows in temporal succession remains, in some sense, subordinate, secondary with respect to what comes first: hence, what follows is placed in the category of "behind" or "below." Clearly, this kind of model presupposes that whatever comes before a certain event can be considered its cause *(post hoc ergo propter hoc),* can contain its grounds, can constitute a precedent to be imitated, and so forth.

The question, naturally, is complex, but a starting point from which one could go on to discuss matters that appear to be very far from one another, although in reality they are closely related from the anthropological standpoint: such as the nearly constant ambivalence of temporal statements, which often cover also the field of causality; the tendency to impose models on the part of ancestral customs *(mos maiorum),* as with ancestors in general (thus the genealogical tree and the funeral cortege, discussed in chapter 13); the social and cultural preeminence of those who can boast of remote origins, by contrast with the son of earth, who cannot count those born before; the general importance of the origin of peoples and cities, with the issue of autochthony, of men without predecessors, in whom one touches the foundations of history and time; of those who are *ab origine;* and so forth.

Clearly, the same criterion ought to be applied to the model "past/future." It links the past with "behind," and the future with "before." Thus, in the personal relationship (with the subject, that is, directly involved) that characterizes the category "past/future," the future, which is the personal "then," gets considered as culturally dominant with respect to the past, which is the personal "first." This time, the "first" is only life used up and dead, enjoyable only through memory: the good part is obviously what belongs to "next, then," that portion of life which still awaits us and which, for this reason, gets associated with "in front, before." An old man, who "we see has already come to the end of human life" (Seneca,

De brev. vit. 3.2, discussed in chapter 8), can do nothing but look back (*respicere*) to call up for accounting all his past life. Before him lies nothing good.

With this cultural model it is more difficult than in the other case to connect further social and cultural ramifications. And this is natural. The model of "anterior/posterior" is objective, independent of shifting introduced by the subject (see chapter 7): "before/behind" works by itself, sets up objective hierarchies, and thus can work as a collective, social model. It can assume a model-setting role, can produce and signify cultural diversity. By contrast, the personal "past/future" is a model that we might call existential. Its best products will be in the field of poetry or philosophical reflection, such as Seneca on the "Brevity of Human Life," in which the philosophical reflections often arise and grow by abruptly displacing the habitual hierarchical order of "past/future" in localizations of time (see chapters 8 and 11).

Here, then, I believe, lie the deepest grounds of the basic localization of "anterior/posterior" and "past/future" (in terms of "before/behind" and "high/low" for the former, and "behind/before" for the latter). These basic localizations are inverted, as we now know, for cultural reasons, to communicate other cultural values: the trait of being knowable in "past/future," the complex semantic vectors of the tree in vertical representations of time, and so forth. In short, the localizations vary according to individual anthropological investments in time. But, as we have seen, even the basic representations of time, what we may call its normal and most common localizations, are determined by similar anthropological investments.

So we return, in closing, to the very workings of culture. It operates by expressing the categories of difference within itself, by signifying them through binary oppositions of a kind that become typical, become examples. Just as the categories "honest/dishonest," "favorable/unfavorable," and so forth, are expressed directly in terms of "right/left" (see chapter 12, n.13); just as the categories "noble/ignoble" and "powerful/weak" can be expressed through the category "high/low"; just as the categories "important/secondary" and "brave/cowardly" (see chapter 12) can get expressed through "before/behind"; in the same way the category "first/then" can get expressed directly through the categories "before/behind" and "high/low." What we have is a continuum of signs which recodifies one and the same cultural opposition into sets that are diverse but corresponding. We have a set that blends into one and the same oppositional category more than one cultural opposition, thus offering the possibility of setting up similarities and correlations, not only at the level of signifiers (in which several sets express one and the same opposition), but also, more importantly, at the level of what is signified (in which one and the same category conveys several cultural contents).

I regret that the oppositions "before/behind" and "high/low" have not been studied as deeply in classical culture as the opposition "right/left."[9] And yet these cultural categories have the same function and the same importance.

Time does not exist, we were saying as we began this study of time: language makes it manifest, gives it place, in the two senses of the expression. Now, however, it is clear that our initial formulation was not clear enough. What gives time place is not language, but culture: the working of the cultural continuum of signs which precedes, in a certain sense, and contains language itself. Time, in short, is an investment on the part of culture. Without its "high/low" and "before/behind," and without the further cultural investments that these categories bring with them, time would have no way of manifesting its hierarchies and internal arrangement. Indeed, it would have no motive for representing itself: it would be something without interest.

Part Three

The Bee, the Moth, and the Bat:
Natural Symbols and Representations
of the Soul

Fifteen

The Bee and the Moth

I f one had to liken the world of the dead to something, it would have to be the sea. Like the sea, the world beyond the tomb is present, but, like the depths of the abyss, it is unknown, impenetrable by the living. Therefore, the world of the dead ends up being imagined as a projection of the world "over here," a mirror sending back images that are ambiguous and sometimes changeable, according to various cultures, beliefs, or even simple states of mind. Metaphor for the world of the living, just as the sea is metaphor for the emerged world, the "over there" is a kingdom imagined by analogies, and its architecture is peopled by beliefs and tales that move the images of the living into the miraculous, with differences more or less pronounced: thus, in Homer's Hades, there are poplars, but white; there are willows, but they lose their fruit; and the souls are in every respect identical to the bodies, only light and without thickness, like dreams. Similarly, ancient culture peopled the sea with maidens and with bearded men endowed with fishy tails, and the names of creatures of the sea echo, with slight differences, those of the creatures of the land, or also of simple objects or characteristics of the emerged world (the blackbird-fish, thrush-fish; but also the ball-fish, shadow-fish, etc.): the

197

earth is mirrored in the sea, and it has seen there the reflection of itself.

In building a metaphorical world, as is the case, then, of the world beyond the tomb, the process of analogy is obviously the main one. Thus, even likeness can become sometimes an actual screen for images, on which to project the construct of abstract ideas which gives the meaning of an eschatology. In the souls that throng the banks of Acheron like fallen leaves, or birds impatient to set out across the sea, something is stored that really would take too long to explain in a philosophical paraphrase: an outlook focussing the ideas of a culture about the conditions of the soul "over there," perhaps the very meaning given this survival.

A Virgilian Simile

One such storehouse of a culture's ideas about the soul must be Virgil's figure of the "clans and peoples without number," which he described as swarming near Lethe (*Aen.* 6.706–9):

> Around it flitted numberless clans and peoples;
> and just as meadows when the bees in tranquil summer
> beset the several flowers, and, gleaming white around,
> lilies get poured out: the field all buzzes with the noise.

In view of the profound cultural implications, it is a bit disappointing the way the main Virgilian commentaries deal with the analogy between souls and bees: they say that the *tertium comparationis*, the basis of comparison, must be the vast number and the buzzing,[1] or that the souls fly.[2] Not that these ideas are wrong; they are just too limited. Actually, Norden's commentary gives a valuable further hint (even though he inserts it in his elaborate reconstruction of a lost Orphic descent tale that supposedly was Virgil's model):[3] "all souls going to be born" were called bees by the ancients, according to Porphyry (*On the Grotto of the Nymphs*, pp. 18ff. [p. 69 N]).[4] So, then, souls on their way to birth were expressly called "bees." And Porphyry himself quotes a verse of Sophocles to the effect that "the swarm of souls buzzes and goes up" (795 N).

Let us widen our base of comparison by reading a little further in Porphyry: the ancients did not use the name "bees" for all the souls on their way to be born, but only for those destined to live justly and return where they came from after having done the will of the gods. Thus, it is the souls of the just that were properly called "bees." But one can add another comparison, lacking in Norden. In Euripides' *Hippolytus,* the hero offers Artemis a wreath of flowers from a unviolated meadow, "where the herdsman does not dare to pasture his flock, where iron has never come. Only the bee in spring frequents this spotless meadow, and modesty tends it with drops of dew" (73ff.). It is, then, a place of great purity where only the bee can go. But in the ancient commentary, the phrase the "bee in spring frequents meadow" gets glossed by "soul": in this environment as untouched as the goddess who is chaste *par excellence,* the bee, then, is interpreted by the scholiast, allegorically, as the symbol of the soul.[5]

Hence, Virgil had good reason to chose the simile he did to represent the souls on the verge of reincarnation. But symbols, by their very nature, tend to fall into obscurity and break down with the passage of time, and something that was instantly perceptible to someone immersed in ancient culture may no longer be so for us. With this in mind, then, it is worth our while to sketch a cultural typology of the bee.

"It seeks out all things pure"

We know the ancients thought the bee contained a divine seed;[6] or, in Virgil's words, "They say bees share in divine mind and ethereal breath" (*Geo.* 4.220–21). The appearance of "ethereal" also in Virgil's account of the souls purified and ready to be reincarnated, spoken by Anchises shortly after the simile of the bees (*Aen.* 6.747), permits a useful remark at the margins of our analysis. No sooner has Virgil in the *Georgics* said that "bees share in divine mind and etherial breath," than he presents the theory of the universal spirit that penetrates the entire world and guarantees the survival in heaven of the souls ("no place for death, but fly alive," *Geo.* 4.226). In other words, this theory resembles that spoken by

Anchises in book six of the *Aeneid,* following the simile of the bees and culminating in the theme of the immortality of the soul. Hence, it is very interesting that, in the *Georgics,* too, the theme of immortality gets associated with the bees, creatures of the soul. In short, Virgil must have been well aware that the bee could symbolize the immortal soul: hence the simile in the sixth *Aeneid* and the point of departure in the fourth *Georgic* for a philosophical theory about the world spirit and the soul's immortality.

Leaving Virgil's texts, now, let us turn to a world of beliefs perhaps more scattered, but for that perhaps even more interesting. Here we shall retrace step by step the threads of a symbolic complex constructed out of a veritable language of "things" and "beings": a language that turns out to comprise objects seen in their cultural interrelationship. For this language it will be necessary each time to seek out the vocabulary and the syntax, but it will be interesting to discover that this vocabulary and this syntax have more or less continued to be organized according to the same rules for a rather long stretch of time, with a tenacity and a durability that ought not to surprise either the classical philologist or the student of symbolic systems in various cultures.

Bees, then, are chaste above all else. Virgil himself tells us that they are not given to coupling (*Geo.* 4.198ff.), do not weaken their bodies in the pleasures of Venus. And they do not give birth with travail (Aristotle, *Gen. an.* 3.10.759a). The customs of the bees were cited by Rufinus of Aquileia when he sought to prove to the pagans the virginity of Mary by means of an instance in nature (*Expos. symb.* 9 = 350 Migne).[7] Moreover, the name "bees" was taken by the women of Athens who participated in the festival of the Thesmophoriae,[8] and these women abstained for three days from all sexual contact, and they fasted for a day and lay down on beds of "chastelamb," an aphrodisiac plant.[9] This explains why Semonides called lucky the man whose wife, among the various kinds of women, came from the bees: "This one does not delight to loiter among the other women when they discourse of love" (7.83 West). The bee seems particularly to hate love relations. Bees are known to attack those who have just had an amorous encounter,[10] as well as those who smell of myrrh or wine;[11] and bees generally hate luxury and softness (Aelian, *Hist. an.* 5.11).

This hatred that bees traditionally have for sexual impurity and transgression gave rise to a German folk belief that placing oneself in front of a hive constitutes a "test of purity" for girls and young brides.[12] In contrast, a Greek myth demonstrates, perhaps better than any other, the bee's stance with respect to love: Rhoikos, so the story goes, had saved a tree from destruction, and the nymph who lived there granted him her love, but on the condition that he never couple with any other female; a bee was their go-between. Rhoikos, however, betrays his promise and sees the bee flying along beside him. The nymph blinds him (Schol. Ap. Rhd. 2.476; Schol. Theocr. 3.13; *Etym. magn.* 78.32). In a variant handed down by Plutarch, it was the bee itself that blinded the traitorous lover (*Quest. nat.* 311).[13]

Blinding is a well-known punishment for sexual crimes and offenses. However, it is interesting that here a bee inflicts the penalty, and in a context in which the transgression is infidelity. As the go-between for the two lovers, the bee symbolizes the bond of purity and fidelity which should bind the one to the other: once this link has been broken, the bee itself can carry out the role of punishing the guilty party. Later (in chapter 17), when we study the adulterous Aristaeus, whose bees get killed by the nymphs, we shall have to remember this myth. One who has anything to do with bees must keep his conduct in love above reproach.

From the sexual code, of course, the step is easy to the alimentary code; here, too, the bee shows an identical cultural profile. Even as it hates every kind of luxury and lasciviousness, it would never gorge on delicacies:[14] and the beekeeper, to approach the hive, must have abstained from every strong or too fragrant food, from sauces that are too spicy,[15] and also from the harsh scent of garlic or onion.[16] The bee also hates every form of bloodiness or rottenness. Never would it settle on a piece of meat, or where there is any blood or fat.[17] Bees feel a like incompatibility with menstruation: Pliny writes, "Nothing can easily be found more terrifying than the flow of women" (*Hist. nat.* 7.64), by which bees can even be killed (7.64, 11.44, 28.79). So, too, they can be killed by the blossoms of the carnelian cherry, a plant characterized as bloody.[18] Nor would bees ever settle on beans, which are known for their complex symbolism associating meat, blood, sex, and putrefaction,[19] as well as their too close connection with the world of the dead.[20]

The rejection of flesh and blood on the one hand and of beans on the other touches a Pythagorean theme *par excellence:* Aelian pointedly underlines how the bee, by abstaining from flesh, applies without knowing it the shibboleth of Pythagoras (*Hist. an.* 5.11). It becomes clear how Virgil closed a symbolic circle when he likened the bee, which avoids flesh, blood, and beans (a substance with Pythagorean significance), to a soul destined Pythagorically for reincarnation. And as bees avoid flesh, fat, blood, and beans, so they also hate every kind of odor which might be traced to the sphere of decay. Not only are we told that they constantly keep their hive clean, taking advantage of leisure moments to carry out waste,[21] but that the beekeeper must also keep far from the hive every foul odor, such as from muck, a marsh, or crabs roasting on the fire; and, finally, that he must build the hive far from latrines, dunghills, and baths.[22]

The bee, then, in keeping with its aversion to sex, highly seasoned foods, meat, beans, and so forth, also hates the odor of decay. And if we recall what was said about the incompatibility between the bee and myrrh (and scents in general), it will be clear how the bee places itself in a position that is perfectly equidistant from the two poles between which stretches the range of the olfactory code, from "rotten" to "aromatic."[23] Creature of the flowers and the dew, creature of honey, the bee cannot help being marked negatively with respect to the two extremes of the olfactory range. Moreover, in this type of cultural identity, which is negative and differentiating (neither aromas nor decay), the bee appears to replicate a position that it fills also in other cultural spaces. Thus, the bee cannot be defined as either masculine or feminine,[24] nor even as either fierce or tame:[25] as if to say, neither on the side of culture nor on the side of nature. The bee is a distant creature, divine, rather enigmatic in the last analysis, certainly not the norm.

The "Wild Moth" and the Girl with Moth Wings

It comes as no surprise that the bee, this creature of ether, symbol of the immortal soul, shows a net detachment from all that recalls the sphere of the dead. Never would bees settle on dead flowers, still less on a corpse (Pliny, *Hist. nat.* 11.18). And during plagues and epidemics they carry out their dead with great care.[26] In contrast, wasps drag the lifeless bodies of spiders into their nests and even make their offspring grow up therein (11.72)! Near the beehive there must grow no yew, which is known as a grim and gloomy plant (16.50) and is often associated with the kingdom of the dead.[27] However, as haters of myrrh and perfumes, bees are especially delighted by the scent of burned *galbanum*:[28] this is the same scent that drives out snakes (12.26), which are the chthonic animal *par excellence*. Indeed, for the same effect, the royal jelly of the bee can be burned instead of *galbanum* (11.16). It is known, too, that among the worst enemies of the bee is the *papilio* (butterfly, moth), which Pliny, in telling of this enmity (11.65), characterizes as "lazy and ignominious, flying in with gleaming eyes." What we have, then, is the night creature that likes to circle around lamps: the moth. It is said to damage bees "in more than one way" (11.65): it eats up the wax, leaves excrement from which gnawing worms are born, and, finally, like a spider, weaves webs wherever it goes.

This enemy of the hive displays a well-stocked series of oppositions to the bee: insect of night, loving the artificial light of lamps, already in this the moth figures as the inverse of the bee, which is not only diurnal[29] but also loves the sun,[30] so much so that it was even considered the sun's daughter,[31] and from the sun could regain life.[32] Furthermore, the moth is characterized by Pliny not only as ignominious, hence the opposite of the bee, which is full of virtues, but also lazy: if there is one thing that bees hate more than any other it is sloth.[33]

Beyond these cultural differences lies another that interests us even more. Pliny classifies this "moth flying in with the lights of its lamps" (*lucernarum luminibus advolans*) among the "evil drugs" (*mala medicamenta*), warded off by goat liver (28.162). Hence, the nocturnal enemy of the bee has qualities that tend to relate it to the sphere of black magic. This invites us to identify it also with that *papilio* which Ovid calls "fierce, of death" (*Met.* 15.374): all the more because it is described as the natural transformation of *agrestes tineae* (wild caterpillars), and it is from these caterpillars that night moths are born (just as Pliny calls both *tineae* and *papilliones* the enemies of the hive). Moreover, the nocturnal moth in general often appears as the grim sign of death or misfortune in not only ancient but also in modern literature.[34]

Yet another cultural difference between the bee and the nocturnal moth thus begins to emerge, an opposition that can already to some degree be related to the axis "life/death." But here a brief parenthesis is appropriate. Only too well known is the ancient belief that the moth symbolizes the soul.[35] This is so to such an extent that the Greek language simply calls this insect *psyche* (soul). The moth symbolizes the soul split off from the body, after death, as in an ironic burial epigram that deserves citation: "Heredibus mando etiam cinere ut me [ra vina ferant] volitet meus ebrius papilio."[36] The speaker commands his heirs to pour pure wine on his ashes, otherwise, how will his "moth" manage to keep flying drunk? But the soul-moth also enters in the iconography of the Prometheus myth of human creation, where it represents the soul that is about to be placed in a body as yet inanimate.[37] Later, we shall see how, within the soul-moth, there has to be established a necessary gradation, with some differences. Now, instead, let us make a brief stop in the world of literature, because a moth iconography is nested, I believe, in a work that bears the "moth" and the "soul" in its very title: the "Tale of Cupid and Psyche" in the *Metamorphoses* of Apuleius.

The beauty of Psyche is a useless beauty: admired by all, praised by all (*Met.* 4.32ff.); however, no one comes to take her to wife. Her splendor is that of a statue; even her two sisters, whose beauty is measured, Apuleius says, have found royal suitors. Psyche, the scorned girl, remains at home to weeps because of her loneliness. Then her father turns to the oracle of Apollo of Didymus, at Miletus, only to receive a terrible reply (4.33):

On the crag of a lofty peak, king, place the girl
  dressed in the garb of a funeral chamber.
Expect a son-in-law not born of mortal stock,
  but savage and a fierce and viperish evil.

Just as Virgil's oracle in the *Aeneid* promised the old king Latinus a foreign son-in-law who would raise his stock to the sky, so
here the suitor is out of the ordinary, no doubt, but monstrous.
The old father of Psyche can hardly suspect that the "viperish evil"
(which, as the rest of the oracle says, terrifies the gods, Jove, even
Styx) is none other than Love camouflaged by the imagery commonly used to characterize him in literature. Hence, for Psyche a
funerary wedding is readied, as the oracle has prescribed: the funeral torches are put out in the darkest gloom, the flutes play melancholy tunes in the Lydian mode, the joyous songs of marriage
end in lugubrious wailing, and the girl dries her tears on her bridal
veil. Like Octavia as described by Tacitus, for Psyche, "the first day
of her marriage began her funeral" (*Ann.* 14.63). Finally, the funeral cortege sets out, while in the city public mourning gets declared. The living funeral slowly climbs the difficult incline of the
mountain, where the girl is to be left to be seized by the monster.
Her retinue sadly departs, having gone so far as to put out the
torches with their tears. Reaching home, the king and queen shut
themselves up forever in their darkened house, never to come out
again.

Psyche, now, is alone: but the feared monster does not come.
Instead, a gentle wind gathers her in its arms (*Met.* 4.35): "Psychen
autem paventem ac trepidam et in ipso scopuli vertice deflentem
mitis aura molliter spirantis Zephyri *vibratis hinc inde laciniis* et
reflato sinu sensim levatam suo tranquillo spiritu vehens paulatim
per devexa rupis excelsae vallis subditae florentis caespitis gremio
leniter delapsam reclinat." The wind places the girl, calm at last, in
the bosom of a clump of flowers at the bottom of a deep valley,
where she falls asleep before going to the enchanted dwelling of
her spouse. But we will pause right at this moment of passage, on
the light and delicate flight that moves Psyche from the funereal
context of her deathlike wedding to her new state as bride, no less,

of the god of love. Zephyr conveys her with a fluttering, here and there, of the borders of his clothes. This is the flight of a moth. Or, better, the flight of a moth insinuates itself into the folkloristic configuration just as, in the personage of Psyche, there begins to acquire body that allegory of the soul which, insistently Platonic, will accompany the entire development of the story. In the classic iconography of Cupid and Psyche (under the form of wedding, struggle, game, etc.), the soul-girl is often represented as a young woman with the wings of a moth.[38] Here Apuleius, by a clever allusion, ritualizes the representation in order to symbolize, in some way, the symbolic turn that the story more and more takes on. Studies by Cumont have shown how,[39] in Roman funerary symbolism, the soul is often represented in the process of flying toward the kingdom of the dead, wafted by the blowing of the wind. Gently gathered up by Zephyr, with garments rippling here and there like the light wings of a moth, it is truly a *psyche,* in the three senses of "soul" and "moth" and character in the story, that flies toward the further narrative development.

So, like the bee, the moth is a symbol of the soul. But within this cultural paradigm of "soul as moth" there must have been variations and differences: differences to some degree reflecting the various values of the soul in the culture (restless soul, soul at rest, soul on the verge of birth, etc.), and in which the opposition between the lively daytime creature and the gloomy nighttime one certainly played its part. At least, that is how things stand in our culture.[40] But it is rather likely that the night moth, counted among the evil drugs and characterized as "fierce," occupied a place rather positioned toward a "fierce" conception of survival as something fearsome and restless. Quite otherwise is the *psyche,* "girl with moth wings," whom we meet in classical iconography or feel moving—almost the trembling and faltering beat of her wings—amidst the rolling swell of Apuleian style. In short, the bee and its nocturnal enemy, the moth, may be opposed to each other also inasmuch they are diverse, but simultaneous, means of conceiving death and survival: the former is the creature of rebirth; the latter is the fierce image of death.

This difference fits naturally into that system of contrastive correlations between the bee and the moth which we described earlier. And now another contrast, too, can be added. From Columella, we hear that in order to drive out the usual caterpillars and moths from the hive, it is useful to burn dried dung mingled with cow marrow (9.14.2). This singular mixture finds a likely explanation if compared with the belief in *bugonia,* which is the miraculous birth of bees from the carcass of a cow: because the two elements of dung and marrow play an important role in this belief. It would appear, then, that the moths, enemies of the bees, held a great aversion for that from which the bees draw life and can be reborn: dung and marrow.

These two diverse conceptions of survival, embodied in the bee and the "fierce moth," appear to fit into a broader cultural framework, and as if at its top. In this framework, one and the same oppositional message gets repeated, transposed each time into diverse codes:

BEE	MOTH
diurnal	nocturnal
sun-loving	lamp-loving
virtuous	ignominious
active	lazy
producer	predator
close to cattle dung and marrow	hates cattle dung and marrow

These correlations constitute an entire system. Level by level it absorbs the insects' appearance and objective (natural) behavior into the cultural modeling process that built on them the beliefs of the ancient world.

"Ox-generation"

The sphere of the putrid and rotten, which we skirted in our pages about the purity of the bees, brings us naturally to the belief about the birth of these insects or, rather, rebirth: *bugonia,* "ox-generation," the swarm that generates itself from a rotting bovine carcass.

The belief is widely attested in ancient texts,[41] and explanations have been sought, perhaps not wholly wrong-headedly, from a scientific, or at least positivistic, perspective.[42] But obviously the latter are not what interests us. The fullest surviving description of the practice comes from the *Geoponica* (15.2.21ff.). It will serve as our point of departure and text of reference, around which to cluster analogues, differences, or variants recoverable from the versions of other authors. I would like, however, first to specify the season in which *bugonia* must take place.

Virgil, in his first version of *bugonia* (*Geo.* 4.281; cf. 305), refers to the beginning of spring, whereas his second version easily allows us to infer that the *bugonia,* the mythical one, as it were, performed for the first time by the hero Aristaeus, is set in the hot summer, the season of the Dog Star. When Aristaeus betakes himself to the grotto of Proteus to interrogate him, Virgil states expressly that "Sirius was scorching the Indians" (*Geo.* 4.531). And the sacrifice to the nymphs, as well as the ensuing *bugonia,* takes place immediately thereafter. The choice of the season of Sirius draws support from what we are told by Columella (9.14.6), who says that Mago and Democritus, as well as Virgil, maintained that the thirty or so days from the summer solstice to the rising of the Dog Star are the most propitious for *bugonia.* Moreover, the period is a crucial one for the cycle of honey because at that time, when the harvests are being gathered, beans are being picked (9.14.6).

Turning, now, to our text of reference, we read in *Geoponica* 15.2 that one has to choose, with Democritus and Mago,[43] a small squarish structure, about ten cubits on a side, having but one door and four small windows. In it gets placed, then, a beef about two and a half years old, rather fleshy, which a throng of youths must beat with clubs: gently at first, then with ever-growing violence. The flesh and bones must be broken down together, but care must be taken that the body not become bloody, because from blood bees would not be born. Then all the orifices of the beef must be blocked with fine, clean cloth soaked in pitch and the body must be laid out supine on a bed of thyme. Then the door and windows must be sealed hermetically and smeared with chalk, so that air and light cannot get in. After three weeks, air and light do get let in, as long as the wind is not too strong. When the larvae begin to come to life,[44] everything is shut again; and, after ten days, upon reopening, the swarm of bees will be found: nothing of the beef remains but horns, bones, and hide.

As for the place selected, we hear that Juba chose a wooden chest (*Geopon.* 15.2.21), whereas Virgil vacillates between two kinds of places. In his first version (which we may call the more technical and didactic), he, too, speaks of a rather small place, with four little windows facing the four winds and admitting an oblique light; in his second version (the mythical *bugonia,* set in the narrative of Aristaeus), there is a shady grove (*Geo.* 4.543). We must, however, keep in mind that here the cattle, besides generating bees, are meant to serve as victims to placate the nymphs, and that they must be sacrificed on four altars set up for the goddesses. The model of sacrifice, bound to the need of the narrative, thus superimposes itself on that of *bugonia.* Hence, in the first version there is a single calf, but in the second version there are four bulls and four heifers. More different still are Ovid's versions (*Fast.* 1.377; *Met* 15.364): in them the carcass gets lowered into a trench and covered with earth. Burial also is prescribed by Antigonus of Carystus (19.23): only the horns must stick out, so that they can subsequently be sawed off. Leaving aside Virgil's second version, which is shaped by the pattern of sacrifice, what all the versions share is obviously that the bovine carcass has to be identified completely with the sphere of earth, darkness, and putrefaction. Light and air must get in only at a later moment, when the larvae and the bees have taken on life.

The beef must be killed by blows. In this, Virgil's first version agrees with the *Geoponica* (*plagisque peremptus,* 4.301), but his second version does not, because there the throats of the sacrificial victims get cut (*Geo.* 4.542). Thus, clearly the pattern of sacrifice, in which the victims' throats are cut, stretches the rules of *bugonia;* this is rather unusual, because in the *Geoponica,* in keeping with the aversion of bees for blood and flesh, there is a pointed warning against bloodying the beef. And, of course, Virgil's own first version quite expressly says that the hide must remain unbroken, with no wounds. Indeed, this allows us to underline an interpretive point concerning the first version: "insincerus apes tulerit cruor" (*Geo.* 4.285). After what we have seen about bees and blood, it is clear that *cruor* cannot here mean "blood" ("for not from blood would the bee be born," says the *Geoponica*), but must mean, more generically, "rottenness, gore," a putrefying liquid (as suggested by the presence of the adjective *insincerus,* "corrupt"), hence the exact equivalent of the "liquefied viscera" (*Geo.* 4.555).

After the killing, the bones and flesh have to be broken down together, into one mass. And generally the writers speak of the birth of bees from a bovine carcass or body.[45] The presence of the bones, however, merits particular emphasis. In Hesychius (s.v. *bougeneon*), the bees are actually born from the bones; Virgil himself in his first version—the most technical—speaks of "moisture warmed in the tender bones" (*Geo.* 4.308). Now we should recall what was said about the use of bovine marrow against moths: if this substance gives life to bees, clearly it is to be feared by the enemies of the bees. The belief in the generative power of marrow seems rather widespread, because Aelian says that the marrow of horses gives birth to wasps (*Hist. an.* 1.28); and it was also generally believed that the snake was generated from the spinal marrow of man.[46]

Let us look, now, at the detail of the carcass placed supine on a bed of thyme. If the presence of thyme may be explained by the particular love that bees bear this plant,[47] the supine position must relate to what the sources say about the function of the viscera in *bugonia*. The supine position leaves the viscera more exposed and better allows the bees to get out: in his second version, Virgil writes of "bees buzzing in the whole womb and boiling out from the burst ribs" (*Geo.* 4.555ff.). Clearly, he emphasizes the viscera. He actually speaks in the first version of "pounded viscera" (*Geo.* 4.302), and in the second version of "liquefied viscera" (*Geo.* 4.555), just as Ovid has the bees born from the decaying viscera of the bull (*Met.* 15.365ff.). Mago would have it that bees could even be born from the belly alone, without the carcass (Columella 9.14.6). This belief appears also in Pliny, with an interesting detail added: "Lost bees can be restored using fresh bovine bellies covered with dung" (*Hist. nat.* 11.70).

Dung also, then, makes its appearance; it is a material of no secondary importance in raising bees. From dung, the hives can even be built (Columella 9.6.6); dried cattle dung gets used to fumigate them[48] and Columella explains this detail by actually alluding to *bugonia:* "Dung, . . . as if by a certain relatedness of race, is especially fit for bees" (9.14.2). Curious, this "relatedness of race" *(cognatio generis)*. Bees are relatives of dung because both, in a way, come from the cow's belly, or something of the sort. The openings of the hive, then, actually are sealed with cow manure *(Geopon.* 15.2.8; Palladius 4.15.4), and it is even believed that the flight of the swarm can be avoided by spreading the hives with the dung of a first-born bull *(Geopon.* 15.4.1; Palladius 1.38.2). The theme of "first-birth" is an express mark of folklore, almost even of fable, added to this complex of beliefs already so unusual in itself. But it is very singular that cow manure constitutes such a powerful attraction for the bees, enough to keep them even from their intentions of emigration. Evidently, it is believed that the "daughters of dung" recognize by its presence their natural dwelling. Thus, the mention of dung in the context of *bugonia,* as given us by Pliny, is by no means a secondary feature. On the one hand, "dung" is related by contiguity to "belly," which plays a preeminent part in this process; on the other hand, "dung" evokes its own wider functions in the general field of apiculture: with cow dung, hives get built and their cracks get sealed; burning it fumigates the hives; smearing them with it keeps the bees that want to leave them; and burning it along with marrow drives out the enemies of the bees. Needless to say, in the variant that makes the bovine belly the specific site of *bugonia,* especially when covered with dung, the theme of the putrescent and rotten reaches its maximum.

All of this allows us, perhaps, a remark about language. In Latin, the hive is called *alvarium* or *alvaria,* but also fairly often *alvus,* which is the term from which the others derive in secondary formation. It can hardly be chance that *alvus* also means "intestinal cavity" and, indeed, that these are its only two meanings. Evidently, the link between viscera and bees or beehive (remember the hives made from dung) was so tight that the cultural model of *bugonia* imposed itself also at the level of language: "intestine" and "hive" thus came to be called by the same term. Some Indo-European languages in the Western group have terms close to *alvus* to indicate the hive, or at least devices used to capture bees:[49] it does not seem, however, that these languages use related terms to indicate the intestinal cavity. Thus, one could even think that in the term *alvus* the idea of "hive" is primary and that it served to prompt the idea of "intestinal cavity," conceived of as a "hive," "belly," following the model of *bugonia*, could be indicated by the same term as "hive" itself.

The *bugonia* proves to be very well-rooted in Roman culture, perhaps even already at the level of the language. And it seems likewise rooted in the practice of raising bees, to judge from the multiplicity of functions for which the beekeeper uses cow dung. This rootedness does not preclude an origin of the legend, that in Egypt, as some sources relate.[50] But certainly one would have to suppose that the legend arrived in Rome early, and not by itself, but incorporated in the ensemble of bee-raising practices.

One further detail remains, the closing one: that is, the necessity of keeping the carcass far from air or wind, and of stopping up the openings of the victim. The two requirements are evidently related, and Virgil reports them together in his first version. Frankly, what comes to mind at once is an explanation that leads, among other things, back to the very cultural meaning of *bugonia*. One must avoid letting the soul of the beef get out of the carcass or, still worse, out of the place in which the carcass has been enclosed.[51] Remember, too, the warning against breaking the hide (which would make further openings for the soul to get out). Ovid comments that "from one killed cow, a thousand souls" (*Fast.* 1.380). And an identical conception is cited from Aeneas of Gaza, actually in a context referring to the reincarnation of souls: "The one soul was broken down and dispersed into thousands that the cow collected and kept" (*Theophr.* 155 = p. 16, 10 Colonna).

Evidently, *bugonia* takes us back to our point of departure: the bee as symbol of the reincarnate soul. In *bugonia*, the bee is reborn because it constitutes in some sense the outcome of a transformation of the soul. The bee is the soul, as Ovid says. Where there is a body subject to death, it frees itself in flight. *Bugonia* thus shows some rather precise correlations with the general categories of beliefs about bees: on the one hand, opposition to every sort of rottenness (and thus an aversion for whatever belongs to the sphere of the dead); on the other hand, the link with the immortal soul. The same categories that we already knew get applied in the myth of the swarm that is born where a body rots. The sphere of the rotten—made even more intense by darkness, by contact with earth and isolation from air, or even by the presence of entrails and dung—contrasts with that of purity and light, represented by the bee, which detaches itself from the carcass and flies off "in longing for light" (*Geopon.* 15.2.34), like the soul.

Ox, Horse, Hornet, Wasp

Why is the ox at the origin of bees? Here, too, we find ourselves facing some categorical oppositions. The sources tell us that bees are born from an ox, bull, or calf, but that wasps,[52] or hornets,[53] are born from a horse. Nor do we lack for yet more confusing reports, as often when Isidore of Seville is involved.[54] Pliny adds, however, that dung beetles come from asses (*Hist. nat.* 11.70), a belief seconded by other sources.[55] We can leave the beetles, which have precious little to do with the world of bees;[56] however, wasps and hornets have rather close ties. Pliny considers them degenerate bees (*Hist. nat.* 11.61); they strongly resemble bees, which were even "daughters of hornets and the sun" for Euhemerus (Columella 9.2.3); and both insects construct cells. However, the offspring of wasps and hornets are not born at set times, but irregularly, "as among barbarians"; both insects even eat flesh ("unlike bees, which touch no body"); and they do not have "kings" and swarms.[57] Although resembling bees, the hornets and wasps hence differ from them as a lower, more barbarous, variant. They, too, like the bee, are born from a putrefying animal carcass, but from that of a horse rather than that of an ox.

Ancient writers give us some interesting hints on the perceived cultural affinities between the horse and the hornets and wasps. According to Ovid (*Met.* 15.368), the horse was used to generate hornets by *hippogonia* because of its warlike nature: hence the war-horse, for hornets, too, are very fierce.[58] A not dissimilar explanation occurs for the link with wasps. "The wasp fashions its passionate stock on the model of the horse," we are told in a discussion of *bugonia* by Nicander (*Theri.* 740); and the soul of Hector, the warrior, bound itself to a wasp, "because both were exceedingly warlike," we hear from Aeneas of Gaza (*Theophr.* 154). Similarly, Artemidorus stated that a dream of wasps foreshadowed meeting cruel and perverse men (*Onir.* 2.22), evidently because of the aggressive nature of this insect.

We must not neglect another route, opened by a scholion to Nicander (*Theri.* 740), which calls the wasps *anaischyntoi* (shameless). The horse is considered a very lascivious beast,[59] as appears, moreover, in the legend of *hippomanes* (horse-madness).[60] Horses often appear in incestuous relationships.[61] Hence, from this standpoint, too, "shameless" wasps and "lascivious" horses go together. Nor can it be chance that the horse, shameless, progenitor of barbarous and degenerate bees, which are indeed inimical to the true bees (Virgil, *Geo.* 4.245), does not get along with the bees: often a swarm has attacked and killed a horse.[62]

Let us return to the war-horse and go on to oxen. The opposition between these two cultural models, horses and oxen, emerges well from a legend concerning the foundation of Carthage, told by Justinus (18.5.15):

> At the first foundation, the head of an ox was found, which was the harbinger of a city to be fruitful, but toilsome and forever enslaved. Because of this, the city was moved to another site, where was discovered the head of a horse, signifying that the people would be powerful and warlike.

The warlike ambitions of the Carthagians found congenial the sign of the horse, not that of the ox, which is, to be sure, a productive beast, but the very type of toil and servitude. Needless to say, for this very reason the ox is a meritorious beast, the closest, at least for man, who uses him. "All useful race" in life, the ox even in death is "noble" and "praiseworthy," because from its remains are born the bees, says Aelian (*Hist. an.* 2.57). And it is superfluous to recall the bonds of trust, respect, and affection which join the ox to the farmer in the ancient world.[63] Enough to make the point is the Athenian Buphoniae, "assassination of the ox," with all its surrounding ritual of horror and expiation.[64] Very beautiful is the praise of the ox by Pythagoras, as imagined by Ovid: "What have oxen earned, creature without treachery or tricks, harmless, frank, born to put up with toil?" (*Met.* 15.120).

Pythagoras, a little further along (*Met.* 15.141ff.), warns that eating the flesh of the ox is like eating your own hired hands, so close is the bond between the farmer and the beast that plows. So there is plenty to motivate culturally the link between the most noble and useful insect, on the one hand, and the most noble and useful of domestic animals on the other. Mild, productive, obedient, the ox is set in contrast to the horse, warlike and shameless, just as the bees are set in contrast to their degenerate and warlike cousins, the wasps and hornets.

One variant of *bugonia* makes even more precise the cultural vectors that touch the ox, in the quadrilateral comprising bees/ox/wasps and hornets/horse, in the specific context of *bugonia*. A story in the Daniel-Servius commentary on Virgil (*Aen.* 1.430) tells how there lived near the Isthmus of Corinth an old women named Melissa. Ceres had confided in her the secrets of her holy mysteries, commanding her to reveal them to no one. Certain women wanted to force Melissa to reveal them: first they tried with prayers and promises, then, seeing that their efforts were to no avail, they grew angry and cut her to pieces. Ceres punished the women by putting a plague on all their people, and she made bees arise from the dismembered body of Melissa.[65]

The analogies are very strong with the pattern of *bugonia* as we have seen it thus far, where bees are born from the body of a killed animal. Here they are born from the body of an old woman who has been killed by the impatient and curious women. In both cases, the bees figure as a rebirth, as the transformation of a body bereft of life. However, this variant of the myth, because it is built on a human being, not an animal, gives more attention to the specific qualities of the generative element. Melissa is a woman who is faithful to her mistress and long-suffering even to the point of sacrificing herself. On the level, then, of function, Melissa seems to present in each and every respect qualities such as those seen thus far in the ox. Through Melissa, we get a kind a of explanation of why bees descend from oxen. As for the plague accompanying the birth of the bees, it clearly takes us back to the link between *bugonia* as rebirth, on the one hand, and the deeds performed on Ceos (affliction by pestilence and salvation by the hero of honey, Aristaeus). But this is discussed more fully later (in chapter 17).

The Foreigners

The bee loves solitude and does not seek human company (*Geopon.* 15.2.9). Enigmatic, exceptional (neither male nor female, neither tame nor wild, far from both the rotten and the aromatic), it is closed in a society so well-composed as to resemble greatly the human one, which can almost mirror itself in the bees. But just because the bee lives a life so well-organized, self-governed, and self-sufficient, the hive is, in effect, distant. The relations between human beings and bees are metaphoric, not metonymic: between the two worlds there is mirroring, but by that very fact no contact, no contiguity. Wearying of one settlement, the swarm can decide to leave. And does, this too, in a terribly human way (especially by comparison with the customs of ancient peoples), that is, getting organized in the fashion of an actual "spring rite," as the Sabines, for example, used to do (Varro, *Rer. rust.* 3.16.29). The beekeepers know that precisely the beginning of spring is the moment in which their swarms may decide to take off (Columella 9.9.1).

This natural custom of migration by the bees may provide the grounds for some legends in which bees play the role of guides to colonizers. It was believed that a swarm of bees guided the Athenians to Ionia[66] and, furthermore, that bees showed the Ionian Timesias the way to get to where he was to found a colony (Plutarch, *De amic. mult.* 7). Because bees themselves found colonies (Varro, *Rer. rust.* 3.16.29), practicing a veritable rite of spring, they fit quite well the role of guides for human colonization.[67] This dual condition of the bee, both near and far with respect to human society, both colonizing and guiding colonizers, is reflected also in a proverb preserved by Photius (s.v. *seiren*): "The siren announces a friend; the bee announces a stranger." The siren is an insect of which we know precious little: only that it is a solitary bee, as Aristotle says (*Hist. an.* 623b). In any case, the bee's skills of colonizing and guiding colonists, as well as the proverb preserved in Photius, may help us to understand better a passage in Virgil and show us another case in which, in the *Aeneid,* beliefs about bees are woven deeply into the narrative texture.

Book seven tells of a prodigy that took place in Laurentum (7.59–70). A swarm of bees, shaped like a bunch of grapes, lodged itself at the top of the sacred laurel that grew in the royal palace. At once the seer prophesied: "We see a foreign hero come and column from the same parts seek the same parts and lord it in the lofty citadel" (7.68–70).

Generally, the prodigy tends to be explained by recalling how the arrival of a swarm of bees was considered a bad sign among the Romans.[68] Only La Cerda thought to recall, in this context, the bees' practice of marching in formation with their king at the head, like the Trojans with Aeneas, and their custom of sending out colonies. Already these remarks of the seventeenth-century commentator should be enough to suggest reasons for Virgil's specific choice of a sign to announce Aeneas's arrival to the Latins. But the device takes on more meaning if we recall what was said about the bees as guides to colonizers, and even more meaning with the proverb preserved by Photius, which Virgil's expression seems almost to retranscribe ("the bee announces a stranger"). In short, there is a bit of folklore in this Virgilian prodigy, as there should be in a prodigy: more folklore, I would say, than ideology.[69] We have seen (in chapter 4) that Aeneas and the Trojans are outsiders and foreigners *par excellence*. We recall that the oracle of Faunus, whom Latinus goes to consult after the disturbing omens in the palace, explains to the old king: "Do not seek to join your daughter in marriage with Latins, o my offspring, or trust in the readied wedding chambers: in-laws will come from afar" (7.96–98). The type of prodigy chosen, a swarm of bees, foreshadows exactly, in symbolic terms, the arrival of the outsider, of the son-in-law from afar. It is one and the same, almost uttered, truth, which from the symbol of the bees gets transcribed into the seer's explanation, into the palace, and into the express warning of Faunus. The content of what is about to happen is revealing itself little by little, in a continuous tension that comes to a head with the arrival of the first Trojan embassy.

Let us remain with the seer's interpretation of the prodigy. I do not believe that the expression "from the same parts" can be explained (along the lines of Servius) as "from the Tuscan sea" (*ab infero mari*), as if the seer wished simply to say that the bees, like Aeneas, come from the sea.[70] In this mirrorlike expression, with its strongly analogical construction (*partes petere agmen easdem/partibus ex isdem*), we should probably see only a vague way, very oracular, of saying, "The foreigner goes toward the same place in which the bees settled, and comes from the same place from which the bees come," without knowing exactly from where, but knowing with certainty only that the stranger (announced by the bees) will follow in every respect their way. Here I think of a passage in which Pausanias describes the Boeotians, who found the oracle of Trophonius only because they were guided by a swarm of bees: it struck their leader as opportune that "wherever the bees turn, they also should follow" (9.40.2). The bees not only announce the stranger but also, in keeping with their capability as colonists and guides to colonists, mark out the way step by step: "wherever the bees turn, they also should follow," without knowing where they come from, when they appear, or where they go. One follows them. That is enough. It is an enigmatic creature, as we have seen.

First Conclusions
(But a Simile, "How does it work?")

The mythic pattern is clear. The bee emerges as an animal that is pure in the sexual, the alimentary, and the olfactory codes. Creature of rebirth *par excellence,* so far from corruption and death that it can launch itself in life right there where a carcass rots, it shows a marked aversion from death and whatever represents death, such as, in particular, the moth. The kind of animal that is closest and most faithful to man, it figures simultaneously as something distant, foreign, in many respects enigmatic: enough to justify the ancient Greek practice of giving the name of bee, *melissa,* to the immortal soul, the just soul on its way to be born; and also to interpret rather more completely, beyond the simple buzz or multitude, the cultural lines that may have guided Virgil in his choice of that particular simile to designate the souls.

One might, indeed, at this point propose something more general about the simile. One might say that this rhetorical procedure is, in reality, a way of placing in comparison two cultural patterns and, by means of the second, putting in focus those semantic and cultural traits of the first that interest the poet. Obviously, we must specify that, in this sense, the procedure of simile has to be related to the familiar problem of authorial viewpoint in writing: by choosing for comparison one certain paradigm instead of another, the writer opens for us a likely access to his way of conceiving, of organizing with a particular sense, what he is telling. His way, or that of the culture that he shares? I do not believe it is always easy to tell the difference (as it never is when we try to distinguish phenomena of *langue* from phenomena of *parole,* the language at large from the individual idiom), especially because a third variable, the pressure of the tradition or of the literary code, here comes massively into play. It remains true, however, that the thing compared works in the simile as an actual translation into a different code of the thing to which it is compared: the hero who fights like a lion amounts to the translation of a notion, courage, or more simply of a certain sequence of courageous acts, into the cultural language of characteristic beliefs about the animal world.[71] In fine, the problem of similes is one of naming, as if it were a matter of establishing what the notion of purified, immortal soul corresponds to in the code of beliefs about insects: naming, of course, as cultural act.

But our journey among the ancient symbolisms of the soul has not yet ended. Further travel remains, which leads us backward from Virgil's poem straight to the *Odyssey.*

Sixteen

The Bee and the Bat

The Weariness of the Dead

omer's world beyond the tomb is a grim place. All of it is so imbued with gloomy sadness as to leave no room even for tragedy. Homer (or, better, that polyphony of nameless voices which produced in the course of time the tissue of the *Odyssey*) even dares to describe there something precious few poets would: the meeting of Odysseus with his mother, a hopeless meeting with a dead mother. The shadows are dense and foggy, and any description of a scene beyond the tomb falls short: only the sequence of a few detached names, mythic, full of significance (Acheron, Pyriphlegethon, Cocytus, Styx), but without so much as a sketch, a draft of a image. Nor do we learn much about the souls and what they are like: no more than what does emerge from certain epithets (the paradigmatic manner, through emblems, that often carries description in Homer), or that gets said fleetingly by one or another questioner of Odysseus. It seems almost as if the poet does not narrate, does not tell, that only grudgingly does he fold out into linear sequence the time of a narrative, of something getting done.

The Homeric shades do not actually get linked to a description of place or to a story; their features conceal themselves, as if slinking off, in some adjective or some qualifying turn of phrase. Yet, if one had to try to define these shades so sketchily described, so as to assemble on one thread their impression on the reader, one might say: etiolated, the Homeric souls resemble beings pitiably weakened and used up. And this matter of weakness, of enfeeblement, is attributed to the shades, from different perspectives, in various codes, almost obsessively. Thus, they are called *eidola* (images), similar in traits and features to what the body was, but reduced to objects of mere sight, and of no other senses. Or they are called *amenena karena* (forceless heads), deprived of their *menos,* "force" (*Od.* 10.521, 10.536, 11.29 and 49). "Forceless," too, are dreams (*Od.* 19.562), which the souls resemble (*Od.* 11.222): and when the shade of Agamemnon vainly tries to hug Odysseus, we are told that "in his limbs he lacked the force of old, his strength" (*Od.* 11.392).

Not dissimilarly, one speaks of the dead also as *eidola kamonton* (images of the tired), as "feeble."[1] "Tiredness" often is a way of conceptualizing illness, the state of prostration into which it causes one to fall.[2] And there comes to mind that passage in the *Odyssey* in which the hero worn out by the sea arrives at the island of the Phaeacians: "But he, breathless and voiceless, lay with little strength, and a terrible tiredness came on him" (*Od.* 5.465). The hero, gripped by this "terrible tiredness," lacks breath and voice, is without force, reduced almost to nothing: and this *oligopelie* (little being) is a condition that could well describe the Homeric shades.

Lacking force, gripped as by a mortal weariness, the shades are like the sick, or people lying without voice or breath, worn out by effort. Thus, the dead also fail to keep intact their spiritual faculties. Only Tiresias has *phrenes empedoi* (sound wits; *Od.* 10.493); the other dead are without senses, lacking in every sort of mental capacity (*Od.* 11.476). Achilles, after the shade of Patroclus leaves him, says that "in Hades, too, there exist a *psyche* and an *eidolon* ('soul' and 'image'), but the mind is no longer there."[3] Nor do these pitiable creatures without their senses have any stability, solidity, or direction. All the shades (except Tiresias, whose wits are firmly on the ground), *aïssousi,* "flit here and there" like "shadows" (*Od.* 10.495). And indeed, after death the soul flees "in the manner of a dream" and "hovers about" (*pepotetai*), wandering vaguely without aim or meaning (*Od.* 11.222).

Deprived of force, feeble, and lacking in senses, stability, and direction, the shades likewise have feeble voices. In the *Iliad*, the soul of Patroclus, like smoke, flees away beneath the earth, "squeaking, gibbering" (*tetriguia*; 23.100). And the same verb is used for the souls of the suitors, who are heard "gibbering" as they are led by Hermes down to Hades (*Od.* 24.5). The sound, *trizein*, is one that Homer elsewhere attributes to bats, or to baby sparrows attacked by a snake.[4] Otherwise, the voices of the dead that flee when Heracles approaches get likened to the sound of birds, this time a *klange*, more of a scream (*Od.* 11.604).

Also outside of Homer, the sound *trizein* gets attributed to birds and animals, such as partridge, swallow, mouse (see the entries s.v. in *LSJ*), and snake (Hermes Trismegistos, in Stobaeus 1.49.44). Why *trizein* got attributed to animals was explained, probably correctly, by Eustathius in his commentary on the *Odyssey*: "Mythically, *trismos* got chosen for souls, because they were deprived of articulated speech and only made noise" (1951.38). The souls lack shaped and distinct utterance, hence they sound like a confused murmur. This remark appears to get the precise sense of *trizein*, to judge also from Herodotus, who speaks of the Ethiopian troglodytes, who "use a language unlike everyone else's . . . twittering [*tetrigasai*] like bats" (IV 183) (where the verb, referring to language, can hardly mean the sound of the bats' wings). Hence the obscure and unknown language of the troglodytes is compared not to an articulated tongue, but to a confused murmur, with a metaphor not unlike that which had led the Greeks to consider those who spoke other tongues as *barbaroi* (stutterers).

Eustathius's explanation gathers yet greater weight if compared with the usage of a term that the poets often apply to the living, to human beings as such; that is, *meropes* (as in *Il.* 1.250, 3.402; *Od.* 20.49, 132, etc.). For the ancient Greeks, *meropes* meant "those of articulated [*mer-*] voice [*op-*]."[5] Thus, humans actually are defined as "those who articulate their speech," and, indeed, *meropes* by itself can stand for "humankind," as does also, for example, *brotoi* (mortal).[6] This definition can be better understood if we compare it with the fact that, in Homer, a particular voice, always called *omphe,* gets attributed to the gods;[7] this voice is perceptible to mortals in their dreams, as when "the divine *omphe* spread around" Agamemnon as he slept and dreamed (*Il.* 2.41). There is, then, a kind of descending progression from the mysterious *omphe* of the gods, through the "articulated speech" of men, to the *trizein* of the shades, who have lost distinct speech, falling back to the level of birds, of bats, or of mice, or of savages such as the troglodytes.

Voice reduced or enfeebled, the hum, the squeaking of the souls is the *vox exigua* that Virgil assigns them in an extraordinary passage of book six of the *Aeneid* (6.492ff.). When the souls of those who fought bravely at Troy, the Greek leaders and the ranks of Agamemnon, see the gleam of Aeneas's armor, they are seized by a great fear: "Some started to turn tail . . . some to raise a tenuous voice: the shout begun trails off to empty mouthing."[8] The voice is weak; the threat sketched out dies in the throat and fails. Nor could one say if the most cruel detail is being unable even to shout (I see no question about the painfully dreamlike character of this), or if it is the fear felt by once brave warriors at the mere sight of arms. Loss of courage, powerlessness to speak, as in a nightmare: among the indirect descriptions of death, among its mythic phantasms, this is one of the most terrible. But let us get back to the squeaking of the dead.

Naturally, to marvel at the fact that the squeaking souls can speak with the living in a normal manner (as does Virgil's Deiphobus just after the poet has referred to the "tenuous voice" of the dead) means in all likelihood to confuse two things. On the one hand are the features of a description that is symbolic or simply paradigmatic, which tends to give in a brief analogical sketch the measure and almost the essence of a condition (the degradation and the enfeeblement of the dead). On the other hand are the requirements of narrative discourse to be linear and syntagmatic, in which not everything that belongs to the symbol or the paradigm has to be reabsorbed: thus it is, in general, for those aspects of mythic discourse which refer us back to the level of the paradigm, of the *langue*, but which can seem incoherent or lacking in verisimilitude when they are read on the level of the narrative.

So, then, the shades in Homer—pure objects of sight, powerless, weakened, lacking sense, stability, direction, and even articulated voice—are only pale and wretched echoes of the living. Here there is no question of another life; there is only this life cruelly diminished and enfeebled. The necessary metaphorical relation that has to be set up, as noted at the beginning of this part, so that the imagination can get at a world unknown and uninhabited except by cultural images, here is established in the most elementary way, and thus the most terrible: simply by systematic subtraction from what characterizes the world of the living.

In various guises, by means of diverse codes, an identical message is repeated: the condition of the shades is like a life emptied of everything; death is a great weariness. It is also on this account, we can imagine, that Odysseus, unlike Aeneas or Dante, practically never asks information about the other world.[9] There is nothing to learn about Homer's Hades; it all is terribly simple. To imagine it, one only need weaken, reduce life here to the point of submerging it in emptiness and filth. An otherworld constructed by subtraction is an otherworld toward which neither hopes nor expectations point, but only a dark projection of washing out. "Over there" no experience exists; there is nothing to learn or to communicate. Memories evaporate; they get lost like the fruits of the willow (*iteai olesikarpoi, salices frugiperdiae*) that line the shore at the edge of Hades: everything there is sterile like the cow that Odysseus sacrifices to the "powerless heads" (*Od.* 10.510)[10]

Like Bats in a Fearsome Cave

Having opened with a simile, I close in the same way. Beginning book twenty-four of the *Odyssey*, the so-called Lesser Nekuia, Hermes Guide-of-Souls leads to Hades the shades of the suitors slaughtered by Odysseus (*Od.* 24.1–9):

> Kyllenian Hermes called forth the souls
> of the suitors. He held in hand the staff,

lovely golden, with which he calms men's eyes,
whose ever he cares to, but rouses others, even from sleep.
With it he drove, pricking on: they followed squeaking.
As when bats in the depth of a fearsome cave
flit squeaking, when one falls from the bunch
that hangs from the rock, then cling one to another again,
so squeaking they went along together.

Here we are, then, arrived at talking about the most dreadful of
flying creatures. Halfway between birds and animals, hence
double natured,[11] the bat therefore is perceived as ambiguous and
monstrous; both night and blindness make it still more repulsive.
Because it retreats from the free spaces of the sky in its love of caves
and grottoes, this creature appears as a flyer quite attached to the
earth: Herodotus, describing the harvest of *casia* in the East, says
that it is protected by bats (3.110); Pliny speaks of bats or "winged
serpents" (*Hist. nat.* 12.85). The association is very suggestive of
the feeling that surrounds the bat in ancient culture: the serpent is
the creature most linked with earth; the bat, as the flying creature
of the grottoes and underground cavities that is functionally analogous to a "serpent with wings," presents itself as an actually
chthonic flyer. Moreover (and here we approach the symbolism for
souls), bats were associated with souls caught up by mad love for
corporeal life; like bats, these souls have "corporeal wings, thick
and earthy" (Proclus, *Comm. in Plat. Resp.* 1.120, 5–10 Kroll). Bats
also have associations with fear and cruelty. Bats were what Min-
yas's daughters turned into (only one of the girls, or all three),[12]
those accursed mother-aunts who sacrificed one of their son-
nephews because of their desire to eat human flesh.[13]

We also know that the bat was often linked to death or to the
shades.[14] On the isle of dreams, where Sleep has his palace, not
trees but tall poppies and mandrakes grow, and on them are bats:
"This is the only bird that inhabits the island" (Lucian, *Ver. hist.*
2.33). Such an association between dream and bat brings us closer
already to Homer, and to his souls "that fly off like dreams."

In the Homeric text are still more specific details that concern
us. Like Homer's souls, the bat is characterized by squeaking,
which it shares with mice and birds. Moreover, in its unbroken

flight, apparently endless and aimless, and therefore mindless, the bat exactly represents the Homeric soul, which darts and flutters mindlessly in the shadows of Hades. A bat that shrieks and flits madly in the dark of a fearsome cave: that is the dreadful survival awaiting the *eidolon* in Hades.[15] Here is the last touch added to the conception of the afterlife in Homer, projected on the image screen of a simile. The very traits of the bat in nature, including its twittering and obsessive flight, combine with its traits in culture, as flyer of earth, as fearsome, as the transform of murderous and cruel sisters, with links to dreams and to the shades, to make the bat a privileged symbol of a certain manner, particularly dreary and dreadful, of conceiving the condition of the soul after death.

Brief Last Remarks

In order to pull together the threads of these sets of symbols, the bee and the bat, nothing remains but to follow step by step the language of the things and the creatures: an entire language made naturally of objects in their cultural interrelation, a language for which now and again we have to seek out the vocabulary and syntax. And it displeases to see this "language of things" subjected to arbitrary and unreasonable symbolistic readings, which pay no heed to the real, attested meanings held by things and creatures in the culture, but batten on unlikely intertextual correspondences or miscellaneous allegorizations.[16] In this language of things, language of culture, the way, then, is long from Homer's bat to Virgil's bee: the horrid bat that flits fitfully in a dreadful cave, but the bee that settles, in quiet summer, on colored flowers, with lilies sprinkled all about. The symbolic gap between the two similes makes perceptible at once, as if these were a kind of geometric topos and cultural focus, an anthropological gap of very great import: between a soul-bat and a soul-bee, the difference is the same as that between a blind and desperate underworld, which is pure survival in exhaustion, and the Orphic-Pythagorean hope of an eternal and purified soul.

Seventeen

The Madness of Aristaeus

T he time has come to speak of something that all along has been flitting (to continue metaphorically our theme) through the pages about bees: their foundation myth, the story of Aristaeus, who lost the bees a nymph once gave him and learned from his mother, Cyrene, how to get them back. Virgil uses the myth to close the *Georgics;* and to give it a title that better than any other points out the impression it makes, I shall call it "The Madness of Aristaeus," because the hero Aristaeus differs so much, here in Virgil, from what he is in other stories that cast him as the leading figure in some cultural undertaking: here he is so guilty, so lacking in direction.

Myth is what we have called the invention of *bugonia* and the story of Aristaeus. Undoubtedly, the story in its function (explaining a cultural practice) is a myth. Yet is it really a myth or a tale? We shall seek to answer this question, too. For the moment, we recall this apt appraisal by Norden: "The finale of the *Georgics* spreads before us a world of fairy tale. Aristaeus, the powerful god of yore, the benefactor of mankind, here takes on the traits of a prince in a tale."[1] The appraisal is apt, both a bit true and a bit false. It is true because the story of Aristaeus really is a tale in certain respects, and the title "The Tale of Aristaeus" has a certain currency. But Norden's remark also is partly false, because the close of the *Georgics* does not have enough of the warm and ingenuous simplicity usually required of a tale: in Virgil, everything is polished and a bit cold. The style might almost be symbolized by the crystalline transparency of the "glassy benches" on which the nymphs take their ease (do not forget the sea-green color with which they dye the wool they spin). Norden's phrase, however, is very suggestive, because it contains the problem or, rather, the two problems we wish to address: first, the fairy tale character of the episode; second, the distance that Virgil's Aristaeus, the fairy-tale prince, marks from the powerful god, the benefactor of mankind: his distance, we could then say, from the myth or complex of myths that identify him.

The Tale of Aristaeus

Let us begin by retelling Virgil's version of the story (*Geo.* 4.315–566). Aristaeus has lost his bees, dead of hunger and disease. In despair, he betakes himself to the river Peneus in Thessaly and there calls out in a loud voice to his mother, Cyrene, a water goddess, reproaching her for failing to keep her promise that he would one day receive divine honors for his accomplishments as a farmer and grower. The scene shifts, and now we are shown the underwater home in which Cyrene sits surrounded by other nymphs: they are engaged in weaving and they listen to the stories of one of their number, Clymene. The mother hears her son complaining; Arethusa, her sister nymph, lifts her head from the waters and actually sees Aristaeus.

Then Cyrene gives the command that her son come to her in her underwater realm (*fas illi limina divum / tangere,* 358–59): the waves open wide, and Aristaeus begins his miraculous descent [ecphrasis of the underwater realms]. Received with great honor by his mother and by the other nymphs, Aristaeus tells Cyrene his misfortunes. His mother orders him then to betake himself to Proteus, the powerful sea god and seer to whom nothing is unknown. Aristaeus will have to take advantage, however, of the seer's slumber (Cyrene herself will lead him, at the noon hour, to the hidden places where the ancient gets his rest) and bind him tightly, because never will the ancient speak of his own free will. As soon as Proteus becomes aware of being bound, he will change himself into the most fearsome beast: but her son must hold on, and Proteus will speak.

Cyrene and Aristaeus betake themselves, therefore, to Proteus's grotto, and everything happens as the mother had said. When the wrath of the ancient has been mastered, Aristaeus asks him to explain to him why his bees have been wiped out by disease and hunger. Proteus reveals to him that he is being persecuted by divine wrath. In fact, Aristaeus caused the death of the nymph Eurydice, wife of Orpheus. Aristaeus was chasing her through the woods to possess her, but the girl did not realize that in the thick grass there lurked a snake; its bite killed her. But the misfortunes caused by Aristaeus in his guilt do not end here. Proteus now tells the tragic tale of Orpheus: how the Thracian singer betook himself to Hades to free his wife, how this privilege was granted him because of the suasion of his song; but, also how Orpheus himself, in his impatience, caused Eurydice a second downfall: for Proserpine had set him as a *lex* not to turn around before leaving the world of the dead (Orpheus was leading; Eurydice, following).[2] Orpheus, however, drawn by excessive love, did turn and so lost Eurydice again. Losing hope, he lets himself go completely in melancholy song, disdaining the love offered him by the Ciconian mothers. Because of this refusal, he is torn apart during a Bacchic orgy.

Having ended the story of Orpheus, Proteus throws himself into the sea and disappears. Then Cyrene gives Aristaeus new instructions: he must make a sacrifice of reparation to the nymphs (because he is guilty of the death of one of them); to this end, he will have to choose four bulls and four heifers that have not yet known the yoke, to cut their throats in a leafy grove, leaving their carcasses there where they fall; after nine days, he must return to the place of sacrifice to placate the ghosts of Orpheus and Eurydice with other offerings. Aristaeus faithfully carries out his mother's prescriptions and, after nine days, returns to the place of sacrifice.

Here he finds, with great wonder, that bees are freeing themselves from the rotting bodies of the animals. Thus originates *bugonia.*

To analyze this story, it behooves us to start from the simple, which is the structure of the tale. For this purpose we shall use the *Morphology* of Propp,[3] which we then shall integrate with the tools of classical philology (in defining the several intertextual loans that Virgil has grafted onto the tale).

Aristaeus violates an interdiction: he tries to possess the nymph Eurydice, who is the wife of Orpheus; he causes her death. These are two paired functions in Propp's morphology: interdiction (g gamma) and violation (d^1 delta[1]):[4] in narrative terms, however, they do not occur at the beginning but come in as if put off until the explanations by Proteus ("You are expiating great sins committed," 454).

After the transgression the punishment gets inflicted on Aristaeus by the nymphs; that is the loss of the bees ("bees lost . . . by disease and hunger," 318): this obviously is Propp's narrative function "lack" (↑).

The hero reacts to the action of the antagonist and betakes himself to his mother ("fleeing Peneian Tempe," 317), stopping at Peneus's source: in order to reach his mother, Aristaeus will undertake a journey that, as often in this phase of a tale, partakes of the miraculous: a wandering in which every sort of adventure may confront the hero, as Propp says (visit to the underwater kingdoms, 360). Again, we have two moments from Propp's schematization: "hero reacts" (E) and "hero departs" (↑).

Learning of the grief of her son, Cyrene urges him to ask the reason for his misfortunes from Proteus and instructs him how to overcome the seer's reluctance ("There is in Carpathian," 387; "to be caught with chains," 396): here in the narrative we have the "first function of the donor" (D), hence the "test of the hero" (D[1]).

Following his mother's advice, Aristaeus passes the test and succeeds in learning the reasons for his troubles (418ff.). Here the narrative function is "hero reacts to donor's act" (E) and precisely "hero's victory in combat" (E[9]).

At this point, for compositional reasons, Proteus inserts the tale of the misfortunes of Orpheus into the main tale. Now Cyrene explains to Aristaeus how to placate the angered nymphs by sacrificing to them four bulls and four heifers not yet set to the yoke (531ff.): here the narrative function evidently is "receipt of magical agent" (F).

Aristaeus follows his mother's dictates in great detail and carries out the sacrifice (548ff.): by now we have reached the narrative moment of "struggles with the villain" (H), obviously a wholly metaphorical clash.

Finally, the bees are reborn from the viscera of the sacrificed animals (554ff.): in Propp's functions. this is "liquidation of misfortune or lack" (K).

The Disharmonic Tale of Orpheus

In similar fashion, we can also subject the tale of Orpheus to morphological analysis. At the beginning, both "interdiction" and "violation" are lacking: we shall find them further along. In compensation, the tale is articulated, unlike that of Aristaeus, into a classic opposition, as described by Propp, between a hero-victim (Eurydice) and a hero-searcher (Orpheus). Orpheus has suffered misfortune, losing his wife, Eurydice, through the fault of Aristaeus ("wife snatched away," 456). First Orpheus reacts to the loss ("consoling himself," 464), then he leaves for the underworld (467ff.). In terms of narrative function, this is not so much "departure, hero's dispatch before encountering donor" (↑) as it is "transference to designated place before struggle with antagonist" (G, H). Thus, the underwater journey (↑) of Aristaeus and the underground journey (G, H) of Orpheus do not correspond functionally in narrative. The two stories differ in this respect. Orpheus already possesses the "magical agent" (the power of song) and thus does not need to encounter a donor. Instead, Aristaeus needs to "make a journey" to meet a donor and thus enter into possession of the "magical agent." Orpheus, in short, functions as his own "helper."

Going on, the hero clashes with the antagonist (471ff.), compelling the underworld gods to give him back Eurydice (485ff.): in this way, the "loss suffered" is repaired. At this point, however, the tale takes its most original turn; for an interdiction is imposed on

Orpheus ("Prosperine set this *lex*," 487), which consists in not turning to look at Eurydice until they are outside of the underworld. Orpheus, however, breaks it by turning (490ff.). At this point the tale, in a certain sense, starts over: or better, ought to start over. The hero undergoes another "misfortune" by losing his wife again (491ff.). He reacts with the sadness of his song (as he had done the first time), weeping for seven months before the solitary Strymon (507ff.). This time, however, his reaction leads to no positive development: instead, Orpheus commits a new violation (520ff.). He scorns the love of the Ciconian mothers[5] and thus undergoes the ultimate loss (killing of the hero, 522ff.).

From the viewpoint of form, the tragedy of Orpheus consists of a tale that ought to start over at a certain point (with the narrative functions of interdiction and violation), but breaks off, with doubling of the loss, followed even by its tripling: a tripling that becomes the hero's fall. In short, this tale snaps and turns back, as if the thread drawn out so far, suddenly rolled itself back into the wool. From the viewpoint of narrative morphology, the phase of inaction (the song, the tears, etc.) displaces the expected "hero reacts" (E), a reaction from which ought to spring the continuation of the tale. The hero's inaction fits, instead, with the statute we may call elegiac that characterizes Virgil's version of Orpheus.

Having conducted a morphological analysis, we may venture some comparative reflections of a more general order. A certain number of sources would have us believe that Orpheus's venture into Hades originally ended in success: that he brought Eurydice back to life.[6] There was a widespread version of the myth in which what we have analyzed morphologically as a second beginning of the tale (interdiction—violation—hero's new loss) did not take place: the tale unfolded in normal fashion from initial loss (death of the heroine Eurydice) to its repair (Orpheus takes her out of the underworld). In contrast, the Virgilian version (which it may be called: even if Virgil did not invent it, he did prefer it, which is enough), with its second beginning left so painfully unrealized, imposes on the story a negative turn, unsatisfying: what comes out (in terms of the structure of the plot) is a form that is disharmonic and in a certain way deformed, a story in which the finale to be expected (after the introduction of the second beginning) does not arrive. At the level of the text, this disappointment means, of course, that a hymn to love, and to happiness in love, gets transformed into a desperate story of unhappiness. We hardly need underline how much this version fits Virgil's way of imagining the affairs of love. But at the level of the structure, this unhappy love, all too Virgilian, corresponds to the disharmony that arises between what is expected from the new beginning launched in the tale and what, instead, does not come.

This same disharmonic structure, however, may actually push, as in the *Orfeo* written by Calzabigi for Gluck's opera, toward the introduction of a second happy ending: Love intervenes and saves the girl a second time from death. This solution, which Calzabigi carries out in a manner far from mechanical,[7] might be said to be naturally implied, at the level of the narrative structure, by the presence of the functions "interdiction/violation/hero's new loss." It is as if "one could not stand to see" a story set up in that way end without repairing the loss. The effort of the post-Virgilian Orpheus appears, then, directed to neutralizing the intrusion of an unresolved second beginning, which had been quite unknown to the story before Virgil. The struggle against unhappy and hopeless love becomes, on the level of narrative morphology, a tiresome and sometimes ingenuous struggle against the painful inventiveness of the poet who turned the blessed descent of Orpheus into a tale with disharmonic structure.

Intertextuality and Folk-Tale Motifs

Our morphological analysis thus far may let us understand better the distribution of the numerous intertextual loans in the Aristaeus episode and, in any case, of the literary inserts into the narrative continuum. Let us begin with the beginning. The paired sequence of functions (interdiction/violation) allows the poet to interpose within the first a second narrative (Orpheus-Eurydice): the technique is well known also to students of folklore and belongs to pretty much any storyteller's bag of tricks.[8] Let us see, then, how the technique actually works out.

Greek literature has no trace of Aristaeus intervening to cause the death of Eurydice.[9] One simply hears that the girl died of snakebite on her wedding day (a relatively frequent motif in folklore).[10] Thus, it is fairly clear how Virgil behaved, if, as we believe, he did take the stitch (but even if someone else did before him, it would hardly matter). He simply added a causal nexus to the familiar motif: Eurydice was bitten by a snake *because* Aristaeus was pursuing her, breaking the ban against committing adultery.

The result is a narrative sequence created by digging, as it were, backward into the chain of events: the narrative pattern employed is evidently that of the nymphs desired and hunted down by pastoral gods. Hence, in this tale the paired narrative functions, interdiction (g gamma[1])/violation (d^1 delta[1]) appears as if stretched out into a bridge leading to the second tale: a tale that contains itself, as in a frame, within the first. This second tale is what would be called a new narrative *partie* in the rather elegant metaphor of Lévi-Strauss: *partie* in the sense of "section" and, simultaneously, "game" (like playing a second hand at bridge, with different cards but the same rules).[11] In Virgil's specific case, the employment of narrative inset is implicit in choosing Proteus, with the activity typical of a seer, to construct the narrative function of the hero's ordeal: already in Homer, the Proteus episode gave occasion to insert into the main body of the narrative more than one further tale (both the betrayal and the death of Agamemnon).

To continue with our analysis, the reaction (E) of the hero Aristaeus appears surrounded by what Propp would call a "rudimentary trebling": the hero's complaints by Peneus's waters, with his calls to his mother, Cyrene.[12] To construct this moment in the tale, which comes at the beginning of the narrative sequence, Virgil works with two Homeric episodes in which Achilles complains by the waters of the sea and is heard by his mother, Thetis (*Il.* 1.348ff., 18.35ff.). Virgil's very "choice of donor" (D), in the figure of a mother from beneath the water, appears to have been implied by the same model. With the hero's reaction and his complaints, we arrive at the beginning of the tale: and Norden put it very well, "It is not always easy for an epic poet to get his narration going."[13]

Onto this general coincidence with Homer's narrative situation (identical reaction by the hero, E; identical "choice of donor," D), Virgil, then, grafted a whole series of quite evident expressive debts, especially to book one of the *Iliad*.[14] Here I shall underline in passing only one trace that is more hidden, and therefore less remarked: little remarked, it seems, even by Virgilian exegetes, who have not, I believe, flagged it so far.

Book eighteen of the *Iliad* seems present, not only in the general motif of the list of nymphs, Ocean's daughters, but also in a singular calque. One verse, *Drymoque Xanthoque Ligeaque Phyllodoceque* (*Geo.* 4.336), reproduces Homer's *Doto te Proto te Perousa te Dynamene te* (*Il.* 18.43): identical the pattern of dactyls alternating with spondees, identical the disposition of the connectives (*-que* and *te*), and, above all, their lengthening, in the arsis of the second foot before a consonantal doublet, X ($= cs$) and Pr.[15] In the lengthy ledger of Homer's loans to Virgil, this entry appears especially strange: here Virgil has borrowed only an empty mold, made of a well-individualized series of longs and shorts, of connectives, of prosodic facts, and so forth, and he has filled it with new contents, changing one for one the names that appeared in Homer and replacing them with others of the same formal properties.

Virgil, however, also transforms Homer's generic gathering of the daughters of Ocean around Thetis (*amphageronto, Il.* 1.37) into a delicate domestic scene of spinning: as if around a *materfamilias* were gathered maids and girls intent on work, but even more enchanted by the tales that one of them was telling. I do not know whether these "sweet thefts" of Mars and Venus and the other loves of gods from Chaos down, which Clymene was spinning out, constitute an echo, almost a downplaying, of the theft attempted by Aristaeus. But certainly this scene, with its mythic simplicity, with the magic of telling stories as a backdrop for the timeless nobility of women's work, was to yield thematic treasure for the poets.[16]

Homer has provided the material for these two narrative functions, "hero reacts" (E) and "choice of donor" (D, the mother);[17] Homer has served to make the connective moment that I styled, in Proppian fashion, "rudiments of trebling" ("hero's lament"). Another author, Bacchylides (a dithyramb, 17 Snell), seems to have been tapped for the loan to construct the function "hero departs"

(↑), the journey of Aristaeus. Generally, Virgil's and Bacchylides' texts are not very profoundly compared by scholars,[18] but they deserve particular attention. Not simply does the legend of Theseus visiting the abyss, known also from other sources, such as Pausanias (1.17.2) and Hyginus (*Astr.* 2.5), show a substantial affinity with Aristaeus's journey to the source of all waters. A series of comparisons can also be made between the text of Virgil and that of Bacchylides, even though the latter is much more elusive and condensed than the former, comparisons that could lead one to think that Virgil actually used this Greek author as his model in reworking for Aristaeus the canvas of the adventure of Theseus.[19]

Bacchylides tells the story thus. Theseus, traveling toward Crete with the youths and maidens destined to become victims of the Minotaur, falls into argument with King Minos over his own origins. The king declares himself ready to prove that he is son of Zeus (and, in effect, a thunderclap will provide proof), hence let Theseus prove that he is son of Poseidon. Minos throws a ring into the sea, and Theseus dives in to fish it out. Led by dolphins to the dwelling of Amphitrite, Theseus is received by her with the gift of a crown, as well as a "fringed scarf" with magical properties.[20] Afterward, he reappears on the surface, to the joy of the youths and maidens. But let us look at the possible points of comparison with Virgil.

When Theseus takes Minos's dare and plunges into the sea, Bacchylides describes his contact with the waters: "sea grove received him willingly" (84–85), which corresponds fairly well to the like moment when Aristaeus ventures into the unknown element: "Him . . . wave received . . . in ample gulf" (360–61). Furthermore, Bacchylides writes of Theseus: "He went to the gods' hall, . . . seeing Nereus's famous daughters, he marveled" (*edeise,* 100–103).[21] And Virgil writes of Aristaeus: "Then marveling, he went to his mother's house and by the waters' monstrous rush was struck dumb" (363–64). Both passages share the theme of the hero's wonder, or reverent fear.

Also from Bacchylides might come certain details of the picture, such as the poet's lingering over the hairdos of the underwater goddesses: Bacchylides says of the daughters of Ocean, "Gold-braided fillets twirled about their locks" (105–6); Drymo, Xanthus, and the others in Virgil are pictured "pouring gleaming hair over white necks" (337).

This section of Virgil's narrative invites us, however, to go deeper still. It is likely enough that Virgil used Bacchylides directly here (even though, on the basis of the comparisons just offered, the matter cannot be called absolutely certain). Nevertheless we would not wish to be reduced to a mere search for sources, which would risk greatly impoverishing Virgil's text and would keep from view what may be the most fascinating side of the episode. Because Greek mythology tells numerous other stories of descents to the depths of the sea, stories that fit, in all likelihood, into the larger historico-religious context of *katapontismos*—a rubric usually comprising the rich complex of rites and beliefs that assigns "descent" and "dive" or just "getting wet" the significance of basic rites of passage.[22] Such stories present quite interesting parallels with Virgil's episode, foremost among them the famous leap into the sea by Dionysus (pursued by Lycurgus), where the god is received "in the bosom" of Thetis (*Il.* 6.130ff.).[23] Also from the *Iliad* comes the story of Hephaestus, driven out by his mother and received at the bottom of the sea by Thetis and Euronyme (*Il.* 18.395ff.): in the depths, the crippled god works on metals for nine years, accomplishing his apprenticeship as a smith.[24] But Eumolpus, too, the mythical progenitor of the Eumolpid priesthood, is another hero thrown into the sea by his mother, received by Poseidon, and entrusted to the care of the daughters of Ocean.[25] As others have underlined,[26] these mythic narratives all share a common trait: their heroes all are young, and in their experiences beneath the sea they are received, or even nurtured, by the daughters of Ocean. Theseus, too, fits perfectly into this category. The function of Ocean's daughters in these myths corresponds—as Jeanmaire remarked,[27] comparing Hesiod, *Theogony* 346ff.—to the quality of "nurse-for-heroes" possessed *par excellence* by these goddesses.

Such journeys into the marine depths bear the stamp of a relationship that is somewhat maternal.[28] The heroes who go through this experience are youths who find, in the depths, certain female beings that receive them in all good will or even bring them up.

For an interpreter to yield to a psychoanalytic temptation in such cases would be only too easy. So we do not. Instead, we underline how the journey or sojourn under water constitutes an experience of passage (well named so by Van Gennep), which has fundamental import: after it, the heroes emerge to a truly new life. Regarding stories of this sort, Jeanmaire has spoken of experience that can lead to "initiations diverses":[29] almost a multifunctional stage able to direct the hero toward new paths of diverse kinds and meanings.

If, therefore, the episode of Aristaeus's descent corresponds in some of its formal traits to Bacchylides' text, this must not make us forget that such a descent finds parallels in a much wider typology of mythic tales. Like Theseus, like Dionysus, like Hephaestus, like Eumolpus, so, too, Aristaeus is a young hero who goes under water to get to a female who is markedly maternal. Like the other heroes, Aristaeus will also emerge from the experience with a new statute (he has learned what to do to overcome his troubles), a statute he actually obtains because of his kind reception by the mistress of the waters. If, then, we must actually speak of the "initiation" of Aristaeus, using a term that is so ambiguous and, frequently, so empty, we ought to speak of it in the way that this mythic tradition suggests and delimits.[30] We must, in other words, compare Virgil's Aristaeus to the type of the young hero who, by means of an underwater journey and meeting with a maternal figure who lives there, accomplishes his symbolic passage toward a successive state of his life.

We should not forget that Aristaeus, in Virgil's story, is on the way to founding a very important institution of ancient culture, the *bugonia*. Evidently, the undersea journey belongs to the process that guides him toward that foundation. Hence, in the structural terminology we have been using, we can say that Virgil constructs the function of "hero departs" (↑) by choosing a motif that conveyed in ancient culture a series of symbolic meanings that were very strong and deeply rooted: undersea journey to meet marine mother figure. It is surprising that readers of what we might call a symbolistic bent pay attention to everything but the symbols that are really authorized by historico-religious tradition. Above all, these symbols are much more beautiful and fascinating than those that, generally speaking, an everyday modern critic can think up sitting at his desk.

Leaving behind Aristaeus's underwater flight, let us continue with our reckoning of Virgil's other debts. Virgil composes his version of Propp's "hero tested by donor" (D¹) with loans from the episode in the *Odyssey* of Menelaus and Proteus, taking some liberties and causing no little trouble for modern interpreters. In particular, some have found the insert superfluous, even a failure.[31] They ask whether Cyrene by herself would not have sufficed to reveal to Aristaeus not only the remedy but also the cause of his trouble. I confess to scant propensity for problems of this sort. Therefore, I limit myself to a consideration at our chosen level of analysis (structure of the narrative; although others, obviously, could be added): Cyrene appears here in the role of "donor of magical agent," whereas Proteus belongs specifically to the segment of the "test" imposed by the donor. Thus, the two personages perform quite different functions in the narrative and do not constitute a mere duplication. Eliminating one to satisfy the taste of some modern reader would result in a story no doubt closer to the economy of verisimilitude, but sure to be infinitely poorer: of the type of Ovid's very brief summary of the myth (*Fast.* 1.363–80).

In other words, those who complain about the overly copious nature of the two episodes risk, at very least, letting themselves be drawn off course by what ought to be defined as "motivations" (again following Propp), which are those "how's" and "why's" that mediate the passage from one sequence to another: motivations that may well show slippage, and sometimes be even contradictory.[32] From the standpoint of narrative structure, Proteus ought not to be seen as the one who knows the cause of Aristaeus's troubles, but rather as one who resists being mastered and thus puts the hero to the test.[33] Proteus knows the cause of the trouble by motivation, but is protean and monstrous by function.

The articulation of narrative segments that emerges in adapting Propp's model to the particular needs and nature of Virgil's narrative, also provides a structure for the individual literary debts, numerous and massive as they are, that figure in this episode. Apply

239

the term "motifs" to these diverse loans and we find something quite familiar, a custom deeply rooted in fairy-tale production. Motifs in the realm of fairy tale pass from one story to another with enormous ease, so much so that folklorists speak of an actual "law of transferability" to describe the phenomenon, which is in some fashion a matter of filling the several functions in the most attractive possible manner and, at the same time, with the greatest possible freedom. It could be this general "fairy-tale morphology," at the level (so to speak) of literary behavior, that actually explains the fullness (read by some as superficiality) with which Virgil filled his plate with others' texts and episodes, indeed picking out episodes—such as the transformations of Proteus, the underwater descent, the girl bitten by a snake the day of her wedding—that show a strongly folkloric and fairy-tale character. The concentration of such episodes in a single text reinforces, of course, the fairy-tale quotient of the episode. Hence Virgil, feeling free from the requirements of the story (or, in any event, from the fixity of a mythic text given once and for all), told a fairy tale. Naturally, he told one that could well conclude an Augustan poem such as the *Georgics,* and in a suitable fashion.

From Tale to Myth

We have seen how morphological analysis of an episode in Virgil can lead to some results and a certain clarification. We cannot stop here, however. To be sure, we have related the story to a familiar, common matrix, providing a solid and useful viewpoint to give focus to individual literary achievements or intertextual loans. But it would be unsatisfying to end without a word about the hero of the affair and what befalls him: without deigning, that is, even one glance at the fact that Aristaeus lost his bees, that he tried to commit adultery and practically made himself responsible for a murder, that he does not know how to regain his property, that he needs to get a seer, and so forth. In short, we know all the resemblances, but not the differences: and yet it is the differences and disjunctions that give grounds for meaning. To be sure, we have employed Propp's work as a "grammar or a textbook of harmony," to recall his own metaphor from music,[34] and now we are clearer about the rules for constructing a piece. But what about the concrete sense, the specificity, of the piece? We could almost wish to expand on the metaphor: by putting aside the characters, attributes, and motivations,[35] in short, by reducing Virgil's episode to its more or less anonymous form, it is as if we had applied the rules of a harmony handbook to a piece meant to be sung.

Analysis of the harmonic base does produce some results and a certain amount of clarity; but hardly enough. What remains outside is the text that combines with that base, as well as the overall meaning of this combination. What remains, then, is that the Aristaeus tale, besides being composed more or less by the typical rules of a certain folkloric base, is always one of the stories that the well-known mythic hero Aristaeus gathers around himself as part of his legend. And, however much Virgil's narrative is a folk tale, it also functions always as a myth: it ends in a discovery; it is the foundation myth of *bugonia*. Only take the paradigm from a different viewpoint, lining up on the grid of analogy no longer the narrative functions, but the names, the attributes, the places, the typical actions that the several variants give us for Aristaeus, and everything changes in our hands: each and every detail, even the slightest, becomes meaningful. Here lies the passage from the narrative functions to the mythic contents: or, if we prefer, to the structures from the forms.

So we set out to reconsider something that until now we had neglected: the personage of Aristaeus; that is, the problem of his present identity as compared with that identity known from the other sources of his legend. Employing this language takes us back, of course, to those valuable handwritten notes that Saussure devoted to the Niebelungs and to the problems of the mythic personage in general.[36] Here we do not need to debate that matter. It is enough to recall that Saussure, before Propp, had intuited, on the one hand, the role of the functions in analyzing legendary personages (function means actions) but, on the other hand, also tied to it the importance of "name," "position with respect to others," and "character." In other words, Saussure reintroduced content into the pure form of the functional relationships.

What is the "character" of Virgil's Aristaeus? One Greek source called him "a man outstanding for intelligence (*synesis*) and discretion (*sophrosyne*) and every sort of discipline (*paideia*)" (Diodorus Siculus 3.70.1); this picture seems very far, not to say completely removed, from that of the *Georgics*. Where is the sagacity of a man who cannot understand what befalls him and has to consult a seer, who cannot figure out how to remedy his ills and has to turn to his mother? Where are the discretion or temperance of an adulterer and involuntary homicide?

The same goes for his *paideia*: in Virgil, Aristaeus really shows none. Yet the characterization by Diodorus fits very well what Greek myths hand down about Aristaeus. Hence, we can begin to see what principle lets us describe Aristaeus's identity in Virgil: reversal. The Latin Aristaeus takes shape, within certain limits, as the opposite of the Greek one. Transplanted into the *Georgics,* the hero is no longer himself. We would like to ask him a very Virgilian question: "What madness seized you?" But let us see more closely what the Greek myth tells us and also look for other signs.

Aristaeus is a great cultural hero. Reared by the Nymphs, he is responsible for not only apiculture but also taming the olive, inaugurating the arts of pasturing and raising cattle,[37] discovering hunting and what curdles milk for cheese, and so on.[38] But other details interest us even more. Aristaeus marries Autonoe in a perfectly regular matrimony (Nonnus, *Dion.* 5.217), which is particularly satisfying for the family of the bride (5.218ff.): the girl was chosen by the Nymphs (scholiast in Apollonius Rhodius 2.511), who in this case, too, play the role of teachers and guides for the hero. The Greek myth involves Aristaeus in no other sentimental relations or sexual adventures—naturally an obvious part of his discretion, his temperance, but one that implies above all a precise cultural meaning. We know that the bees, chaste animals *par excellence* (e.g., *Geo.* 4.197ff.), hate those who let themselves go in luxury and lust.[39]

The sexual temperance of Aristaeus, master and founder of apiculture, hence stands as an essential corollary to the cultural picture from which the figure arises. In Virgil, by contrast, Aristaeus becomes an adulterer. Moreover, he rises against the Nymphs, his nurses and protectresses, seeking to possess one of their number and causing her death. No wonder they show outrage against their ward: Aristaeus is not only an intemperate and adulterous bee-keeper but also an ungrateful rebel. The reversals in Virgil follow a rather clear line. The sexual behavior of this Latin Aristaeus resembles that of his son, Acteon. Acteon also became guilty of a transgression of this sort, and was punished for it, when he lusted for the goddess Artemis,[40] chastity itself.

In Virgil's version, once the bees are lost, Aristaeus cannot understand why. His bewilderment is strange. The Nymphs had taught him the prophetic art (Apollonius Rhodius 2.512).[41] In Virgil, however, he cannot see anything without the help of a personage gifted with divinatory powers, Proteus. The Nymphs had also taught Aristaeus the art of medicine (2.512): an ample account of his capability in this field appears in Nonnus (*Dion.* 17.357ff.). Aristaeus even knows the secret of bringing back to life rams that have been killed and even cut apart (Oppian, *Cyn.* 4.280). What should be said, then, of a medical man capable of nothing less than bringing animals back from the dead, yet not knowing how to proceed when his own bees perish of disease and hunger? He will need help from his mother, Cyrene, who tells him what to do. Let us dwell for a moment on this point because it is especially instructive.

Cyrene and Proteus fill specific functions in the narrative: as donor and as object of test. Now we look at them as contents of the narrative; that is, bearers of meaning. They are the ones that bring out Aristaeus's loss of powers to work wonders (Cyrene) and to prophesy (Proteus), which typify the hero elsewhere, but here are assigned to other personages. This double focus of Proteus and Cyrene, both narratological (as functions) and anthropological (in competency, powers), does not detract from either viewpoint: the narrative forms and mythic contents do not exclude each other, but, indeed, must be imagined as fused into one. In other words, a text can organize its narrative according to the patterns identified by Propp, or their variants. But as in the language, so also in the literary text (which is, after all, a hierarchically more organized formation of the language) the morphologico-syntactic and the semantic aspects are not distinguishable, if not with respect to the two viewpoints of the analyst. One has to find the meaning of that which is organized according to a certain syntax.

This problem of the disease and the famine that wiped out the bees, which is central in Virgil, reminds us of one of the most famous deeds of Aristaeus, carried out on Ceos. The island was tormented by the raging rays of Sirius (Apollonius Rhodius 2.216), and indeed a raging plague was ravaging all of Greece (Diodorus Siculus 4.82). On the advice of Apollo, his father, Aristaeus betakes himself to the island, where he carries out a sacrifice to Zeus Ikmaios; then the Etesian winds come up, counteracting the furious influence of Sirius and halting the plague. Aristaeus also teaches the inhabitants of Ceos the rite to make the miracle repeat year after year, summoning the benign breezes.[42] Parenthetically, let us add that the episode in question is recalled by Virgil, who translates the allusion, however, into the oblique form of a determination of time. And it does not seem that Virgil's interpreters have remarked on this link between texts. When Aristaeus betakes himself to Proteus's grotto, we read, "And now blazing Sirius, scorching the thirsty Indians, was burning in the heaven" (*Geo.* 4.425–26).

These specific indications have no counterpart in the Homeric original. Instead, Virgil's text seems modeled on a verse that Apollonius used just where he began describing Aristaeus's exploit on Ceos: "When from heaven Sirius was burning the Minoan islands" (2.516–17). Evidently, Virgil changed the use of the citation, for it no longer serves to describe an event inserted in the narrative (Sirius infesting the Minoan islands), but simply specifies the time (the season in which Sirius torments the thirsty Indians): the relations between the two texts, however, are only too clear. What follows, then, in Virgil ("and the fiery sun had finished half its round"), is a well-known paraphrase of the like temporal sign that tells Menelaus it is time to hasten to Homer's version of the grotto of Proteus: "But when the sun had reached midheaven" (*Od.* 4.400). In short, Virgil has combined in one passage both the letter and the structure of his two sources. From Apollonius comes the indication of the season;[43] from Homer, the time of day. With this addition of the season, not in Homer and suggested by Apollonius, Aristaeus carries out his undertaking under the sign that best represents him: Sirius.

Let us return to the myth we were analyzing. In his Cean adventure, Aristaeus faces a plague from which he frees the islanders and all Greece by carrying out a sacrifice. The skeleton of the story is absolutely identical to that in our Virgilian variant: by skeleton, I mean, of course, not the formal pattern (Propp) filled by no matter what contents at various times, but the structure that organizes certain particular and motivated contents (plague, rules of sacrifice, liberation, founding a stable cultural institution). However, from the Greek version of the Cean undertaking to Virgil's *bugonia,* change occurs on a large scale in the specific capacities of the hero. In Virgil, Aristaeus cannot see the reasons for the plague on his bees and gets others to tell him the rules of the saving sacrifice. In the Greek myth, Aristaeus in person saves an identical situation and carries out the liberating sacrifice.

By now we have a reference myth by which to interpret Virgil's variant as a reversal. Around this basic reversal are arrayed all the collateral reversals we have discussed, such as "marriage/adultery," "temperate beekeeper/illicit sex," "nurture by nymphs/pursuit to death of nymph," "gift of prophecy/need of prophet," "capability of restoring animals to life/incapability of restoring bees": all these reversals constitute the cultural score, with the key signature of reversal set at the head of the staff, that gets performed in Virgil's text.

This key signature may need some explanation. Myth is not an empty pattern that each person uses, filling it out it at will. To assert that means probably confusing the generic nature of the form with the specific nature of the structure (in a certain sense, the abstract with the concrete). Recalling the problem formulated by Saussure, which was mentioned earlier, I remain convinced that the mythic personage must vary "within certain limits."[44] These limits are imposed by the basic skeleton of the myth, and their validity is certainly not weakened by transformations describable as a correlated set.

The key employed in the Virgilian text changes from what we find in the Greek variants, but it does constitute a system in equilibrium with respect to the precedents. Aristaeus remains ever a cultural hero, and to him, now, gets attributed an accomplishment that had not been assigned (so it seems) to the Greek Aristaeus: *bugonia*. Virgil's hero, however, accomplishes this by following the devious route of crime and reparation. The adventure of Virgil's Aristaeus thus takes shape as a story of madness and its progressive and laborious redemption in culture. The moment of the invention, the event that marks the beginning of a new cultural practice, gets presented, with a strong narrative twist, in the form of a passage from one state of calm, in which there were no problems but also no techniques (in particular, that special technique), to a state that was ambiguous but, by that very fact, comforted by cultural inventiveness. The nucleus of this twist, which is both narrative and cultural, is specifically constituted by the presence of crime. Actually having committed a crime that weakens the canny inventor and "lord of techniques" to the point of making him into his opposite: an incapable—or, perhaps better, a kind of mediated—inventor, who only by steps, and with the decisive help of others, manages to master the new technique he needs.

Hence, the crime holds the key to the entire series of reversals which characterize the Virgilian variant (in the pattern of correlations we mentioned). An Aristaeus transgressor and criminal is, correlatively, an Aristaeus nonprophet, nonphysician, and so forth. The result is a singular story about a cultural hero who does the opposite of what he usually does, in order to present humanity with a gift like the many others he has already given. The formal structure of this story is, in many respects, that of folk tale, of a story like many others. But now that we have reintroduced attributes, names and contents generally, we can realize also how much this story differs from so many others.

Notes

Preface

1. F. Schlegel, "Frammenti del 'Lyceum,'" in *Frammenti critici e scritti di estetica,* ed. V. Santoli (Florence, 1937 = 1967), p. 20.

Part One. "Uncle me no uncle!": Relatives in the Archaic Roman Family

1. Which does not mean that study of such contingencies might not uncover the sort of characteristics that are systematic, although unperceived. But this is another matter.
2. I refer to the well-known study by C. Lévi-Strauss, "Structural Analysis in Linguistics and Anthropology," in *Structural Anthropology,* tr. C. Jacobson and B. G. Schoepf (Garden City, N.Y., 1963), pp. 29ff., in which he first worked out the notion of "Atom of Kinship," which I discuss in detail in chap. 6 below. Lévi-Strauss refined this concept, in response to various critics, in "Reflections on the Atom of Kinship," in *Structural Anthropology,* tr. M. Layton (New York, 1963), 2:82ff, and in "Un 'atome de parenté' australien," in *Le regard éloigné* (Paris, 1983), pp. 93ff. Also by Lévi-Strauss, see the essay "La famiglia," in *Razza e storia e altri studi di antropologia* (Turin, 1967), pp. 147ff., as well as the chapter on interindividual relations in *La vita familiare e sociale degli indiani Nambikwara* (Milan, 1970), pp. 81ff. Also on the question of attitudes, see bibliographical notes in chap. 6 below.
3. *Frater (soror) patruelis* (descended from a father's brother), *consobrinus* (descended from a mother's sister), *amitinus* (descended from a fa-

ther's sister), and *avunculi filius* (descended from a mother's brother). But *consobrinus* was becoming widely used for all four types of cousins by the first century B.C. (On the terminology for cousins, I intend to publish a special study in *Athenaeum*: see also the discussion of *matruelis*, which remains problematic, in chap. 4 below.)

4. Cf. the precise remarks in J. Goody, *L'evolution de la famille et du mariage en Europe* (Paris, 1984), pp. 265ff.

5. R. T. Anderson, "Changing Kinship in Europe," *Kroeber Anthr. Soc.* 28 (1963):1ff.; also Goody, *L'evolution,* pp. 365ff. Only recently, too late to utilize it here, have I seen Judy Hallett, *Fathers and Daughters in Roman Society* (Princeton, 1984).

Chapter One. Father: Pater

1. Cf. also Livy 2.41.10 (the private trial undergone by Spurius at his father's hands and his sentence to death), 8.7.1, and so forth. Concerning the severity of fathers in Rome, see also R. Önnerfors, *Vaterporträts in der römischen Poesie* (Stockholm, 1974), pp. 11ff., a work carried out, of course, from a viewpoint quite other than the anthropological one of interest us here. But see, above all, A. Peruzzi, *Le origini di Roma* (Florence, 1970), pp. 150ff., on the father's power over the sons.

2. Cf. also Valerius Maximus 5.10.1: "Concerning Parents Who Brought About Their Children's Death with a Stern Spirit."

3. Livy 2.8.8; cf. E. Pais, *Storia di Roma* (Rome, 1927), p. 109.

4. Besides, the instances of the indulgence and moderation of fathers toward their children, given in Valerius Maximus (5.7.1, 5.8.1), point to a much later historical time. On the evolution of the father figure in Rome, see Önnerfors, *Vaterporträts in der römischen Poesie.*

5. Cf. Cicero, *Off.* 3.112; Livy 7.4.1 and 7.5.7; Valerius Maximus 5.4.3 and 6.9.1; Auctor, *Vir. Ill.* 3.28.1; Appian, *Samn.* 2; Zonar. 7.24; and Münzer, *RE* 14.1179. On the theme of sons rusticated by fathers, see Cicero, *Sext. Rosc.* 42.

6. Cf. Cicero, *Off.* 3.112; and Valerius Maximus 5.4.3.

7. Cf. Livy 8.6.14 and 7.22; 11.7; 12.1, 4; 30.13; 34.2; 35.9; and 24.37.9. Cf also Frontinus, *Stat.* 4.1.40; Cicero, *Fin.* 2.60; Valerius Maximus 5.8.3; Gellius, *Noct. Att.* 1.13.7; and so forth.

8. On the like behavior of Postumius Tubertus, see Livy 4.9.6; and Valerius Maximus 2.7.6 ("generals' axes flowing with their own blood").

9. On the imperiousness of the Manli (besides Önnerfors, *Vaterporträts in der römischen Poesie*), see also the acute remarks in R. G. Nisbet,

CQ 9 (1959):73ff.; following a suggestion in Münzer (*RE* 14.1193), he finds an ironical hint of this theme in Horace, *Epist.* 1.5.5.

10. Valerius Maximus 5.8.3; Livy, *Perioch.* 54; and cf. Münzer, *RE* 14.1210ff.

11. Cf. Lévi-Strauss, "Reflections on the Atom of Kinship," 2:82ff.

12. On the concept of avoidance, see ibid.

13. A famous study of avoidance occurs in J. G. Frazer, *The Golden Bough* (London, 1911; reprint, 1966), 3:83ff., pp. 338–346; but see, above all, H. A. Junod, *Moeurs et coutumes des Bantous* (Paris, 1936), 1:224ff.

14. S. Freud, "Totem and Taboo," in *The Standard Edition of the Complete Psychological Works of Sigmund Freud,* ed and tr. J. Strachey et al., 24 vols. (London, 1953–73), 13:21ff.

15. Cicero, *De orat.* 2.224; *Off.* 1.129; *Pro Cluent.* 141; *De Rep.* 4.4; and Valerius Maximus 2.1.7. The passage in Plutarch goes unremarked by Rose in his commentary. We should recall, too, that father-in-law and son-in-law could not even exchange gifts, according to Plutarch, *Quaest. Rom.* 8.

16. Plutarch, *Cato Maior* 20. Particularly interesting is the context of reflections in which Cicero mentions this avoidance (*Off.* 1.128.)

17. See A. R. Radcliffe-Brown, "Le parentele di scherzo," in *Struttura e funzione nella società primitiva* (Milan, 1972), pp. 105ff. and 119ff. (*Altre osservazioni sulla parentela di scherzo*). Useful remarks are in J. Cazeneuve, *La sociologia del rito* (Milan, 1974), pp. 119ff. See also E. C. Parson, "Vitance," *L'anthropologie* 19 (1918–19):288ff. (cited in Cazeneuve); and L. Lévy-Bruhl, *Soprannaturale e natura nella mentalità primivita* (Milan, 1973), pp. 245ff.

18. M. Granet, *La civiltà cinese antica* (Turin, 1968).

19. Ibid. p. 293.

20. Ibid., p. 279.

21. Ibid., p. 303.

22. Lévi-Strauss, "Structural Analysis in Linguistics and Anthropology," pp. 29ff; and Lèvi-Strauss, "Reflections on the Atom of Kinship," 2:82ff.

23. For discussion of this passage, see G. Guastella, "I Parentalia come testo antropologico: L'avunculato nel mondo celtico e nella famiglia di Ausonio," *MD* 4 (1980):97ff., and 7 (1982):141ff.

24. Rose's reference to Horace, *Epist.* 2.1.109, is irrelevant.

25. In all likelihood, avoidance between father and young son among the Gauls formed part of the institution of fosterage, which had deep roots in Celtic society, whereby boys were reared by the maternal uncle or the mother's family (see remarks in Guastella, "I Parentalia come testo antropologico," and the references he cites). In this sys-

tem, there were close bonds between maternal uncle and nephew while the child was being reared, but avoidance between father and son (something analogous existed in ancient China according to Granet, *Catégories matrimoniales et relations de proximité dan la Chine ancienne* [Paris, 1939], pp. 278). This avoidance would diminish (or vanish, we do not know which) when the boy reached military age and left the mother's family. Something like the reverse appears to have been the case in Rome. We cannot say whether there was a corresponding reversal of the roles of maternal uncle and nephew during the different ages. If there was, we would have to assume that the nephew was close to his father and distant from his maternal uncle during childhood, then, as an adult, close to his maternal uncle and distant from his father. For this, we lack evidence. But we shall look at cases of close bonds between maternal uncles and adult nephews.

26. The differentiation of the ways in which *pater* and *mater* are expected to treat a son is spelled out well in Seneca, *Prov.* 2.5ff.; cf. Terence, *Heaut.*

27. See also Terence, *Heaut.* 101, which speaks of the "very familiar forceful way of fathers."

28. I have dealt with this subject in "Verso un'antropologia dell'intreccio: Le strutture semplici della trama nelle commedie di Plauto," *MD* 7 (1982):39ff., in which I also study other cases of father/son conflict in sexual matters.

29. The case of the new pedagogy of Terence differs greatly, especially in comedies such as *Adelphoe* or *Heauton timoroumenos*: see L. Perelli, *Il teatro rivoluzionario di Terenzio* (Florence, 1973): Terentian comedy documents a remarkable cultural change, especially in the relations between fathers and sons.

Chapter Two. Father's Brother: Patruus

1. Desiderius Erasmus, "Collectanea Adagiorum Veterum," in *Opera Omnia* (Leiden, 1703), 2:535.

2. The mistake is hardly rare. It occurs, for example, in the commentary of Kiessling-Heinze on Horace, *Sat.* 2.2.96, "der *patruus* . . . um das wohl des *nepos* . . . am meisten besorgt ist." Interestingly enough, the mistake occurs already in the two Paris manuscripts of Acro's commentary on Horace: "iudex durus quia patrui severiores sunt in nepotes" (7971 and 7973: Bphi Havthal). For the meaning and use of *nepos,* see below.

3. "Childhood games," literally, *nuces,* "nuts," with which the Roman

child played so commonly that they can mean, as here, simply "toys" or "games": cf. Seneca, *De ira* 1.14: Martial, 5.84.1; and Suetonius, *Aug.* 83.

4. The manuscript tradition troubled A. E. Housman, *M. Manilii Astronomicon,* vol. 5 (London, 1930), who shifted our verse (454) to after 457. Concerning the constellation of Cepheus and its relation to stern customs, see Th. Breitner, *M. Manilii Astronomicon* (Leipzig, 1908), 2:167. See below on *tutor.*

5. Although it is peripheral to our theme, for completeness we should mention here a brief mythological romance sprung from this Ciceronian speech. The rhetor Fortunatianus (*Rhet. Lat. Min.* 124, Halm) tells us that Atratinus called Caelius "pulchellum Iasonem." However, Quintilian reports that Caelius used the phrase "Pelias cincinnatus" (1.5.61), which could reasonably be taken as a rebuttal to Atratinus. Add Cicero's barb, "Palatine Medea" (18), aimed at Clodia, and a Jasonic plot emerges from behind the events. This mythological irony, above all so coherent and elegant, may be suggestive; but for our inquiry, the fact (noted in R. G. Austin, *Pro Caelio* [Oxford, 1933], p. 67) that Pelias was also Jason's paternal uncle is only accidental, as Austin observed, and irrelevant, because Atratinus ought to be "Pelias" and not "Herennius," the one whom Cicero termed a *patruus.*

6. On Gellius, see T. P. Wiseman, "Who Was Gellius?" in *Cinna the Poet* (Leicester, 1974), pp. 119ff.; and F. Della Corte, *Personaggi catulliani* (Florence, 1976), pp. 67ff.

7. I do not believe that the brother of Gallus here can be identified with the *patruus* of Gellius, or that the "charming son" in question is Gellius. At least the latter cannot be proven. Baehrens, *Catulli Veronensis Liber* (Leipzig, 1876), on 89.3f., thought that the two wives of fathers' brothers whom this epigram supposes as the young man's lovers (one actual, one potential) could be identified with the kindred girls of 89.3, with whom Gellius makes love. But Catullus would not call kindred (*cognatae*) women who for Gellius were only related by marriage (*adfines*). By the same token, I do not believe that the Catullan Gellius can be identified with that son of L. Gellius who was accused of illicit relations with his stepmother (Valerius Maximus 5.9.1), a hypothesis that goes back at least to L. Schwabe, *Questionum Catullianarum Liber* (Gissae, 1862), 1:110ff., and is repeated more or less by successive commentators. See, however, the historical-chronological discussion in Wiseman, "Who Was Gellius?" pp. 119ff. Catullus, in *Carm.* 88, 89, and 91, speaks expressly of "mother." Nor is this term applied to the "stepmother" to intensify the insult, as Baehrens by sleight of hand would have it: this we know from *Carm.* 90,

which declares that the unspeakable union between Gellius and his mother could produce a *magus,* according to the Persian tradition. Thus, it has to be a case of true incest with the mother.

8. The commentary of Plessis-Lejay (Paris, 1911), p. 347, evokes the figure of the "celibate uncle in a rural family" and assigns to the "neighbors" the character of "principle that regulates the morality of the country and small towns": an appropriate idea, though unprovable.

9. "Amori dare ludum" was studied in G. Pasquali, *Orazio lirico* (reprint, Florence, 1964), p. 87; and in C. W. Nauck, *Q. Horati Flacci Oden un Epoden* (Leipzig, 1889), p. 158, who writes: "*Dare ludum* witzig, nach der Analogie von *operam dare.*"

10. The role and figure of *patruus* here were studied in Pasquali, *Orazio lirico,* pp. 86ff., with useful comparisons of Greek and Roman practice, especially with regard to the differing position of the maternal uncle in tutelage of the child. See also the following note and below.

11. Cf. Polybius, 6.2.5, also in Athenaeus, 10.440; Plutarch, *Quaest. Rom.* 6; Gellius, 10.23; Pliny, *Hist. nat.* 14.90. See also the classic remarks in P. Noailles, *Fas et Ius* (Paris, 1948), pp. 1ff. (on the bar against wine). The same question is discussed in Pasquali, *Orazio lirico,* pp. 90ff. (although he does not relate the Horatian passage to the *ius osculi*). A broader and more generic sociological perspective is brought to bear on the two themes in S. B. Pomeroy, "The Relationship of the Married Woman to Her Blood Relatives in Rome," *Anc. Soc.* 7 (1976):215ff. More recently, see also L. Minieri, "Vini usus feminis ignotus," *Labeo* 28 (1982):150ff. Very interesting remarks on the women's position in archaic society are in A. Peruzzi, *Le origini di Roma* (Florence, 1970), pp. 75ff., with remarks on the bar to wine on pp. 40, 68, and 148.

12. Juan Luis de La Creda, *P. Vergili Maronis Opera Omnia* (Cologne, 1642), 2:676.

13. The union of niece with *patruus* was considered incestuous before the marriage between Claudius and Agrippina, daughter of his brother; afterward, it was permitted: Tacitus, *Ann.* 12.7; Gaius, *Inst.* 1.62; and Suetonius, *Claud.* 26. Clear testimony in this regard comes from Catullus 111, on Aufilena who is united with her *patruus:* "Sed cuiuis quavis potius succumbere par est / quam matrem fratres [te parere] ex patruo." Any union is preferable, says Catullus, to that of a niece who, by uniting herself with her uncle, produces "brothers" for herself: the sons of the *patruus* are classified as *fratres patrueles,* so Aufilena would at the same time have "brothers" in her own sons. What we need to remember, to understand this play on words, is its Oedipal nature, long before Seneca let loose on the incest *par excellence:*

for example (of Oedipus), "Fratres sibi ipse genuit . . . " (*Oed.* 640); and (of Oedipus again), "Frater suorum liberorum et fratrum parens" (*Phoen.* 125). Vertical incest consistently mingles brothers with sons (parallels that one would expect to find in the commentaries). In the case of Aufilena, then, we cannot interpret *patruus* as not her uncle, but as uncle to her sons; in other words, brother of her husband, as argued in W. de Grummond, *CW* (1970):120ff., properly corrected, with citation of numerous cases in which *frater = frater patruelis,* in A. C. Bush, *CW* 65 (1972):148ff.

In the case of Claudius and Agrippina, they were received with disfavor, and it was feared that the incest would cause natural calamities (on the Oedipal wordplay, see M. Bettini, "L'arcobaleno, l'incesto e l'enigma," in *Atti del Convegno di Siracusa sul Teatro Antico, Testo e Communicazione* [Siracusa, 1983–85]; and idem, "Lettura divinatoria di un incesto," *MD* 12 [1985]:145ff.). For the comic side of all this, which provokes witticism, see M. Bettini, "La stirpe di Iuno ovvero il metodo nella follia," forthcoming in *Studi in Onore di F. Della Corte.*

14. The whole question is quite complex and intricate, and it need not be addressed here: in general, see J. Perret, *Les origines de la légende Troyenne de Rome* (Paris, 1942).

15. Cf. M. Bettini and A. Borghini, "Il bambino e l'eletto," *MD* 3 (1979):121ff.

16. Whether the son of Numitor was called Lausus or Aigestos, Ainitios, or whatever: see the note in F. Bömer, *P. Ovidius Naso Die Fasten* (Heidelberg, 1958), 2:110, on *Fast.* 2.283.

17. If one were to take this line, one would have to see in Pelias, maternal uncle of Jason and his persecutor, an example of the severity of a *patruus.*

18. Cf. Plutarch, *Quaest. Rom.* 3.4. It would be interesting to study the attitudes among *fratres (sorores) patrueles.* The case of Rhea Silvia and her cousin seems to suggest that they behaved toward each other like *fratres germani (sorores germanae),* and this would appear to be the general situation: see the information collected in Bush, *CW* 65, which is useful, but to be used with caution because the interpretations are not always careful. See further below.

19. V. Propp, *Morphology of the Folktale,*[2] ed. Louis A. Wagner and tr. Laurence Scott (Austin, 1968), pp. 75–78; Italian trans., *Morfologia della fiaba* (Turin, 1966). See chaps. 3 and 17 below.

20. M. Barchiesi, *Nevio Epico* (Padova, 1962), pp. 524ff.

21. Gaius Claudius Salanus Inregillensis was consul in 460: see Münzer, *RE* 3 (1899):2863.

22. Nothing on this matter appears in the valuable work of R. M. Oglivie, *A Commentary on Livy, 1–5* (Oxford, 1965), p. 471. Oglivie notes only

that in Dionysius, G. Claudius pronounces a "long and turgid speech," in which Livy "casts him in a different mold, as the sententious appeaser, anxious to avoid trouble and violence." But I believe that, in Dionysius's version, G. Claudius is poured into the traditional mold of the *patruus,* whereas in Livy this model is overlooked (even if a probable trace survives).

23. Plutarch cites, among the examples of the mildness of uncles toward nephews, the relations between Plato and Speusippus; however, Plato was Speusippus's maternal uncle (unlike the uncle of Aleva, "his father's brother," 492 B): see Stenzel, *RE* 3A.1636. This inconsistency may reveal Plutarch's way of considering the whole matter. He draws no distinction between paternal and maternal uncles, moving unconsciously between them, quite in the Greek manner, in which *theios* refers to either. The loss of opposing terms reflects the lack of opposing models of behavior.

24. A curious old remark of Casaubon's may be noted here, from his *A. Persi Flacci Saturarum Libri* (Paris, 1605), p. 52; on *Sat.* 1.12, he wrote, "Patruus et tutor saepe idem sonant ac gravis censor et obiurgator . . . ideo Graeci patruum dixerunt *theion:* etsi aliter paullo Plutarchus in finem libri *Peri Philadelphias.*" Casaubon's keen sense did not fail to note the extreme difference between the two types of paternal uncle offered by the Roman tradition and the exhortations of Plutarch.

25. Discussed in Bettini, "Verso un'antropologia dell'intreccio," *MD* 7 (1982):39ff.

26. Evidently, Plautus identifies *frater patruelis* with *frater germanus* and treats Hanno for all intents and purposes as the brother of Iaon, father of Agorastocles. This elasticity in the usage confirms what we speculated earlier about the equivalence of attitudes between *frater (soror) patruelis* and *frater germanus (soror germana),* in n.19 above. Really, in the kinship terminology of the jurists, Hanno would be for Agorastocles *propius sobrino,* and vice versa: see, for example, Gallus Aelius in *Fest.* 379.6, s.v. "sobrinus." Many texts have been gathered by the following: J. M. André, "Le nom du collateral au 5° degré," *Rev. Phil. lit. hist. anc.* 42 (1968):42ff.; A. C. Bush, *AJP* 93 (1972):568ff.; and idem, *TAPA* 103 (1972):39ff., with original remarks; and R. Röhle, "*Propior sobrino, propius sobrino* in der römischen Rechtssprache," *Zeitschr. f. Rechtg.* 98 (1981):341 ff., a very careful piece of work.

27. What I have said so far about Roman comedy in Greek dress (*comedia palliata*) may help us to deal with a small puzzle in Apuleius, which may well be destined to remain just that, or to evaporate, because chances are even that it may not exist.

In the *Florida,* Apuleius offers a long critical judgment on the comic writer Philemon: although clean and chastened himself, his plots represent the "treacherous pimp, fervent lover, clever slave, deceitful girlfriend, restrictive wife, indulgent mother, reprimanding paternal uncle *(patruus obiurgator),* helping companion, combative soldier, but also greedy hangers-on and grasping relatives and forward whores" (16.64).

Apuleius lets himself go in a breathless catalogue rather suited to what we know of his style: see M. Bernhard, *Der Stil des Apuleius von Madaura* (Stuttgart, 1927), pp. 74ff.), who begins with the possible Greek models for these many-membered Apuleian utterances. But what is the reproachful *patruus* doing in this company? Isn't he a typically Roman character? Apuleius's list had caused wonder, too, in Ph. Légrand, *Daos: Tableau de la comédie Greque pendant la période dite nouvelle* (Paris, 1910), p. 181. Légrand remarked that no traces of a reproving *patruus* seem to appear either in what remains of Philemon or generally in other texts of new comedy, including those translated into Latin comedies: on this idea, see also Pasquali, *Orazio lirico,* p. 88, who was a bit less skeptical than Légrand about the worth of the report in Apuleius.

Reproachful, in any case, is what the two *patrui* in Roman comedy are not, as we have seen. So where did Apuleius get his reproachful uncle? Because we, alas, cannot check the texts of Philemon directly, our judgment must remain suspended. We cannot rule out, of course, that Apuleius assimilated to Roman tradition some Dutch uncle (whether paternal or maternal) encountered in Philemon. In this light, we may recall a fragment from Menander's *Thuroros:* "Ouk adelphos, ouk adelphe parenochlesei, tethida / oud'heoraken, to sunolon, theion oud'akekoen. / eutuchema d'estin oligostous anagkaious echein" (208 Körte).

One might suppose that the use of the verb "to hear" for the uncle could refer to his having "too much to say," in which case this fragment might be taken as evidence for the existence of the type of the Dutch uncle in new comedy. But the fragment comes from Menander, and the whole matter is suppositious. Besides, the subject is a generic uncle (as we could have predicted), neither maternal nor paternal and, above all, an uncle considered a nuisance in the same way as a brother, a sister, and an aunt.

A further and simpler explanation could be that Apuleius erred. In his catalogue of comic types, he may have slipped a Roman type into a Greek taxonomy, no doubt seduced by his own craze for balanced phrasing and rhyme. In any case, when Ovid gives a brief sketch of

Menandrian types, he mentions "tricky slave, harsh father, wicked pimp, . . . coaxing whore" (*Amores* 1.15, 17ff.), which are more or less the same types, but instead of the "reproachful uncle" we have the more natural "harsh father."

28. "Si stud nimium" is Lachmann's correction for the reading of the manuscripts of Nonius, "si studium," which Lindsay kept. I give Ribbeck's text more out of convenience than conviction.
29. See the admirable sketch of young Quintus in Münzer, *RE* 7A.1306ff.
30. Cf. Cicero, *Att.* 2.2.1, 4.7.3, 4.9.2, and so forth.
31. Cf. Münzer, *RE* 7A.1306ff.
32. Having reached the end of our study, we are in a better position to realize how weak was the usual explanation for the severity of paternal uncles. In the most common view, the proverbial severity of the *patruus* depended simply on the fact that he, more than anyone else, was likely to become a nephew's guardian in the event of the father's death. See, for example, A. Otto, *Die Sprichwörter der Römer* (Leipzig, 1890), p. 268; Plessis-Lejay on Horace, *Serm.* 2.2.96; and Pasquali, *Orazio lirico*, p. 89.

    This mere presumed likelihood was thought to account for a relationship of contrasting attitudes that function within a real affective system. This is not to deny that the potential responsibility for guardianship could have influenced the behavior pattern of the *patruus:* but so would being next of kin to the father, and the contrast with the maternal uncle, and belonging to the male line, and so on. See below.

    Opinion erred yet further when it assumed that the *patruus* was legally defined as first in line to become the guardian of a minor. Since the time of the Twelve Tables (5.6), legal guardianship was assigned on the basis of closeness in the male line, beginning with the minor's brother, then his *patruus*: Gaius, *Inst.* 1.156ff.; Justinian, *Inst.* 1.15; *Cod.* 30.5; and so forth. See M. Kaser, *Das römische Privatrecht*[2] (Munich, 1971), 1:88.

    Although those who hold the view never cite it, the only text I know that considers the *patruus* as the child's natural guardian comes from Isidore: "Patruus frater patris est, quasi pater alius. unde et moriente patre pupillum prior patruus suscipit, et quasi filium lege tuetur" (*Et.* 9.6.16). But this is Isidore, don't forget.

    Legal questions aside, it would be still be superficial to derive the severity of the *patruus* from an eventual guardianship. First we would have to ask whether the guardian (*tutor*) in Rome was a severe, reprimanding figure. Otto and the others cited above seem to have taken this so much for granted that they never asked. Yet if we read the evidence, we realize that things stand differently. In the *Aulularia* of Plautus, Euclio asks the cook: "Quid tu malum curas / utrum crudum an coctum edim, nisi tu mihi es tutor?" (429ff.). Again, in *Vidularia* 20ff. (with Studemund's supplement):

NI: Te ego audi[vi di]cere
operarium te velle r[us cond]uc[ere].
DI: Re[ct]e audivisti. *NI*: Quid vis operis [fie]ri?
DI: Qu[id t]u istuc curas? An mihi tutor additu's?

In these two passages, there is not the least trait of reprimand or severity: simply someone who tends to not mind his own business is compared to a *tutor.* A *tutor,* then, is one who is too curious, not an unbending judge. So, too, when someone shows too much concern for Persius's health, he retorts sharply, "Ne sis mihi tutor" (3.96). Far from reproachful or wrathful, the *tutor* annoys because he is too concerned for his ward.

Chapter Three. Mother's Brother: Avunculus

1. See B. Delbrück, "Di indogermanischen Verwandtschaftsnamen," *Abhandl. phil. hist. cl. Kön. Säch. Ges. Wiss.* 11 (Leipzig, 1889); and A. Meillet, *Mel. Soc. Ling.* 9 (1895):141ff., on which see below.
2. E. Benveniste, *Le Vocabulaire des institutions indoeuropeénnes* (Paris, 1966), 1:172ff. Benveniste's explanation had been suggested already in essence, though more briefly, in G. Thomson, *Studies in Ancient Greek Society* (London, 1949), 1:79, as remarked in O. Szemerényi, "Studies in the Kinship Terminology of the Indoeuropean Languages," *Textes et Memoires* 6, *Acta Iranica* 7 (1977):1ff.
3. The choice of names, Durand and Dupont, clearly reflects the practice of C. Lévi-Strauss, *The Elementary Structures of Kinship,* J. H. Bell, tr., and J. R. von Sturmer and R. Needham, eds. (Boston, 1969). pp. 160ff, a quite different context, dealing with systems of exchange limited to four classes of the Kariera type.
4. Benveniste, is, however, a bit too hasty: in *Le Vocabulaire des institutions indoeuropeénnes,* he states that "in this system, kinship is established between brother and sister's son, between maternal uncle and nephew." And further, that "the etymological relationship with *avunculus* implies and reveals another type of filial relationship," s.v. *nepos, avunculus.*
5. One may take the examples of *avus* given in the thesaurus: none imposes the meaning of "maternal grandfather" (ibid., p. 174).
6. Lévi-Strauss, *The Elementary Structures of Kinship,* pp. 304ff.
7. Although these proposals in Benveniste are unfounded, his chapter on kinship in *Le Vocabulaire des institutions indoeuropeénnes* (to say

nothing of the entire work) retains enormous worth. Every scholar in this area must feel his or her debt, almost at every line, to Benveniste's clarity and generally to his method.

8. R.S.P. Beekes, "Uncle and Nephew," *Journ. Ind. Eur. Stud.* 4 (1976):43ff.

9. I refer to the well-known work by A. Piganiol, *Essai sur les origines de Rome* (Paris, 1917), pp. 145ff., who believed that the Roman patricians traced descent through fathers, and the plebs traced descent through mothers (but see p. 156, in which the obscure and unfortunate term *matriarchal* is already qualified as "a type of family characterized by the almost exclusive regard for kinship through the womb"). The hypothesis that differing criteria for kinship distinguished patricians and plebeians goes back at least to J. Binder (*Die Plebs* [Leipzig, 1906 = Rome, 1965]), who argued that the plebs passed from matrilinear to patrilinear descent when the Laws of the Twelve Tables were promulgated.

10. The patrilineal logic of Roman culture comes out also in many other documents of the most diverse sorts; consider only the position of the woman in matrimony *cum manu:* she is no longer *agnata* of her own *agnati;* does not keep the cult of her own ancestors, but takes part in the cult of her husband's; and will belong to the *dei parentes* of her sons, and becomes a "daughter" to her husband. See P. E. Corbett, *The Roman Law of Marriage* (Oxford, 1969), p. 108.

11. Take, for example, Paul.: "Avus est patris vel matris meae pater" (*Dig.* 38.10.10). The fact that *avus* most often means "paternal grandfather," even as *avi* are often "ancestors on the father's side," simply depends on the intrinsic patrilinear bias of Roman culture, which always puts the male lineage to the fore. Nonetheless, *avus* remains a semantically undifferentiated term.

12. Lévi-Strauss, *The Elementary Structures of Kinship,* pp. 438ff.

13. Beekes, "Uncle and Nephew," p. 46, in which evidence is drawn primarily from India.

14. M. Granet, *La civiltà cinese antica* (Turin, 1968).

15. Ibid., p. 137.

16. Ibid., p. 380.

17. M. Granet came back to Chinese kinship structures in *Catégories matrimoniales et relations de proximité dans la Chine ancienne* (Paris, 1939), in which he substantially modified his earlier reconstructions: see a chapter that Lévi-Strauss, *The Elementary Structures of Kinship,* pp. 311ff., devotes to this book.

18. Benveniste's thesis was accepted in Y. Thomas, "Mariages endogamiques à Rome," *Rev. hist. de droit franç. et étr.* 58 (1980):345ff. (p. 358, n.35). P. Moreau, "Plutarque, Augustine, Lévi-Strauss," *Rev. belg.*

phil. 56 (1978):41ff., suggests the existence in archaic Roman society of a regulated form of marriage with the daughter of the father's sister, although I do not know whether he was inspired by Benveniste; see also P. Moreau's useful reflections in *Rev. Et. Lat.* 56 (1978):41ff.

19. F. G. Lounsbury, "The Structural Analysis of Kinship Semantics," in *Proceedings of the Ninth International Congress of Linguistics,* ed. H. G. Hunt (The Hague, 1964), pp. 1075ff.; and F. G. Lounsbury, "The Formal Analysis of Crow- and Omaha-Type Kinship Terminologies," in *Explorations in Cultural Anthropology,* ed. W. Goodenough (New York, 1964), pp. 351ff. Lounsbury well describes rules that show how the system works and that predict individual shifts within the general classification: Crow appears as the matrilineal counterpart to the patrilineal Omaha. On the anthropological and sociological reasons of this type of classification, see A. R. Radcliffe-Brown, "Le parentele di scherzo," in *Struttura e funzione nella società primitiva* (Milan, 1972) (*Altre osservazioni sulla parentela di scherzo*), pp. 69ff.; and Lévi-Strauss, *The Elementary Structures of Kinship,* pp. xxvii-xlii; and, above all, F. Héritier, *L'exercise de la parenté* (Paris, 1984).

20. P. Friedrich, "Proto-Indoeuropean Kinship Terminology," *Ethnology* 5 (1966):1ff.

21. H. P. Gates, "The Kinship Terminology of Homeric Greek," suppl. to *Int'l Journ. Am. Ling.* 37 (1971).

22. Szemerényi, "Studies in the Kinship Terminology," 1ff.

23. See also the references to C. Lévi-Strauss in part 1, n.2 above, and see also below, chap. 6.

24. Beekes, "Uncle and Nephew."

25. Radcliffe-Brown, "Le parentele di scherzo," pp. 39ff.; cf. p. 47.

26. Ibid.; see also the works by Lévi-Strauss cited above in part one, n.2, and further below.

27. "Katacharizesthai tais gynaixi tous prodotas": these women can be none other than the sisters of Collatinus, who were said to be the mothers of Aquilli and Vitelli.

28. Lévi-Strauss, "Structural Analysis in Linguistics and Anthropology," in *Structural Anthropology,* tr. C. Jacobson and B. G. Schoepf (Garden City, N.Y., 1963) pp. 29ff., and also below in chapter 6.

29. From our viewpoint, Livy gives a less interesting version (1.3ff.), making the exile of Collatinus, for example, precede the plot. J. Gagé (*Matronalia* [Brussels, 1963], pp. 233ff.) found in this legend a kind of patronage by the maternal uncle of his nephews "pour le passage de puberté" (p. 235).

30. See Paulus-Festus 163 L: "Nepotes luxuriosae vitae homines appellati, quod non magis his rei suae familiaris cura est, quam is, quibus pater avusque vivunt." In the corresponding passage of Festus 162 L,

the Farnese codex appears to read "Tuscis dicitur," which, however, must not have had anything to do with our metaphor. The reading here, as we see in Paulus, is plural, "nepotes," which cannot go with "Tuscis dicitur." The cut made by Paulus, to say nothing of the corruption in the Farnese codex, is quite unfortunate for us, because it would have been interesting to know what Festus said about *nepos* and some Etruscans. Their language, by the way, seems to have borrowed *nepos* as *nefts*, even as it turned *pronepos* into *prumts*: see A. Ernout and A. Meillet, *Dictionnaire étymologique de la langue Latine* (Paris, 1967), p. 438, although I do not share their view that Festus indicated an Etruscan origin for the metaphor *nepos* (wastrel). For other contexts in which *nepos* means "wastrel," see Cicero, *Quinct.* 40 and *Leg. agr.* 1.2; Horace, *Serm.* 1.4.49 and *Epod.* 1.34; Propertius 4.8.23; Seneca *Dial.* 4.16.3; and Pliny, *Hist. nat.* 10.133, among others. These passages are carefully gathered and well discussed in J. L. Heller, *TAPA* 93 (1962):61ff. The use of *nepos* in this sense thus seems not to have been archaic, at least to judge from the surviving evidence (certainly the metaphor does not occur in Plautus, *Miles* 1413, "Veneris nepotulum," although Beekes, "Uncle and Nephew," seems to find it there: see E. Löfstedt, *Syntactica* 9.86). But the absence of archaic evidence may be accidental, if we remember that the analogous metaphor, *patruus* (severe), also lacks archaic examples, even though it reveals an extremely old anthropological pattern (the severe *patruus*, like the *pater*, and both counterposed to the indulgent *avunculus*). In any event, Porphyry says on Horace: "Nepotem autem veteres ut prodigum . . . dixerunt" (*Epod.* 1.4).

31. A. Pariente, "En torno a *nepos*," *Emerita* 11 (1943):60ff.
32. The hypothesis seemed credible, for example, to Beekes ("Uncle and Nephew," 51), although he was nonetheless quite cautious in considering it.
33. For the quantity of *nepos* (wastrel), no doubts can be entertained: see, e.g., Propertius 4.8.23.
34. Pariente, who in "En torno a *nepos*" invoked such an analogy with *nepos* (nephew), to motivate the phonetic change, extricated himself from the impasse by asserting that "saria absurdo pretender reducirlo [this phonetic shift] a los métodos de explicación corrientes en gramatica." His whole article, if truth be told, takes a haughty and frankly unpleasant tone, as when, for example, he judges "completamente pueril" (p. 68) the explanation of *nepos* given by Ernout and Meillet in the *Dictionnaire*. Nor does Pariente add much that is new in "Mas sobre nepos," *Emerita* 21 (1953):18ff. To the contrary, his hypothesis had been formulated before him by at least L. Müller, *Altitalisches Wörterbuch* (Göttingen, 1926), s.v. "nepos."

35. Benveniste, *Le Vocabulaire des institutions indoeuropeénnes*, s.v. *nepos*.
36. Radcliffe-Brown, "Le parentele di scherzo."
37. Beekes, "Uncle and Nephew"; and Szemerényi, "Studies in the Kinship Terminology," 1ff.
38. Jerome, *Ep.* 14.2.3 and 60.9.1; and Orosius 7.28.11.
39. Latin does not distinguish between maternal and paternal at the level of *avus* and *avia*, or *nepos* and *neptis*.
40. Radcliffe-Brown, "Le parentele di scherzo."
41. Granet, *La civiltà cinese antica*, p. 271.
42. E. Benveniste, "Termes de parenté dans les langues indoeuropéennes," *L'homme* 5 (1965):5ff. On the links between grandfather and grandson, see Ausonius: "Pappos aviasque trementes / anteferunt patribus seri, nova cura, nepotes" (*Protr. ad Aus. nep.* 18).
43. Besides referring to anonymous sources, Dionysius expressly mentions Polybius.
44. J. B. Hofmann, *Lateinische Umgangsprache*, trans. L. Ricottilli, *La lingua d'uso latina*[2] (Bologna, 1985), with an introductory essay, "Hofmann e il concetto di lingua d'uso" (pp. 26ff.), which points out some of the limits and risks, as well as the sources, of Hofmann's concept of "affective language."
45. Hofmann, *La Lingua d'uso latina*,[2] pp. 296ff. For ample notes on the problem of the diminutive in Latin, which are beyond our present scope, see Ricotilli, *La lingua d'uso latina*, pp. 297, 299, 300, and 380ff.
46. M. Leumann, *Lateinische Laut- und Formenlehre*[2] (Munich, 1977), p. 307.
47. By a different route, however, A. Meillet, *Mél. Soc. Ling.* 9 (1895):141ff., sought in *avunculus* the suffix *-tero*, "marquant opposition" (as in *matertera*); he thus postulated *awontro-* becoming *awontlo-*, hence *avunculus*: "Sous l'influence du suffixe de diminutifs que le latin s'est créé." But, all other considerations apart, in forming kinship terms on the maternal side, it would be difficult to employ one and the same suffix *-tero*, marking otherness, for both the like aunt, mother's sister (*matertera*), and the unlike uncle, mother's brother (*avunculus*). I am uncertain whether Meillet's suggestion relates to the fact that he began by defining *matertera* erroneously as "soeur de pére." However, *avunculus* is commonly accepted as a normal diminutive of *avus*; see Benveniste, *Le Vocabulaire des institutions indoeuropeénnes*, s.v. *avus*; Szemerényi, "Studies in the Kinship Terminology," pp. 53ff.; and Ernout and Meillet in the *Dictionnaire*, p. 91, explaining *avunculus* as "diminutif familier": as the dictionary's first edition dates from 1932, Meillet seems to have given up or forgotten his note of nearly forty years earlier.

48. Cf. also Festus 492 L, on *tagax; TLL* 6.1650.
49. *Lembunculus: Gloss. Ansil.* 51.300, and so forth; *lenuculus:* Caesar, *Bell. civ.* 2.47.3; Sallust, *Hist.* fr. 1.25; and so forth. Cf. Ernout and Meillet in the *Dictionnaire,* s.v.
50. Formed on the model of *ambulatiuncula,* according to J. B. Hofmann, *Ind. Forsch.* 38, p. 177n.1; also in the form *domucula, TLL* 5 (1949):7.
51. "Ob natale Aprunculorum": see *Rev. Arch.* 15 (1910):325ff. The same expression recurs in the inscriptions numbers 1, 2, and 6, the former two datable to 175 and 191 B.C. Evidently the allusion is to the *natalicium* of the standards, a custom well known for the *natalis aquilae.*
52. *CIL* 8.2601 and 18233. On *statunculum,* which is also attested in the glossographers, see W. Heraeus, "Die Sprache des Petronius und die Glossen," in *Kleine Schriften* (Heidelberg, 1937), p. 137.
53. *Sangunculus* occurs, too, in the *Acta fratrum Arvalium* of 240 B.C.: Dessau, *ILS* III–2.CLXVI ff. Cf. Heraeus, "Zu Petronius und die neuen Arvalakten-Fragmenten," in *Kleine Schriften,* pp. 227ff. The Traguriensis Codex of Petronius reads *saucunculum,* which Heraeus emended.
54. See Cicero, "humilem et abiectam orationem" (*Orat.* 192); Quintilian, "Et humilibus interim et vulgaribus est opus" (10.1.9,); and idem, "Humile et quotidianum sermonis genus" (11.1.6). Remember, too, the passage in which Horace warns the would-be poet against letting a god or hero slum with low speech in dim taverns (*Ars* 227ff.).
55. Cicero, *De rep.* 2.63 and *De fin.* 2.66 and 5.64; Diodorus 12.24; and Pomponius, *Dig.* 1.2.2, 24, et. Cf. Gundel, *RE* 16.1530ff.; and Münzer, *RE* 3.2700.
56. In Livy, Numitorius is once the *avus* of Virginia (3.45.4), and once her *avunculus* (3.54.11). In their note to 3.45.4, Weissenborn and Müller try to show that he must have been the girl's *avunculus magnus,* although the parallel texts they cite show nothing of the sort. Furthermore, an *avunculus magnus* could easily be called simply *avunculus,* as in, for example, Suetonius, *Aug.* 8 and 10, but hardly *avus,* which would change collateral relationship into descent. In all likelihood, Livy just slipped. Numitorius is called *ho pros metros theios* by Dionysius (11.30.1) and refers to Numitoria, Virginia's mother, as *ten adelphen ten heautou.*
57. For example, Münzer, *RE* 2.2700 and 6.45; and E. Pais, *Ancient Legends of Roman History* (London, 1906), pp. 185ff.
58. Livy 3.44.1; Cicero, *De fin.* 2.66; Silius Italicus 13.821; and Valerius Maximus 6.1.1. See also the general remarks on Lucretia in S. Pomeroy, "The Relationship of the Married Woman to Her Blood Relatives in Rome," *Anc. Soc.* 7 (1976):215ff.

59. Diodorus (10.20.1) calls Collatinus "cousin of the king": in Roman terms, the two would thus have the relationship of *propius sobrino* (cf. chap. 2, n.26 above, and Dionysius of Halicarnassus, *Ant. Rom.* 4.64.4). On the genealogical problems of the Tarquin family, see L. Bessone, "La gente Tarquinia," *RFIC* 110 (1982):394ff.

60. See M. Bettini, "Verso un'antropologia dell'intreccio: Le strutture semplici della trama nelle commedie di Plauto," *MD* 7 (1982):39ff., with particular reference to plots such as those of *Curculio* and *Poenulus*.

61. For the importance of the number three as a device in composition, particularly in folklore, see chap. 9 below.

62. See Bessone, "La gente Tarquinia," 394ff. In Dionysius, Brutus expressly denies that he is related to Lucretia: "Kai pantes hymeis hoi te gynaiki prosekontas" (*Ant. Rom.* 4.70.3).

63. Other sources also speak of the call to the *propinqui*: Dionysius of Halicarnassus, *Ant. Rom.* 4.66.2, 3; Diodorus 10.10.1; and Valerius Maximus 6.1.1.

64. With regard to the Servian variant, which appears also in *Myth. Vat.* 1.74 (vol. 1, p. 25 Bode), Münzer speaks of "ganz späte un geschmacklose Erweiterungen" (*RE* 13.1962). On the same passage, totally useless observations were offered in C. Appleton, "Trois épisodes de l'histoire ancienne de Rome: Les Sabines, Lucrèce e Virginie," *Rev. hist droit franç. et ètr.* 3 (1924):239ff., because he fails to note the role of *avunculus* donned by Brutus, fixing instead on the role of "negro" played by the Ethiopian slave.

65. I am thinking of the express attempt made in J. Bédier (*Les Fabliaux* [Paris, 1895], pp. 186ff.), who even used the textual critics' criterion of *error coniunctivus* to establish relations of "kinship" and derivation among diverse versions of a fable. The "archetypes" Bédier reconstructed almost always hovered between logical and chronological ordering, so it was unclear whether a certain variant came before another because historically earlier or because its structure seemed presupposed by the other: a kind of blind alley that can hardly be avoided with this approach.

66. See Bettini, "Verso un'antropologia dell'intreccio," in which I attempted to show the network of reciprocal assumptions which links the action of a story, on the one hand, with the cultural system, on the other, taking my examples from Plautine plots.

67. V. Propp, *Morphology of the Folktale*,[2] *Morfologia della fiaba* (Turin, 1966).

68. R. M. Oglivie, *A Commentary on Livy, 1–5* (Oxford, 1965), p. 226. Also on the oath, see E. von Lasaulx, "Der Eid bei den Römern," in

Studien des classischen Altertums (Regensburg, 1854), pp. 208ff. (Brutus's oath, p. 213). Brutus swears "by Ares and all the other gods," not on Lucretia's blood, in Dionysius, *Ant. Rom.* 4.70.5.

69. The opposition, *sanguis/cruor,* is the object of a study by F. Menacci, in preparation for the volume *Il sanguee l'identità nella cultura romana,* in collaboration with G. Guastella and M. Bettini. Note that Ovid could not have employed in this syntactic nexus the form *sanguinem,* which is cretic and cannot be used or elided in the dactylic hexameter. On *castus* and the notion of chastity, see L. Beltrami, "*Castus e incestus:* Problemi linguistico-antropologici," forthcoming in *MD.*

70. On *adulterium* and *turbatio sanguinis,* see also M. Bettini, "Lettura divinatoria di un incesto," *MD* 12 (1985):145ff.

71. For example, Leumann, *Lateinische Laut- und Formenlehre,* p. 307, "Kleiner *avus* als Sohn des *avus*"; also Szemerényi, "Studies in the Kinship Terminology."

72. Lévi-Strauss, *The Elementary Structures of Kinship,* pp. 304ff.

73. This kind of terminology, in which relatives of both mother and wife fall together, implies in all likelihood a system of generalized exchange; that is, one takes a wife from the same group from which one's father took.

74. Lévi-Strauss, *The Elementary Structures of Kinship,* pp. 305ff.

75. *The Tale of Genji,* trans. E. G. Seidensticker (Tokyo, 1978), 2:886, cited in C. Lévi-Strauss, "Lectures croisées," in *Le regard éloigné* (Paris, 1983), p. 114.

76. Lévi-Strauss, "Structural Analysis in Linguistics and Anthropology," p. 120.

77. Lévi-Strauss, *The Elementary Structures of Kinship,* pp. 304ff., saw the maternal uncle's protection and domination of his niece, together with his often preferential right to the bride price, as a trait related structurally to simple systems of generalized exchange, an argument that he applied, of course, only to the cases of the Gyljiaki, the Lushai, and so forth.

Chapter Four. Mother's Sister: Matertera

1. M. Mead, *Sex and Temperament in Three Primitive Societies* (New York, 1935).

2. Ibid., p. 72.

3. On the formation of the substantive *matertera,* see E. Benveniste, *Noms d'agent e noms d'action en Indo-éuropéen* (Paris, 1948), p. 118, partially modified, however, in *Le Vocabulaire des institutions indoeuropeénes* (Paris, 1966), s.v. *matertera,* 1:177. Still useful are the ex-

amples gathered by A. Meillet, *Mél. Soc. ling.* 9 (1895):141. I find not wholly pertinent the comparisons offered by M. Leumann, *Lateinische Laut- und Formenlehre*[2] (Munich, 1977), p. 318.

4. L. Mair, *Il matrimonio: Un'analisi antropologica* (Bologna, 1976), p. 39.
5. Turnus is called *consobrinus* (seemingly of Lavinia) by the *Origo gentis Romanae* (13.5), which later calls him Amata's *matruelis* (13.8), citing the evidence of "Piso" (which, however, Peter does not accept as authentic). *Consobrinus* is a rare term, hard to delimit, even if V. Bulhart, *TLL* 8.490, 57ff., does not hesitate to equate it with *avunculi filius,* for which I find no proof. *Matruelis* does recur in Marcianus (*Liber XIV institutionum,* cited by *Dig.* 48.9.1), who gives the *lex Pompeii de parricidiis* in a fairly obscure and almost certainly lacunose passage, at least in the view of Th. Mommsen, *Römisches Strafrecht* (Leipzig, 1899), pp. 664ff., from which, nonetheless, on the basis of the succession of degrees, one might most easily argue that the subject is the *matertera*'s son; and perhaps the apposition with *frater* suggests the same thing.

   This, in any event, appears to be the explanation given by the glosses. Ugutio Pisanus, cited by the *Novum glossarium mediae latinitatis* (Hafniae, 1959–69), p. 270, stated: "Matrueles dicuntur filii vel filiae materterae: adj.: ad materteram pertinens." In the *Gloss. Lat. Gall. Sang.* (cited by Du Cange, s.v. "matruelis"), the word is explained as *pertinens ad materteram* or related to the "marratre" ("filz ou filles de marratre"): this semantic shift from *matertera* to "stepmother" might constitute an interesting trace of sisterhood. If, then, *matruelis* indicates the son of the *matertera,* one must infer that, in the view of "Piso," Turnus was son of the *matertera* of Amata; in other words, *consobrinus* not of Lavinia, Amata's child, but of Amata herself. In short, this "Piso" has pushed Turnus up a generation (but we are going to have to come back to the terms for cousins).

   From this viewpoint, it is interesting that Dionysius of Halicarnassus considers Turnus, whom he calls Tyrrhenus, the *anepsios* (cousin) of Amata (*Ant. Rom.* 1.64.2): hence, if the purported citation of "Piso" did not come from such an untrustworthy medium as the *Origo,* it would be tempting to think that here Dionysius actually followed "Piso" in making Turnus not the nephew of Amata, but her cousin. Dionysius is known, after all, to have shown a certain predilection for "Piso," especially where genealogy is concerned, a matter I shall return to (in chap. 5 below), because Dionysius follows "Piso" against the tradition in turning the sons of Tarquinius Priscus into his grandsons; namely, sons of a son who died before Priscus did.

   In the manuscripts of Dionysius, a joint reading of both the Chigianus and the Urbinas, Amata's name takes the form Amitas, which

Jacoby accepts, attributing a correction, Amatas, to Cobet, *Obs. crit. et pal. ad Dion. Hal. Ant. Rom.* (Leiden, 1877), p. 33; but the correction probably is earlier; Amates Stephanus. This may indeed be a banal mistake, of the sort that systematically turned Turnus Herdonius into Tyrdos Erdonios (*Ant. Rom.* 4.45, 47, 48): after all, only in this passage do we get the queen's name. And if it were a respectable variant, it would still be a scribal twist for a proper name, like hundreds in Greek writers on Roman subjects, which certainly would not let us think Dionysius thought Amata was the *amita* (paternal aunt) of Turnus. What could it mean, after all, to write something such as "tina tes Latinou gynaikos amitas anepsion"? Thus, I can hardly subscribe to the thesis of Y. Thomas ("Mariages endogamiques à Rome," *Rev. hist. de droit franç. et étr.* 58 [1980]:363 with n.40), who turns Amata into Turnus's *tante paternelle,* a proposal made earlier by Klausen, *Aeneas und die Penaten* (Hamburg and Gotha, 1840), 2:875n.1701.

Finally, Zonara defines Turnus as "tw Latinw prosekontos" (kinsman of Latinus, 7.1). This must be a generic statement of what the other sources also tell us, rather than a version relating Turnus to the Lavinate royal family through the king instead of the queen, as suggested by Ehlers, *RE,* s.v. "Turnus." Even in the *Aeneid,* Amata says to Latinus: "quid cura antiqua tuorum / et consanguineo toties data dextera Turno?" (7.365ff.) (cf. 12.40). Latinus, too, speaks of Turnus "cognato sanguine victus" (12.29). These are generic and broadened turns of language that in all likelihood presuppose what we would call acquired kinship. The same terminological latitude underlies expressions such as one in Paulus-Festus: "Adfines in agris vicini, sive consanguinitate coniuncti" (10 L). Strictly speaking, of course, *adfines* are not joined by blood but, just as Turnus to Latinus, get assimilated to the status of blood relatives. Evidently this stretching of terminology presupposes cultural models of behavior in which such assimilation was practiced: for example, the festival of Cara Cognatio, commemorating the dead on 22 February, the day after the Feralia: on this occasion the blood relatives (*cognati*) took part (Ovid, *Fast.* 2.617), offerings were made to the *dis generis,* and the *gradus* of the *genus* were counted. In short, it was a celebration of kinship which involved the members of a group linked by *necessitudo,* and yet Valerius Maximus describes it as "convivium . . . cui praeter cognatos et adfines nemo interponebatur" (2.1.8).

6. On Amata, see below. "Qualcosa di erotico, di sessuale" in Amata's affection for Turnus has been found by R.O.M. Lyne, "La voce 'privata' di Virgilio," *Mus. Pat.* 2 (1984):5ff.: cf. the remarks by A. Traina, *RFIC* 112 (1984):249n.2.

7. Whether the actual title referred to one or more *materterae* is uncertain: see the textual notes in Ribbeck's edition.
8. Cf. Tacitus, *Dial de orat.* 28; likewise, Ausonius told of having been reared under the aegis of his maternal grandmother: "Hae me praereptum cunis et ab ubere matris / blanda sub austeris imbuit imperiis" (*Par.* 5.9).
9. Cf. Horace, *Epist.* 1.4.8; and Seneca, *Epist.* 60.1.
10. *CIL* 3.8551, 12962; 6.12251, 14243, 11854; 7.1934, 2916, 3434; 9.3483; 12.3925; and so forth.
11. *CIL* 3.8551; 10.7640; and so forth.
12. In inscriptions, *tata* may mean variously "father" or "grandfather" or simply "nurse-attendant," according to S. G. Harrod (*Latin Terms of Endearment and of Family Relationship* [Princeton, 1903], p. 53n.44), although "father" is most common.
13. See the examples gathered by Thylander, *Études sur l'épigraphie Latine* (Lund, 1952), pp. 85–91.
14. To cite a emblematic case, C. Favez, *Mus. Helv.* 3 (1946):118ff.; however, see G. Guastella, "Non sanguine sed vice," *MD* 7 (1982):141ff.; and idem, "I Parentalia come testo antroplogico: L'Avunculato nel mondo celtico e nella famiglia di Ausonio," *MD* 4 (1980).
15. See, however, my two-part discussion "Su alcuni modelli antropologici della Roma più arcaica," *MD* 1 (1978) and especially 2 (1979):9ff., generous parts of which are reproduced here. But there I have left the more narrowly linguistic examination of the meaning of *matuta*, its relations with *manus, maturus*, and so forth, for which I lack space here; nor could I bring over my attempt to interpret the "expulsion of the female slave" during the Matralia, an attempt that today, were I to do it again, I would at least rewrite and enlarge.
16. The two most detailed and important works on this ritual are still the following: M. Halberstadt, "*Mater Matuta*," in *Frankf. St. z. Rel. und Kurt. d. Antike*, 8 (Frankfort, 1934); and the part devoted to the goddess by G. Radke, *Die Götter Altitaliens* (Munich, 1965), pp. 206ff. On the relations of the ritual with Fortuna, see J. Champeaux, *Le culte de la Fortune à Rome et dans le monde Romain* (Rome, 1982), pp. 308ff.
17. On the special relationship between Camillus and Mater Matuta, much has been written by G. Dumézil: *Mythe et Epopée* (Paris, 1973), 3:93ff.; and "*Mater Matuta*," in *Déesses Latines et mythes védiques* (Brussels, 1956), pp. 9ff.
18. See the synthesis by Halberstadt, "*Mater Matuta*," pp. 49ff.; see also Radke, *Die Götter Altitaliens*, p. 207. Excavations at Satricum brought to light an archaic inscription of remarkable value for history and linguistics made public by Dr. Stibbe, whose report is discussed by C.

de Simone and M. Pallottino, *Quaderni del centro di studio per l'archeologia etrusco-italico* 1 (1978):95ff. Above all, see A. Peruzzi, "On the Satricum Inscription," *Parola del Passato* 33 (1978):346ff.; J. A. De Waele, "I templi della Mater Matuta a Satricum," *Med. Ned. Inst. Rom.* 8 (1981):1ff.; and the discussion and bibliography in A. Prosdocimi, "Sull'inscrizione di Satricum," *Giorn. It. Fil.*, n.s. 15 (1984):183ff.

19. Halberstadt, "*Mater Matuta*," p. 51.
20. But the text presents problems: see Livy 32.30.10, with the commentary by Weissenborn and Müller.
21. Radke, *Die Götter Altitaliens*, p. 206.
22. See Halberstadt, "*Mater Matuta*," pp. 65ff.; and Radke, *Die Götter Altitaliens*, p. 207.
23. Ibid.
24. Here we face an uncertainly caused by the language of the sources: Plutarch always speaks of the children *twn adelphwn*, which obviously could mean children of either sisters or brothers. Ovid speaks generically of women praying to the goddess on behalf of "alterius prolem" (*Fast.* 6.559ff.), as opposed to their own children. In theory, then, the women at the Matralia might have prayed also for their brothers' children (a possibility not ruled out by Dumézil, *Mythe et Epopée*, p. 327n.1). In short, they could have acted as both *materterae* (mothers' sisters) and *amitae* (fathers' sisters). However, the latter must absolutely be excluded. The constant parallelism between Mater Matuta and Ino Leucothea restricts the field to only the sons of sisters because Ino Leucothea, as Semele's sister, is the *matertera* of Dionysus ("Quid petis hinc . . . *matertera* Bacchi?" Ovid, *Fast.* 6.523): the parallel was rightly underlined by J. G. Frazer, *The Fasti of Ovid* (London, 1929), 4:289n.2. In any case, a sister's concern for her sister's children fits perfectly into the functions of the *matertera* as sketched thus far. Moreover, we shall see, there is a certain parsimony in relations between the paternal aunt and the nephew, which makes it even less likely to have been the type of relation underlying the *Matralia*.
25. See Dumézil's ample appendix on Mater Matuta and all the related problems in *Mythe et Epopée*, pp. 305ff. See also Bettini, "Alcuni modelli," part 2, 36ff.
26. Radke, *Die Götter Altitaliens*, p. 208.
27. Radke refers on this to his "Introduction" in ibid., p. 17, in which he gathers examples of past participles in -*to* with active force: *cenatus, consideratus, desperatus, iuratus, obstinatus, patratus, potus, pransus.* However, all of these refer to an action that remains in the actor and describes some situation of his: he has dined, despaired, sworn, drunk. Not so *matuta*, which would have to be transitive. But even if

Radke's interpretation is correct, the goddess must still "have done good" to others, not herself.

28. See Bettini, "Alcuni modelli."
29. H. J. Rose, *Mnemosyne*, n.s. 53 (1925):407ff. and 413ff.; and idem, *CQ* 28 (1934):156ff.
30. K. Latte, *Römische Religiongeschichte* (Munich, 1960), p. 97. Dumézil, *Mythe et Epopée*, pp. 309ff., disagrees with this view. Yet Latte's view is accepted by M. Torelli, *Lavinio e Roma* (Rome, 1984), pp. 125ff.
31. In the two contexts, the two verbs do not follow each other in the same order: thus *sororiabant . . . fraterculabant* in Paulus, but *fraterculabant . . . sororiabant* in Festus, reconstructed from the surviving *so*[. . .] that can still be read. Meter (iambic senarius) gives no help, because the two forms are interchangeable. I think that Paulus is more likely to have erred and that Lindsay was correct to follow Festus's order in his edition of Plautus (frr. 82ff.). Although Leo followed Paulus, he read Festus in the edition by Therwick, who saw less than Lindsay and missed that *so*[. Which hardly matters for us, or rather it would if this were one of those Plautine plays on words, in which a linguistically false word gets coined on the spot, after which the real form gets juxtaposed, underscoring and telegraphing the coinage, as in the case of *Rudens* 422, which is discussed below. If this, then, were such a game of coinage, the relative position of the words would be crucial: the first false, the second true. But luckily, as we shall see, both verbs here are authentic, not neologisms; so the only problem lies with the point of the witticism, and the glimpse of plot it gives, which concerns editors of Plautus, not us.
32. See A. Ernout and A. Meillet, *Dictionnaire étymologique de la langue Latine*[4] (Paris, 1967), s.v. "frater" and "soror."
33. Rose, *Mnemosyne*.
34. Radke, *Die Götter Altitaliens*, pp. 290ff.
35. See Leumann, *Lateinische Laut- und Formenlehre*, p. 210; and M. Niedermann, *Précis de phonétique du Latin*[2] (Paris, 1968), p. 140.
36. Niedermann, *Précis de phonétique du Latin*, p. 162. Radke, *Die Götter Altitaliens*, cites lilium from Greek *leirion* with "Fernassimilation." This would be an isolated case: see F. Sommer, *Handbuch der Lateinischen Laut- und Formenlehere*[3] (Heidelberg, 1914), p. 211. But more important, the sequence of the liquids is just the reverse of that in the supposed *sorolia*: from *leirion*, an *l . . . r* would become an *l . . . l*, while from *sorolia* a *r . . . l* would have to become a *r . . . r*. In realty, too, Latin lilium and Greek *leirion* must be separate borrowings of a non-Indo-European word, as often happens with names of plants: see A. Meillet, *Lineamenti di storia della lingua greca* (Turin, 1976), p. 90.
37. More on this garment is in J. Gagé, *Matronalia* (Brussels, 1963), p. 31.

38. Cf. *TLL* 6.1257.82ff.; 1258.1ff.
39. J. Manacorda, ed., *J. W. Goethe: Il Faust*, (Florence, 1940), 1:409n.6.
40. Cited from S. Freud, "Introductory Lectures on Psychoanalysis," in *The Standard Edition of the Complete Psychological Works of Sigmund Freud*, ed. and tr. J. Strachey et al., 24 vols. (London, 1953–73), 15:196.
41. "Cum segetes novis aristis aequantur, quia veteres aequare hostire dixerunt, deam Hostilinam [coluerunt]": on *hostire*, see chap. 12 below.
42. Thus the account by B. Gutmann, "Feldbausitten und Wachstumsgebräuche der Wadschagga," *Zeitschr. f. Ethn.* 45 (1913):475ff., commented on by J. Cazeneuve, *La sociologia del rito* (Milan, 1974), pp. 119ff.
43. Bettini, "Alcuni modelli," *MD* 1 (1978):178.
44. Pliny, *Hist. nat.* 7.15, citing Aristotle; see also Augustine, *Civ. dei* 16.8; and idem, *Libr. monstr.* 1.19.
45. Or, accepting the order given by Paulus, Plautus "forgetfully" put the term for male breasts in the place of the term for female ones; again, this issue is the concern of the editors of Plautus.
46. On slips of this sort, see Bettini, *RFIC* 101 (1973):324, with note. Freud, who took his sample slips from literature of the period between Shakespeare and Schiller, might have found examples perhaps even more interesting in Plautus.
47. Dumézil, *Mythe et Epopée*, pp. 315ff. For the dawn character of the goddess, compare the discovery at Satricum of bronze votive figures representing a nude female with her head capped by a more or less oval disk: see E. Richardson, "Mooned Astaroth?" in *In Memoriam O. J. Brendel: Essays in Archaeology and Humanities* (Mainz, 1976), pp. 21ff.
48. Degrassi I, p. 47; cf. K. Meister, *Ind. Forsch.* 26 (1909):69ff.; Halberstadt, "*Mater Matuta*," pp. 48ff.; and G. Cresci-Morrone and G. Mennell, *Pisaurum* (Pisa, 1984), pp. 138ff.
49. Although Krahe had the linguistic evidence concerning *deda* (aunt), he took it to mean *nutrices*, imagined thus as cooperating with the *matronae* in the offering. In this belief he was misled by Halberstadt, "*Mater Matuta*," pp. 53ff., for whom the Matralia was a festival of *nutrices*, a baseless interpretation already undercut by Dumézil in *Déesses Latines et mythes védiques* and *Mythe et Epopée*, p. 308. Hence, Krahe's conclusion comes as a surprise. The only text Krahe might have cited in his favor is Soranus, *Gyn.* 114, with the term *dida*. It usually means "mother," as in *CGL* 3.12.50; Soranus 44.46.108, and so forth; cf. C. Paucker, *Rh. Mus.* 38 (1883):313. But *dida* means *nutrix* in *Gyn.* 114, which may be compared with the Catalan *dida*

(nursemaid), noted by Ernout and Meillet, *Dictionnaire,* s.v. *dida.* In any case, we are dealing with *dida* and not *deda;* but above all, pace Halberstadt, *"Mater Matuta,"* our sources speak of a festival not with "nurses," but with "aunts."

50. For example, *deda(s)* was taken as a form of verb by A. Ernout, *Recueil de textes latins archaïques* (Paris, 1947), p. 42, following F. Ritschl, *Opuscula philologica* (Leipzig, 1897), 4:407; cf. Bücheler, *CIL* 1.².379, p. 407. These and other similar interpretations had already been condemned, though with another not much better advanced, by Meister, *Ind. Forsch.*, who also addressed the problem in morphology constituted by -*a*-: see also A. Ernout, *Meg. Soc. ling. Par.* 13 (1905–6):324; H. Petersen, *Zeitschr. verge. Sprachf.* 65 (1938):256; V. Pisani, *Testi latini arcaici e volgari* (Turin, 1950), p. 19; R. Lazzeroni, *St. sagg. ling.*, n.s. 2 (1962):106ff.; and I. Kajanto, *Arctos,* n.s. 5 (1967):72ff. (who thinks of the singular).

51. R. von Planta, *Litteris* 6; Krahe, *Ind. Forsch.* 55 (1937):121ff. Von Planta took *deda* as an Illyrian equivalent of the Greek *tethe,* evidently an oversight to be corrected, because *tethe* means "grandmother." Instead, *deda* must be related to the Greek group *tethis, theia,* discussed by O. Szemerényi, "Studies in the Kinship Terminology of the Indoeuropean Languages," *Textes et Memoires* 6, *Acta Iranica* (1977), pp. 61ff., although without reference to *deda.* Here one might mention also the reflections, wildly imaginative though they are, of W. Borgeaud (*Les Illyriens en Grèce et en Italie* [Geneva, 1943], pp. 85ff. and 139ff.), who would trace the Pesaro inscription to a special bond with Mater Matuta, as dawn goddess, on the part of the Ausones, who were "sons of dawn" (**auson-es | ausos-*), according to an old hypothesis of F. Ribezzo, *Riv. Ind. Gr. It.* 15, 3–4 (1931):65.

52. The dialects are found in southern Lombardy and western Veneto: see the *Sprach- und Sachatlas Italiens* I, K. 20, pp. 275 and 330.

53. This line of interpretation has been broached by some of the scholars who have studied Mater Matuta, although their perspectives remain partial or outmoded. Thus, the special relationship between aunt and nephew was seen as a trace of an archaic and matriarchal kinship system by G. Wissowa, *Religion und Kultus der Römer*² (Munich, 1912), p. 111. This view was rejected by H. J. Rose in his commentary on Plutarch's *Quaestiones Romanae,* p. 176, and by Frazer, *The Fasti of Ovid,* 4:280. Of course, the rite was read as an overt trace of "Mother-rule" by J. J. Bachofen, *Das Mutterrecht,* ed. K. Meuli (Basel, 1948), pp. 107n.2 and 151.; and so, too, Halberstadt, *"Mater Matuta,"* who had the merit to focus on the relationship of aunt and nephew only to come to the astonishing conclusion we have seen (nursemaids' rite).

Although confusing *materterae* with *amitae* and reducing the whole matter to the putative care of Roman aunts for orphaned nephews, one of the best approaches may still be that of A. Hild (*Daremberg-Saglio* 6 [1904]:1626a, n.7), taking a hint from the old but valuable remarks of Klausen, *Aeneas und die Penaten,* pp. 875ff., above all n.1701, in which he gathered a good part of the comparative evidence that fed the ensuing debates. Klausen's pages bear reading again not only for the archaeology of the problem but also for the discovery, perhaps not without emotion, of Professor F. Ritschl sending invaluable information from the manuscripts of Dionysius of Halicarnassus concerning the name Amata.

Failure to explain the ritual was confessed by W. Warde Fowler, *The Roman Festivals* (London, 1899), p. 155n.9. The hypothesis of group matrimony in archaic Rome met with moderate favor from L. R. Farnell, "Sociological Hypothesis concerning the Position of Women in Ancient Religion," *Arch. Rel. Wiss.* 7 (1904):70ff., an hypothesis taken up, independently I believe, by G. Franciosi, *Clan gentilizio e strutture monogamiche*[2] (Naples, 1978), pp. 57ff.

Various contributions to the discussion of Mater Matuta are gathered also by Dumézil, *Mythe et Epopée,* pp. 308ff. As for his interpretation, judgment is difficult. He rightly restored the value of the relationship between nephew and aunt to the rite, only to uproot it completely from its anthropological context, reducing everything to an astral content of ritual: birth of Day, the newborn cared for by Dawn, the sister of Night.

Mater Matuta receives only passing mention from S. B. Pomeroy, *Goddesses, Whores, Wives and Slaves: Women in Classical Antiquity* (New York, 1975), p. 207.

54. That Caecilia was Metellus's wife seems to appear from Valerius Maximus, although Cicero speaks only of "Caecilia Metelli." See Münzer *RE* 3[1].1234. The practice of taking *uxor* as implied occurs, for example, in Virgil, "Hectoris Andromache" (*Aen.* 3.319); Tacitus, *Ann.* 4.11.5; Pliny, *Hist. nat.* 28.12.

55. Only in these sources do we hear of such a custom, which thus must be treated with caution: it could be that *priscus mos* refers merely to the taking of omens for matrimony, with no necessary involvement of the *matertera,* who might appear in the tale for other reasons. Yet the way the story is told, especially by Valerius Maximus, makes our interpretation likely: it is accepted also by Rose, *Quaest. Rom.,* p. 174; Gagé, *Matronalia,* pp. 225ff.; and others—e.g., Klausen, Hild, and others mentioned in chap. 4, n.53 above.

56. A. De Marchi, *Il culto private di Roma antica* (Milan, 1896), 1:153ff. The relevant passages and bibliography were very carefully gathered

by A. S. Pease in the margins of Cicero, *Div.* 1.28, and Virgil, *Aen.* 4.166 ("pronuba Juno"). See also A. Rossbach, *Untersuchungen über die römische E he* (Stuttgart, 1853), pp. 294ff.

57. *Omen* etymologically means "declaration of truth," *o-* comparing directly to the Hittite verbal theme *ha-* (believe, consider true), according to a famous interpretation by E. Benveniste, *Hittite et Hindo-Européen* (Paris, 1962), pp. 10ff.; cf. idem, *Le Vocabulaire des institutions indoeuropeénes,* 2:255ff. However, it seems necessary to keep in mind the existence of *omentum* ("omenta sunt autem membranae quae exta continent" [membrane that contains the intestines], Schol. Persius 2.47): the term seems to be the doublet of *omen,* like the pairs *cognomen/cognomentum* and *termen/termentum,* and to belong to the augural language of the *extispicina.* In short, the matter may be a bit more complex that it seems. On the divinatory qualities of *omen,* see A. Bouché-Leclerq, *Histoire de la divination dans l'antiquité classique* (Paris, 1882), 4:77ff; and R. Bloch, *Les prodiges dans l'antiquité classique* (Paris, 1973), pp. 79ff.

58. See P. E. Corbett, *The Roman Law of Marriage* (Oxford, 1969), pp. 1ff.

59. See Münzer *RE*3[1].1234; and yet Metellus was called a "Vetter" of Caecilia, without explanation, by W. Kroll, *Die Kultur der Ciceronischen Zeit* (Leipzig, 1933), 2:37. On this marriage and the broader endogamic strategies of the Roman aristocracy in the first century B.C., see Thomas, "Mariages endogamiques à Rome," p. 354.

60. Münzer *RE* 3[1].1234.

61. Gaius, *Inst.* 1.156; Justinus, *Inst.* 3.5.4; and so forth. Cf. G. Hanard, "Observations sur l'adgnatio," *Rev. int. droit. anc.* 27 (1980):169ff.

62. Kroll, *Die Kultur der Ciceronischen Zeit,* 2:37. The phenomenon must be listed among the pushes toward bilateralization of Roman kinship, as marriage and divorce became ever more common, while frequency declined for marriages *cum manu,* and so forth. Cf. Thomas, "Mariages endogamiques à Rome," pp. 350ff., 357ff., and 375ff.

63. J. E. Phillips, "Roman Mothers and the Lives of Their Adult Daughters," *Helios* 6 (1978):69ff.

64. This anecdote is told also by Plutarch, *Tib. Gracch.* 4.3, with variations in the persons between Livy and Plutarch, and within the latter, which perhaps support the inference that the anecdote was traditional in character, reflecting not an actual and identifiable fact, but the general problem, or model, of relations between father and mother regarding the daughter's prospects.

65. We are not too far in this from two omens reported by Cicero in his work *On Divination:* "Persa perit" (1.103), uttered by the daughter of L. Paullus about her puppy, but applied by her father to King Persa, whom he was about to fight; and "Cauneas!" (Figs of Caunus) (2.84),

but also "Cav(e) ne eas!" which a nameless vendor at Brindisi was shouting as Crassus readied his ill-fated campaign in the East.

66. Amata is an extremely complex and rich figure, whose significance is certainly not exhausted in the following few pages. On her, see, at least, R. Heinze, *Vergils epische Technik³* (*Leipzig, 1915*), pp. 182ff.; H. Boas, *Aeneas' Arrival in Latium* (Amsterdam, 1938), pp. 80ff., especially for the Dionysiac character, genuine or not, of the orgy; R. Pichon, "L'episode d'Amata dans l'Eneide," *Rev. hist. anc.* 15 (1913):164 ff., on Amata as an ancient divinity or priestess of Dionysus; W. H. Friedrich, "Amatas Raserei," *Philol.* 94 (1939–41):142ff., seeking to draw improbable political implications from the figure; S. Patris, "Amata, reine des Latins," *Les ét. class.* 13 (1945):40ff.; and V. Buchheit, *Vergil über die Sendung Roms* (Heidelberg, 1963), pp. 102ff. For obvious reasons, I have not examined the relations between the Virgilian queen and the vestal *te amatam capio.*

67. See Gagé, *Matronalia,* pp. 236ff. This marriage is one of the many cases in Rome in which a royal succession passes from father-in-law to son-in-law, with the latter often appearing in a weaker position, that of the outsider, which constitutes less of a threat to the king as giver of the girl and to his group. The prime example is Servius Tullius, even the "son of a slave woman," and hence a zero on the father's side, a "son of earth," as a man without ancestors is called in Latin: Servius is born of a slave and a coal from the hearth.

The relative weakness of Servius with respect to the Tarquins emerges also from the kind of marriages he arranges for his two daughters by Tarquinia: they will marry the brothers of their mother (so Livy) or her brother's sons (Dionysius: see nn. 52 below and 4.5 above). In any event, the case is one of the maternal group reclaiming the ceded mother by taking her daughters and with them the temporarily ceded royal power. Likewise Aeneas, as outsider, must have weak contractual power if his descendants are to be called by his wife's father's name, Latini, rather than Troiani: it is as if the right to pass the father's family name to the children had been ceded to the mother's group. Similarly, the new city founded by the people born of this union will be called by her name, Lavinium: see A. Borghini, "Elementi di denominazione matrilaterale alle origini di Roma," *Stud. Urbin.* 57 (1984):43ff.

This aspect of the legend closely resembles the story that, after the slaughter of Cremera, the sole survivor of the *gens Fabia* contracted marriage with the daughter of Numerius Otacilius Maleventanus, but with the pledge that the first-born son be named for the maternal grandfather ("Incertum de praenominibus," 6). Again, we see a case of a son-in-law's weakness with respect to the maternal, or giving, group. We hardly need underline that these stories are not traces of an ancient matrilineality in Rome, before patrilineality took over.

Here, then, is the framework in which to apprise Aeneas's matrimony "willed by fate" and with an outsider, as opposed to nuptials with a member of the family of the mother of the girl. The latter choice would have blocked Latinus and his group from maintaining royalty, which they would have ceded to the group from which he had taken his wife.

68. Unlikely is the suggestion that in early Latium it was customary for first cousins on the mother's side to marry, made by Franciosi, *Clan gentilizio e strutture monogamiche*, pp. 82ff. However, this work has the merit of focusing interest on generally neglected subjects. His ideas on archaic marriage between matrilateral first cousins are taken up by J. C. Richard, *Origo Gentis Romanae* (Paris, 1983), p. 153. Yet the case of Turnus and Lavinia represents a union proposed but doomed, and thus a mythic warning that such marriages were prohibited.

Of the same type is the other legendary union between matrilateral first cousins, Horatia promised to a Curiatius, in which Horati and Curiati are sisters' children. Hence, the betrothed couple are in the same position as Turnus and Lavinia; and again it is a prospective marriage, never realized; and here, too, one of the partners, the girl this time, suffers a violent death, killed by the brother she refused to kiss because he had killed her fiancé (Dionysius of Halicarnassus, *Ant. Rom.* 3.21ff.; Livy, 1.26ff.; and Festus 380 L).

To invoke these legends, which weave tragic and negative events around the type of custom under discussion, as evidence that the custom existed means at very least to neglect the fact that myth may not only found a positive institution but also propound the contrary, warning against cultural choices that are in theory possible yet in practice disapproved. Who, for instance, would claim that the Oedipus myth proves the existence in Thebes of a historical phase characterized by a custom of matrimonial preference for the mother? A myth's cultural meaning, like any story's, as Propp used to say, must be measured from the end: the results reveal the intentions, and hence the cultural semantics. Yet there is a persistent tendency to consider institutions that are present in myth but not in real historical circumstances as traces of an earlier period, even though this tendency will always obstruct understanding of the world of legend and so, too, block a genuine historical grasp of a people's past. The surest way to falsify history is to historicize, arranging everything that cannot stand together according to the categories "first" and "then," thus binding every fact or mythic motif to a fixed historical phase.

69. "Mother-right" is little remarked in commentaries: remarks on *ius*

only are in C. J. Fordyce, *Aeneidos libri VII-VIII* (Oxford, 1977), p. 136; and also in Patris, "Amata, reine des Latins."

70. Cf. Virgil's use of *remordeo* in Jupiter's address to Venus, who is concerned about the future of her son, Aeneas: "Fabor enim, quando haec te cura remordet" (*Aen.* 1.261). In both contexts, then, there is a *cura* that *remordet,* an insistent anxiety. But already in Lucretius is: "Praeteritisque male admissis peccata remordent" (3.827); "Cum conscius ipse animus se forte remordet / desidiose agere aetatem" (4.1135); or, especially interesting, from Livy: "Sin autem tandem libertatis desiderium remordet animos" (8.4.3: also, the desire, or regret, for freedom is something that can never be quenched: it will repeatedly return to *remordere* the spirit).

Some of the subjects discussed here were treated in a baccalaureate thesis: E. Peranzi, "Il ruolo della mater nella cultura romana arcaica" (Pisa, 1981–82).

71. E. De Martino, *La terra del rimorso* (Milan, 1961), pp. 199ff.

72. Women overwhelmingly predominate in the phenomenon of tarantism: ibid., pp. 50ff. In 1959 De Martino found that, of thirty-seven participants identified in the Chapel of Saint Paul at Galatina, thirty-two were female (p. 48).

73. De Martino, *La terra del rimorso,* pp. 95ff. However, the "scorzoni," a kind of small snake, play an important function in the fantasies of the possessed.

74. De Martino, *La terra del rimorso,* p. 95: Rosaria, age thirteen, reported that "un serape celeste" blocked her path and put her under a spell.

75. The analogy, to be sure, may be accidental and must not be overvalued, although any valuation would be premature before going more deeply into the symbolic function of blue (and *caeruleus*) in contexts of *mania*. As for snakes, Virgil's language ("fit tortile collo / aurum ingens coluber, fit longae taenia vittae / innectitque comas ... ," 7.351ff.) led Heyne to comment that this detail was unworthy of Virgil's usual epic style. In effect, the ambiguous nature of the snake, at once alive and golden, lingering between the reality of the necklace and the fearsome imaginary identity that Allecto's action confers, creates an impression that is strongly perturbing (*unheimlich,* in Freud's sense, in "The Uncanny," in *The Complete Psychological Works of Sigmund Freud,* ed. and tr. J. Strachey et al. [London, 1953–73], 17:230). The ambiguity arouses that "doubt that a lifeless object may not in reality have a soul," which for Jentsch was the essence of *unheimlich*.

On this lingering between life and object, or, better, between reality and its image, as a source of perturbance, see M. Bettini, "Tra Plinio e S. Agostino: F. Petrarca sulle anti figurative," in *Memoria dell'antico nell'arte italiana,* ed. S. Settis (Turin, 1984), 1:222ff. Nor would I rule out the possibility that this ambiguity, too, belongs to the symbolic and religious framework of the episode. For example, De Martino *(La terra del rimorso,* pp. 91ff.) examines the case of Carmela: the possessed person, who saw her scorpion during her dance, holds in her hands a black rag and a gray one in relation to the color of the animal. Evidently, such behavior is a question of "really" wearing, in the form of objects that expressly recall its features, the mythic animal that causes one to be possessed.

76. De Martino, *La terra del rimorso,* pp. 127ff.
77. "Symbolism in Music and Dance," in ibid., pp. 132ff.
78. De Martino, *La terra del rimorso,* pp. 209ff.
79. A link between Amata's mode of suicide and her madness was posited by Warde Fowler, *The Death of Turnus* (Oxford, 1919), pp. 113ff., whereas her *letum informe* is simply "a mark of the queen's unallayed evil, not merely . . . a mode of death usual in tragedy," for V. Pöschl, *The Art of Vergil* (Ann Arbor, 1966). The aristocracy in Rome despised suicide by hanging, which was frequent among the lower classes, according to Y. Grisé, *Le suicide dans la Rome antique* (Paris, 1982), pp. 107ff.; remarks on Amata are on p. 148. Amata starved herself to death, according to Fabius Pictor (fr. 1 Peter). For other comments on her suicide, see G. Thaniel, "Nodum informis leti," *Act. Class.* 19 (1976):75ff.; J. L. Voisin, "Le suicide d'Amata," *Rev. ét. Lat.* 57 (1979):254ff.; and idem, "Pendus, crucifiés, 'oscilla' dans la Rome paienne," *Latom.* 38 (1979):422ff.
80. De Martino, *La terra del rimorso,* pp. 196ff., cites the mythic *aria* of Sardinia and other folklore.
81. On Virgil's poetry as copresence or plurality of viewpoints, see G. B. Conte, *Virgilio: Il genere e i suoi confini* (Milan, 1984), pp. 72ff.
82. Servius transmits the variant version by overinterpreting a Virgilian expression in which the poet certainly did not mean to allude to Amata's other crime: "Filius huic fato divum prolesque virilis / nulla fuit primaque oriens erepta iuventa est." Servius remarks, "Per transitum tangit historiam."
83. I use the text of Thilo-Hagen, which conflates Servius and Daniel's Servius. Square brackets indicate material appearing only in the latter.
84. On the *avunculus* in Roman legend, see A. Piganiol, *Essai sur les origines de Rome* (Paris, 1917), p. 146ff.; and Benveniste, *Le Vocabulaire des institutions indoeuropeénes,* s.v. *avunculus.*
85. "Matriarchal" interpretations of the *matertera* are discussed in chap. 4, n.53 above.

86. The Amata legend reveals "der Begriff des Muttertums in seiner ur-
sprünglichen Hoheit," according to J. Bachofen, *Das Mutterrecht*, p.
375; see also Boas, *Aeneas' Arrival in Latium*, pp. 80ff. Against the
method of matrilineal survivals, already there was a warning by H. J.
Rose, "On the Alleged Evidence for Mother-Right in Early Greece,"
Folklore 22 (1911):12ff.; on the antimatriarchal studies of Pembroke,
see E. Cantarella, *Introduzione a J. J. Bachofen: Il potere femminile*
(Milan, 1977), p. 44n.64. On Bachofen, see also O. Wesel, *Il mito del
matriarcato* (Milan, 1985).

    Not to be read as a trace of matriarchy is the frequent succession
from father-in-law to son-in-law in Roman royal legend: see the useful observations by Thomas, "Mariages endogamiques à Rome," pp.
375ff. and n.213. Beyond classical studies, the problem of matrilineal
survivals has often been treated with the institutions surrounding the
maternal uncle; for example, C. Lévi-Strauss, "Structural Analysis in
Linguistics and Anthropology," in *Structural Anthropology,* tr. C. Jacobson and B. G. Schoepf (Garden City, N. Y., 1963), pp. 37ff. But where
the maternal uncle predominates, a matrilineal succession may or
may not exist: the avuncular role occurs in both matrilineal and patrilineal societies and reflects the general tendency to associate certain
social relations with certain kinship roles: see R. H. Lowie, "The Matrilineal Complex," *Univ. Cal. Publ. in Am. Arch. and Ethn.* 16
(1919):29ff. Yet the role of maternal uncle among the Germans as
described by Tacitus was seen as a trace of "mother-kin" by J. G.
Frazer, *The Golden Bough,* part 1, vol. 2 (London, 1913), pp. 285ff.
However, Tacitus was a model of ethnographic clarity: "Sororum filiis
idem apud avunculum qui apud patrem honor. Quidam sanctiorem
artioremque hunc nexum sanguinis arbitrantur et in accipiendis ob-
sidibus magis exigunt, tamquam et animum firmius et domum latius
teneant. Heredes tamen successoresque sui cuique liberi, et nullum
testamentum" (*Germ.* 20.3). With this remark, Tacitus shows that he
perfectly understood that a privileged relationship with the maternal
uncle can peacefully coexist with a rule of inheritance of goods
through the father.

87. What I have in mind are the contrary fates of Bachofen's "Mutterrecht," which has been accepted by the socialist historians and soci-
ologists, but also by the virile faith of J. Evola, as remarked in Cantarella, *Introduzione a J. J. Bachofen.*

88. See the remarks by C. Lévi-Strauss, "Du mariage dans un dégré rap-
proché," in *Le Regard éloigné* (Paris, 1983), pp. 132ff. Here we cannot
report, even in terms of naked bibliography, the anthropological debate on filiation (unilineal, bilineal, indifferent, etc.). The absolute
importance of the concept, however, needs to be lessened in favor of

careful study of the relations between "givers" and "takers": see ibid., following Richards and Evans-Pritchard, also idem, *Structure elementaire,* pp. 164ff. Also important here is J. Goody, *L'Evolution de la famille et du mariage en Europe* (Paris, 1984), pp. 225ff.
89. See chap. 3, n.10 above; and on the importance of the mother-line, see chap. 13 below.

Chapter Five. Father's Sister: Amita

1. The sole text that may suggest a close relationship between paternal aunt and nephew is, I believe, *CIL* 3.12286 (Issa, Dalmatia): "Valentina mater et Crescentilla amita Praeponti filio," in which the child is treated as *filius* with respect to the *amita,* as well as the *mater.* In *CIL* 3.1038 (Reatinum, Dalmatia), "amitae dicnissime et nutrici," but *nutrici* is a correction for *aiutrici.* On the *amita* in the *Parentalia,* see G. Guastella, "Non sanguine sed vice," *MD* 7 (1982).
2. On the problems raised by this genealogical leap, see L. Bessone, "La Gente Tarquinia," *RFIC* 110 (1982).
3. See M. Bettini, "Su alcuni modelli antropologici della Roma più arcaica," *MD* 1 (1978) and 2 (1979).
4. On the degrees of kinship, see *Dig.* 38.19.1.
5. On Calpurnia Hispulla, see also J. E. Phillips, "Roman Mothers and the Lives of Their Adult Daughters," *Helios* 6 (1978). Tender behavior between nephew and *amita* are also recorded in the case of Nero and Domitia Lepida, who virtually reared the future emperor (Suetonius, *Div. Ner.* 6.5). The aunt employed all manner of *blandimenta* and *largitiones* toward him, according to Tacitus (*Ann.* 12.64). The intimacy of their relationship appears also in the story that once, while ill, she took between her fingers the first down on the young man's cheeks "per blanditias" (*Div. Ner.* 34.5); however, their behavior toward each other appears very corrupt. Of this, Tacitus informs us: "Et utraque impudica (Agrippina and Domitia), infamis, violenta, haud minus vitiis aemulabantur quam si qua ex fortuna prospera acceperant. Enimvero certamen acerrimum, amita potius an mater apud Neronem praevaleret: nam Lepida blandimentis ac largitionibus iuvenilem animum devinciebat, truci contra ac minaci Agrippina" (*Ann.* 12.64). The affectionate and indulgent aunt offers a contrast to the harsh mother: neither pattern of behavior is spontaneous; each seeks a result. As always, it is difficult to draw pure sociological inferences about the Julio-Claudian family: the same is true of their marriages, divorces, incestuous relations, and so forth.

Chapter Six. Conclusions

1. E. E. Evans-Pritchard, *Kinship and Marriage among the Nuer* (Oxford, 1951), p. 157–58.
2. Ibid., pp. 160–61.
3. Ibid., pp. 162–63.
4. Ibid., p. 167.
5. H. A. Junod, *Moeurs et costumes des Bantous* (Paris, 1936), 1:211ff. Here we find, in contrast with a severe father–paternal uncle, an indulgent and affectionate maternal uncle: Junod's data were utilized also by A. R. Radcliffe-Brown, *Le Parentele di scherzo,* in *Struttura e funzione nella società primitiva* (tr. Ital., Milan, 1972). Junod also makes interesting remarks on the difference between maternal and paternal grandfathers in their respective attitudes toward their grandchildren.
6. According to the well-known hypothesis of C. Lévi-Strauss ("Structural Analysis in Linguistics and Anthropology," in *Structural Anthropology,* tr. C. Jacobsen and B. G. Schoepf [Garden City, N.Y., 1963]; "Reflections on the Atom of Kingship," in *Structural Anthroplogy,* in ibid., 2:82ff.; and in "Un 'atome de parenté' australian," in *Le regard éloigné* [Paris, 1983], pp. 93ff.; "La famiglia," in *Razza e storia e altri studi di antropologia* [Turin 1967]; and *La Vita familiare e sociale degli indiani Nambikwara* [Milan, 1970]), the relations between maternal uncle and nephew must be included in a system of four elements, also consisting of father-son, husband-wife, brother-sister: among these four sets, the relationships are correlated. I believe that likewise it would be possible to find some traits of rather detached and severe relations between husband and wife in archaic Rome: after all, the foundation myth of Roman matrimony is a kidnapping, the so-called Rape of the Sabine Women, which is also reenacted in many parts of the ritual. Evidence also exists for rather tender relations between brother and sister. Thus, the Roman system appears to correlate a positive relationship between maternal uncle and nephew with a positive relationship between brother and sister, but a negative relationship between father and son with a negative relationship between husband and wife (the content of "positive" and "negative" requiring, naturally, to be filled in and made explicit from case to case). Such bonds are what Lévi-Strauss means by "atom of kinship": the notion has often been questioned, and underwent refinements by its author in successive works as cited above, yet still can offer guidance and very interesting solutions. This, too, is a subject to which I hope to return.

Part Two. "The future at your back:
Spatial Representations of Time in Latin

1. "(Tempus) fallit autem illos, quia res incorporealis est, quia sub oculos non venit." See the commentary of A. Traina in S. Mariotti, C.
   Questa, A. Traina, *Una maschera, una coscienza, un popolo* (Turin,
   1981), p. 123; see also "Introduction," p. 92.
2. It is well known that the linguistic system of temporal relations is by
   and large spatial: see the introductory remarks in the fundamental
   study by E. C. Traugott, "On the Expression of Spatio-Temporal Relations in Language," in *Universals of Human Language,* ed. J. H.
   Greenberg (Stanford, 1978), 3:369ff. For classical languages, the spatialization of temporal categories has been addressed, but quite inad-
   equately, by M. Treu, *Von Homer zur Lyrik* (Munich, 1968), pp. 123ff.
   Treu believes that Greek spatialization of time was the reverse of ours.
   Also interesting is G. E. Dunkel, *"Prosso kai opisso,"* Zeitschr. vergl.
   Sprachf. 96 (1982–83):67ff. On the other hand, not our problem, but
   the system of prepositions in Homer is studied by G. Horrocks, *Space
   and Time in Homer* (New York, 1981).

Chapter Seven. Localizing Anterior and Posterior

1. E. C. Traugott, "On the Expression of Spatio-Temporal Relations in
   Language," in *Universals of Human Language,* ed. J. H. Greenberg
   (Stanford, 1978), 3:176ff.
2. Ibid.: "Sequencing, as opposed to tense, is the system whereby events
   or situations $E_1 E_2 \ldots$ are ordered with respect to each other."
3. Evidently, the augural space is marked here so the south is ahead and
   the north behind: "Sic etiam ea caeli pars, quae sole inlustratur ad
   meridiem, antica nominatur, quae ad septentrionem postica"
   (Paulus-Festus 244 L). Useful remarks on the orientation of the augural space, as well as the shifts between south and east as "before"
   the augur, are in A. L. Frothingham, "Ancient Orientation Unveiled,"
   AJA 21 (1917):55ff., 187ff., and 420ff. In contrast, misleading considerations are raised by C. O. Thulin, *Die etruskische Disziplin* (Gö-
   teberg, 1926), 1:21. Above all, see G. Wissowa, *Religion und Kultus
   der Römer*[2] (Munich, 1912), p. 525 and 525n.
4. "Et quae ante nos sunt antica, et quae post nos sunt postica dicuntur"
   (Paulus-Festus 244 L).
5. See *TLL* 2.177.24ff.
6. The minimal pair (/ + / -/) rounded off in case of velars is hardly un-

known in Latin: cf. *sequor/secor, loquor/locor, coquo/coco.* On labiove-
lars in Latin, see A. Devine and L. D. Stephens, *Two Studies in Latin
Phonology* (Saratoga, Fla., 1977); and G. Marotta, "Il problema delle
labiovelari latine nel confronto di due teorie fonologiche," *ASNP* 12
(1982):1183ff.

7. See *TLL* 1.128, 21ff. Likewise the superlative *antiquissimus* can take
   on the sense of "best, extraordinary."
8. A. S. Pease, *M. Tulli Ciceronis De Divinatione Libri Duo* (reprint;
   Darmstadt, 1977), p. 131, on 1.27. See also Herodotus 5.63; Plato,
   Symp. 218 D, and so forth. Analogous, on the Greek side, is the explanation by H. Stein, *Herodotus* (Berlin 1963), 3:62.
9. P. Chantraine, *Dictionnaire étymologique de la langue Greque* (Paris,
   1974), s.v. "presby."
10. See chap. 12 below.
11. For this sense of the word "discourse," see E. Benveniste, "The Corre-
    lations of Tense in the French Verb," in *Problems in General Linguistics*
    (Coral Gables, Fla., 1971), pp. 208ff.
12. R. Jakobson, "Commutatori, Categori Verbali e il tempo in Russo," in
    Problemi di Linguistica Generale (Milan 1971), pp. 149ff.; on "yester-
    day/tomorrow," see Benveniste, "L'experience humaine et le langage,"
    in *Problèmes de linguistique générale* 2:67ff.
13. A. Ernout and A. Meillet, *Dictionnaire étymologique de la langue Latine*[4]
    (Paris, 1967), s.v. "primus."
14. S.v. "Primus."
15. See chap. 12 below. *Pro-* does not have a specifically temporal em-
    ployment, unless one is assigned by derivation, as we shall see.

Chapter Eight. Localizing Future and Past

1. E. C. Traugott, "On the Expression of Spatio-Temporal Relations in
   Language," in *Universals of Human Language,* ed. J. H. Greenberg, vol.
   3 (Stanford, 1978), following B. Comrie, *Aspect* (London, 1976), pp.
   1ff.
2. Traugott, "On the Expression of Spatio-Temporal Relations in Language," p. 374.
3. R. Jakobson, "Commutatori, Categori Verbali e il tempo in Russo," in
   Problemi di Linguistica Generale (Milan 1971), pp. 149ff. On "yester-
   day/tomorrow," see E. Benveniste, "L'experience humaine et le lan-
   gage," in *Problèmes de linguistique générale,* vol. 2 (Paris, 1972); and
   Traugott, "On the Expression of Spatio-Temporal Relations in Language," p. 374.
4. See also Cicero: "Hic error et haec indoctorum animis offusa caligo

est, quod tam longe retro respicere non possunt" (*Tusc.* 5.6), and "Deinceps retro usque ad Romulam, qui ab hoc tempore anno sescentesimo erat" (*De rep.* 1.58).

5. See the fine remarks by A. Traina, "Il tempo e la saggezza," in S. Mariotti, C. Questa, and A. Traina, *Una maschera, una coscienza, un popolo* (Turin, 1981).

6. See also Seneca, *Ad Lucil.* 49.2, 99.7, and so forth.

7. Seneca, "Pervenisse te ad ultimum aetatis humanae videmus . . . agedum, ad computationem aetatem tuam revoca" (*De brev. vit.* 3.2). Here the metaphor is financial, but is modified by the superimposed temporal image. In *revoca* "there is further a glance backward, without which it would read *ad computationem aetatem tuam voca,*" remarks Traina, in *Una maschera, una coscienza, un popolo.* On this theme, I cannot help recalling, too, a thrust by Hermerotes in Petronius: "Tu autem tam laboriosus es, ut post te non respicias? In alio peduclum vides, in te ricinium non vides" (57.7). Clearly, the theme of the man too busy to look back (here "laboriosus" expresses the idea of "occupatus") belongs also to the humble stock of popular wisdom.

8. Plautus, *Rud.* 1316; and Terence, *Phorm.* 817. A good part of the material presented here is owed to G. Guastella, who is preparing a comprehensive study of *respicere.*

9. Cicero, *De leg.* 2.11.28; see J. Champeaux, *Fortuna: Le culte de la Fortune à Rome et dans le monde Romain* (Rome, 1982), 1:37, 49ff.216, and so forth.

10. Cf. Apollodorus, *Bibl.* 1.3.15. On the theme of prohibition against turning, copious material appears in E. Rhode, *Psiche* II, p. 417; A. S. Pease, *M. Tulli Ciceronis De Divinatione Libri Duo* (reprint; Darmstadt, 1977), on Cicero, *De div.*, pp. 182ff.; J. G. Fraser, "Some Popular Superstitions of the Ancients," *Garnered Sheaves* (London, 1931), pp. 136ff.; and Th. Köves-Zulauf, *Reden und Schweigen* (Munich, 1972), pp. 122ff. The theme intertwines naturally with that of the symbolic functions of the eye: see S. Seligmann, *Der böse Blick und verwandtes* (Berlin, 1910); idem, *Die Zauberkraft des Auges und das Berufen* (Hamburg, 1922); and W. Deonna, *Le symbolisme de l'oeil* (Bern, 1965). For the dream of Hannibal and other implications of turning around, see chap. 11 below.

11. As Tertullian adds: see the full discussion in Köves-Zulauf, *Reden und Schweigen*, pp. 122ff.

12. See Traina, in *Una maschera, una coscienza, un popolo*, pp. 96ff.; and the image "in se . . . descendere" (Persius 4.23), which is analogous in some respects and constitutes another metaphoric way of reestablishing contact with oneself.

13. Properly speaking, *bruma* is the winter solstice, reckoned by the Julian calendar to 25 December. Probably Ovid superimposes two models of the year's ending and beginning: that reckoned on 1 January and that reckoned on the winter solstice, which is shared by many cultures: cf. Frazer's comment in *The Fasti of Ovid* on *Fast.* 1.136; "tempus a bruma ad brumam, dum sol redit, vocatur annus" (Varro, *Ling. Lat.* 6.8,); and Plutarch, *Quaest. Rom.* 19.

14. See L. A. Holland, *Ianus and the Bridge* (Rome, 1961), p. 276. To the same class of representations belong two epithets of Patulcius and Clusius (or Clusivius) attributed to the god *in sacris:* Macrobius, *Sat.* 1.9.15. See also Ovid, *Fast.* 1.129; Servius on Virgil, *Aen.* 7.610; and so forth. Clearly, the god that opens and closes has every type of passage in his power. His attributes, not surprisingly, are the keys and the staff (Ovid, *Fast.* 1.99.228, 254): according to Macrobius, "Cum clavi ac virga figuratur, quasi omnium et portarum custos et rector viarum" (*Sat.* 1.9.7) (here, too, passing and going). Seeking to explain why opening the temple of Janus Quirinus signified war, Servius wrote on *Aen.* 1.291: "Quod ad proelium ituri optent reversionem" (the same explanation appeared already in Ovid, *Fast.* 1.279).

    In other words, the passageway left open in the temple of Janus Quirinus suggested, by a kind of sympathetic analogy, the return of the soldiers going out to war, because it did not shut them out. The model of *pro itu et reditu* (going and coming) continues to work.

    On the temple of Janus Quirinus *ad infimum argiletum,* see Holland, *Ianus and the Bridge,* pp. 108ff. Generally on Janus, see the well-balanced work by R. Schilling, "Janus," in *Rites, cultes, dieux de Rome* (Paris, 1979), pp. 220ff.; G. Capedeville, "Les épithètes cultuels de Janus," *Mat. éc. Fr. Rome* 85 (1973):395ff. On the imperial period, R. Turcan, *ANRW* 2, 17.1, pp. 374ff.

15. See J. Wackernagel, *Vorlesungen über Syntax*[1] (Basel, 1925), 1:149, 154.

16. See E. Benveniste, *Noms d'agent e noms d'action en Indo-éuropéen* (Paris, 1948), p. 104; and M. Bettini, "Su alcuni modelli antropologici della Roma più arcaica," *MD,* 160ff.

17. Such a periphrasis is employed also outside the infinitive mood; for example, by Cato: "Quae [contumelia] mihi factum itur" (*Orat. fr.* 176 Malc.). The quite unusual construction is discussed by M. T. Splendorio Cugusi, *M. Porci Catonis orationum reliquiae* (Turin, 1982), p. 424, with preliminary bibliographical guidance. Again in the infinitive, but outside the passive construction, is the type *ultum ire:* see J. B. Hofmann and A. Szantyr, *Lateinische Syntax und Stilistik* (Munich, 1965), p. 381.

18. This type of syntax is briefly discussed, though not always clearly or

convincingly, by Hofmann and Szantyr, *Lateinische Syntax und Stilis-tik*, p. 381.

19. In *Una maschera, una coscienza, un popolo*, Traina says that "*rapidissimi* does not say the same thing as *celeritatem*, because it adds the etymological notion of 'theft'" (p. 167); see also p. 105.

Chapter Nine. "On the way":
Reflections in Literary Anthropology

1. See Paolo Fedeli, "Petronio: Il viaggio, il labirinto," *MD* 6 (1982):91ff.

2. From the anthropological viewpoint, this episode illustrates in a most interesting way the well-known tendency for groups or peoples to identify themselves as "human beings," while denying this quality to those around them: thus, "others" are identified as "eggs of lice" and "sharks" and "dead men in lion forms" in cases gathered by C. Lévi-Strauss, *The Elementary Structures of Kinship*, tr. J. H. Bell and J. R. von Sturmer and ed. R. Needham (Boston, 1969), pp. 87ff. See also L. Lévy-Bruhl, *La mitologia primitiva* (Rome, 1973), pp. 92ff.; to which add the comments on the name *arya* by E. Benveniste, *Le Vocabulaire des institutions indoeuropeénes* (Paris, 1966). On the ancient world, see S. Ferri, "Esigenze archeologiche V," *St. Class. Or.* 12 (1963):254ff.

    The proliferation of imaginary beings in folklore, such as dwarfs, giants, monsters, resulted from an inability to conceive of strangers in the same manner as citizens, according to a hypothesis of Gobineau, cited by Lévi-Strauss. This hypothesis fits well with the picture of peasants in *Oblòmov*, mistaking the unlucky outsider for a werewolf.

3. Petronius in the *Satyricon* makes many specific allusions to the *Odyssey*, beyond a simple working analogy at the level of plot, though such an analogy may be one of the reasons for explicit allusions: see Fedeli, "Petronio: Il viaggio, il labirinto"; A. M. Cameron, "Myth and Meaning in Petronius," *Latom.* 21 (1970):25ff., who extends the comparison to Joyce; and A. Barchiesi, "Poetica dei nomi in Petronio," *MD* 12 (1984):169ff.

4. The scheme is very old and widespread in folklore: see D. L. Page, *Racconti populari nell'Odyssea* (Naples, 1983), p. 16 and n.3, with ample bibliography.

5. Even a linguistic link between the wisdom, *noos*, of Odysseus and his experience as a hero of "return home," *nostos*, has been suggested by D. Frame, *The Myth of Return in Early Greek Epic* (New Haven, 1978), who argues not only that *noos* and *nostos* both derive from the root *nes-*, from which would come even *asmenos*, and which is found in

the verb *neomai,* but also that this linguistic link still operates in the many episodes in which the superior *noos* of Odysseus allows him to further his *nostos,* even though Homer himself was not conscious of the link. All this is developed in the light of a solar mythology that we thought had set forever (if a pun can be forgiven) in the study of classical myth.

6. E. Balensiefern, "Die Zeitgestaltung in Homers Iliad" (Diss., Tübingen, 1955); I. Schudoma, "Naturerscheinungen und Naturgeschehn bei Homer" (Diss., Tübingen, 1960); and, above all, B. Hellwig, *Raum und Zeit in homerischen Epos,* Spudasmata II (Hildesheim, 1964).

7. See the computation by Hellwig, *Raum und Zeit in homerischen Epos,* pp. 40ff., which is based in turn on Balensiefen, "Die Zeitgestaltung in Homers Iliad," pp. 3ff.

8. Hellwig, *Raum und Zeit in homerischen Epos,* pp. 42 and 45.

9. Ibid.

10. Ibid, p. 45.

11. Ibid.

12. "Rückweise," a term taken from E. Lämmert, *Bauformen des Erzählens* (Stuttgart, 1955).

13. "Rückgriff," in Hellwig, *Raum und Zeit in homerischen Epos,* p. 45.

14. Hellwig, *Raum und Zeit in homerischen Epos,* pp. 28ff.

15. Ibid., p. 35.

16. K. Reinhardt, "Die Abenteuer des Odysseus," in *Von Werken und Formen* (Bad Godesberg, 1948), p. 73.

17. Hellwig, *Raum und Zeit in homerischen Epos,* pp. 35ff.

18. Ibid., p. 38. Hellwig also makes productive remarks in general on events that remain in the background during passage from one action to another, with return, then, to the first: awareness of such background events appears more pronounced in the *Odyssey* than in the *Iliad* (p. 75).

19. See Ju. Nekljudov, "Il sistema spaziale nell'intreccio della bylina russa," in *Ricerche semiotiche,* ed. J. M. Lotman and B. A. Uspenskij (Turin, 1973), pp. 107ff.

20. Ibid., p. 108.

21. Hellwig, *Raum und Zeit in homerischen Epos,* pp. 35ff.

22. Ibid., p. 58.

23. Concerning the *Geistesgeschichtliche* mode in classical philology, I think first of Bruno Snell, *La cultura greca e le origini del pensiero europeo* (Turin, 1963). But, above all, it is impossible not to cite Herman Fränkel, *Wege und Formen frühgriechischen Denkens* (Munich, 1960). Its first chapter, dealing with "Zeitauffassung" from Homer to the lyric poets, makes a well-known statement that today requires review with other eyes. Fränkel remarked that in Homer the word *chronos* is

used only to indicate time that is empty or negative (sleep, useless agonizing, failed efforts, etc.: pp. 2ff., with evidence on pp. 15ff.), so "beim Warten hat also man die Zeit entdeckt" (note the use of "entdecken," a buzzword in this type of study). In short, the Greeks are supposed to have discovered time in those moments when it was *absent*. Or, in the words of Edmund Leach, paraphrasing Fränkel, "in Homer, *chronos* refers to moments of time's absence," in "Due saggi sulla rappresentazione simbolica del tempo," in *Nuove vie dell'antropologia* (Milan, 1973), p. 202. But in this way, the "history of the spirit" improperly took the place of study of the workings of literature and built, among other things, a false history of psychology.

In Homeric *epos* it is natural that *chronos* is mentioned almost entirely in moments when the action to some degree *slackens off*, so there is a need to show expressly the amount of time that passes. In moments of action, because action is identified with narrative time and carries it along, time does not need to be mentioned. If a hero fights before our eyes, and the poet describes it, there is no need for the story to tell how long the fighting lasted; the time appears directly through the action, as its understood premise. However, if a hero sleeps or vainly weeps, then the time taken by this empty action, inactive action, has to be spelled out. But how can anyone identify these niceties of narrative, these necessities of composition, with "discoveries" of the "spirit," with nothing less than the "discovery" of a category such as Time?

The paradox of *Geistesgeschichte*, as applied to the ancient world, lay just here, in identifying the "spirit" (or whatever) with certain literary texts, as if Greek culture were not far wider and the series of literary texts not a merely partial metonomy (made, above all, according to precise laws that themselves ought to have been studied) for the cultural manifestations of religion, work, daily life, the law, and so on, which are the boundless material of literature. And yet it was thought that a certain poet, or a certain literary text, was needed to "discover" what thousands of unknown Greeks employed every day to be themselves and live the way they did. But to return to *chronos* and Homer, Fränkel himself noted cases in which it was mentioned in apparently "positive" contexts (pp. 15ff.): the problem really was badly posed.

24. Narrative repetition has an intensifying character that was already clear to the older students of folklore. "To show that an action is important, [folk literature] employs repetition: in this way attention can stay longer on the same fact," according to A. Olrik, "La costruzione del racconto: Le leggi epiche," *Uomo e cultura* 11–12 (1973):197ff. (a partial version of a study first published in 1921).

Again, "the chief means of ballad style is a sort of progressive itera-
tion," according to Gummere, *Old English Ballads* (1894), p. xxxii,
cited by Olrik. Homer's triple repetition of the name Nireus (*Il.*
2.671) was, in Aristotle's view, an attempt at the "effect" of fullness
(*Rhet.* 3.12 = 1413b 23): see F. Leo, *Analecta Plautina* (Göttingen,
1906), 3:5ff.; and M. Bettini, "A proposito dei versi sotadei greci e
romani," *MD* 9 (1982):82n.9.

25. See the fine remarks on time and repetition in oral poetry by H.
Scheub, "Body and Image in Oral Narrative Performance," *New Lit.
Hist.* 8 (1977):345ff., based on direct observations among the Xhosa
of South Africa. According to Scheub, the repetition of "image-sets"
serves to establish a continual tension with the duration of narrative
time without breaking off artificially its flow, something not allowed
in oral performance. In this way, the narrative can really convey a
message or content that, allowing time to flow in perfect accord with
the normal logic of events, could not be fixed. The fact that repetition
is one of the ways to create narrative isotopy, which is more or less
what Scheub was getting at, has rightly been underlined by A. Grei-
mas, *Semantica strutturale* (Milan, 1969), as well as by Bettini, "A proposito dei versi sotadei greci e romani."

I would further insist that in *epos,* as in myth, repetition also and
above all achieves the paradigmatic stamp of the narrated events. If,
also from a linguistic standpoint, analogy is the realm of paradigm,
even as opposition is the combinatory, syntagmatic, realm, it is very
likely that also on the compositional level repetition is related to the
paradigmatic pole, so in some sense it exalts the meaning and the
very presence of the narrated events.

This ought to be more emphasized in studies of Homeric formula:
among much else that conditions the use of this poetic technique
must be, unavoidably, the paradigmatic effect produced in the listener. The formula, the "repeated," is what creates in the hearer the
suggestion that the actions being told are unfolding in a paradigmatic
world, quite detached and different from everyday life, in the space of
the code, beyond that of its manifestations in particular events or
individual tales. See M. Bettini and C. Questa, "Nuovi Studi su
Plauto: Grammatica poetica e fortuna letteraria di un testo esem-
plare," *MD* 14 (1986).

26. On folk trebling, see V. Propp, *Morphology of the Folktale,*[2] ed. Louis
A. Wagner and tr. Laurence Scott (Austin, 1968), pp. 74–75; Olrik,
"La costruzione del racconto," pp. 197ff.; copious material, obviously,
in H. Usener, *Dreiheit* (Hildesheim, 1966); M. Vendryes, "L'unité en
trois personnes chez les Celtes," *Compt. rend. Ac. Inscr.* (1935):324ff.;
W. Deonna, "Trois, superlatif absolu à propos du taureau tricornu et

de Mercure trifallique," *Ant. Class.* 23 (1954):23ff. On the Roman world, see F. Menna, "La ricerca dell'adiuvante," *MD* 10–11 (1984):105ff., particularly 126ff.; see also P. Fedeli, "Il cedimento dell'incrollabile," in *Miscellanea Della Corte* and chap. 17 below.

From a slightly different viewpoint, more focused on three than on trebling as a narrative device, see also for bibliography from the field of psychology, V. N. Toporov, "L'albero universale: Saggio di interpretazione semiotica," in *Ricerche semiotiche, pp.* 180ff. The trebling of objects, magical devices, and so forth in folklore as possible survivals of trifunctional structures is discussed by G. Dumézil, "Les objects trifonctionnels dans les Mythes indo-européens," in *Strutture e generi delle letterature etniche: Atti del simposio internazionale* (Palermo, 1970 [1978]), pp. 45ff.; idem, *Heur et malheur du guerrier* (Paris, 1969), pp. 20ff., also *Mythe et épopée,* 1:540ff. Useful remarks appear, too, in the commentary on Antonius Liberalis by M. Papathomopoulos, *Metamorphoses* (Paris, 1968), pp. 90–91. On Amor and Psyche, see R. Roncali, *Sileno* 7 (1981):81.

27. E. M. Meletinskij, *La Struttura della fiaba* (Palermo, 1977), p. 132.
28. These successive displacements of the hero in fable follow a repeated pattern of the type A-B-A, in which A is the place of the hero's passivity, from which he is expelled, to get to B and get back; in this, the Russian magic fable differs from the *bylina,* in which the hero, at the start, is represented as not home (passive position), but in movement along the field: Nekljudov, "Il sistema spaziale nell'intreccio della bylina russa."
29. See the remarks above (in n.23) on *chronos* in Homer appearing essentially in moments of empty or negative time and concerning H. Fränkel.

Chapter Ten. "On the way": Generational Time and the "Review of Heroes" in Book Six of Virgil's Aeneid

1. See also Seneca, "Dimisimus illum, immo consecuturi praemisimus" (*Ad Marc.* 19.1); idem, "Non reliquit ille nos, sed antecessit" (*Ad Pol.* 9.9); Augustine, "non amisimus, sed praemisimus" (*Ep.* 92.1): see A. Traina, *Lo stile drammatico del filosofo Seneca* (Bologna, 1978), p. 190.
2. "Standi ordine, non nascendi, nam sextus est rex Albanorum," remarks Servius. Let us set aside his historical detail, which interests us less here, and note that Servius rightly underlines that Virgil is describing an *ordo standi:* "proximus ille" are Virgil's words, giving demonstrative concreteness to the reference: see J. Henry, *Aeneidea*

(New York, 1972), 3:407, and the note by R. G. Austin, *P. Vergilius Maro Liber VI* (Oxford, 1977), ad loc.

3. E. Norden, *P. Vergilius Maro "Aeneis" Buch VI²* (Stuttgart, 1967), p. 315, speaks of "gewaltigen Eindruck, den diese Partie . . . auf der Leser gemacht hat" and finds the reasons in the grandeur of composition and the elevated language. See also E. Skard, "Die Heldenschau in Vergils Aeneis," *Symb. Osl.* 11 (1965):51ff.: "Eine der grossartigsten Szenen in der Literatur des Abendlandes."

4. Norden, *P. Vergilius Maro "Aeneis" Buch VI*, p. 312.

5. G. N. Knauer, *Die Aeneis und Homer* (Göttingen, 1964), pp. 124ff.

6. Gilbert Highet, *The Speeches in the Aeneid* (Princeton, 1972), p. 241.

7. L. Delaruell, "Souvenirs d'oeuvres plastiques dans la révue des héros au livre VI de l'Enéide," *Rev. Arch.* 21 (1913):153ff.; and H. T. Rowell, "Vergil and Augustus," *AJP* 62 (1941):261ff.

8. Skard, "Die Heldenschau in Vergils Aeneis"; on the models of the "Review of Heroes," see the careful discussion by W. P. Basson, *Pivotal Catalogues in the Aeneid* (Amsterdam, 1975), pp. 37ff. Only a few stylistic remarks appear in J. Gassner, "Kataloge in römischen Epos" (Diss., Munich, 1972), pp. 64ff.

9. Austin, *P. Vergilius Maro Liber VI*, 233ff.

10. Already Servius commented on *Aen.* 6.752: "Qui bene considerant, inveniunt omnem Romanam historiam ab Aeneae adventu usque ad sua tempora summatim celebrasse Vergilium. Quod ideo late, quia confusus est ordo: nam eversio Ilii et Aeneae errores, adventus bellumque manifesta sunt; Albanos reges, Romanos etiam consulesque, Brutum, Catonem, Caesarem, Augustum et multa ad historiam pertinentia hic indicat locus; cetera, quae hic intermissa sunt in aspidopoiia commemorat." Through oversight, Servius's "confusus ordo" gets taken as referring to chronological discrepancies in the "Review of Heroes" rather than Virgil's scattering of Roman history in various contexts, which Servius clearly meant, by Basson, *Pivotal Catalogues in the Aeneid*, p. 39n.11.

11. See Highet, *The Speeches in the Aeneid*; and Basson, *Pivotal Catalogues in the Aeneid*, p. 29n.11.

12. The funeral of Augustus appears to be the sole exception to the practice, if we believe Dio Cassius (56.34.2), cited in chap. 13 below: Augustus's bier opened the procession, rather than closing it as was usual, and images of all the great Romans, not only those of Augustus's family, were carried. If this was the case, one might assert for the sake of paradox, to be sure, that Skard's thesis ("Die Heldenschau in Vergils Aeneis") should be turned inside out: it was not the funeral of Marcellus that inspired Virgil's "Review of Heroes," but the "Review of Heroes" that inspired a funeral—Augustus's.

13. See Polybius (6.54.3) on the love of excellence inspired in the young by the ceremony of the aristocratic funeral. See also below, chap. 13 below.
14. The differences are easy to appreciate when one reads the imitations, which, in similar reviews of heroes or heroines, left before the readers' eyes only a little band of immobile figures (Manilius 1.758ff.; and Silius Italicus 13.806); see also Dante, *Inf.* 4.115ff., and *Purg.* 7.88ff. Nor could Petrarch, of course, in the *Africa,* fail to allude to this scene: "Aeternum cupitis producere nomen / secula demulcent animos numerosa venitque / posteritas longa ante oculos" (2.408ff.): Petrarch adheres to the model of posterity coming before one's eyes, its movement.
15. On the frequent use of verbs of motion in this entire Virgilian episode, see Basson, *Pivotal Catalogues in the Aeneid,* p. 432n.22; and Austin, *P. Vergilius Maro Liber VI,* p. 233. The internal chronology of the procession is violated, as Servius notes on 6.754; see also Norden, *P. Vergilius Maro "Aeneis" Buch VI,* p. 314; and, above all, the long discussion by Basson, pp. 49ff., which gives a very clear account of the arrangement of the several heroes and groups, with plausible explanations, too, of Virgil's choices in the internal arrangement.
16. On *legit,* see Conington-Nettleship, ad loc.: it means, of course, "to run over with one's gaze, recognize one by one"; see also remarks by Parsons and Nisbet in R. D. Anderson, P. J. Parsons, R. G. M. Nisbet, "Elegiacs by Gallus from Qasr Ibrim," *JRS* 69 (1979):142.

Chapter Eleven. Other Aspects of Time: "The future at your back"

1. S. Freud, "Jokes and Their Relation to the Unconscious," in *The Standard Edition of the Complete Pyschological Works of Sigmund Freud,* ed. and tr. J. Strachey et al., 24 vols. (London, 1953–73), 8:26, "he has a great future behind him."
2. A. Borghini, "Dietro le spalle: Sul significato delle pietre dietro le spalle nel mito di Deucalione," *MD* 10–11 (1983):319ff.
3. Cicero's source is Coelius Antipater (fr. 11 Peter²). Cf. also Livy 21.22; Valerius Maximus 1.7.1; Silius Italicus 3.163ff.; and Dio Cassius in Zonar. 8.22. For interpretations of Hannibal's dream, above all the guide's rule and its violation, see E. Meyer, *Kleine Schriften* (Halle, 1924), 2:369ff.; F. Ribezzo, "Elementi di romanzo ellenistico in Livio," *Riv. Ind. Grec. It.* 5 (1921):9ff.; F. Altheim, *Epochen der römischen Geschichte* (Frankfort, 1935), 2:63; G. Stäubler, *Die Religiosität des Livius* (Amsterdam, 1941; reprint, 1964), pp. 95ff.; J. Vogt, *Das Hannibal-Portrait im Geschichtswerk des Livius und seine Ursprünge*

(Freiburg, 1953), pp. 102ff. Interesting comparisons with Artemidorus in the light of the old theme of not turning back have been proposed by G. Cipriani, *L'epifania di Annibale* (Bari, 1984), pp. 103ff.

4. See n.5 below and chap. 8, n.10 above.

5. This interpretation by Artemidorus must certainly be compared with the folkloric belief that it is a bad sign to turn back on leaving one's own house or parting for a journey; to recall one instance for all, there is the well-known Pythagorean *symbolon,* "apodemon tes oikias me epistrephou" (Iamblichus, *Protr.* 21, p. 107 Pistelli). To begin to go more deeply into the matter, see Pease on Cicero, *Div.* 1.49 (pp. 182ff.); for other bibliography, see chap. 8, n.10 above.

6. Generally speaking, the device of inversion and reversal appears to play a very important role in dreams or in the ancient and modern interpretative representations of them. The theme is huge, and goes beyond my scope here, so I shall give only a few indications. See, for example, Pliny the Younger, on an unfavorable dream that caused Suetonius to postpone a legal case he was to argue: "Refert tamen, eventura soleas an contraria somniare" (*Epist.* 1.18). Still more technical and exegetical is the precept of Artemidorus: "In the interpretation of dreams, one must consider them once from beginning to end, once from the end to the beginning" (1.9). And S. Freud noted, in "Jokes and Their Relation to the Unconscious," in *The Complete Psychological Works of Sigmund Freud,* ed. and tr. J. Strachey et al., 24 vols. (London, 1953–73), 8:89: "Representation by the opposite is so common in dreams that even the popular books of dream-interpretation, which are on a completely wrong track, are in the habit of taking it into account"). In his *The Interpretation of Dreams,* he gave some concrete examples of dream analysis by reversal of the type, such as "Freud dreams that Goethe is attacking a young writer = a young scholar has attacked his friend Fleiss, who is older" (4:98–99). In this context, Freud cited Artemidorus 1.9, which is quoted above. It is well known that Th. Gomperz brought Artemidorus to Freud's attention: see H. Blumenberg, *La leggibilità del mondo* (Bologna, 1984), pp. 348ff.; and, on the relations between Gomperz and Freud, see S. Timpanaro, *Aspetti e problemi della cultura ottocentesca* (Pisa, 1980), pp. 414ff.

7. P. Riccardi, *Pregiudizi e superstizioni del popolo modenese* (Florence, 1891), p. 27, quoted by A. Borghini, "Una credenza modenese e una tradizione antica: La 'perdita' dell'ombra," to appear in *Annali della Biblioteca civica di Massa.*

8. Cf. "quidam ideo eum dici bifrontem putant, quod et praeterita sciverit et futura providerit" (1.9.4).

9. See G. Wissowa, *Religion und Kultus der Römer*[2] (Munich, 1912), p.

221; and G. Radke, *Die Götter Altitaliens* (Münster, 1965), pp. 81ff.

10. On *porro*, see chaps. 8 above and 12 below. Here it is remarkable that *porro* is applied to the past, not the future, as in the cases studied earlier. The reason, naturally, is once again provided by the change in the pattern of spatial localization of temporal relations: from the normal pattern, with the future "before," to the cognitive pattern, with the past "before" and what is to come "behind the back."

11. A. Bouché-Leclerq, *Histoire de la divination dans l'antiquité* (Paris, 1882), 4:120; Peter in Roscher 2.216, s.v. "indigitamenta." Rather strange is Radke's objection, "Man . . . nicht ansehen kann, wozu Gottinnen gedient haben sollen, die das Vergangene wussten" (*Die Götter Altitaliens*, p. 260). It is well known that Etrusco-roman divination dealt not only with the future but above all with the past, because of the need to discover the sins or the mistakes committed previously, which might have aroused divine ire, which conditions the difficulties of the present: see, for example, Bouché-Leclerq, pp. 17 and 82. One could say that, from this viewpoint, divination about the past works as a kind of feedback which can find out the previous error and get the process underway again.

12. From a different context, though perhaps less distant than might seem, comes the pair Prorsa/Postvorta, which presided over the position of the fetus in the mother's womb, a fetus that might present itself either head first or feet first (Varro, fr. 145 Funaioli, in Gellius 16.16; Tertullian, *Ad nat.* 2.11). Some relation between this pair and the one we are studying must have existed, because Varro identifies Prorsa and Postvorta as Carmentes, and we have seen that Antevorta (or Porrima) and Postvorta (or Postverta) were companions to Carmentis. Moreover, Carmentis is also known as a goddess of both prophecy and childbirth (Plutarch, *Rom.* 21.2, *Quaest. Rom.* 56; Augustine, *Civ. Dei* 4.11), in line with the recurrent linkage between goddesses of springs, of birth, and of prophecy (Wissowa, *Religion und Kultus der Römer*, p. 221).

A separate problem is posed by the use of the name Agrippa for children born feet first: explained by Gellius as deriving "ab aegritudine et pedibus" (loc. cit.), but by Pliny from "aegre partus" (*Hist. nat.* 7.45). Above all, we know that this kind of birth was considered a bad sign for the child. One reason for this, apart from the generic unnaturalness of the birth, which already rendered it suspect, might reside in the Roman custom of placing a corpse on view with its feet toward the door (*collocatio*) and carrying it out (*efferri*) still in the same position: see J.M.C. Toynbee, *Death and Burial in the Roman World* (London, 1971), p. 44 and n.126, citing only Persius 3.105; but we should add at least Seneca, *Ep.* 12.3, and Pliny, *Hist. Nat.* 7.46.

In other words, coming out feet first, a child risked appearing immediately like a corpse and his birth coincided with a death. Precisely
this aspect is emphasized by Pliny: "ritus naturae hominem capite
gigni, mos est pedibus efferri." For various beliefs concerning birth
feet first, see N. Belmont, *Les signes de la naissance* (Paris, 1977); and
C. Lévi-Strauss, "Lectures croisées," in *Le regard éloigné* (Paris, 1983),
pp. 277ff. (analogies between "feet first," twinhood, harelip, reverse
coitus, etc.).

13. What we have, evidently, are deities of the type called *indigitamentum*:
one of the most exciting and difficult subjects in archaic Roman religion, it cannot be examined in detail here. For its linguistic aspect
(but the linguistic side, also in the philosophical sense, has always
dominated studies of these religious representations: to recall the famous work by E. Cassirer, *Language and Myth,* which made great use
of H. Usener, *Götternamen* [Bonn 1929]), see, at least, J. Grassmann,
"Italische Götternamen," *Zeitschr. vergl. Sprachf.* 16 (1867):108ff.; F.
Stolz, "Zur Bildung und Erklärung der römischen Indigeten-Namen,"
Arch. lat. lex. 10 (1898):172ff.; H. Usener, op. cit., pp. 75ff.; Radke,
Die Götter Altitaliens, pp. 10ff.; and S. Timpanaro, *Contributi di filolo-
gia e di storia della lingua latina* (Rome, 1978), pp. 436ff. See also Peter
in Roscher 2.210ff.; and Kraus *RE* 22.987ff.

14. Cf. Catullus 22.21; Persius 4.24; and Seneca, *De ira* 2.28.

15. Although wrong, this explanation corresponds by and large to that
given for the spatial localization of time in Homer by M. Treu, *Von
Homer zur Lyrik* (Munich, 1968). See also G. E. Dunkel, "Prosso kai
opisso," *Zeitschr. vergl. Sprachf.* 96 (1982–83):67ff.

Chapter Twelve. *The Cultural Preeminence of*
"Before": Linguistic and Anthropological Analysis

1. E. Benveniste, "The Sublogical System of Prepositions in Latin," in
Problems in General Linguistics (Coral Gables, Fla., 1971), pp. 114ff.
Useful remarks appeared already in B. Kranz, "De particularum 'pro'
et 'prae' in prisca latinitate vi atque usu" (Diss., Vratislaviae, 1907),
pp. 33ff. On *pro* and *prae,* a more recent work is E. D. Francis, "*Particularum quarundarum varietas: Prae* and *pro,*" *YCS* 23 (1972):1ff.,
which is ample but difficult to use because of its extremely uncertain
and haphazard methods and its truly flabbergasting number of interpretive errors. A complete review being pointless, I give only a
taste. For faulty methodology, I would point to the interpretation of
praegnas, praesens, and *praesto* as stemming from expressions of the
type **praegnatid,* *prae sente and **prae situ:* on the grounds of what

rule, what pattern? As for the indefensible interpretations: p. 8, on Cicero, "ipsum dolorem tulit paulo aperte" *(Planc* 14.34), in which "tulit" does not mean "made public" but, as is perfectly usual, "endured"; p. 36, on Plautus, "Iam linguam praecidam atque oculos ecfodiam" *(Aul.* 189), it is impossible to maintain that this usage implies that "*praecido* . . . becomes comparable in meaning . . . with *ecfodio*"; p. 41, the absence of **adsens* as a opposite to *absens* cannot be explained by asserting that "*adsens* and *absens* would have been virtually homophones," simply because they would never have been homophonic (-*bs*- versus -*ss*-), indeed, there exist *adsum* (= *assum*) and *absum* with no problem of homophony; and, finally, p. 41, in Plautus *Pseudo.* 293, *praevortere* does not mean "to be more important than," but has the usual transitive value: one has to introduce as subject of the infinitive *te,* which clearly fell out after *pietatem,* also in order to avoid scanning the first syllable of *pietatem* as long.

2. O. Riemann, *Syntaxe latine*[5] (Paris, 1908), p. 179n.2; E. Benveniste, "The Sublogical System of Prepositions in Latin," pp. 114ff. The counterexamples cited by Francis, "*Particularum quarundarum varietas: Prae* and *pro,*" are not valid: for instance, Cicero, "Non tu quidem vacuus molestiis [es], sed prae nobis beatus" (You have your troubles, but with respect to us [sc., the number of troubles we have] you are happy) *(Ad fam.* 4.4.2). The style is rather elegant and ironical, but hardly a counterexample (and the others, too, are fallacious).

3. The value of *prae* (extremity) is related to the causal value of the preposition by Benveniste, *Problèmes de linguistique générale.*

4. But see Kranz, "De particularum 'pro' et 'prae,'" pp. 1ff.: "'pro' idem fere est atque 'ante.' At ei non est contrapositum 'post.' sed 'intra.' Dici enim potest 'pro' de ea re, quae ante eum locum est, intra quem fuit antea." This is a suggestive distinction that cannot always be demonstrated. The diverse values of *pro* were already of interest to Aulus Gellius, who reported a list of examples from which emerged "qualis quantaque esset particularum quarundam in oratione latina varietas" *(Noct. Att.* 11.4) in the case of *pro.* Gellius did not explain the possible relations among various differentiated uses and their distribution, but he expressed himself in a way that merits mention: "Varietatem istam eiusdem quidem fontis et capitis, non eiusdem tamen esse finis putabam" (11.3).

5. Gloss.[L] I Ansil. HO 177; cf. Nonius 3 and Servius Auct. on *Aen.* 2.156. See also M. Bettini, *Studi e note su Ennio* (Pisa, 1979), pp. 94ff.

6. Still worse than the explanation of Ernout and Meillet is that of Delbrück, who would have it that *pro*- in *proavus* even preserves the Indo-European value of the preverb, analogous to the Greek *pro,* implying an idea of anteriority which is foreign to the Latin: "Die indo-

germanischen Verwandschaftsnamen," *Abh. d. sachs. Gesel. d. Wiss.* 11.476.

7. Kranz, "De particularum 'pro' et 'prae,'" p. 16. See also Sallust: "verum providet" (*Catil.* 51), in the sense of "discern the truth," not "foresee" it.

8. See *porro* in J. B. Hofmann and A. Szantyr, *Lateinische Syntax und Stilistik* (Munich, 1965).

9. See A. Ernout and A. Meillet, *Dictionnaire étymologique de la langue Latine*[4] (Paris 1967), s.v. "palam."

10. The first and last example of *anticum* seems to be *Anth. Lat.* 21.131; nothing can be extracted from Paulus-Festus 26 L, in which the text is corrupt.

11. On this honorable conduct of the soldiers in death, see A. Borghini, "Codice antropologico e narrazione letteraria," *Lingua e stile* 14 (1979):165ff.

12. Borghini, "Codice antropologico e narrazione letteraria," 173. For the cultural preeminence of "before," see also chap. 7 above.

13. M. Lurcat, *Il bambino e lo spazio* (Florence, 1980), tr. into Italian, with a handsome "Introduction" by R. Tom.

14. See, above all, R. Hertz, "La preminenza della mano destra," in *Sulla rappresentazione collettiva della morte* (Rome, 1978); also, R. Needham, ed., *Right and Left* (Chicago and London, 1973); V. V. Ivanov, "La semiotica delle opposizioni mitologiche di vari popoli," in *Ricerche semiotiche,* ed. J. M. Lotman and B. A. Uspenskij (Turin, 1973), pp. 130ff. On the ancient world, see C. B. Gulick, "Omens and Augury in Plautus," *HSCP* 7 (1896):235ff.; A. L. Frothingham, "Ancient Orientation Unveiled," *AJA* 21 (1917):55ff.; S. Eitrem, *Opferritus und Voropfer der Griechen und Römer* (Oslo, 1918), pp. 29ff.; X. M. Walters, *Notes on American Folklore* (Amsterdam, 1935), pp. 49 and 77ff.; A. F. Braunlich, "To the Right," *AJP* 57 (1936):245ff.; and J. Cuillandre, *La droite et la gauche dans les poèmes homeriques* (Paris, 1944).

Chapter Thirteen. Vertical Time:
From the Genealogical Tree to the Aristocratic Funeral

1. No further examples of *maiores* meaning "ancestors" are needed; for *minores* meaning "descendants," see, for example, Virgil, *Aen.* 1.532, 753, and so forth. Some interesting reflections on the meaning and notion of *minores* are in V. V. Ivanov, "La semiotica delle opposizioni mitologiche di vari popoli," in *Ricerche semiotiche,* ed. J. M. Lotman and B. A. Uspenskij (Turin, 1973), pp. 139ff. However, Ivanov imputes to *minores* a positive character, in contrast to a negative charac-

ter for *maiores*; this holds only within the framework of folkloric plots, in which the smallest of three brothers often is the third and the winner (see chap. 9 above). But the mechanism cannot be extrapolated from folkloric narrative without an adequate series of comparative examples.

2. *See also* Virgil, "demissaeque ab Iove gentes" (*Geo*. 3.35); and Tacitus, "Nero . . . Romanum Troia demissum et Iuliae stirpis auctorem Aeneam . . . executus" (*Ann*. 12.38). On *profundus* and the notion of profundity in Latin, we have the well-stocked work of P. Mantovanelli, *Profundus* (Rome, 1981), with remarks on *profundus/altus*, pp. 23ff. Concerning *altus*, see E. Benveniste, "Language in Freudian Theory," in *Problems in General Linguistics* (Coral Gables, Fla., 1971), pp. 70ff.

3. The list of the honors which conferred the right to images was drawn up by Th. Mommsen, in Mommsen and Girard, *Droit public romain* (Paris, 1892), 2:84ff. See also F. Walbank, *A Historical Commentary on Polybius*, vol. 1 (Oxford 1957), on Polybius 6.54.

4. The main ceremonial use of ancestral masks was to accompany the dead in the funeral procession: see Mommsen and Girard, *Droit public romain*, 2:88; J. Marquardt, *La vie privée des Romains* (Paris, 1892), 1:283ff.; and J. Toynbee, *Death and Burial in the Roman World* (London, 1971), pp. 47ff.

The problem of the *imagines* in Roman culture is quite complex (partially because of the importance assigned to the custom by art historians for interpreting Roman portraiture): here I cannot go beyond the concerns of this study with the spatial representations of time. For a work on the specific subject, which offers useful orientation and observations, see R. Daut, *Imago* (Heidelberg, 1975), especially pp. 42ff.; also Walbank, *A Historical Commentary on Polybius*, 1:737ff. A quite particular slant appears in M. Rambaud, "Masques et imagines," *Les Et. class*. 46 (1978):3ff. For further discussion, see B. Schweizer, *Die Bildkunst der römische Republik* (Leipzig, 1948), pp. 19ff.; F. Brommer, "Zu den römischen Ahnenbildern," *Röm. Mitt.* 60–61 (1953–54):163ff.; and R. Bianchi-Bandinelli, *L'arte romana nel centro del potere* (Milan, 1969), pp. 75ff., with brief information on related art-historical issues. In general, see E. Courbaud, *D. S.* 3, pp. 413ff.; K. Schneider (with additions by H. Meyer) in *RE* 9.1097ff.; K. Schneider, *Die Tugenden der Römer* (Heidelberg, 1930), pp. 4ff.; and E. Bethe, *Ahnenbild und Famliengeschichte bei Römern und Griechen* (Munich, 1935), pp. 80ff.

5. See S. Ferri, *C. Plini Secundi Naturalis Historiae quae pertinent ad artes antiquorum* (Rome, 1946), p. 119. On the genealogical stemma in Rome, see L. Friedländer, *Darstellungen aus Sittengeschichte Roms*[10]

(Leipzig, 1922), 1:120ff.; and T. P. Wiseman, "Legendary Genealogies in Late-Republican Rome," *Greece and Rome* 21 (1974):153ff., although concerned more with separate genealogies than with the general type of the genealogical stemma. Other useful evidence, in addition to that cited in the text, includes Seneca, *Epis.* 44.5; Persius 3.28 with scholion; Statius, *Silvae* 3.2.6; Juvenal 8.1 with scholion; Suetonius, *Div. Ner.* 37 and *Div. Galb.* 2; and Martial 4.40, 5.35, and 8.6. Also Prudentius, *Cath.* 7.81; and Martianus Cap. 2, p. 35.

6. Ancient examples of genealogical representations of the degrees of relationship in the legal writers are collected by P. Huschke, *Iurisprudentiae quae supersunt* (Leipzig, 1886), p. 628. The most famous and most accessible examples appear in the manuscripts of Isidore's *Origines* (9.6.28), illustrating the *ramusculi*, which are discussed below. Reproductions are in Lindsay's classic edition. The drawings are designed not to show the evolution of a family, but to place together all relatives who are equally distance from the focal person. I was not able to use H. Schadt, *Die Darstellungen der Arbores Consanguineitatis und der Arbores Affinitatis* (Tübingen, 1982).

7. Among the genealogical trees showing degrees of relationship which appear in the manuscripts of Isidore mentioned in n.6 above, there is one with the look of a stylized tree, like a fir cut out in paper. The focal person is placed in the middle, with his children and grandchildren in a line below him (the trunk), while his forebears, arranged above him, form the peak of the tree. Hence, in this tree, too, the orientation of development is from high to low (on this configuration, see Huschke, *Iurisprudentiae quae supersunt,* pp. 631ff).

8. See A. E. Douglas, *M. Tulli Ciceronis Brutus* (Oxford, 1966), ad loc., citing Pliny, *Hist. nat.* 17.120.

9. V. N. Toporov, "L'albero universale: Saggio di interpretazione semiotica," in *Ricerche semiotiche,* ed. Lotman and Uspenskij, pp. 167ff.; see also V. Pâques, *L'arbre cosmique dans la pensée populaire et dans la vie quotidienne du Nord-Ouest Africain* (Paris, 1964).

10. On the presence of a label for each image, the sources are clear: see Marquardt, *La vie privée des Romains,* 1:285ff.; and Mommsen and Girard, *Droit public romain,* 2:87 and n.2.

11. Following, above all, Pliny, *Hist. nat.* 35.6, and Seneca, *De ben.* 3.28 (cited above). Scholars have even thought that the stemmata actually joined the waxen images: thus Mommsen and Girard, *Droit public romain,* 2:88; Courbaud, *D. S.* 3, pp. 413ff.; K. Schneider (with additions by H. Meyer) in *RE* 9.1097ff.; and so forth. However, this frankly seems impossible. The nobles' masks were lifesize. One is hard put to imagine them arranged in a genealogical tree. Besides, Pliny and Polybius (6.58) expressly say that they were stored in their

own cupboards or armoires. How to reconcile the two things? The problem had not escaped an archaeologist of the level of Ferri, *C. Plini Secundi Naturalis Historiae*, pp. 119, on 35.6: "Certo è che non si può pensare all'utilizzazione pratica per l'albero gentilizio delle immagini ceree." I think that the two passages in question rather clearly distinguish between the waxen images and the genealogical stemma: Pliny speaks first of "expressi cerae vultus" that "singulis disponebantur armariis"; then he adds "stemmata vero discurrebant ad imagines pictas." Hence, the *vultus* of wax, stored in the *armaria*, are one thing; the *imagines pictae*, which evidently must have been little painted representations inserted in the stemma, are another: note that the two statements are separated by *vero*.

Pliny maintained at the beginning of the paragraph that "aliter apud maiores in atriis haec erant quae spectarentur" (in polemic with the effete and Hellenizing practices of modern times, which love statues of athletes and *Epicuri vultus*). This assertion is followed by the example of the *cerae vultus* of the ancestors and their *imagines pictae*, both of which exemplify the fact that the ancestors kept in their halls images nobler than those commonly put there in modern times (hence the translation attempted by Ferri does not satisfy: "Del resto gli alberi genealogici, con le loro ramificazioni di linee, costituivano già dei quadri." Indeed, Ferri underlined its uncertainty in a note). Furthermore, in one of the most famous mentions of stemmata, Juvenal speaks of the *vultus pictos* of the ancestors: "stemmata quid faciunt? quid prodest, Pontice, longo / sanguine censeri, pictos ostendere vultus / maiorum?" (8.1–3).

No different is the case in Seneca: "Imagines in atrio exponunt, et nomina familiae suae longo ordine ac multis stemmatum inligata flexuris in parte prima aedium collocant" (*De ben.* 3.28). Here, too, the distinction is clear. The images displayed in the hall are one thing; the family names woven into the twists of the stemma and placed at the front of the *aedes* are another. Indeed, Seneca seems here to have in mind a tree without images, with nothing but names: an even clearer distinction. A painted image, such as those described by Pliny, must be what is meant by Suetonius: "Cassio Longino obiectum est quod in vetere gentili stemmate C. Cassii percussoris Caesaris imagines retinuisset" (*Div. Nero* 37). We do not know, then, what the aged Messala saw when he grew angry "cum Scipionis Pomponiani transisset atrium vidissetque Salvittones . . . inrepentes Scipionum nomini" (Pliny, *Hist. nat.* 35.8). Names, or painted images (the problem was framed in exemplary fashion by O. Jahn, *Auli Persi Flacci saturarum liber* [Leipzig, 1843], pp. 149ff.).

Among the older dissertations on *imagines* and their function, even though it does not deal with *imagines/stemma,* that of Justus Lipsius should be recalled, *Electorum* 1:29, cited from Justi Lipsi *Opera* (Lugduni, 1613), p. 623. Instead, one dissertation that did deal with a proposition more ingenious than convincing was Lessing, "Über die Ahnenbilder der Römer," in *Sämtliche Schriften,* ed. K. Lachmann, 11–1 (Leipzig, 1857), p. 261. In Lessing's view, the *imagines pictae* Pliny mentions must have been the waxen images, however "mit natürlichen Farben übermalt," in keeping with the ancient ancestral practice of coloring sculptured images. It is possible that the waxen images of the ancestors were colored: see Polybius 6.53 and Nicolet's note in R. Weill, *Polybe. Histoires VI* (Paris, 1977), p. 136n.2. But Pliny and Juvenal hardly seems to be referring to this.

12. It seems quite reasonable to suppose that genealogical representation, with its close linkage to the images stored in the hall, comprised also relatives *per cognationem* and related in-laws (*adfines*) of the agnatic line, introduced through matrimony. Speaking of C. Antonius, whose niece (brother's daughter) got married to Vatinius, Cicero remarks: "C. Antonius . . . imagines patris et fratris sui fratrisque filiam non in familia sed in carcere collocatam audire maluit quam videre" (*In Vatin.* 28). From this we can easily infer that Antonia, by marrying Vatinius, took with her the *imagines* of her father and grandfather. In the same way, Ancus Martius, son of a daughter of Numa, is described by Livy: "Sabina matre ortum nobilemque una imagine Numae" (1.34.6). This assertion presupposes that, in line with Livy's lore concerning *imagines,* Ancus Martius kept in his house also the image of his maternal grandfather, or that his mother must have brought with her, when she married, her father's image.

It is reasonable to suppose that this grafting of images from the maternal side was also reflected in some way in the genealogical stemma, so every member of the line could be identified in terms of maternal relatives, as well as paternal ones. This is consistent with the remarkable, if subterranean, importance of cognate relationships that we have studied (in chaps. 3 and 4). Statius addresses Victorius Marcellus as "stemmate materno felix, virtute paterna" (*Silv.* 4.4.75). Other examples of cognate relatives among the *imagines* are not lacking (see Mommsen and Girard, *Droit public romain,* 2:84n.2). For example, Tacitus tells us that present at the funeral of Junia, the sister of Junius Brutus and wife of Cassius, were the *imagines* from a good twenty noble families, among them the Manlii and Quinctii (*Ann.* 3.76). It is possible that these included some of the families that had become related to the Junii through successive marriages. In this case, too, it is difficult to imagine that the genealogical stemma of the Junii preserved no trace of these connections: for reasons of prestige (the same that led to carrying the images in procession, to display them), and simply for reasons of arrangement within the patrimony of images owned by the family. Speaking of the same Junia, Tacitus remarks: "Catone avunculo genita."

Hence, the fact that the woman, at marriage, brings with her some images of her ancestors (something, let me repeat, that could have repercussions also on the stemma) ought not to be considered as a fact in itself but as an operation serving the prestige and identity of the stock as of the individual. By means of this transfer, one made it possible for one's children and grandchildren to display the images of both maternal and paternal ancestors (on this score, then, appear inadequate the remarks of Mommsen and Girard, *Droit public romain,* 2). We are not talking here merely about a girl who brings some family pictures with her when she gets married; this is an investment in the future, a concrete token of the link through marriage which will permit successive generations to establish their identity and raise their prestige by drawing also on the maternal line: their own and those of each of their predecessors in the male line. Thus brought together, this heritage of images on the female side constitutes a fundamental support for the patrilineal line, which joins the bearers of one and the same name. Carried in procession, the impressive crowd of what I would like to call cognate images constitutes a massive and irrefutable proof of the nobility of the family as a whole, a still further sign of the importance of cognate and maternal relations in a society apparently as rigidly agnatic as the Roman (see chaps. 3 and 4). From a general point of view, useful remarks on matrilineal insertions in patrician genealogies, whenever the maternal side enjoyed greater prestige than the paternal one, appear in G. Duby, "Remarques sur la littérature généalogique en France," *Hommes et structures du Moyen Age* (Paris, 1979), pp. 287ff.

13. Truly entertaining must have been the scene that provoked the old Messala to write his books *De familiis:* "Cum Scipionis Pomponiani transisset atrium vidissetque adoptione testamentaria Salvittones— hoc enim fuerat cognomen Africanorum dedecori—inrepentes Scipionum nomini" (Pliny, *Hist. nat.* 35.8).

14. See Ferri, *C. Plini Secundi Naturalis Historiae.*

15. J. Goody, "Mémoire et apprentissage dans les societés avec et sans écriture: La transmission du bagre," *L'homme* 17 (1977):29ff. On the genealogical question, see J. Goody and I. Watt, "The Consequences of Literacy," in *Literacy in Traditional Society,* ed. Goody (Cambridge, 1968), pp. 32ff.; and M. Detienne, *L'invenzione della mitologia* (Milan, 1983), pp. 35ff.

16. We know that this spatial arrangement was violated on an occasion

that, precisely because it is exceptional, may be especially revealing about the meaning that such an order had in Roman practice. According to Cassius Dio (56.34.2), the images of the ancestors came after the bier at Augustus's funeral. Indeed, they numbered not only the ancestors of Augustus but also of all the great Romans, starting with Romulus: "starting," however, with Romulus, so that here, too, the oldest was first. The procession thus resembled the one in book six of Virgil's *Aeneid,* which passed before the eyes of the hero (see chap. 10 above). If the report can be believed (and reserve in general was expressed by Mommsen and Girard in *Droit public romain,* 2), the unusual order of the procession, like the presence of images from beyond the family lineage (supplemented by images of the great), might have been adopted precisely in order to indicate the absolutely exceptional nature of the dead man: a personage who, by being placed ahead of his own ancestors, and accompanied to his last resting place by all the great men of Rome, as if greatness itself, rather than blood, became here a sign of kinship, achieved in all this the confirmation of his absolutely leading position in the history of his people.

17. See the note of H. Furneaux, *The Annals of Tacitus* (Oxford, 1934), 1:503.

18. See Paulus-Festus 247 L; and F. Bömer, *Ahnenkult und Ahnenglaube im alten Rom* (Leipzig, 1943), p. 6.

19. From the language of lineage, Plautus draws an elegant and amusing line: "pater, avos, proavos, abavos, atavos, tritavos" (*Persa* 56). E. Benveniste, "Termes de parenté dans les langues indo-européennes," *L'homme* 5:102ff.; and Ulpian: "Quidam parentem usque ad tritavum appellari aiunt, superiores maiores dici" (*Dig.* 2.4.4.2).

20. Suetonius, *Nero* 37; and Mommsen and Girard, *Droit public romain,* 2.

21. On the funeral masks, see the brief but penetrating remarks of M. Mauss, "Una categoria dello spirito umano: La nozione di persona, quella di 'io,'" in *Teoria generale della magia e altri saggi* (Turin, 1965), pp. 371ff.

22. On the link of likeness between father and son, see, for example, Catullus: "Sit suo similis patri / Mallio, et facile inscieis / noscitetur ab omnibus" (62.221–23); Horace, *Carm.* 4.5.23; Ovid, *Tris.* 4.5.31; Martial 6.27.3; and so forth. Many passages are gathered together by E. Baehrens, *Catulli Veronensis liber* (Leipzig, 1876), ad 61.221. For resemblances of family, see Plutarch (*Brut.* 1), who cites Posidonius: some of the Junii Bruti contemporary with Posidonius were said to bear a great likeness to the statue of the elder Brutus in the Capitol; this likeness freed the family from accusations that it was not descended from the liberator of Rome. See also Pliny, *Hist. nat.* 33.9.

23. Here I use a somewhat extended notion of Jakobson's "shifter," which I have previously employed and sought to define in the workings of some metrical structures: M. Bettini, "A proposito dei versi sotadei, greci e romani," *MD* 9 (1982):59ff., especially 98ff.

24. On the paradigmatic and modeling character of the *imagines maiorum*, see Polybius 6.54; Sallust, *Iug* 4.5; and also Pliny, *Hist. nat.* 35.8, who, with the go-ahead of the old Messala (cf. n.13 above), forgave even the practice of faking *imagines*, for this had always been a sign of love for manliness. On the stern tradition of the Torquati, see chap. 1 above.

25. For certain typical traits of epitaphs, and of self-representation in poetry, see M. Bettini, "L'epitaffio di Virgilio, Silio Italico e un modo di intendere la letteratura," *Dial. di Arch.* 9–10 (1976–77):439ff. Note also the exemplary commentary on this elogium by A. Traina, *Comoedia: Antologia della palliata*[3] (Padova, 1979), p. 169. [Now see also two studies by the translator: "The First Hellenistic Epigrams at Rome," *Bull. Inst. Class. Stud.,* suppl. 51 (1988):152–53; and "The Elogia of the Cornelii Scipiones and the Origins of Epigram at Rome," *AJP* 108 (1987):41–55.]

26. Cicero recalls instead the case of Scipio Africanus's son, who "propter infirmitatem valetudinis, non tam potuit patris similis esse quam ille fuerat sui" (*De off.* 1.121): this time the preformed mold could not be filled as it should. I owe this and other passages cited in the last part of this chapter to G. Guastella, who is working on the notion of *persona* in the *De officiis* and Roman culture.

27. *Neque* is the manuscript reading; *Atque* was Leo's conjecture: see M. Bettini, *Plauto, Mostellaria e Persa* (Milan, 1981), p. 258.

28. On this genealogical tour de force, see M. Bettini, "Il parasito Saturio, una riforma legislativa e un testo variamente tormentato," *St. cl. or.* 26 (1977):83ff.; idem, *Plauto, Mostellaria e Persa,* p. 439; and G. Chiarini, *La recita*[2] (Bologna, 1983), pp. 90ff.

Chapter Fourteen. Spatial Localizations of Time:
Closing Remarks and Anthropological Reasons

1. E. C. Traugott, "On the Expression of Spatio-Temporal Relations in Language," in *Universals of Human Language,* ed. J. H. Greenberg (Stanford, 1978), 3:127n.2.

2. Although the concept is clear in itself, here we refer to the work of M. Lurcat, *Il bambino e lo spazio* (Florence, 1980); trans. into Italian, with an "Introduction" by R. Tom.

3. Lurcat, *Il bambino e lo spazio.*
4. I can cite only one example of modular exchangeability between diverse temporal localizations: the cortege of generations, in which "past/future" and "anterior/posterior" combine to create the representation of the *comitatus.* But this is a particular combination, not a primary model. See chap. 10 above.
5. While taking the discussion a step further, I want to underline the quality and the intrinsic importance of Traugott, "On the Expression of Spatio-Temporal Relations in Language," for both for its approach and its abundant material.
6. Remarks on this theme of "higher" as a dominant category in culture are in V. N. Toporov, "L'albero universale: Saggio di interpretazione semiotica," in *Ricerche semiotiche,* ed. J. M. Lotman and B. A. Uspenskij (Turin, 1973), pp. 153ff. An entire, suggestive book has been built turning on the axis "high/low" by M. Bachtin, *L'opera di Rabelais* (Turin, 1979). See also M. Bettini, "Un'utopia per burla," in *Plauto, Mostellaria e Persa* (Milan, 1981).
7. Accepting the supplement of Müller: "Ordo sacerdotum aestimatur deorum [ordine, ut deus] maximus quisque."
8. On the order at banquet, see J. Marquardt, *La vie privée des Romains* (Paris, 1892), 1:356ff.; likewise Bettini, "Un'utopia per burla," pp. 265ff.
9. The "high/low" axis in the designation of cardinal points has been studied by J. A. Huisman, "Ekliptic un Nord/Südbezeichnungen in Indogermanischen," *Zeitschr. vergl. Sprach.* 71 (1953):97ff.; H. V. Velten, "The Germanic Names of Cardinal Points," *JEPB* 39 (1940):443ff. On Nerthus, goddess of the "nether" and "vital force" in relation to the North, see E. Palome, "A propos de la déesse Nerthus," *Latom.* 13 (1954):167ff.; and Toporov, "L'albero universale," pp. 182ff.

Chapter Fifteen. The Bee and the Moth

1. E. Norden, *P. Vergilius Maro "Aeneis" Buch VI*² (Stuttgart 1967), ad loc., p. 305.
2. F. Fletcher, *Virgil Aeneid VI* (Oxford, 1966), ad loc. A swarm of bees in a simile relating to the world of the dead (and precisely to the extraordinary number of the souls called up by the seer in the presence of Creon) appears also in Seneca, *Oed.* 602: there, however, the comparison turns on the innumerable flowers of Ida (toward which the swarm directs itself).
3. Norden, *P. Vergilius Maro "Aeneis" Buch VI,* 2:306.
4. Remarks on this text of Porphyry's, together with a translation and

interpretation, appear already in a valuable study by A. B. Cook, "The Bee in Greek Mythology," *JHS* 25 (1895):1ff. (esp. 16ff.). The passage had already been pointed out by the article on *melissa* in Roscher's lexicon of myth (by C. Weniger, who also wrote a specialized monograph on the bee in Greek mythology); it had been related to Virgil's simile by M. G. Verrall, "Two Instances of Symbolism in the Sixth Aeneid," *Cl. Rev.* 24 (1911):43ff. This relation, then, was touched on, but in quite summary fashion, by D.E.W. Wormell, *"Apibus quanta experientia parcis,"* in *Vergiliana,* ed. E. Bardon and R. Verdière (Leiden, 1971), pp. 429ff.

On the symbolic link between bees and souls in other cultures, a few hints appear in the Roscher article on *melissa.* A singular song of Engadina invokes, in the form of an apostrophe to the bee, the soul of someone recently deceased: "Bienchen, unser Herr ist Todt / verlass mich nicht in meiner Noth," cited by A. De Gubernatis, *Zoological Mythology* (London, 1872), 2:218. See also O. Waser, "Über die äussere Erscheinung der Seele," *Arc. Religionw.* 16 (1913):337ff. Abundant if not always scientifically ordered material on the bee is in A. Siganos, *La mythologie de l'insecte* (Paris, 1985), pp. 111ff.

5. On the scholion, see Cook, "The Bee in Greek Mythology," 16ff.
6. Aristotle, *Gen. an.* 3.10.761a; Petronius, *Sat.* 56.6; and so forth. See, above all, Olck, *RE* 3–1.431ff., s.v. "Biene."
7. I have not been able to consult the specialized commentary on the bee in late-ancient and medieval literature by E. Misch, *Apis est animal, apis est ecclesia* (Bonn and Frankfort, 1974).
8. Apollodorus of Athens, *Fr. Gr. hist.* 244.89; Callimachus, *H. Apol.* 110ff.; and so forth. See M. Detienne, *I giardini di Adone* (Turin, 1975), pp. 104ff.; and P. Scarpi, *Il picchio e il codice delle api* (Padova, 1984), pp. 94ff.
9. Detienne, *I giardini di Adone,* pp. 110ff.
10. Varro, *Rer. rust.* 16.6; Columella 9.14.3; Plutarch, *Praec. con.* 44; Palladius 1.37.4 and 4.15.4; *Geopon.* 15.2.19. See also Pliny, *Hist. nat.* 11.44: see chap. 17 below.
11. Aelian, *Hist. an.* 1.58; *Geopon.* 15.2.19; and Palladius 4.15.4. For the opposition, "bee/wine," with the bee as the sober animal *par excellence,* see Porphyry, *De antr. Nymph.* 19. The dominant cultural opposition pairs wine with honey: see Plutarch, "antitheton fusin malista tou melitos pros ton oinon echontos" (*Symp.* 4.6.672b) (on which see Cook, "The Bee in Greek Mythology," 20). Remember, too, the myth of Aristaeus, hero of honey, defeated by Dionysus in the contest between wine and honey water.
12. E. Fehrle, *Die kultische Keuscheit im Altertum* (Giessen, 1910), p. 56n.2.

13. Plutarch's variant survives only in the Latin version by Gisbertus Langolius: see R. Ellis, *AJP* 20 (1899):75ff.
14. Aristotle, *Hist. an.* 625b; and *Geopon.* 15.3.4.
15. Virgil, *Geo.* 4.230; Columella 9.14.3; and Palladius 4.15.4
16. Columella 9.14.3.
17. Aristotle, *Hist. an.* 535a; Varro, *Rer. rust.* 3.16.6; Aelian, *Hist. an.* 5.11; *Geopon.* 15.3.4; and so forth.
18. Pliny, *Hist. nat.* 21.72: see J. Bayet, "Le rite du fécial et le cornouiller magique," in *Croyances et rites dans la Rome antique* (Paris, 1971), pp. 9ff.
19. Porphyry, *De antr. Nymph.* 19: materials on the beliefs about beans are gathered by A. Delatte, "*Faba Pythagorae cognata*," in *Serta Laodensia* (Paris, 1930); see Detienne, *I giardini di Adone*, pp. 60ff., and C. Lévi-Strauss, *Le regard éloigné* (Paris, 1983, pp. 263ff.
20. Porphyry, *De antr. Nymph.* 19: beans are the only plant in which the stem is not interrupted by any knot, hence they offer a direct passage between the two worlds.
21. Aristotle, *Hist. an.* 627a; Pliny, *Hist. nat.* 11.25; Aelian, *Hist. an.* 1.10; and so forth.
22. Virgil, *Geo.* 4.47; Pliny, *Hist. nat.* 11.62; Columella 9.5.6; and *Geopon.* 15.3.4; for the bad odor of the swamp, see Martial: "Quod siccae redolet palus lacunae" (4.4.1) (in an epigram that is a veritable catalogue, or handbook, of bad odors.).
23. Look at the contrasting case of the dung beetle: an insect rather close to excrement, it avoids perfumes and can even be killed by them: Aelian, *Hist. an.* 1.38 and 6.46.
24. Aristotle, *Gen. an.* 759b; and Augustine, *Civ. dei* 15.27.4.
25. Pliny: "Neque mansueti generis neque feri" (*Hist. nat.* 11.11). Differently, Varro distinguishes between bees that are *cicures* (tame), because they graze in cultivated places, and wasps that are *ferae* (wild), because they graze in wild places (*Rer. rust.* 3.16.19).
26. Aristotle, *Hist. an.* 626a; Virgil, *Geo.* 4.256; Columella 9.13.7; Pliny, *Hist. nat.* 11.63; and so forth.
27. See, for example, Silius Italicus 13.595ff.; Lucan 6.645; and Seneca, *Oed.*
28. Virgil, *Geo.* 4.264; and Columella 9.13.7.
29. At twilight, the humming of the hive little by little dies down, then it ceases altogether: Aristotle, *Hist. an.* 627a; Virgil, *Geo.* 4.186ff.; Pliny, *Hist. nat.* 11.10; and so forth.
30. *Geopon.* 15.2.34.
31. Columella 9.2.3; Pliny, *Hist. nat.* 11.11.
32. Columella 9.13.4.

33. Pliny, *Hist. nat.* 11.25; and *Geopon.* 15.39.
34. G. Gozzano, in his entomological phase, devoted one entire piece ("Della testa di morte" in *Le farfalle*) to *Acherontia atropos,* the sphinx with the skull on its back. Nor should we forget the famous *Sphinx* of E. A. Poe. It is also well to recall the *Vecchi versi* of E. Montale, the poem that opens *Le occasioni:* and also *La primavera hitleriana* begins (*La Bufera e altro*) with a flight of "falene impazzite," a gloomy prelude to the Hitlerian chill that encircles Florence that night. One could go on ad infinitum, but I conclude by recalling the thematic function of the black moth ("vattene, diavolo!") in J. Machado de Assis, *Memorie dell'aldilà* (Milan, 1953), e.g., p. 72. Much material appears in Siganos, *La mythologie de l'insecte,* pp. 68ff.
35. Cook, "The Bee in Greek Mythology," 10ff.; Waser, "Über die äussere Erscheinung der Seele," pp. 382ff., who reports various beliefs, coming from different peoples; idem in Roscher, s.v. "Psyche," pp. 3234ff.; and F. Cumont, *Le symbolisme funeraire des Romains* (Paris, 1942), pp. 319, 346, and 412.
36. *Carm. ep.* 2.1851; cf. 2.1069.
37. See Nicole in Daremberg-Saglio, "s.v. Psyche"; also Waser in Roscher.
38. See Nicole, in Daremberg-Saglio, loc. cit.; Waser in Roscher; and above all, E. Collignon, *Essai sur les monuments Grecs et Romains relatifs au mythe de Psyché* (Paris, 1877).
39. Cumont, *Le symbolisme funeraire des Romains,* pp. 110ff.; likewise P. Grimal, *Apulei Met. IV 28-VI 24* (Paris, 1969), ad 4.35, who recalls also the epitaph of Regilla, 1049, 21 Kaibel.
40. The cultural difference between "daytime" and "night" is, in this sense, fairly obvious, and I shall use a few examples only from the authors cited in chap. 15, n.34 above: the symmetry will appear even more clearly. Thus, in Gozzano, *Delle crisalidi,* which speaks of the chrysalises of five hundred light "Vanesse Io" that are about to open into moths, the poet feels himself a "necromancer" who "keeps safe the captive spirits / of those who have gone, of those about to appear." Again, in E. Montale, one sees the little moth, calm and happy, that gives its name to the prose collection *Farfalla di Dinard* and to the story that closes it.
41. See Olck, *RE* 3–1., 434ff., s.v. "Biene": medieval survivals of the belief (ox skull and golden bees in the tomb of King Childeric), are cited by Cook, "The Bee in Greek Mythology,"; see also T. F. Royds, *The Beasts, Birds and Bees of Virgil* (Oxford, 1914), pp. 57ff. (esp. pp. 82ff.). As for the scholarly discussion of some of these literary sources (the mythic *Bugonia* of Eumelos, etc.), it always behooves one to look again at E. Norden, "Orpheus und Eurydike," in *Kleine Schriften* (Ber-

lin, 1966), pp. 468ff. (esp. pp. 483ff.): a magisterial demonstration of the fact that the subject of *bugonia* never received specific treatment from Philitas. See also A. Seppilli, *Poesia e magia*² (Turin, 1971), pp. 341 with nn. 237, 468, and 567 with n. 373.

42. An attempt at such scientific, or positivistic, explanations, was made by J. Michelet, *L'insetto* (Milan, 1982), chap. 23; see also Cook, "The Bee in Greek Mythology," 18; Frazer on Ovid, *Fast.* 1, p. 372; and K. A. Hoffmann, in Norden, P. *Vergilius Maro "Aeneis" Buch VI*, p. 475. But all these are rather tentative and generic. Much different is the older work of C. R. Osten Sacken, "On the So-called Bugonia of the Ancients and Its Relation to Eristalis Tenax," *Bull. Soc. Entom. di Firenze* (1893):186ff.: the writer complains that *Eristalis Tenax,* a fly that strongly resembles the bee, actually lays its eggs in the carcasses of dead animals. As an explanation, this is a bit too positivistic; and the grounds for the belief must be sought rather in the complex and the very structure of beliefs about bees, not expressed in terms of origins or causes but in terms of cultural correlation. This is not to deny that Osten Sacken's scientific remarks remain quite interesting, especially because they are strengthened by an admirable attentiveness to the classical sources, noteworthy hints of the belief in *bugonia* from Africa and the East (obtained from the work of Eastern specialists who were his colleagues at Heidelberg), and interesting reexaminations of this belief in the works of the great naturalists of the cinquecento and later.

43. The *Baron* preserved in the manuscripts must be a mistake for *Magon:* see A.S.F. Gow, *CR* 58 (1944):14ff.

44. One must read *hai eulai* for the manuscript reading *hai hulai:* see Gow, *CR* 58 (1944):14ff.

45. King Archelaus of Macedon, mentioned in Varro, *Rer. rust.* 3.16.4; cf. also 2.5.5 and 3.2.11; Nicander, *Ther.* 740ff. and *Alexi.* 446ff.; Ovid, *Fast.* 1.379ff.; Sextus Empiricus, *Pyr. ypot.* 1.41; Aelian, *Hist. an.* 2.57; and so forth.

46. Ovid, *Met.* 15.390; Plutarch, *Cleom.* 39; and Origen, *Contr. Cels.* 4.57. See R. B. Onians, *Origins of European Thought* (Cambridge, 1951), pp. 57ff.

47. Cook, "The Bee in Greek Mythology": the bee's predilection for thyme is very abundantly documented. Virgil (*Geo.* 4.304) adds *casia* to boot.

48. Columella 9.15.5; *Geopon.* 15.4.1; and Palladius 4.15.4.

49. See Lithuanian *aulys* (apiary) and *avilys* (braided apiary); Latvian *aulis* (apiary of fir bark, or made of a rotten stump, to catch bees) (F. Fraenkel, *Litauisches Etym. Wörterbuch,* s.v. "aulas"). For the names of "hive" in the Romance languages, see G. Bottiglioni, *L'ape e l'alveare*

nelle lingue romanze (Pisa, 1919); for "wasps," idem, "La vespa e il suo nido nelle lingue romanze," *Zeitschr. röm. Phil.* 42 (1922):291ff.

50. Virgil, *Geo.* 4.281; Antigonus of Carystus 19; see the brief remarks by Gow, *CR* 58 (1944):14ff. Very vague, and certainly a bit too symbolistic, are the remarks by J. Chomarat, "L'initiation d'Aristée," *Rev. Et. Lat.* 52 (1974):186ff.

51. See Cook, "The Bee in Greek Mythology," but his explanations for the ban on spilling blood are a bit too generic and very animistic. We hardly need recall the Homeric belief that the soul of a stricken warrior leaves by the mouth or by the wound just inflicted: *Il.* 9.408, 14.518, and 16.505. This belief can be connected, in my opinion, with the practice of closing the mouth of the dead, along with the eyes: *Od.* 11.426. Because it was believed that the soul fled through the "hedge of the teeth," closing the mouth and eyes acquired the specific function of signalling and hallowing the death: indeed, the gesture translates into action the thought that "once the soul has crossed the hedge of the teeth, it cannot be retaken or caught and made to return" (*Il.* 9.408). The mouth is closed, then, to signal the irreversibility of the passing: the soul leaves by the mouth, but cannot turn back through (and the theme is always that of *unde negant redire quemquam*). Scarcely exact, in this regard, are the remarks of T. D. Seymour, *Life in the Homeric Age* (New York, 1907; Oxford, 1963), p. 473; in general, see also E. Rohde, *Psyche*[2] (Bari, 1950), 1:24n.1.

52. Archelaus in Varro, *Rer. rust.* 3.6.4; idem in Antigonus of Carystus 19; Nicander, *Theri.* 740 (and scholia); Plutarch, *Cleom.* 29; Origen, *Contr. Cels.* 4.57; and Suidas, s.v. "bougeneon." From this ancient belief in the hippogenesis of wasps, Lessing took the germ of a story, rather nasty, against the Italians ("Die Wespen," *Die Fabeln*, 1.16).

53. Ovid, *Met.* 15.361; and Pliny, *Hist. nat.* 11.70 (both wasps and hornets from horses).

54. *Orig.* 11.4.3 (from horses are born dung beetles; from mules, locusts) and 12.8.2 (from horses, hornets; from mules, drones; from asses, wasps): Isidore, from one context to another, seems to have confused the relation "ass - dung beetle" with "horse - hornet, wasp"; for "dung beetle - ass," see further below. Concerning the relation "mule - locust," I do not know, but certainly "mule - drone" could have some basis: like mules, drones are viewed as not productive.

55. Plutarch, *Cleom.* 39; Origen, *Contr. Cels.* 4.57; and Sextus Empiricus, *Pyr. ypot.* 1.41.

56. Between the dung beetle and the ass some sort of link runs, perhaps mediated by the beetle's connection with dung: remember the resemblance between *kanthon*, a Greek name for "ass," and *kantharos* (dung beetle); also Hesychius, *kanthis - onis* (ass dung): see R. Strömberg,

Griechischen Wortstudien (Göteborg, 1944), pp. 10ff. In Aristophanes, Trygaeus, who rises to heaven on the back of a huge dung beetle, speaks as follows to his mount: "hesychos, hesychos, erema, kanthon [and not *kantharos*]" (*Peace* 82).

57. Pliny, *Hist. nat.* 11.71ff. On "wasp" meaning "undertaker," see E. Benveniste, *Bull. Soc. Ling. Par.* 24 (1923):124ff.; and L. Deroy, *Ant. Class.* 52 (1983):9.

58. Virgil, "asper crabro" (*Geo.* 4.245); and Columella, "violentia crabronum" (9.14.10). Plautus, "inritabis crabrones" (*Amph.* 707) is used as a proverb by Sosia, "Stir up a hornets' nest," urging Amphytruo not to reproach his wife, Alcumena, whom Sosia considers mad.

59. Mares are "lagnistatai" (Aelian, *Hist. an.* 4.11): thus, the nickname "mare" is given to sensual women.

60. "Hippomanes" produces in men a passionate love close to "equinae cupidini" (Columella 6.27.3).

61. Aristotle, *Hist. an.* 576a; and Aelian, *Hist. an.* 4.8.

62. Aristotle, *Hist. an.* 626a; *Anth. Pal.* 9.302 (Antipater) and 9.548 (Bianor); and Pliny, *Hist. nat.* 11.60.

63. Still suggestive are the pages of G. Murray, *Le origini dell'epica greca* (Florence, 1964), pp. 83ff.; see also J. Illies, *Anthropologie des Tieres* (Munich, 1973), passim. For the Pythagorean precept, see Detienne, *I giardini di Adone,* pp. 62ff.; also U. Dierauer, *Tier und Mensch im Denken der Antike* (Amsterdam, 1977), pp. 285ff.

64. Bibliography on the subject of ox-assassination is immense: see, however, Detienne, *I giardini di Adone,* p. 78n.115.

65. The myth receives some remarks from Cook, "The Bee in Greek Mythology," especially on the link between Demeter and the bees (which we have no way of examining here): *melissai* was the name of the priestesses of this goddess as of others (Magna Mater, perhaps Artemis, etc.); see Weniger, n.4 above; Olck, *RE* 3–1., 434ff.; Fehrle, *Die kultische Keuscheit im Altertum*; and W. Elderkin, "The Bee of Artemis," *AJP* 60 (1939):204ff.

66. Phil., *Im.* 2.8.5; and Himer., *Or.* 10.1; 28.7.

67. On the role of animals as guides for colonizing, and their affinities with helpful animals that occur in the mythic type of the exposed child, see M. Bettini and A. Borghini, "Il bambino e l'eletto," *MD* 3 (1979):121ff.

68. Conington-Nettleship, ad loc.; and no differently Heyne or Forbiger. So, also, B. Grassmann-Fischer, *Die Prodigien in Vergils Aeneis* (Munich, 1966), pp. 164ff.

69. Grassmann-Fischer, *Die Prodigien in Vergils Aeneis*: there is the problem of the swarm with a king (a negative conception or not for Virgil?), and so on.

70. One cannot rule out, although it seems less likely, that the expression also implies that the Trojans, inasmuch as they were originally autochthonous, not only come to Laurentum but also return to it: see Grassmann-Fischer, *Die Prodigien in Vergils Aeneis.*

71. On the general relations between "figure" and "belief," see also the remarks by D. Sperber, *Per una teoria del simbolismo* (Turin, 1981), pp. 103ff.

Chapter Sixteen. The Bee and the Bat

1. *Il.* 3.278, with Leaf's note, and 23.72; and *Od.* 11.476 and 24.14. The expression *eidola kamonton* is much debated, and its interpretation cannot be called definitive.

2. Aristophanes, *Nub.* 708; and Herodotus, "hoi kamontes" (the sick) (1.197)

3. *Il.* 23.103. The scene poses several problems: see, for example, A. Schnaufer, "Frügriechischer Totenglaube," in *Spudasmata* 20 (Hildesheim, 1970), pp. 67ff. and 71ff.

4. *Il.* 2.314. Schnaufer, "Frügriechischer Totenglaube," p. 65n.215, underlines that in reality bats do not emit squeaks, but ultrasonic tones imperceptible by the human ear. Thus, *tetriguia,* said of the soul of Patroclus, cannot mean "squeaking like a bat": yet "fledermausgleich piepsend" is the translation by U. Wilamowitz, *Die Ilias und Homer* (Berlin, 1916), pp. 110. Bats in fact do not squeak, and the soul of Patroclus speaks with a perceptible human voice. Thus, Schnaufer would understand *trizein* as the rustling emitted not by speaking, but simply by moving. However, I believe that the difficulty raised seems too positivistic and that the solution proposed is pretty unconvincing.

5. See the scholion to *Il.* 1.250; Hesychius, s.v. *merops;* and *Etym. mag.,* s.v. *merops.* However, the opinions of modern linguists are many and contradictory, because there is the bird *merops* (the Latin *apiaster*), the hero Merops, and the people Meropes. Frisk, s.v., fully reviews the matter; see also P. Ramat, "Nuove prospettive per la soluzione del problem dei *Meropes* di Cos," *Atti e mem. dell'acc. tosc. La Columbaria* 24, n.s. 10 (1959–60):131ff. The problem of ethnic names in *-op-* receives very interesting treatment by P. Ramat, *RFIC* (1952):150ff.

6. But *merops* does not mean simply "humankind" in Homer: see Musaeus fr. 13 D.; Aeschylus, *Choeph.* 1018; and so forth.

7. *Il.* 2.41 and 20.129; *Od.* 3.215 and 16.96: omphe indicates also the oracular response or the divine will read in the flight of birds.

8. E. Norden, *P. Vergilius Maro "Aeneis" Buch VI*[2] (Stuttgart 1967), makes

an interesting comparison with Lycophron, *Alex.* 686ff., which speaks of the "opa lepten" of the shades, and the metrical setting is identical: citing the Homeric parallel, Norden, through an oversight, speaks of "phone tetriguia" instead of "psyche tetr." Recall, too, Ovid, in which the "umbra cruenta" of Remus speaks in a dream to Acca and Faustulus "exiguo murmure" (*Fast.* 5.457ff.).

9. Underlined by E. Rohde, *Psiche*² (Bari, 1950), 1:53ff.

10. *Od.* 10.521 and 11.30. Aeneas, too, sacrifices a sterile cow to Proserpine before he descends to the underworld: "sterilemque tibi Prosperina vaccam" (*Aen.* 6.251). And Servius comments "deae congruam, numquam enitenti" (ad loc.).

11. The Greeks viewed the bat as a source of riddles and wordplays, as do we: Plato, *Respub.* 5.479b; see also Aesop 307.

12. Ovid, *Met.* 4.389ff.; Aelian, *Hist. an.* 3.42; Anton. Lib. 10; and Plutarch, *Quaest. graec.* 38.

13. I believe that the Minyades can be called *materterae* (sister-aunts), because the motif "two sisters murder son of one" joins this myth with that of Procne and Philomel, in which a comparable ornithotropic metamorphosis occurs: in this sense, the Minyades, as well as Procne and Philomel, shape up as the exact reverse of the Roman women at the *matralia* (see chap. 4 above). The relation between the myth of the Minyades and Dionysus, who grows angry and changes them to bats, can also depend on the three women's condition as *materterae*: Dionysus had been saved and brought up by the sister of his mother, and on this account was called *bimatris* (Ovid, *Met.* 4.12).

14. See O. Waser, "Über die äussere Erscheinung der Seele," *Arc. Religionw.* 16 (1913):337ff. Generally, this Homeric simile has been studied from the standpoint of the survival in Homer of the figure of an ancient "Seelenvogel": G. Weicker, *Der Seelenvogel* (Leipzig, 1902), p. 21; Waser in Roscher, s.v. "Psyche," pp. 3213ff.; E. Bickel, *Homerische Seelenglaube* (Berlin, 1925); and Schnaufer, "Frügriechischer Totenglaube," n.215. Thus, one can understand the emphatic position taken by W. Richter (*Der Kleine Pauly,* s.v. "Fledermaus"), to the effect that this simile "lacks all historico-religious significance." Much material and many remarks occur, *quae semper,* in V. J. Propp, *Le radici storiche dei racconti di fate* (1949; reprint, Turin, 1972), pp. 329–33. There are representations of the soul with bat wings on Mycenean chests: see E. T. Vermeule, "Painted Mycenean Larnakes," *JHS* 85 (1965):146ff.

I recall E. Montale, "Il pipistrello," in *Farfalla di Dinard*³ (Milan, 1976), p. 145: in a hotel room, a newly married couple receives a visit from a bat: the husband confesses that he fears to drive it away or kill it because he considers it the soul of his father.

15. It is difficult to know whether these resemblances reflect beliefs in an older "Seelenvogel," although it cannot be wholly ruled out. In any case, it behooves us to keep to the analogies that we may call synchronic which run between the natural and the cultural characteristics of the bat, on the one hand, and the description of the soul in Homer, on the other. Indeed, it is worthwhile remarking expressly that, at least in the choice of this simile of bats, the second or Lesser Nekuia corresponds fairly well to the representations of the soul and its survival found elsewhere in the poems.

16. I am referring, for example, to R. B. Hornsby, *Patterns of Action in the Aeneid* (Iowa City, 1970), pp. 51ff., who sets up incomprehensible relations between the simile of the bees in book 6 and the other in book 4, 401ff. (the repetition of the same point of comparison ought to tell the reader that Aeneas "comes from very far away" and is undergoing a kind of intellectual and emotional education). Not too different is W. W. Briggs, Jr., *Narrative and Simile from the Georgics to the Aeneid* (Leiden, 1980), pp. 68ff.: here, too, there is a tendency to make the function of the bees in the two poems symbolic by studying in a certain way the thematic value, but without seeking to correlate the single traits with the cultural models attested for the ancient world. Thus, the simile of the bees in book 6 is arbitrarily said to regard "idle souls," in contrast with "men at work" who appeared in book 4, and the bees become a generic symbol of "concord among fellows" (p. 76). That is, traits get brought out that are irrelevant because they are not obtained from oppositive and correlative processes within ancient culture, but simply worked out by the external intuition of the critic. It might be well to avoid just this: to study symbols (like the similes) utilizing not the symbolic language really attested in the ancient systems of beliefs, but letting oneself go at the suggestion of what we may call private reading of the text; out of it come some things even intelligent, but often useless. In B. Grassmann-Fischer, *Die Prodigien in Vergils Aeneis* (Munich, 1966), pp. 66ff., it is maintained that the miraculous bees of Laurentum symbolize also the heroes described by Anchises in book 6 and destined to be reincarnated (the hint is offered, this time, by some verbal analogies between the two texts). This tendency is still more evident in J. Chomarat, "L'initiation d'Aristée," *Rev. Et. Lat.* 52 (1974):186ff.

Chapter Seventeen. The Madness of Aristaeus

1. E. Norden, "Orpheus und Eurydike," in *Kleine Schriften* (Berlin, 1966), pp. 468ff. and esp. 525. Norden's study remains the most

complete, rich and important devoted to the episode, in part because scholarship has only recently begun to get free from its obsession with those unreal problems of the *laudes Galli* and the "lost Hellenistic poem." In the bibliography known to me, the following stand out for diverse points of interest: C. Segal, "Orpheus and the Fourth Georgic," *AJP* 87 (1966):307ff.; G. B. Conte, "Introduzione," in *Le Georgiche*, ed. A. Barchiesi (Milan, 1980), pp. xxii ff.; and A. Perutelli, "L'episodio di Aristeo nelle Georgiche: Struttura e tecnica narrativa," *MD* 4 (1980):59ff.

In contrast, little more than an unbroken paraphrase of Virgil's text, with a few hints that are interesting, but by and large ingenuous, is all we get, frankly, in the "new interpretation" by G. B. Miles, *Virgil's Georgics* (Berkeley, 1980): For example, how can one claim that the struggle to master Proteus is "symbolic of mankind's efforts to subdue the forces of disorder and destruction in nature"?

It is surprising, although here the criticism takes a little different tack, that phenomena such as hiatus in cesura after a long vowel or a diphthong, the heterosyllabic scansion of "muta cum liquida," and other absolutely permissible things ("atque Getae atque Hebrus et Actias Orithyia," *Geo.* 4.463) could be considered "alien to Latin metrics" by A. Parry, "The Idea of Art in Virgil's Georgics" *Arethusa* 5 (1972):35ff. Almost worse is what Parry infers from this alienness, if he really means what he writes ("The language, that is to say, in fairly direct fashion presents Orpheus as the essence of poetry," p. 48): so the poetic quotient rises with the poetic license.

2. On the theme of *ne respexeris*, see chap. 8, n.10 above, and chap. 11, with nn. 5 and 6 above.

3. V. Propp, *Morphology of the Folktale*,[2] ed. Louis Wagner and tr. Laurence Scott (Austin, 1982).

4. Ibid., pp. 26–27. However, the interdiction is not expressed as such, but in a certain sense culturally implied: the hero Aristaeus tries to commit adultery with a married woman and causes her death (moreover, he is a beekeeper and, as such, ought not to let himself go in lust: this is discussed in chap. 15 above and is touched on again below). Propp lists cases in which the first half of the paired functions, the interdiction, is missing: "The tsar's daughters go into the garden [beta[3]]; they are *late* in returning home. Here the interdiction of tardiness is omitted" (p. 27). Here is a real limitation in Propp's method, which may be explained by his lack of interest in the attributes (in this case, the qualifying marks) of the persons. However, the qualifying marks, or other forms of content set aside by Propp, sometimes actually influence the absence or presence of certain functions, or

their specific realization (a problem to which I have given consider-
able attention in "Verso un'antropologia dell'intreccio: Le strutture
semplici della trama nelle commedie di Plauto," *MD* 7 [1982]:39ff.,
with special regard for the underlying plots in Plautus). Thus, in regard to characters who have the qualifying mark of "daughters," it is
clear that one hardly need mention expressly the interdiction, because it goes without saying that daughters must always come home
at the set time. Something like this also comes up when Propp,
speaking of motivations, gives the example in which the hero's request is not motivated by any "feeling of shortage": "The tsar calls
children together, saying 'do me a service' etc. and sends them out on
a quest" (p. 78). Again, by anthropological statute, a father can ask
his own sons any service whatsoever and has no need to give a motive.

5. This is another interdiction that is anthropologically implicit: one
cannot refuse love. Orpheus is committed to the funereal duty of
homage (*quo munere*) that binds him to the dead Eurydice; this duty
consists of weeping and lamenting her loss. Taken up by this commitment, he does not accept the other bond of amorous reciprocity
which the local women offer him. The theme of biunivocality, of a
right and necessary reciprocity in the love relationship, has received
much study, especially for the case of archaic Greek elegy: see the
synthesis by M. Vetta, *Theognis, Elegiarum liber secundus* (Rome,
1980), pp. xxxv ff.; cf. Plutarch, *Erot.* 766 c-d.

6. J. Heurgon, "Orphée et Eurydice avant Virgile," *Mél. Arch. Hist.* 49
(1932):6ff.; G. Paduano, *Noi facemmo ambedue un sogno strano* (Palermo, 1982), pp. 178ff. (a chapter on the *Orfeo* by Calzabigi for
Gluck: see especially pp. 180ff. with notes); also, generally, W. S.
Anderson, "The Orpheus of Virgil and Ovid," in *Orpheus: The Metamorphoses of a Myth,* ed. J. Warden (Toronto, 1982), pp. 25ff.

7. Paduano, *Noi facemmo ambedue un sogno strano,* has written well on
this in pages to which my own structural remarks constitute, so to
speak, a brief morphological commentary. Naturally, Calzabigi's effort consisted in working out successful "motivations" for introducing the happy ending that the structure in some way required. But I
cannot repeat enough that the motivations actually make the texts
and artworks, which otherwise would be reduced to an ill-omened
gallery of bare canvases for the functions of Propp.

8. In Virgil's particular case, the technique closely resembles that of Catullus 64: see Perutelli, "L'episodio di Aristeo nelle Georgiche."

9. Norden, "Orpheus und Eurydike," pp. 499ff.

10. Ibid., p. 505. The attention given to folklore by this grand philologist

is admirable (still worthy of study are pp. 524ff., in which Norden underlines the importance of this discipline for deeper understanding of classical texts).

11. C. Lévi-Strauss, "Reflections on the Atom of Kinship," in *Structural Anthropology,* tr. M. Layton (New York, 1963), 2:124.

12. On trebling, see chap. 9 above; and Propp, *Morphology of the Folktale,* p. 97, analysis of point 8.

13. Norden, "Orpheus und Eurydike," pp. 479ff.

14. Thus, *Geo.* 4.317ff. recalls *Il.* 1.349ff.; also, Aristaeus's reproach to his mother, "mater, Cyrene mater," is a precise echo of *Meter* (*Il.* 1.352ff.), with a similar return of the concept of honor, which has been taken from both (*honorem,* 326; *timen,* 353); and likewise Homeric is the moment in which the mother hears the son's complaints (*Geo.* 4.333ff. and *Il.* 1.357ff.; cf. also *Il.* 18.35ff.).

15. Already the very use of such a refined allusive technique would invite one here to expunge *Geo.* 4.338, a verse that gets repeated in *Aen.* 5.826, but is not present for the *Georgics* in the manuscripts M, R, and P, and is not interpreted by the scholiasts. The verse is formed by a simple addition of the first half of *Il.* 18.39, and the second half of the following verse. And although it fits well in the *Aeneid,* in which there is no express situational reference to the episode in the *Iliad,* it does not sound well here, where the debts to Homer are already too massive to swell by also reprising almost verbatim.

16. I believe that Dante remembered the passage, when Cacciaguida nostalgically evokes old Florence: "l'altra, traendo alla rocca la chioma, / favoleggiava con la sua famiglia / de' Troiani, di Fiesole e di Roma" (*Par.* 15.124ff.). The subject of the tales changes, but the picture remains the same (I do not find the comparison in the commentaries I have seen, including that of Gmelin, who sometimes offers these hints, or in Moore's *Studies in Dante,* or in P. Renucci, *Dante Disciple et Juge du Monde Gréco-Latin* (Paris, 1954).

17. On this theme of relations with the mother, Virgil appears to have respected the traits of the Greek Aristaeus, for whom the advice and intervention of his parents often play a decisive role. In Apollonius of Rhodes, Aristaeus betakes himself from Phthia to the island of Ceos (for an undertaking to be discussed in a moment) actually "patros ephetme" (at his father's behest) (2.519). From Servius's commentary on *Geo.* 1.14, in a rather different variant of the myth (Aristaeus betakes himself to Ceos from Thebes, not Phthia; moreover, the island is "adhuc hominibus vacuam"), we learn instead that Aristaeus betakes himself to the island "matris instinctu." Finally, Diodorus tells us: "hypo tes metros nymphes ten anagogen poiesamenon eis ten Sardo" (4.82.4) (where that "hypo" was emended to "apo" by Wessel-

ing, Dindorf, and Vogel: but the comparisons I have adduced show that one must not emend, lest one misread a rather important feature of the Aristaeus myth).

18. Norden, "Orpheus und Eurydike," pp. 482ff.

19. Already Norden, loc cit., thought it likely that Virgil knew Bacchylides directly. To Norden's considerations, it should be added that Hyginus knew Bacchylides (see Webb's introductory note to Bacchylides): see, above all, B. Gentili, *Encyclopedia virgiliana,* 1:446ff.: the dithyramb is referred to by Servius on *Aen.* 6.21.

20. Interpreters have had some difficulty with the term *aion* (v. 112): Jebb's edition placed it among the cruces. Here I follow the interpretation of B. Gentili in *Arch. Cl.* 6 (1954):121ff., which proposed a suggestive comparison with the crater from Tricase di Ruvo, which shows Theseus in the act of taking his leave from Poseidon, with the crown and, around his neck, the fringed scarf: it looks like a life-saving *kredemnon,* a typical gift of a sea divinity, like the one that Ino gives Odysseus (*Od.* 5.531); see Gentili's article just cited in *Encyclopedia virgiliana,* 1:446ff; also K. Latte, *Philol.* 87 (1932):271; and idem, *Glotta* 34 (1955):192.

21. This parallel is already in part given value by Norden, "Orpheus und Eurydike," pp. 482ff.

22. S. Wide, "Theseus und der Meersprung bei Bachkylides," in *Festschr. Benndorf* (Vienna, 1898), pp. 13ff.; G. Glotz, *L'ordalie dans la Grèce primitive* (Paris, 1904), pp. 34ff. (on Theseus's dive as an ordeal, see p. 44); J. Hubaux, "Le plongeon rituel," *Mus. Belge* 17 (1923):5ff.; H. Jeanmaire, *Couroi et Courètes* (Paris, 1939), pp. 323ff.; C. Gallini, "Katapontismos," *St. mat. st. Rel.* 34 (1963):61ff.; and A. Seppilli, *Sacralità delle acque e sacrilegio dei ponti* (Palermo, 1977), pp. 141ff. and 181ff. (that also considers Aristaeus).

23. Dionysus's leap in the sea is discussed above all by Jeanmaire, *Couroi et Courètes,* pp. 336ff.

24. See M. Delcout, *Héphaistos ou la légende du magicien* (Paris, 1957), p. 43.

25. Apollodorus 3.15.4; and Euripides fr. 349 N. The bath of the Eumolpids ritualized the adventure of their mythic progenitor: see Gallini, "Katapontismos."

26. Jeanmaire, *Couroi et Courètes,* pp. 283ff., and Gallini, "Katapontismos."

27. Jeanmaire, *Couroi et Courètes,* pp. 283ff., comparing Hesiod, *Theog.* 346ff.

28. Gallini, "Katapontismos," 68ff., who underlines well the function of these goddesses: they receive the hero, give him their treasures, carry him to his wedding, and so forth.

29. Jeanmaire, *Couroi et Courètes,* pp. 337ff.; and see his discerning re-

marks on the function of the waters in the initiatory ceremonies, with many ethnographic parallels (pp. 330ff.).

30. J. Chomarat, "L'initiation d'Aristée," *Rev. Et. Lat.* 52 (1974):186ff. It is remarkable that an article entitled "L'initiation d'Aristée" and even containing a paragraph on "Cyrène, les nymphes et le symbolisme de l'eau," does not mention either this series of myths or the functions that water really had in religious symbolism. See also J. G. Campbell, "Initiation and the Role of Aristaeus in Georgics Four," *Ramus* 11 (1982):105ff.

31. See, above all, Norden, "Orpheus und Eurydike," pp. 500ff.; L. P. Wilkinson, *The Georgics of Virgil: A Critical Survey* (Cambridge, 1969), p. 113. However, see the stylistic and compositional considerations of Perutelli, "L'episodio di Aristeo nelle Georgiche," pp. 63ff.

32. On motivations, see chap. 2 above, and Propp, *Morphology of the Folktale,* cited in n.35 below.

33. "Il duca aggiunse alla scelta del luogo e della data dell'avvenimento una finta *prova* [emphasis added] della devozione della ragazza. Le racconta la storia del vecchio mago, macilento ed esangue, al quale essa deve recarsi da sola al fine di fargli una domanda della massima importanza per lui, Carl [here the motivation is expressly fictitious]. Il feroce vecchio cercherebbe di sfuggire con terribili minacce, si cangerebbe in tutto o in parte in disgustosi animali. Essa dovrebbe serrarlo ancor più tenacemente; alla fine l'incanto sarebbe rotto, egli cederebbe, ridiventerebbe un giovane e le darebbe la risposta desiderata": W. Pater, "Carl duca di Rosenmold," in *Ritratti immaginari,* trans. M. Praz (Milan, 1980), p. 153. As we see, Proteus (or in this case the Protean personage) seems naturally predisposed to take on the role of donor and of person who puts one to the test.

34. Propp, *Morphology of the Folktale,* p. 117, where Propp speaks of "disharmony" when the first half of a fairy tale "does not evoke the usual response or else replaces it with a response that is completely different and unusual for the tale norm" (with which already is worked out the so-called system of expectations, which has played its proper role in modern literary criticism: as a concept, "disharmony" is rather self-evident if seen from the viewpoint of tonality in music).

35. It is well known that Propp did not neglect these elements on principle, but considered it appropriate to deal with them in a different place (see, above all, his "Foreword," in *Morphology of the Folktale,* pp. xxv-xxvi): this self-limitation is naturally subject to criticism, yet it did let Propp write his book. He correctly judged that the study of the attributes opened the way to reconsidering the folk tale as myth. His distinction between form and content provoked criticisms from C. Lévi-Strauss ("La struttura e la forma," pp. 165, in V. J. Propp,

Morfologia della fiaba [tr. Ital., Turin 1966]). And Lévi-Strauss is proven still more correct once we read Propp's *Le radici storiche dei racconti di fate* (1949; reprint, Turin, 1972), accessible in Italy since 1949, but apparently not in France, where Propp sets out to deal with motifs and attributes, hence reconsidering the folk tale as myth. Instead, everything is reduced to a forced and conjectural re-creation of historico-evolutionary contexts for the various folklore elements within the heterogeneous body of primitive peoples' beliefs published by anthropologists throughout the world. In this respect, Propp differed little from Andrew Lang, as Benedetto Croce was well aware in *Quad. della Crit.* 16 (1949):102ff. In spite of such drawbacks, we must not forget, of course, the overall usefulness of the book, and they cannot diminish that sense of respect and liking stirred by the cultural tension that permeates these pages.

36. I have used the translation with commentary of D. S. Avalle, *L'ontologia del segno in Saussure* (Turin, 1973), pp. 59ff.; see also R. Jakobson, *Lo sviluppo della semiotica* (Milan, 1978), pp. 50ff. Strong criticisms of Avalle's edition and interpretation have been formulated by R. Engler, *Cahiers F. de Saussure* 19 (1974–75):45ff.: but such problems touch us quite marginally here.

37. From Aristaeus's introduction of the acts of pasturing and raising cattle may come, perhaps, a small contribution to Virgilian exegesis. Virgil calls Aristaeus "cultor nemorum, cui pinguia Ceae / ter centum nivei tondent dumeta iuvenci" (*Geo.* 1.14–15). In the wake of Daniel's Servius, *cultor* is usually taken as synonymous with *incola,* hence "woodland dweller," and rightly so; but we may try perhaps to add some complementary senses required by the figure of the cultural hero, which is what the rest of Virgil's description suggests, relating the woodland character of the hero to cattle-raising.

Aristaeus's herds pasture in "dumeta," scrubby pasture that seems to point to the "nemora" of which he is "cultor": for example, from "greges . . . culta et dumeta pascentium" (Columella 1.2.5), we see clearly that the "dumetum" is conceived as the complementary opposite of "cultum." We know from Oppian (*Cyn.* 4.269) that Aristaeus founded the art of pasturing. And Nonnus (*Dion.* 5.261ff., 16.108) says that Aristaeus taught herdsmen to use their pasturage well. Thus, Aristaeus figures as the hero who taught the use for pasturage even of uncultivated lands: under his guidance, even the scrubland, which is uncultivated *par excellence,* became cultivated. This latter art perhaps, then, must be read into Virgil's "cultor nemorum," and the allusion to the fatness of his herds is the proof, moreover, of his ability as a cultivator. Virgil expressly refers to this founding and experimental pastoral activity when he makes Aristaeus speak of "vitae mortalis honorem" that "pecorum custodia sollers" gave him "omnia temptanti" (*Geo.* 4.327–28). In short, one may conclude that Aristaeus is "cultor nemorum" because he not only dwells in woodlands but also invents a particular woodland culture: a complex sense that well reflects the two semantic vectors of the verb *colo,* both "inhabit" and "cultivate."

38. For example, see the scholiast to Apollonius of Rhodes (2.500: p. 169, 13 Wendel); for rennet, see Oppian, *Cyn.* 4.271; for hunting, see Nonnus, *Dion.* 5.229ff., and Diodorus Siculus 4.81ff.

39. Aelian, *Hist. an.* 5.11; *Geopon.* 15.2.19; Plutarch, *Prae. con.* 44; Palladius 1.37.4 and 4.15.4; Pliny, *Hist. nat.* 11.44; and M. Detienne, "Orphée au miel," *QUCC* 12 (1971):7ff. See also chaps. 15 and 16 above.

40. Acteon may have lusted after Semele too: Apollodorus, *Bibl.* 3.4.4.

41. See also Clement of Alexandria, *Strom.* 1.21.132.

42. See the scholiasts to Apollonius Rhodius: every year it was necessary "meth'hoplon epiterein ten epitolen tou kynos" (2.526: p. 172, 6 Wendel); Nonnus speaks of waiting for Sirius "siderochiton" (*Dion.* 13.281). In the Loeb edition of Nonnus (1:449), H. J. Rose reports a remark of Von Scheffer and thinks that Nonnus had misunderstood the scholiast, who must have meant rather a noise to be made with the shield and weapons to ward off the threatening atmospheric event, according to a model in folklore which is both familiar and widespread: see C. Lévi-Strauss, *The Raw and the Cooked,* tr. J. and D. Weightman (New York, 1970), pp. 300ff. But it is not necessarily the case that "meth'hoplon" meant a noise. It might have meant a generic "armed vigil" at the rise of the baleful star.

43. The comparison between Apollonius and Virgil shows clearly that it is wrong to identify Sirius here with the sun, as does Richter, *Der Kleine Pauly,* ad loc. Already Heyne had remarked that "ita otiose bis dictum: sol ardebat et sol caelum medium tenebat." Indeed, let me point out a detail that may prove useful. According to Columella 9.14.6, Virgil, as well as Mago and Democritus, claimed that the season of Sirius was the most propitious for *bugonia.* Evidently, the ancient commentators had reasoned very simply because Aristaeus betakes himself to Proteus when Sirius is scorching, and *bugonia* takes place immediately thereafter, it must take place under this sign. Thus, clearly Sirius was understood as a seasonal sign, not as the sun. Elsewhere, Virgil associates Sirius directly with plague: *Aen.* 3.141 and 10.273.

44. F. de Saussure, in Avalle, *L'ontologia del segno in Saussure,* pp. 67ff.: "There is no method in maintaining that the symbol (here = 'mythic personage') must remain fixed, or that it must fluctuate endlessly; it must vary within certain limits."

Index of Passages Cited

General Index

Adultery, 63–64; and Aristaeus, 234,
240, 242, 314n.4; and Nuer mater-
nal uncle, 109
Aeneid (Virgil): "Review of Heroes" in,
xiii, 144–50, 178; and time, 139.
See also Virgil *below and in Index of
Passages Cited*
Aequales, 167
Agnatio, 2, 91, 106, 107–8, 175
Altus, 169
Amata (Queen), 68, 87, 88, 92–99,
265–66n.5, 274n.66, 278n.86
Amita (father's sister), xiii, 2, 39–40,
100–105, 106; and *matertera,* 105,
110, 111; and *socrus,* 41, 44
Amitinus, 247–48n.3
Amulius, 23–25, 26
Ante, 158–61, 162, 179
Ante/post, 116–20, 184
Anterior/posterior, 115–20, 122, 157,
184–92
Antevorta (Porrima), 154, 155–56,
164–65, 293n.12
Antiquus (ancient), 117–19, 120
Apuleius, 141
Aquilli, 49–51, 111
Arapesh of New Guinea, 67
Aristaeus, 227–31, 233–34, 235–36,

238–39, 240–46, 314n.4, 316–
17n.17; as "cultor," 319–20n.37;
and Melissa myth, 216; and Ocean's
daughters, 235; and Rhoikos myth,
201; and Sirius, 208, 320n.43
Atom of kinship, 45, 247n.2, 280n.6
Atta, 70
Attitudes, 1; and *avunculus,* 45; different sets of, 2; as system, 107, 112
Aunts, 2; among Nuer, 109, 110; wives
of siblings excluded, 1. See also
Amita; Matertera
Avoidance, 9–10; between fathers and
sons, 9–13, 250n.3; and *patruus,* 17
Avunculi filius, 248n.3
Avunculus (mother's brother), xiii, 2,
39–46, 106, 107, 261n.47; and Cicero as *patruus,* 37; as "defender," 59–
66; "familiarity" with, 46–52; and
intimate diminutive, 52–58, 64–65;
and *matertera,* 91–92, 97; and *patruus,* 39, 57, 105; and Plutarch, 31
Avus, 41, 258n.11, 261n.39

Baggara of the Sudan, 67–68
Balbus, L. Herennius, 15–16, 47
Bathing, avoidance in, 10–13

ANCIENT SOCIETY AND HISTORY

The series Ancient Society and History offers books, relatively brief in compass, on selected topics in the history of ancient Greece and Rome, broadly conceived, with a special emphasis on comparative and other nontraditional approaches and methods. The series, which includes both works of synthesis and works of original scholarship, is aimed at the widest possible range of specialist and nonspecialist readers.